Marx, Engels, and Marxisms

Series Editors
Marcello Musto
York University
Toronto, ON, Canada

Terrell Carver
University of Bristol
Bristol, UK

T0349178

The Marx renaissance is underway on a global scale. Wherever the critique of capitalism re-emerges, there is an intellectual and political demand for new, critical engagements with Marxism. The peer-reviewed series Marx, Engels and Marxisms (edited by Marcello Musto & Terrell Carver, with Babak Amini, Francesca Antonini, Paula Rauhala & Kohei Saito as Assistant Editors) publishes monographs, edited volumes, critical editions, reprints of old texts, as well as translations of books already published in other languages. Our volumes come from a wide range of political perspectives, subject matters, academic disciplines and geographical areas, producing an eclectic and informative collection that appeals to a diverse and international audience. Our main areas of focus include: the oeuvre of Marx and Engels, Marxist authors and traditions of the 19th and 20th centuries, labour and social movements, Marxist analyses of contemporary issues, and reception of Marxism in the world.

Gianni Fresu

Antonio Gramsci

An Intellectual Biography

Gianni Fresu
Universidade Federal de Uberlândia
Santa Monica, Brazil

ISSN 2524-7123 ISSN 2524-7131 (electronic)
Marx, Engels, and Marxisms
ISBN 978-3-031-15609-0 ISBN 978-3-031-15610-6 (eBook)
https://doi.org/10.1007/978-3-031-15610-6

Cover illustration: The History Collection / Alamy Stock Photo

This Palgrave Macmillan imprint is published by the registered company Springer Nature Switzerland AG.
The registered company address is: Gewerbestrasse 11, 6330 Cham, Switzerland

Contents

PART I

The Young Revolutionary

CHAPTER 1

The Premises of an Uninterrupted Discourse

Antonio Gramsci was born in a context of deep crisis in the young Italian state, which was particularly serious in Sardinia as it was historically shaken after centuries of colonial rule and affected by such chronic misery and structural underdevelopment that left him no way out.[1] In 1891, Italy had for a few years been plunged into a customs war with France, which was waged by Crispi[2] to defend the burgeoning industry and Italy's large agricultural production, but with very serious consequences for the Italian South.

[1] Antonio Gramsci was born in Ales (Oristano), a small village in the interior of Sardinia, on January 22, 1891. Born to Giuseppina Marcias and Francesco Gramsci, he was the fourth of seven children. Three years later, the family moved to Sorgono, near Ghilarza, Giuseppina's hometown, where little Antonio Gramsci spent all his childhood and adolescence.

[2] After the collapse of the last right-wing government in Cavour, Agostino Depretis, the new president of the council of ministers, abandoned the policy of free exchange in favor of customs protectionism. Aimed at protecting the burgeoning national industry of the North and large-estate farming in southern Italy, and maintained by Francesco Crispi, the new prime minister, this policy led to the denouncing of old trade treaties and to a customs war with France and thus to the closure of this key market to some Italian products (citrus fruits, olive oil, cattle, wine, cereals, leather), which were particularly important to the *Mezzogiorno* region.

© The Author(s), under exclusive license to Springer Nature Switzerland AG 2023
G. Fresu, *Antonio Gramsci*, Marx, Engels, and Marxisms, https://doi.org/10.1007/978-3-031-15610-6_1

As explained by Gramsci in the first notes of *Notebook 1*, the hierarchical system of privileges established during the *Risorgimento*[3] had made the South's economic and social backwardness structural and led to the ever-increasing use and depletion of huge portions of its savings, which were reinvested in northern Italy. There was some important agricultural production in the *Mezzogiorno*[4] region, and its main market was France. The protectionist policy and the denunciation of the trade treaty signed with France affected this high-level production adversely. This meant a decrease of around 40% in exports in Italy, and of 70% in Sardinia and other southern regions. Customs duties on industrial products and large agricultural production favored the North and the interests of the large-estate owners of the South, but at the same time they ended up stifling the more dynamic classes of agriculture and livestock production, the only ones that invested capital in southern production. However, as Gramsci wrote in his *Notebooks*, this conciliatory approach historically proved to be ineffective because it became an obstacle to the development of the industrial and agricultural economy at several stages, leading to critical levels of class struggle and thus to the state's increasing and overbearing pressure on the masses. In the decades following Italian unification, this contradiction was felt more severely and dramatically in Sardinia.[5]

As Depretis revealed, the three regulations that standardized the tax regime and the registration of rural properties, the legislation of 1864, significantly led not only to great confusion, but also to the adoption of a tax regime completely unrelated to existing conditions and to actual potential. Aiming to face the state budget deficit, the legislation of 1864, which suddenly increased land taxes, was out of touch with the reality in which it would be enforced and came as a final blow to the purposes of economic and social renewal of the fields:

> There was a mortgage debt in Sardinia that, in 1870, amounted to 76,664,027 lire, that is, a tax of 3,161 lire for each hectare of land, which was over four times the value of the land. Nine years have gone by and this debt is very likely to be even greater today, and the situation is not only

---

[3] The term *Risorgimento* refers to the process of Italian unification, which began in the first war of independence in 1848 and led to the proclamation of the Kingdom of Italy in 1861.

[4] The Mezzogiorno region comprises Italy's southern continental area (also called *Italia meridionale, Suditalia, Bassa Italia* or just *Sud*) and the island provinces of Sardinia.

[5] For more details on the contemporary history of Sardinia, see Gianni Fresu, *La prima bardana. Modernizzazione e conflitto nella Sardegna dell'Ottocento* (Cagliari, Cuec, 2011).

worsening, but beginning to deteriorate [...]. Everyone can and must be convinced that rural property is in a pathological state and that measures to correct the table and reduce taxes are warranted.[6]

The large swaths of territory (about 80 thousand hectares) transferred to the state due to unpaid tax debts are a clear sign of the economic depression. Besides being excessive, taxes were collected in a way that proved unfeasible for Sardinia's taxpayers. Sardinian peasants did not produce enough to pay taxes every two months in the winter, and to do so they were forced to turn to usurers. Lending institutions charged interest rates of up to 50% per annum for overdue taxes, not to mention additional costs, and that quickly threw small- and middle-scale landholders onto the streets.[7]

Later, in the 1870s and 1880s, the economy seemed to be recovering due to the export of livestock, olive oil, wine, cork and leather to the French market. However, in 1881 and 1882, Sardinia was struck by a series of endless misfortunes: first, an unexpected drought in the winter, which stretched into the following seasons and destroyed cereal crops; then, cyclones and floods, agricultural pests such as mildew and phylloxera, plague epidemics that destroyed farms, the bankruptcy of lending institutions and eventually the sudden closing of the French market due to the failed protectionist policy adopted by Italian governments.

As was thoroughly documented in Antonio Zanelli's 1879 report to the Ministry of Agriculture, in the previous year Sardinia had significantly increased its exports to France, which forced farmers to borrow so as to increase land for cattle breeding and grazing—land that was leased to meet French demands. Therefore, the customs war wiped out the entire sector, and it also hurt the export of wines, cereals, olive oil, leather and coal, for which France was a unique market. As if this were not enough, in June 1887, Sardinia saw the collapse of its industrial agricultural credit, on which the entire system of financing for rural enterprises in the region depended, and consequently the bankruptcy of countless farming enterprises, the collapse of exports and productive activities, the volatility of

---

[6] Francesco Salaris, "Atti della Giunta per la Inquiesta Agraria", in *Le inchieste parlamentari sulla Sardegna dell'Ottocento* (Sassari, Edes, 1984), 172.

[7] Antonio Zanelli, *Condizioni della pastorizia in Sardegna*, report to the Ministry of Agriculture, Industry and Trade (director of the animal husbandry division of Reggio Emilia; printed under the supervision of the Agrarian Committee of Cagliari, Tipografia Editrice Dell'Avvenire di Sardegna, 1880).

smallholders' slowly accumulated savings, and the unfettered expansion of usury. This led to the pauperization of the population and the abandonment of the Sardinian rural areas where the only alternative was grazing, an activity hindered by the establishment of the first dairy industries between 1885 and 1900, which imposed such a low price on milk that it precluded any possibility of development. The alternative to hunger was mining, but living and working conditions in this activity were also terrible and, with the constant increase in exploitation, wages in Sardinia, already much lower than elsewhere in Italy, were reduced even more. The calamity was analyzed by Gramsci in an article published in 1918:

> These were terrible years that in Sardinia, for example, left the same memory of 1812, when people would die of hunger in the streets and a *starello*[8] of wheat was clandestinely exchanged for its corresponding arable field. Representative Pais's inquiry into Sardinia is a document that will continue to leave an indelible mark of infamy on Crispi's policy and on the economic classes that supported it. The island of Sardinia was literally razed to the ground as in a barbarian invasion; the forests, which regulated the climate and atmospheric precipitation, were torn down to make way for profitable merchandise; now corpses proliferate, and political customs and moral life are corrupted.[9]

With the economic, political and moral crisis that hit Sardinia after unification, criminal issues gained momentum. The *Sardinian question* was seen as a public concern, and banditry was seen as the cause, not the effect, of underdevelopment. This line of reasoning was pseudo-scientifically supported with the development of criminal anthropology and positivist sociology. According to these theories, the causes of crime should be sought in the congenital and biological-racial characteristics of the Sardinian people.

The state considered the island a large open-air prison, to which even corrupt civil servants and those involved in scandals of various types were transferred, while continuing to perform their duties. Among the grassroots and even middle strata, the state had very low prestige, and its authority was restricted to fiscal rapacity and brutal repression. Those

---

[8] An old unit of measure adopted in the region of Sardinia, equivalent to 3,986.75 square meters.

[9] Antonio Gramsci, "Uomini, idee, giornali e quattrini", *l'Avanti!*, 23 jan. 1918, em Guido Melis (org.), *Gramsci e la questione sarda* (Cagliari, Edizioni della Torre, 1977), 88.

years were marked by the Buggerru massacre,[10] which by no mere chance led to the first general strike in the history of Italy, and by the insurgencies of 1906, which began in Cagliari.[11]

This is all very relevant to Gramsci's human biography and intellectual development. Indeed, his production is not the linear, complete plan of a brilliant intellectual; it starts on the battlefield, in the midst of social struggles, from his direct experience of a condition of misery and social marginalization.[12] As has been argued many times, the organic relationship between Gramsci and the subaltern group was marked by affinity, not mere intellectual representation, and this was largely due to the social and cultural background and due to his personal knowledge of the injustices suffered by the voiceless masses in his homeland. Togliatti himself confirmed this close relationship between theoretical-political concepts and human participation in the fate of the humblest, in his very first article after Gramsci's arrest, which was published in the May-June 1927 issue of *Lo Stato Operaio*:

> Having just arrived in the large industrial city in the interior of Sardinia, where the injustice of a social order and the hope of a new order translated into the misery and the instinct of rebellion and solidarity of a population of downtrodden peasants and shepherds, the man destined to understand and effectively communicate with those oppressed by capitalist society had bonds of reason, of passion, and of deep feelings with those people willing to fight. This fight will lead to the renewal of modernity by workers.[13]

---

[10] On September 4, 1904, the police violently suppressed a demonstration for wage increase for miners in front of the company's headquarters in Buggerru, the mining center of southwestern Sardinia. That resulted in three deaths and dozens of people injured.

[11] These themes were thoroughly discussed in the works of Girolamo Sotgiu, one of the most influential historians, from our point of view, of contemporary Sardinia. We are referring especially to the following works: *Lotte sociali e politiche nella Sardegna contemporanea* (Cagliari, Edes, 1974); *Movimento operaio e autonomismo* (Bari, De Donato Editore, 1975); *Storia della Sardegna sabauda (1720–1847)* (Bari, Laterza, 1984); *Storia della Sardegna dopo l'Unità* (Bari, Laterza, 1986).

[12] "Those who know Gramsci's thought and practice will understand that it can be correctly asserted that the origin of his thought and practice lies not only in the factories in Turin, but also in Sardinia, in the conditions imposed by Italian capitalism on the island" (Palmiro Togliatti, "Ho conoscio Gramsci sotto il portico Dell'università di Torino", in Cesare Pillon, *I comunisti nella storia d'Italia*, Rome, Edizioni del Calendario, 1967, 81).

[13] Togliatti, *Gramsci* (Rome, Editori Riuniti, 1972), 4.

This relationship marked by affinity was therefore directly confirmed by so many who lived or worked with him. Among these accounts, some of the many workers in Turin, main figures in the red biennium, agreed on something distinctive in his character; while so many leaders of the movement were eloquent speakers, Gramsci had a unique quality: "he knew how to listen". In his frequent visits to laborers at work, the Sardinian intellectual enjoyed talking, showing interest in every aspect of their existence: the psychophysical effort of production; the geographical and social reality of their origin; the psychological implications of their work; the relationship between all that and their private and family lives. That is what Togliatti confirmed, once again, in 1927:

> Communicating with workers. "Debating" with workers. Among the most notable leaders of our party [...] some are noticeably able to speak to a crowd. But talking to workers individually, plainly, not as a master or an employer, but as a fellow worker and, so to speak, an apprentice, not only seeking, while in contact with workers' consciousness and will, the most fundamental reasons for our faith, not only putting our own ability and will to the test in this contact, but also engaging with workers in the pursuit of a new path for their class in order to test the accuracy of counsel, of guidance, of command—this is quite rare among us, and Gramsci is probably the only one who knows how to do it.[14]

Gramsci arrived in Cagliari in 1908, after a period in *Santu Lussurgiu*, a deteriorating secondary school, and after a particularly difficult childhood in Ghilarza due to his health problems and the difficult economic conditions of the family resulting from the arrest of his father.[15] Back then, Cagliari[16] was, in every sense, the capital of the region, shaken by social

---

[14] Ibid.

[15] In 1897, Francesco Gramsci, working at a registry office in Ghilarza, engaged in a fierce clash involving the many liberals who controlled the electoral college. In the quarrel between Francesco Cocco Ortu, who was an elected member of parliament, and the young Enrico Carboni Boi, the latter's claims, supported by Francesco Gramsci, led to a backlash from the losing faction. For this reason, that same year, Francesco was the subject of an investigation and was subsequently arrested on a charge of embezzlement, extortion and forgery of official documents. In 1905, he was sentenced to five years in prison.

[16] In the capital of Sardinia, Gramsci first shared a room at 24 *via* Principe Amadeo, then he moved to a damp room at 149 *Corso* Vittorio Emanuele, and attended the Liceo Classico Dettori. On a tight budget, he was hardly able to afford any luxury, which usually consisted of just coffee at Tramer, a café at *piazza* Martiri, or a frugal meal with his brother at the *trattoria* at *piazza* del Carmine.

ferment, by the first manifestations of mass politics, and by some cultural activity, which is evidenced by the existence of at least three daily newspapers and several periodicals devoted to political controversy. In Cagliari, where his older brother, Genaro, had become secretary of the socialist section and treasurer of the Chamber of Labor, Gramsci came into closer contact with socialism, not abandoning, however, Sardinian issues and claims.

During his years in the liceo, he and his companions organized the circle "Martyrs to Free Thought Giordano Bruno", in which he assumed his first political responsibility as treasurer, came into contact with the most influential magazines of the national intellectual debate (*l'Unità, Il Marzocco, La Lupa, La Voce*) and conducted, with the socialist press, his first philosophical investigation, which led him from the idealism of Benedetto Croce to the historical materialism of Marx.[17] Cagliari also gave Gramsci the first opportunity to experience journalism when he wrote his first pieces for *L'Unione Sarda*.[18] As for the events that left a mark on his biography, the Cagliari episodes can probably be considered secondary; however, it was in those years that Gramsci's character was formed and his intellectual aptitudes and his propensity for political militancy began to take shape. In a letter to Tania dated October 12, 1931, about his condition as a Sardinian, although Gramsci stated that he belonged to Italian culture and did not feel "torn between two worlds",[19] we cannot consider his education in Sardinia mere accident, which was definitively and

---

[17] Gianni Francioni, Francesco Giasi and Luca Paulesu (eds.), *Gramsci. I quaderni del carcere e le riviste ritrovate* (Catalogo della mostra, Cesena, Biblioteca Malatestiana, 17 jan.–31 mar. 2019, Rome, MetaMorfosi, 2019).

[18] *L'Unione Sarda*, Sardinia's main newspaper, published Gramsci's first article in 1910.

[19] "I myself have no race: my father is of recent Albanian origin (the family fled from Epirus after or during the wars of 1821 and soon became Italian); my grandmother was a Gonzalez and descended from some Italian-Spanish family from southern Italy (many remained there after the end of Spanish rule); my mother was Sardinian, born to Sardinian parents; and Sardinia was united with Piedmont only in 1847, after having been a personal fief and property of Piedmontese princes, who received it in exchange for Sicily, which was very distant and less defensible. However, my culture is Italian and this is my world: I have never felt torn between two worlds, although the *Giornale d'italia* affirmed that in March 1920. In this newspaper, a two-column article attributed my political activity in Turin, among other things, to the fact that I am Sardinian and not Piedmontese, or Sicilian" (Antonio Gramsci, *Lettere dal carcere*, Turin, Einaudi, 1975, 506–7).

organically overcome by the "deprovincialization" experienced by a young man who escaped the insularity of his homeland.[20]

Given this premise and its meaning, his arrival in Turin,[21] which he defined as "the Petrograd of the Italian revolution", was a turning point in the life of Antonio Gramsci, who from then on had the opportunity to be part of an incomparably wider cultural and political horizon. The importance of this existential shift can be noticed in a rare autobiographical passage of the *Prison Notebooks*, in which, referring to *Ricordi politici e civili* by Guicciardini,[22] Gramsci addressed the literary genre of *memoirs*.

> "Memoirs" have the peculiarity of telling us not only autobiographical facts, in the strict sense, but also civil and moral experiences associated with life itself and its events, considered in their universal or national value. In view of that, this style of writing may be more useful than autobiographies, considered in the strict sense, insofar as it refers to vital processes characterized by continuous attempts to overcome a backward way of life, such as that of a Sardinian at the beginning of the century, to develop a way of living and thinking that is no longer provincial, but national, all the more national as it sought insertion into a European way of living and thinking [...]. If it is true that one of the most pressing needs of Italian culture was to become deprovincial, even in the most advanced and modern urban centers, this process was all the more evident when experienced from a "triple or quadruple provincial" as was the case of a certain young Sardinian at the beginning of the century.[23]

In those years, the previous capital of the kingdom was the spearhead of Fordist development in Italy; therefore, that was where class conflicts reached deeper and more conscious levels. This fact played an essential formative role: in Turin, the young Gramsci—whose sociopolitical genetic code embodied the endemic spirit of the pastoral and peasant rebellions of

---

[20] In addition to the great and unsurpassed work of Giuseppe Fiori (*Vita di Antonio Gramsci*, Rome/Bari, Laterza, 1989), which is methodologically halfway between the accurate reconstruction of history and the meticulous investigation of the journalist who availed himself of a multitude of unique first-hand accounts, Angelo D'orsi's biography is an important attempt to go deeper, not only formally, which was able to show the effective weight of Gramsci's years in Sardinia. *Gramsci Una nuova biografia* (Milan, Feltrinelli, 2017).

[21] In 1911, after school holidays, Gramsci won a scholarship intended for the kingdom's needy youth, which allowed him, despite enormous financial difficulties, to enroll in the Facoltà di Lettere of the University of Turin.

[22] Francesco Guicciardini, *Ricordi politici e civili* (Lanciano, Rocco Carabba, 2008)

[23] Antonio Gramsci, *Quaderni del carcere* (Turin, Einaudi, 1977), 1776.

his homeland—came into contact with the organizational power of the workers' movement. The result was a very coherent conception of class conflict and of the very idea of revolution, according to which an organic synthesis between the demands of the working masses of the North and the disordered desires of the rural masses of the *Mezzogiorno* was indispensable. Without taking this landscape into account, it is very difficult to fully understand Gramsci's struggles and theoretical production. From our point of view, the whole of Gramsci's legacy was built within a framework of deep continuity. This does not mean Gramsci always remains the same; on the contrary, his questions and his conclusions develop, become more complex, and take new turns, and he changes some of his initial assumptions (such as his assessment of Jacobinism). The Gramsci of the *Notebooks* does not contradict the political leader and, above all, does not deny the revolutionary ideals of his youth and his worldview.

The Sardinian intellectual's existence, as well as that of so many young people in his generation, was marked by the drama of the First World War, the first mass conflict in which the scientific knowledge of previous years was applied on a large scale and in which millions of peasants and workers were literally sent to slaughter. An expression characteristic of that conflict, often used by Gramsci, perfectly illustrates the instrumental use of subaltern classes by their leaders: "cannon fodder". In Gramsci's reflections, this dual relationship goes beyond trench wars, finding full expression in the fundamental relations of modern capitalist society. In this sense, as we will see in detail, Gramsci used the category of "Cadornism" as a synthesis of the strained sociopolitical relations between rulers and those ruled, unilaterally established by the former over the latter. As opposed to this idea of social hierarchy, considered natural and immutable, he affirmed the need to overcome the historical split between intellectual and manual work, which necessitates a priesthood or a separate caste of experts in politics and knowledge. The essence of human nature is not determined by specific activity, whether material or spiritual. Contrary to what is generally thought and claimed, "every man is a philosopher". This dictum, present in the *Notebooks*, probably contains the definition that best summarizes Gramsci's ideas on "human emancipation" and on the historical—one might even say programmatic—need for an "intellectual and moral reform" capable of putting an end to the exploitation of man by man, as well as to the dualistic relationship between rulers and those ruled.

Between these two phases there is a logical and political continuity that led to the conceptions in the *Prison Notebooks* that constitute the crowning of, not as some maintain the dramatic split between, conceptions "before" and "after" 1926. We are referring to the debate that arose in the various re-readings of Antonio Gramsci's work and political biography, in which a tendency centered on an alleged discontinuity between reflections before and after 1926 developed over time. Not many years later, this tendency, which corresponds more to political demands than to scientific evidence, proved to lack philological and conceptual rigor, and its fragility was evidenced.

As Garin stated, "Gramsci did not intend to be a scholar: his conception of thought and history was permeated by the concrete situation, by real choices."[24] Gramsci, Garin went on, "was a politician, not a philosopher, so he did not bother to collect a simple bouquet of themes that were undiscussed, because they were alien to everyone; rather, he fought on the ground, in the real situation".[25] In Gramsci's work, analytical reading was closely linked to the political battle, and this distinction between the two phases can be explained both by the immediate demands of politics, in the case of the first phase, and by the greater analytical freedom, precisely *für ewig*, seen in the reflections during the time he spent in prison. However, the continuity between the two phases is evident and documentable.

One of the most common claims in the re-readings of the last few decades seeks to purge Gramsci's work of any link with Lenin's theoretical and political legacy, sometimes attributing to him political considerations and analyses peculiar to a later period. Especially in Italy, there is currently a category of scholars specialized in speculating on Antonio Gramsci's so-called political, if not religious, conversion. That has even led some of these scholars to research letters, documents and even an allegedly missing

---

[24] Eugenio Garin, *Con Gramsci* (Rome, Editori Riuniti, 1997), 48.
[25] Ibid.

Notebook, which would prove this rejection, but none of them found what they were looking for.[26] Some have sought evidence of this rupture on the pages of the *Prison Notebooks* and in the poorly used concepts of "hegemony" and "war of position" in order to justify such discontinuity, if not absolute incompatibility, with the "devil of the twentieth century". However, in the *Notebooks* there are plenty of references to Lenin as the "theorist of hegemony" and passages in which Gramsci identifies him as being chiefly responsible for the renewal and continuity of historical materialism after Marx. Contrary to interpretations that support discontinuity, in the *Notebooks*, the relationship between the philosopher from Trier and Lenin is described as the synthesis of a process of intellectual evolution that is manifested in the passage from utopia to science and from science to action.

The proposition in the introduction to the *Critique of the political economy* that men develop awareness of structural conflicts in the field of ideologies must be considered a gnosiological statement, not merely a psychological and moral one. Hence, the theoretical-practical principle of hegemony also has a gnosiological objective and, therefore, it is in this field that one can find the most important theoretical contribution of Ilyich to the philosophy of praxis. Indeed, Ilyich made philosophy progress to the extent that he advanced political doctrine and practice. By creating a new ideological domain and determining the renewal of consciousness and of methods of

---

[26] That is the case of Franco Lo Piparo's book, *L'enigma del quaderno* (Rome, Donzelli, 2013), which, to support his thesis on the disappearance of one of the *Prison Notebooks*, hands down three unappealable, and overall unsubstantiated, sentences regarding the reason for this disappearance and those responsible: a notebook is missing; it was Togliatti who made it disappear; Gramsci repudiates communism and his party in this missing notebook. Paradoxically, to support his arguments, the author used the very absence of documents capable of proving them. The logical structure of his reasoning is the following: if these documents were not found, that means they were destroyed, and therefore, there were things to hide, and certainly the culprit was Palmiro. All the assumptions made about this unbelievable tale of Gramscian espionage would have stemmed from the conspiracies of the communist ruling group, especially Togliatti, which would have planned everything and eliminated the clues with the complicity of poor and helpless Gramsci's wife, sister-in-law and close friend (Piero Sraffa), all KGB agents watching Gramsci under Stalin's command. Even if one admits that one notebook is missing, why would Gramsci concentrate all his criticisms of communism in this single volume? This hypothesis contradicts even the structure of the *Notebooks* and the working method adopted by Gramsci. In all other volumes, nothing is found on this alleged issue.

knowledge acquisition, the materialization of a hegemonic apparatus is a philosophical fact.[27]

From this point of view, the notes entitled "Posing the issue", in *Notebook 7*, are even more explicit and enlightening:

> Marx is the creator of a weltanschauung, but what is Ilyich's position? Is it purely subordinate and subaltern? The explanation lies in Marxism itself—science and action. The passage from utopia to science and from science to action. The establishment of a class of leaders (that is, of a state) is equivalent to the creation of a weltanschauung. [...] For Ilyich, this actually transpired in a particular territory. I have referred elsewhere to the philosophical importance of the concept and fact of hegemony, attributable to Ilyich. The realization of hegemony means the real critique of a philosophy, its real dialectic. [...] To set up a comparison between Marx and Ilyich [...] is foolish and pointless. They are the expression of two phases: science and action, that are simultaneously homogeneous and heterogeneous. [28]

In the following passage, Gramsci draws a curious parallel between the relation between Marx and Lenin and that between Christ and Saint Paul, thus refuting certain interpretations, which still exist, of his distance from a category that emerged after Lenin's death: Marxism-Leninism.

> Likewise, from a historical standpoint, a parallel between Christ and St. Paul would be absurd. Christ—weltanschauung; and St. Paul—organization, action, expansion of the weltanschauung. They are both equally necessary and of the same historical stature. Christianity could be called, historically, Christianity-Paulinism, which would be a more accurate appellation. (The only thing that has prevented this from happening is the belief in the divinity of Christ, but this belief is itself a historical factor, not a theoretical one.)[29]

One of the reasons for this operation must be sought in the cultural and political climate arising from the so-called end of the driving force of the October Revolution and, above all, in the failure of real socialism; nevertheless, regardless of our individual judgment, the philosophical and political science categories of the past cannot be distorted to meet situational

---

[27] Antonio Gramsci, *Quaderni del carcere* (Turin, Einaudi, 1977), 1249–50.

[28] Antonio Gramsci, *Quaderni del carcere*, trans. Joseph Buttigieg, *Prison Notebooks*, v. 3 (New York, Columbia University Press, 2007), 183.

[29] Ibid., 183–184.

requirements. The legacy of the October Revolution represents a real watershed in Gramsci's political thought, between those who reaffirm his adherence (never denied) to this process and those who intend to reduce the value of its centrality by limiting it to a phase of his existence. Around this fundamental core, many of the interpretative nuances related to Gramsci's legacy emerge, though we do not intend to review that on these pages.[30] Starting from our personal point of view, we will limit ourselves to describing Gramsci's process of intellectual development, in an attempt to provide a conceptual and analytical framework as useful as possible to understand his thinking.

---

[30] For those wishing to venture into this territory, we suggest Guido Liguori's volume *Gramsci conteso. Interpretazioni, dibattiti e polemiche 1922–2012* (Rome, Editori Riuniti/ University Press, 2012).

CHAPTER 2

Dialectics *Versus* Positivism: The Young Gramsci's Philosophical Background

In the several phases of his analytical and political activity, Gramsci always identified the origin of Italian socialism's many shortcomings in the philosophically narrow conceptions of the theorists of the Second International. Although he joined the Italian workers' party, that did not mean close and organic adherence to its ideological and cultural horizons precisely because Gramsci only got to socialism after engaging in intellectual debates: that can be confirmed by the type of magazine he had already collaborated with or the periodicals he had read during his years in Sardinia. Thus, we do not agree with the statement that, in his first phase in Turin, Gramsci was influenced not only by "Croce and Italian idealism, but also by the theoretical legacy of the party in which he was active, still linked to the myths, vocabulary and worldview originating from evolutionary positivism".[1]

The young Gramsci's initial contact with idealism resulted from his radical refusal of positivist culture. In the notes of *Notebook 10*, Gramsci himself recalled the importance of this influence, citing an article on Croce, entitled "Religione e serenità" [Religion and serenity], written by him in 1917:

---

[1] Michele Filippini, *Una politica di massa. Antonio Gramsci e la rivoluzione della società* (Rome, Carocci, 2015), 39.

G. Fresu, *Antonio Gramsci*, Marx, Engels, and Marxisms, https://doi.org/10.1007/978-3-031-15610-6_2

> I wrote that just as in the nineteenth century, in the origins of contemporary civilization, Hegelianism had been the premise of the philosophy of praxis, Crocean philosophy could be the premise of a resumption of the philosophy of praxis in our days, for our generations. I merely alluded to the issue, certainly in a primitive and obviously inappropriate way, because at the time the concept of unity between theory and practice, between philosophy and politics, was not clear to me, and I was above all a Crocean.[2]

Although he acknowledged that his view as a young man was still developing, Gramsci considered it beneficial to resume the issue and develop it again, this time critically:

> In short: with regard to Croce's philosophical conception, it is necessary to carry out the same reduction made by the first theorists of the philosophy of praxis with respect to the Hegelian conception. This is the only historically effective way to appropriately resume the philosophy of praxis, to elevate this conception (which, due to the needs of practical life, has been "vulgarized") to the level that it must achieve to be able to solve the most complex tasks proposed by the current development of the struggle, that is, the creation of a whole new culture, with the mass features of Reformation and the French Enlightenment and with the classical features of Greek culture and of the Italian Renaissance, a culture that, in Carducci's words, synthesizes Maximilien Robespierre and Immanuel Kant, politics and philosophy into a dialectic unity that is intrinsic not only to a French or German social group, but to a European and global one. [3]

To build a critical and coherent worldview capable of fighting in the terrain of the hegemonic struggle with liberalism, it was necessary to elevate Italian Marxism to the highest level reached by philosophical thought:

> It is necessary not only to inventory the heritage of classical German philosophy, but to convert it into active life; and for this purpose, it is necessary to settle accounts with Croce's philosophy. In other words, for us Italians, being heirs of German classical philosophy means being heirs of Crocean

---

[2] Antonio Gramsci, *Prison Notebooks* (Turin, Einaudi, 1977), 1233.
[3] Ibid.

philosophy, which represents the current global moment of classical German philosophy.[4]

Gramsci's successive approach to Lenin's thought is, first of all, part of a new cultural environment, a phase of historical change for the workers' movement, which impacts the young Sardinian intellectual by creating a rejection of the deterministic and positivist culture that had penetrated deeply into Italian socialism. This rejection can also be attributed to the strong influence that idealistic Italian philosophy, particularly Benedetto Croce's and Hegel's, had on Gramsci. These relations are clearly represented by the article "Il Sillabo e Hegel", published in *Il Grido del Popolo* on January 15, 1916, as a critique of Mario Missiroli's book *Il Papa in guerra*,[5] about which Domenico Losurdo's reflections are very timely:

> Croce and Gentile are connected by Gramsci to the Italy that emerged from the Risorgimento: they face the opposition of clerical circles, which in Sardinia (and in Italy) of those times constitute a decisive conservative force, due to their terror of all social change, seen as a frightening leap in the dark. These environments see the beast in Hegel and, along with Hegelian philosophy, intend to reject everything modern. However, in the struggle between the Syllabus[6] and Hegel, it was Hegel who won. It was the victory not only of a philosopher, but of a historical development and a real historical world that found its theoretical expression in the system of the German thinker. [...] It is above all the victory of the historical consciousness which, in that situation, refuses to see and suffer from an immutable nature.[7]

Between the nineteenth and twentieth centuries, Marxism established itself within the labor movement largely due to the influence of intellectuals who came to Marx from Darwin and the positivist studies of the social sciences. The spread of Marxism in the German workers' movement took place through two extraordinary publications, namely the weekly *Sozialdemocrat*, published in Zurich under the supervision of Wilhelm Liebknecht, and the journal *Neue Zeit*, launched in September 1882 in

---

[4] Ibid., 1235.

[5] Bologna, Zanichelli, 1915.

[6] *Sillabo* is the pontifical document published by Pius IX in 1864, together with the encyclical *Quanta cura*. The document condemned dozens of "errors" of thought seen as the evil of those times, among them rationalism, scientism, socialism, etc.

[7] Domenico Losurdo, *Antonio Gramsci dal liberalismo al comunismo critico* (Rome, Gamberetti, 1997), 19.

Salzburg by a circle that included such figures as Kautsky, Liebknecht, Bebel and Dietz.

Neue Zeit established itself as the first theoretical journal of a labor party and became the main means for Marxism to gain ground in the Second International;[8] this magazine's diffusion of Marxism was greatly influenced by the intellectual stance of its founders, in which the close relationship with Marxism was linked to positivist conceptions, such as boundless faith in science and progress and in the absolute primacy given to the social sciences. The very history of this magazine, of its debates and of its changes is the history of Marxism of the Second International. In this regard, Ernesto Ragionieri came to a definition that is both concise and precise:

> By Marxism of the Second International what is generally understood is an interpretation and conceptualization of Marxism that claims that its conceptions of history are scientific at the same time that it sees development as a necessary succession of systems of economic production, according to an evolutionary process that only at its limit encompasses the possibility of revolutionary ruptures, which emerge from the development of objective conditions.[9]

From Gramsci's viewpoint, Marxism represented a fundamental moment of modern culture, capable even of influencing some very important currents, external to the Marxist field itself. However, the "official Marxists" of the late nineteenth century neglected this phenomenon because the link between Marxism and modern culture was represented by idealistic philosophy. In his notes, Gramsci resumed several times the double revision of Marxism between the nineteenth and twentieth centuries: on the one hand, some of its elements were taken from certain idealistic currents (Croce, Sorel, Bergson); on the other, the so-called official Marxists, concerned with finding a philosophy capable of encompassing Marxism, clung to modern derivations of philosophical materialism or even neo-Kantianism. The "official Marxists" sought a unitary philosophical conception outside of historical materialism precisely because their conceptions were based on the idea of the absolute historicity of Marxism,

[8] Ernesto Ragionieri, *Socialdemocrazia tedesca e socialisti italiani 1875–1895* (Milan, Feltrinelli, 1961); ibid., *Il marxismo e l'Internazionale* (Rome, Editori Riuniti, 1968).

[9] Ibid., *Alle origini del marxismo della Seconda Internazionale* (Rome, Editori Riuniti, 1968), 47.

as a historical product of the combined action of the French Revolution and the Industrial Revolution, completely ignoring German philosophy. In this context, according to Gramsci, in the Italian Marxist landscape, Labriola was the only one who differed by presenting Marxism as an independent and original philosophy and striving to "scientifically build" the *philosophy of praxis*. This characteristic definition of Labriola in the *Notebooks*, which Gramsci considered more accurate than *historical materialism*, was adopted not only due to its ability to better explain the unitary relationship between theory and practice: it is the organic expression of a conception of Marxism as an autonomous and (philosophically) self-sufficient worldview. As was clearly explained in the important book by Marcello Mustè, dedicated precisely to the intellectual path of the *philosophy of praxis* of Labriola and Gramsci, this is not just a theoretical nuance. We are facing an authentic watershed in the way of understanding Marxism, which provided an absolutely original feature to Italian historical materialism:

> Antonio Labriola employed the expression "philosophy of praxis" in the third Marxist essay, at the end of the fourth letter to Georges Sorel, defining it as the "backbone" of historical materialism. Although antecedents have been sought among the writers of the Hegelian left (August von Cieszkowski, Moses Hess), there is no doubt that Labriola gave this formula a particular tone, either by proposing Marxism as an independent theory, against any "combination" with positivism or with neo-Kantianism, or by mediating between Marxism and national philosophical tradition, from the beginning to the end. These two characteristics—Marxism as philosophy and the relationship with Italian thought—remained decisive throughout subsequent history, at least until Gramsci. Praxis, initially distinguished by Labriola as the beginning of a new conception capable of eschewing the aporia of materialism and idealism simultaneously, would become the core of a long intellectual history, in which Italian culture would develop a particular relationship with the work of Marx.[10]

According to the Sardinian intellectual, Labriola represented the highest product of Marxist philosophical tradition in Italy. Not by chance, in *Notebooks 3* and *11*, he polemicized harshly against Trotsky, who dared to define Labriola's approach to Marxism as "dilettante". In these notes

---

[10] Marcello Mustè, *Marxismo e filosofia della praxis. Da Labriola a Gramsci* (Rome, Viella, 2018), 19.

dedicated to Labriola, opposing and complementing the Russian revolutionary's negative judgment, Gramsci felt the need to face the problem of the double revision suffered by Marxism: that of vulgar materialism, which was unable to encompass the issue of Marxist philosophical culture, and that of the neo-Kantian current, which sought to amend historical materialism and integrate it with other philosophies.

According to Gramsci, in the romantic phase of the struggle, Labriola's little influence on the social-democrat press was a consequence of the excessive importance attached to tactical issues and the lack of will to confront theoretical debates. This contradiction would be overcome with the emergence of new problems associated with the construction of the socialist state, an unprecedented context in which Labriola should be revisited to disseminate his approach to the philosophical issue underlying the tendencies of Marxism.[11] With the conscious and planned development of productive forces, the most mechanistic and primitive stances of Marxism should necessarily be overcome. In this attempt to advance the socialist movement, Gramsci believed that Labriola's philosophical view could play a central role, and therefore insisted on the need for an objective and systematic study of his work to understand his path of development and his theoretical thought.

As Marco Vanzulli adequately explains, Labriola's little success stemmed from his marginal position in relation to the two main Marxist currents of the time: Kautsky's orthodoxy and Bernstein's revisionism. In addition, Labriola's theoretical legacy had in Croce an "ambiguous" curator who "neutralizes the Labriolan work that he intended to administer".[12] Nonetheless, in spite of the result obtained, Labriola's work took on a central role both because of the development of Italian historical materialism and because of the attempts of "revision" made by Benedetto Croce and Giovanni Gentile.

> The longstanding issue of Labriola's reception must be approached from the double perspective of his internal theoretical characteristics and of his stance on the theoretical struggle inside and outside Marxism. The fact that Labriola was isolated and that his thought had no followers is not due to the fact that it was not read. Indeed, it was Labriola who introduced historical materialism in Italy. As previously mentioned, the anti-Marxist revisionists,

[11] Antonio Gramsci, *Quaderni del carcere*, cit., 309.

[12] Marco Vanzulli, *Il marxismo e l'idealismo. Studi su Labriola, Croce, Gentile e Gramsci* (Rome, Aracne, 2013), 23.

Croce and Gentile, started from Labriola's conception of historical material-ism to criticize Marx, nevertheless not being able to master and critically focus on the critical exposition of Marxism in the Saggi [sul materialismo storico]. Thus, they simultaneously revisioned Marx and Labriola: Marx through their misunderstanding of Labriola, and Labriola through their reductio ad unum of Marx (Marx only historical, Marx only philosopher, Marx only metaphysical etc.).[13]

Evidence of such centrality, regardless of philosophical accomplish-ment, is provided by the fact that Antonio Labriola, a disciple of the great philosopher Bertrando Spaventa, was practically the only point of refer-ence within Italian Marxism for the youngsters of *L'Ordine Nuovo* and particularly for Gramsci.

In the Neapolitan Hegelianism of the nineteenth century, two oppos-ing currents developed: a right-wing current, associated with Augusto Vera, and a left-wing one, led by Spaventa. When talking about the sources of Gramscian Marxism, in an interview in 1953,[14] Togliatti stated that in Italian historical materialism, Spaventa was to Labriola what Feuerbach had been to Marx. Therefore, Labriola's intellectual transition was the same as Marx and Engels's, and to this context Togliatti added Gramsci's path of theoretical development.

In addition to their own criticism of positivism and economic deter-minism, both intellectuals had multiple affinities. They shared the idealis-tic starting point, which was overcome due to the discovery of Marxism, as well as the same interest in the studies of glossology and comparative linguistics.[15] They had in common an aversion to the dilettantism of Achille Loria, who was considered by both a representative figure of the

---

[13] Ibid., 24–5.

[14] Marcella Ferrara e Maurizio Ferrara (eds.), *Conversando con Togliatti. Note biografiche* (Rome, Editori di Cultura Sociale, 1953), 29.

[15] "In my youth, I witnessed the Neapolitan revival of Hegelianism. For a long time, I was divided between glossology and philosophy. When I came to Rome as a professor, I was an unconscionable socialist and an avowed opponent of individualism solely on abstract grounds. Then I studied public law and, between 1879 and 1880, was already practically converted to a socialist conception, but much more by the general conception of history than by the internal impulse of a true personal conviction. A slow and continuous approach to the real problems of life, a disgust for political corruption, and contact with workers gradually transformed the scientific socialist *in abstracto* into a true socialist." (Antonio Labriola, "Lettera a F. Engels", April 3, 1890, in *Scritti filosofici e politici*, Turin, Einaudi, 1973, v. I, 256).

then predominant intellectual backwardness. Both highlighted several times how the success of Loria's work among socialists, despite the anti-socialist nature of his criticism of Marx, attested to the theoretical fragility of Italian socialism under the auspices of Filippo Turati.[16] According to Labriola, the theoretical limits of Italian socialism were the logical premise of all the political degeneration of the Italian Socialist Party (PSI)—whose horizon was delimited by parliamentary positivism-evolutionism—as well as its inability to interpret reality and therefore transform it.

Another point of emphasis of Labriola for the youngsters of *L'Ordine Nuovo* was his constant polemic against the Turatian assertion about the absolute superiority of the parliamentary representative system, from which the impossibility of overcoming liberal-democratic institutions through revolution would derive. Turati's gradualism did not contemplate at all the structural nature of the capital-labor conflict, which is why, according to Labriola, his claims for social justice ended up acquiring a sense that is not only abstract but also inhibitory. Precisely because of this contradiction, Labriola constantly invoked the complete autonomy of Marxism in relation to any liberal and bourgeois influence. This requirement of self-sufficiency should be expressed both in terms of categories and in the vocabulary used. In this sense, for example, in a letter to Engels of 1894, on the new edition of the *Anti-Dühring*, Labriola referred to the rhetorical and inferior use of the term "dialectics" in the social-democratic movement, advising its replacement with the term "genetic method". In addition to its higher or lower accuracy, this suggestion meant to highlight the distance between historical materialism and its mechanical interpretation by the disciples of Darwin and Spencer. If the dialectical method expressed the thought process as motion, the genetic conception could more fully encompass the real and material content of things: the former

---

[16] "In the three thousand pages he has published so far, [Loria] has always fought socialism and at least three hundred times accused Marx of being a sophist, a mystifier, etc. Loria is not a politician, has no popularity, does not speak to the general public, has no influence and, as a professor, has only one remarkable characteristic, the unwillingness to teach. His writings are rarely read because they are illegible, and the man is not at all esteemed: quite the contrary! This cheering squad was created—and in bad faith—by the ignorant priests of socialism, and he adapted to it because, as he himself told me, 'great men (*sic*), such as Bismarck, take care of their ideas and not of their followers'. He said this to me in response to the question I had asked him: 'Why do you tolerate socialists calling you a socialist if you are not a socialist?'" (Ibid., "Lettera a F. Engels", August 11, 1894, in *Scritti filosofici e politici*, cit., 401).

would indicate only the formal aspect, while the latter would not harm the empirical nature of each creation, which was further evidence of the misery of positivism and the deterministic vulgarization of historical materialism.[17]

Addressing this question in another letter of 1894, Labriola highlighted in *Capital* a case that illustrated it all: "in fact there is nothing perfect in the method of thinking. Not in a specific form, but in all forms. The concrete genesis (English accumulation); the abstract genesis (commodity analysis etc.); contradiction, which leads it out of the scope of a concept or a fact (money-commodity-money)".[18] The problem lay in the need to refine the definitions and categories used to explain this process and thus show the metaphysical deviations present in the popular adaptations made by intellectuals such as Kautsky. For Labriola, "the comparative logic of language is not only an indispensable discipline, but also the key to finding the causes, that is, the reasons for each metaphysical deviation of thought".[19]

Based on this fruitful debate, Gramsci admitted, in the *Notebooks*, the difficulty in understanding why Marxism, given some of its non-negligible aspects, was assimilated by both idealism and vulgar materialism, because this type of investigation should not only explain which elements had been "explicitly" incorporated by idealism and other currents of thought but also reveal the "implicit" and unacknowledged incorporations. Indeed, Marxism was a moment of culture, a diffuse atmosphere that, as such, changed the old ways of thinking in a previously inconceivable way. Building a history of modern culture after Marx and Engels required a rigorous study of the practical lessons bequeathed as a legacy by Marxism to the parties and currents of thought that oppose it.

The reasons why the "orthodox" of the Second International combined the *philosophy of praxis* with other philosophies and conceptions could be found in the need to combat, among the popular masses, what was left of the pre-capitalist world and derived particularly from religious conceptions. At the same time, Marxism had the task of combating the "higher ideologies of the cultivated classes" and of removing the masses from a still medieval culture, giving them conditions to create their own group of organic intellectuals, independent of the ruling classes. It was

---

[17] Ibid., "Lettera a F. Engels", June 13, 1894, in *Scritti filosofici e politici*, cit., 393.
[18] Ibid., 402.
[19] Ibid.

precisely this second goal of pedagogical nature that ended up absorbing much of the "quantitative" and "qualitative" energies of the movement:

> For "pedagogical reasons", the new philosophy combined with a form of culture slightly superior to the popular average (which was very low), but was totally inadequate to combat the ideology of the cultivated classes, although the new philosophy had come into existence to overcome the highest cultural manifestations of the time, German classical philosophy, and to create a group of intellectuals within the social group that originated the worldviews.[20]

In Gramsci's view, Antonio Labriola was the only Italian philosopher who was fully aware of these contradictions. Indeed, he came into contact with socialism after a long and planned philosophical and political approach, which greatly differentiated him from the theorists of *Neue Zeit*, with whom he was embroiled in countless controversies, and that emphasized the need for an approach to Marxism that he defined as "critical communism". We turn to the remarkable work of Marcello Mustè to show the originality of such approach:

> The criticism of Darwinism led Labriola to identify the truly essential point of human historicity, which meant, in the categories he used, the relations between progress and becoming, or (in the terms characteristic of Spaventa's thought), between thought and being. The differentiation in relation to animal nature occurred when human beings, reacting to their own needs, transformed matter through work, not repeating the form of nature, but replacing it and confusing its own form: natural becoming was transcended here by progress as an essential aspect of human history.[21]

In his struggle against the "dilettantism of certain neophytes of the socialist cause", Labriola opposed the spurious combinations between Marxism and the necessarily unitary and systemic constructions, which were characteristic of the positivism and evolutionism applied to social theory. In his view, one of the most nefarious historical products of the culture of that time was *verbalism*, that is, the exaggerated cult of words, which leads to the corrosion of the real and living sense of "real things" by

---

[20] Antonio Gramsci, *Quaderni del carcere*, cit., 1858.
[21] Marcello Mustè, *Marxismo e filosofia della praxis*, cit., 47.

hiding them and transforming them into abstract and conventional terms, words and ways of saying:

> Verbalism tends to be limited to purely formal definitions; it misleads the mind into thinking it is easy to reduce the immense, intricate complex of nature and of history to terms or phrases that are simple and concrete; and it leads to the belief that the multiform and complex, most complex, linkage between cause and effect are understandable at a glance, as if it were a theater performance; or, more directly, it conceals the meaning of issues because one cannot see anything beyond words.[22]

When verbalism joins the theoretical assumptions of a false opposition between matter and spirit, it immediately claims to explain everything about man, based only on the calculation of material interests, to the point of contrasting them with ideal interests and mechanically reducing the latter to the former. This way of understanding historical materialism originated from the unpreparedness and improvisation of many intellectuals that spread Marxism, who tried to explain to others what they did not fully understand yet, which extended to history the laws and conceptual models that had been appropriately applied to the study and explanation of the natural and animal world. But human history is the result of the process in which a subject can create and perfect his working instruments and change, with these very instruments, the environment where he is inserted, so as to create another, new and artificial. This environment, in turn, reacts and produces multiple effects on the individual. Told from the perspective of the use of the word, that is, the part of the human process that is expressed in traditions and memory, history begins when the creation of this terrain has already occurred, when the economy is already in progress. Historical science has as its fundamental object precisely the knowledge of this artificial terrain, its original forms, its transformations, and only the abuse of analogies and the rush to reach conclusions could lead to the inference that this is all nothing more than a part and extension of nature. Thus, according to Labriola, there was no reason to convert this evolutionary process involving human beings and their environment—that is, history— into a mere struggle for existence. There was no reason to confuse Darwinism with historical materialism, nor even to evoke and use any kind of "mythical, mystical or metaphorical" fatalism. Therefore, claiming that

---

[22] Antonio Labriola, *La concezione materialistica della storia* (Bari, Laterza, 1965), 62.

human will plays no role or attempting to replace it with automatism was in direct conflict with Marx's thought. The tendency to transform every conclusion of thought into pedantry and "Scholastic novels" made all purposes possible, leading "the imagination of the inexperienced in all artistic and historical research and the zeal of fanatics to find encouragement and opportunities, even in historical materialism, to shape a new ideology and extract from it a new, systematic philosophy of history, that is, one that is schematic, with trends and their respective outline." In Labriola's view, on the contrary, historical materialism is not, and does not intend to be, the intellectual vision of a master plan or design, but a method of investigation and conception. Despite being contradictory and ineffective in theoretical terms, the various criticisms of the several detractors of Marx had devastating repercussions in the ranks of the socialist movement, freely exercising their own hegemony, especially among the young intellectuals who would later serve the working class in the last thirty years of the nineteenth century:

> Many of the most ardent reformers of the world at the time began to proclaim themselves followers of Marxist theory, embracing the Marxism that was somewhat invented by their adversaries, and that is how they, by mixing old things with new ones, came to believe that the theory of *surplus value*, as it is usually presented, simplified in simple explanations, encompased *hic et nunc* the practical canon, the driving force, even the moral and legal legitimacy of all proletarian claims.[23]

Between the 1870s and 1880s, a form of *neo-utopianism* was created, driven by a mediocre "universal philosophy", in which socialism should be inserted as part of the whole—literally the ideal breeding ground for all enthusiasts of socialist determinism. In a letter to Turati[24] Labriola describes his philosophical path, refusing to be rechristened by Darwin and Spencer because, while he could call himself a socialist for a little more than a decade, since graduation he had settled accounts with positivism and neo-Kantianism. He did not intend to learn the rudiments of knowledge from Marxism, and he sought only what it offered, that is, the critique of political economy, the features of historical materialism, the stated politics of the proletariat. According to Luigi Dal Pane, one of the leading

---

[23] Ibid., 200.

[24] In this letter, Labriola polemically responds to an article by Antonio De Bella, published in *Critica Sociale* on June 1, 1897, which mentioned him.

experts in Labriola, he saw in historical materialism "the starting point for unexpected developments" because in the work of Marx and Engels materialism was a guiding thread, a guideline, not a pragmatic connection of principles expressed in a precise and, above all, definite manner:

> Indeed, Marx and Engels did not consider systematically organizing the new doctrine, and at different moments of their lives, depending on the circumstances, they focused on one or another aspect of historical human life, without a pre-established and strict logical order. By doing so, they came up with a great scheme, some really useful and important guiding principles for those who are able to revive them, but of little importance for those who announce them in an abstract way.[25]

Marxism, therefore, could not be reduced to a doctrinal formula devised by the clear distinction between, and mathematical succession of, economic and ideological categories. On the contrary, it was an "organic conception of history" as the unity and totality of social life, in which even the economy, instead of extending abstractly to everything else, is historically conceived.[26] Being a disciple of the great philosopher Bertrando Spaventa and having graduated in Naples, the very seat of the second wave of Hegelianism,[27] Labriola approached Marx already having deep knowledge of dialectics.[28] In Labriola's view, that explained the difference between his conception of the philosophy of praxis and that of so many Marxist-positivist intellectuals of the new generation, who were responsible, according to him, for confusing "the line of development, which is typical of historical materialism [...] with that brain pathology that, a few years ago, invaded the brains of many Italians, who now speak of some mother-evolution and worship it".[29] This is an essential point highlighted by Labriola that Gramsci sometimes revisits: the encounter between positivism and Marxism, from which it follows that deterministic vulgarization

---

[25] Luigi Dal Pane, *Antonio Labriola nella politica e nella cultura italiana* (Turin, Einaudi, 1975), 340.

[26] Antonio Labriola, *In memoria del Manifesto dei comunisti* (Rome, Newton Compton, 1973).

[27] In this regard, we recommend the book by Domenico Losurdo, *Dai Fratelli Spaventa a Gramsci. Per una storia politica della fortuna di Hegel in Italia* (Naples, La Città del Sole, 2006).

[28] Antonio Labriola, *Opere*, v. I, v. II and v. III (ed. L. Dal Pane, Milan, Feltrinelli, 1959–1962).

[29] Ibid., *La concezione materialistica della storia*, cit., 240.

derives from, among the many motivations behind it, the ignorance of Hegelian dialectics on the part of many of those who set out to spread Marxism.

This perspective is evidenced by the afterword to the second edition of *Capital*, of 1873, in which Karl Marx—referring to criticism that had been made thirty years before against the mystifying facet of Hegelian dialectics—thought it necessary to treat Hegel as a "dead dog". In this afterword, in addition to admitting that he agreed "here and there" with Hegel's manner of expression, Marx explicitly considered himself a disciple of the "great thinker" in the section concerning the theory of value:

> The mystification which dialectic suffers in Hegel's hands, by no means prevents him from being the first to present its general form of working in a comprehensive and conscious manner. With him it is standing on its head. It must be turned right side up again, if you would discover the rational kernel within the mystical shell. In its mystified form, dialectic became the fashion in Germany, because it seemed to transfigure and to glorify the existing state of things. In its rational form it is a scandal and abomination to bourgeoisdom and its doctrinaire professors, because it includes in its comprehension and affirmative recognition of the existing state of things, at the same time also, the recognition of the negation of that state, of its inevitable breaking up.[30]

But the most significant text from this perspective is "Ludwig Feuerbach and the end of German classical philosophy", of 1886, in which Engels deemed it necessary to take the essential elements of Hegelian dialectics to reaffirm its primacy in the face of the conceptions of materialism in its crudest and most mechanical form. Engels was careful to resume the project that he and Marx set out to accomplish: to settle accounts with their own philosophical development, to face the ideological conception of German philosophy.

Clearly, Engels began to publish his essay on Feuerbach in *Neue Zeit* exactly when the last excerpts of Kautsky's essay on *The Poverty of Philosophy* were being published, in which this conception was entirely and systematically clear. In "Ludwig Feuerbach and the end of German classical philosophy", Engels referred to Hegel and the revolutionary nature of his dialectic, recognizing in the German labor movement the legacy of

---

[30] Karl Marx, *Capital*, vol. I, in MECW (New York, International Publishers, 1996, vol. 35, 19–20.

German classical philosophy. According to several scholars, especially Ernesto Ragionieri, the reference to the philosophical development of scientific socialism was Engels's response to the conceptions held by the new generations approaching Marxism.[31]

Thus, if in "Ludwig Feuerbach" the homage and constant reference to Hegel's philosophy took on a controversial sense in the face of the new socialist vulgate, the criticism of its unforgivable simplifications was even more explicit in a letter by Engels of October 27, 1890:

> What all these gentlemen lack is dialectics. All they ever see is cause on the one hand and effect on the other. But what they fail to see is that this is an empty abstraction, that in the real world such metaphysically polar opposites exist only in a crisis, that instead the whole great process takes place solely and entirely in the form of interplay—if of very unequal forces of which the economic trend is by far the strongest, the oldest and the most vital—and that here nothing is absolute and everything relative. So far as they are concerned, Hegel might never have existed.[32]

However, the most interesting explanation for this is in an exchange between Engels and Marx in two letters written between May 8 and 9, 1870. In the first letter, Engels complained to Marx that Wilhelm Liebknecht, in his capacity as editor, had decided to add to the publication *The Peasant War* a footnote with an explanation (unsolicited and, above all, contested) about Hegel. This comment unleashed Engels's fury, who, after defining Liebknecht as a "dunderhead" and the note as "complete nonsense", expresses himself in the following terms:

[31] This is what Ernesto Ragionieri affirmed in this regard: "on the other hand, it is not strange that at the end of this text on Feuerbach, Engels claimed, in the famous sentence *the German workers' movement is heir to German classical philosophy*, a relationship of ideal heredity that official science rejected or left aside. The linkage between the proletariat and German philosophy, which runs throughout the activity of Marx and Engels and often reappears in their texts, is here formulated in such a way that reaches a critical point as it explains and updates one of the terms of the German workers' movement, that is, the politically organized and unionistic German working class, and with this announcement, it calls on the Social-Democratic Party to prove theoretically equal to this historical legacy" (Ernesto Ragionieri, *Il marxismo e l'Internazionale*, cit., 147).

[32] Friedrich Engels, *Engels to Conrad Schmidt*, 5 Aug 1890, in MECW (New York, International Publishers, 2001, vol. 49, 63).

Ad vocem Hegel, the fellow glosses: known to the general public as the discoverer (!) and glorifier (!!) of the royal Prussian state concept (!!!) [...] This dunderhead, who has been jogging around helplessly for years on the ridiculous contradiction between right and might, like an infantry man placed upon a horse with the staggers and locked in the riding-school—this ignoramus has the insolence to wish to dispatch a man like Hegel with the word 'Preuss' and, at the same time, suggests to the public that I had said it. I have now had enough of the whole thing. If Wilhelm doesn't publish my declaration, I shall turn to his superiors, the 'Committee', and if they also get up to tricks, I shall prohibit any further publication. I would rather not be published than let Wilhelm proclaim me a jackass thereby. [33]

In the same exchange, Marx's answer of May 10 is as harsh:

Yesterday I received the enclosed screed from Wilhelm. An incorrigible South German bumpkin. [...] I had written to him that if, when he wrote about Hegel, he knew nothing better than to repeat the old Rotteck-Welcker muck, then he would do better to keep his mouth shut. He says that this would be 'making rather informally short work, etc' of Hegel, and when he writes stupidities beneath Engels' articles, then 'Engels can of course (!) say something at greater length (!!)'. The fellow really is too stupid.[34]

Marx, in turn, responding to Engels's letter, ends the whole case by defining Liebknecht as an "incorrigible South German bumpkin". In addition to this specific case, this understanding of historical materialism was, for both Engels and Marx, the result of a serious misunderstanding. This is what the letter from Engels to Bloch of September 20, 1890 clearly confirms:

According to the materialist view of history, the determining factor in history is, in the final analysis, the production and reproduction of actual life. More than that was never maintained either by Marx or myself. Now if someone distorts this by declaring the economic moment to be the only determining factor, he changes that proposition into a meaningless, abstract, ridiculous piece of jargon. The economic situation is the basis, but the various factors of the superstructure [...] have a bearing on the course of the

---

[33] Friedrich Engels, *Engels to Marx*, 8 May 1870, in MECW (New York, International Publishers, 1988, vol. 43, 509).

[34] Karl Marx, Marx to Engels, 10 May 1870, in MECW (New York, International Publishers, 1988, vol. 43, 511).

historical struggles of which, in many cases, they largely determine the form. It is in the interaction of all these factors and amidst an unending multitude of fortuities (i. e. of things and events whose intrinsic interconnections are so remote or so incapable of proof that we can regard them as non-existent and ignore them) that the economic trend ultimately asserts itself as something inevitable. Otherwise the application of the theory to any particular period of history would, after all, be easier than solving a simple equation of the first degree.[35]

This intense dialectic, in which a figure like Lenin is inserted with disturbing effects,[36] would be the background of Gramsci's future polemics since all deterministic tendencies of historical materialism took place in the general part of the Erfurt program of 1891, written by Kautsky himself, which was not only approved by German social democracy but also soon transformed into a reference point for all other socialist parties, including the Italian one. Antonio Labriola was a separate case in the landscape of Italian socialism, both because of his philosophical development and because he reached a prominent position in the midst of the most advanced debate within the Second International. For all these reasons, Gramsci considered Labriola a reference, almost an antidote to the main philosophical limits of socialism between the nineteenth and twentieth centuries.

---

[35] Friedrich Engels, *Engels to Bloch*, 21–22 Sep 1890, in MECW (New York, International Publishers, 2001, vol. 49, 33–34).

[36] Gianni Fresu, *Lénin leitor de Marx: dialética e determinismo na história do movimento operário* (trans. Rita Matos Coitinho, São Paulo, Anita Garibaldi, 2016).

CHAPTER 3

Self-education and Autonomy of Producers

The young Gramsci, an avid reader of philosophical and political journals since his years in Cagliari, found in historical materialism, understood as a unitary vision of the world, and in the dialectical conception of history a concrete foundation for his intellectual development. In addition to the aforementioned "Il Sillabo e Hegel", this is further illustrated in the article "Socialism and culture",[1] published in *Il Grido del Popolo*, in which his distancing from the predominant cultural matrices in Italian socialism is closely linked to the denunciation of the dualistic relationship between rulers and those ruled that characterized it. Reformist socialism considered culture too complicated for "the grass roots". The involvement of the masses had nothing to do with empathy; it had to take place gradually and through the popularization (trivialization) of concepts and principles reduced to a scholastic and mechanical dimension, as it was believed knowledge should be presented to them in small doses. Maximalists, in turn, merely rejected culture, considering it hopelessly bourgeois and contrary to the interests of the revolutionaries of the proletariat. In this context, the young Gramsci actively engaged in polemics, denouncing an external and encyclopedic idea of culture, which served pedantic and

---

[1] Antonio Gramsci, "Socialism and culture", *Il Grido del Popolo*, 29 Jan 1916, in *Scritti* (1910–1926), volume I (1910–1916), Istituto della Enciclopedia Italiana, Roma, (Treccani, Roma, 2019), p. 128–133.

© The Author(s), under exclusive license to Springer Nature Switzerland AG 2023
G. Fresu, *Antonio Gramsci*, Marx, Engels, and Marxisms,
https://doi.org/10.1007/978-3-031-15610-6_3

presumptuous pundits who use their knowledge to differentiate themselves from the masses, not to put themselves at their service.

Criticism of encyclopedic culture, of scholarship built on citation-dropping and minor concepts, was certainly not new. It was even found in the philosophy of education of a liberal like John Locke and that of a radical democrat like Rousseau. However, Gramsci criticized this attitude toward culture for being typical of the lack of organic connection between intellectuals and the masses.

> We need to free ourselves from the habit of seeing culture as encyclopedic knowledge and men as mere receptacles to be filled with empirical data and accumulated, unconnected raw facts, which must be piled up in the brain as in the columns of a dictionary so as to make it possible to respond to the various stimuli from the outside world. This form of culture is really harmful, especially for the proletariat. It only serves to create people who are out of place and believe they are superior to the rest of humankind because they have committed to memory a certain number of facts and dates, and they take every opportunity to build a wall between themselves and others. It serves to create the kind of coarse and dull intellectualism that Romain Rolland has flayed so unsparingly, which has resulted in a mass of conceited and vain people who affect social life more deleteriously than tuberculosis or syphilis germs have affected the beauty and physical health of the body. The student who knows a little Latin and history, the lawyer who has only managed to get a degree due to the negligence of his professors, they end up seeing themselves as different from and superior to even the best-skilled worker, who fulfills a very precise and indispensable task in life and is a hundred times more valuable in his activity than they are in theirs. This is not culture, but pedantry, not intelligence, but intellect, and it must be fought on an equal footing.[2]

Criticism of an idea of culture understood as the preserve and monopoly of the high castes of intellectuals was thus combined with the polemic against socialist positivism, which applied the categories of natural sciences to the history of humanity. Despite the still present and strong influence of idealism, we already find in this article some characteristic concepts and themes that Gramsci would develop next.

> Culture is something quite different. It is organization, discipline of one's self, ownership of one's own personality; it is the achievement of greater awareness which helps one understand one's own historical value, one's own purpose in life, one's own rights and obligations. But none of this can result

[2] Ibid.

from spontaneous evolution, from actions and reactions which are independent of one's own will, as is the case in the animal and vegetable kingdoms, in which every specimen selects and specifies its own organs unconsciously and fatalistically. Above all, man is spirit, that is, he is a product of history, not nature. There is no other way to explain why, as there have always been exploiters and exploited, creators of wealth and its selfish consumers, socialism has not yet come into being. Only one step at a time has humanity become conscious of its own value and earned the right to free itself from the rules and rights created by a minority that is foregrounded. And this consciousness was developed not under the brutal imperative of physiological necessity, but as a consequence of intelligent reflection, at first just by some but later by the whole class, on the reason behind certain conditions and on how to transform this vassalage into signals of rebellion and social reconstruction. That means every revolution has been preceded by strong criticism, cultural penetration and the spread of ideas among masses of men who once were resistant and only thought of dealing with their own immediate concerns, their own economic and political problems by themselves, with no bonds of solidarity with others in the same condition.[3]

The young Gramsci did not deem it possible to interpret the French Revolution in a natural sense, as a product of the fatalistic development of things. It resulted from a patient work of cultural penetration and construction of collective consciousness.

In December 1916, in the Piedmontese edition of *L'Avanti*, Althusser published an article, "Uomini o macchine" [Men or machines], which is most interesting at least for three reasons: 1) it highlighted the absence of the idea of school reform in the program of the Italian proletariat party; 2) it described the class-bound nature of the Italian school structure and the social selection that it entailed; 3) it identified in the division between the school of the ruling classes and the vocational schools of the masses an instrument at the service of the division and specialization of labor that made the barrier between intellectual work and manual work unsurmountable.

Gramsci saw the horizon of socialists as limited to a vague propaganda in favor of a ghostly popular culture, riddled with paternalism and abstract principles, but empty of substance. In fact, the school remained a bourgeois institution, but the PSI was unable to propose the new to replace the old, just as it generally lacked an organic and coherent strategic perspective.

[3] Ibid., 129.

> Secondary and higher education, which is state-run and thus financed by state revenues, including taxes paid by the proletariat, is only accessible to the children of the bourgeoisie, who enjoy the economic independence needed for tranquil studies. A proletarian, however intelligent, even if endowed with everything necessary to become a man of culture, is forced to either use his qualities in some other activity, or to become a self-taught rebel, that is (apart from some exceptions), a half-man, one who cannot be all he could have been had he been made full and strong by the discipline of the school. Culture is a privilege. And we do not want it to be so. All young people should have equal access to culture.[4]

The rulers-ruled theme, as a consequence of the artificial (unnatural) division between intellectual and manual work, finds in these lines an in-depth anticipation of future Gramscian writing in the *Notebooks*.

> The proletariat, which is excluded from secondary and higher education as a result of the present social conditions that determine some specialization of man—which is unnatural, as it is based on different capacities, and thus harmful to and destructive of production—must seek education in the marginal educational system: technical and vocational schools. Technical schools, established along democratic lines by Minister Casati [Casati Act of 1859—Gabrio Casati (1798–1873), Minister of Public Education in 1867–1888], have undergone a transformation, given the anti-democratic needs of the state budget, that has largely distorted their nature. In most cases, they have become a mere shadow of classical schools and an innocent outlet for the petty-bourgeois mania for landing a job.[5]

The bifurcation, imposed since childhood, between a school of classical culture and one of professional training was the seal historically stamped on productive relations so that the very institution that by nature should favor human emancipation through full conditioning was at their service. In Gramsci's view, as in Marx's, the integral and one-sided development of man could only result from the overcoming of this historically determined rupture. The school should thus combine theoretical and technical knowledge, freeing people from social conditioning and the state of need. Without this molecular transformation of humanity, it would not be possible to eliminate the dominance of man over man and the division between rulers and those ruled.

[4] Ibid., 797–798.
[5] Ibid.

What the proletariat needs is an unbiased educational school system. A school in which children are allowed to develop, mature and acquire the general features that serve to develop character. In short, a humanistic school, as conceived by the ancients and more recently by the men of the Renaissance. A school that does not mortgage children's future and does not force them against their will, their intelligence and their growing awareness to conform to established standards. A school of freedom and free initiative, not a school of slavery and mechanization. The children of proletarians too should have all possibilities and fields open to them to be able to develop their own individuality as best as they can, and hence in the most productive way for both themselves and society. Technical schools should not be allowed to become a breeder of little monsters rigidly trained for a job, with no general ideas, no general culture, no soul, but only infallible eyes and precise hands. Professional culture can also help children blossom into adulthood as long as it is educational and not simply informative, practical and manual. Councillor Sincero,[6] who is an industrialist, acts like a petty bourgeois when protesting against philosophy. Of course, petty-bourgeois industrialists might prefer to have workers who are more machine than man. But the sacrifices made willingly by the whole of society to perfect itself and to nourish the best and most perfect men who will further improve it must bring benefits to the whole of society, not just to one category or one class. It is an issue of rights and of strength. The proletariat must stay alert so as not to be more abused than it already is.[7]

As we have shown, the emphasis on the dialectics (from an anti-positivist perspective) of Marxism was constant in the various moments of Gramsci's thought. In the single issue of *La Città Futura*, entirely written by Gramsci in February 1917 and regarded by most scholars as the point of arrival of his youth, Gramsci celebrated the debunking of the socialist myth of blind faith in everything that comes with the attribute "scientific". It was an antidialetic and superstitious view, in which the active and conscious role was not taken into consideration at all, to the point of making it seem that man's role was passive and subordinate to economic laws. Thus, ideal

---

[6] Reference to Councillor Francesco Sincero, member of the Turin City Council. At the end of 1916, the programs for vocational education were the subject of debate between those who wanted a humanistic education combined with professional education, not immediately subjecting man to the machine, and those who wanted to relegate workers to strictly vocational education, as is the case of Sincero.

[7] Antonio Gramsci, "Socialism and culture", cit., 128–133.

society, socialism, was imagined on the basis of a mystical philosophical positivism, "barrenly mechanical", and very unscientific.

This *débâcle* of science in socialism, or rather of its myth, was seen by Gramsci as a profound renewal causing social subjects leading revolutions to regain consciousness of their own role, hitherto crushed by the weight of *insurmountable natural laws*. "Natural laws, pseudoscientists' fatalism of things, have found a substitute: the tenacious will of man."[8]

Opposing these stances, Claudio Treves accused Gramsci and the youngsters of *L'Ordine Nuovo* of voluntarism and unculture. In the article "La critica critica" of 1918, Gramsci replied that the new generation, by reading and studying the works published throughout Europe after the golden age of positivism, had definitely become aware of the sterilization to which deterministic socialists subjected Marx's work with no cultural achievements or sociopolitical advances. Treves replaced the truly existing individual man with determinism, reducing Marx's thought to an external scheme, to a natural law that develops from the outside and regardless of human will, which attributed to Marxism the doctrine of the inertia of the proletariat.

Treves did not eliminate *voluntarism* as a whole; he limited himself to turning it into the will of small ministerial concessions, of small achievements, "of today's egg is better than tomorrow's chicken, even if it is a louse egg".[9] Thus, positivist socialists abandoned the party to the work of proselytizing the masses, instilling in them a sense of helplessness before the great *historical and natural laws* of economic evolution. Against this view, Gramsci reaffirmed the creative centrality of man in the historical process, which was central to the reflections of *The German ideology*, a work unknown at the time.[10] In this work, Marx and Engels spoke of the development of society and historical becoming as a result of permanent interaction between man and the surrounding reality, because of which the first historical act of individuals, which distinguished them from animals, was not thought, but the production of one's own means of

---

[8] Antonio Gramsci, "La Città futura", 11 Feb 1917, in *Scritti giovanili*, cit., 85.

[9] Idem, "La critica critica", *Il Grido del Popolo*, 12 Jan 1918, in *Scritti giovanili*, cit., 155.

[10] *The German ideology* was originally published in 1932, in German, on the initiative of the Moscow Marx-Engels-Lenin Institute (the first translation into Russian dates from 1933). Recent studies have shown that Gramsci knew significant parts of this work (before it was fully published) through a 1924 Russian anthology of texts by Marx and Engels. Francesca Antonini, "Gramsci, il materialismo storico e l'antologia russa del 1924", *Studi Storici: Rivista Trimestrale dell'Istituto Gramsci*, v. 59, n. 2, 2018, 403–36.

livelihood. Production is the dynamic and creative origin of new needs and capacities from which society emerges; it is the first historical action and the premise of all other activities. Man produces not only goods but also ideas and representations of reality.

Against all deterministic reductionism of becoming, Gramsci attributed to the "new generation" the will to resume Marx's genuine doctrine, "according to which man and reality, the instrument of work and will, are not eliminated, but identified in historial action" and by which "the canons of historical materialism should be used only *post factum*, to study and understand past events, and should not mean mortgaging the present and the future".[11]

Official Marxism's deformation of Marx's work was responsible for its great loss of vitality, which transformed the deepest sense of historical materialism into "parables" marked by categorical and indisputable imperatives, external to every category of space and time. In Gramsci's view, Marx was neither a messiah nor a prophet, but a historian; therefore, Marxism needed to be cleansed of the multiple metaphysical incrustations and appropriately recast so as to consistently encompass general values and serve as a scientific method of historical assessment:

> Before Marx, history was the domain of ideas alone. Man was considered pure spirit, pure consciousness. Two flawed consequences derived from this conception: the ideas being demonstrated were often arbitrary, fictitious. Attention was paid to anecdotal, not historical facts. With Marx, history continues to be the domain of ideas, of the spirit, of the conscious activity of individuals, whether alone or in cooperation. But ideas, the spirit, take on substance and lose their arbitrary character; they are not mere abstract religious or sociological fiction. Their substance can be found in the economy, in practical activity, in systems and relations of production and exchange. [...] The adverbial "in a Marxist sense" is useless and can lead to misconceptions and to an effusion of facts and parables. Marxist, in a Marxist sense... the adjective and the adverbial are tarnished like coins passing from hand to hand.[12]

With this premise, the October Revolution of 1917 and the role of its main leader inspired the young Gramsci, eliminating the dogmatic constraints of determinism and its alleged historical linearity, which was

---

[11] Antonio Gramsci, "La critica critica", cit., 155.
[12] Idem, "Il nostro Marx", *Il Grido del Popolo*, 4 May 1918, in *Scritti giovanili*, cit., 220.

inspired by the natural sciences. Because of this linearity, the transition from feudalism to capitalism, and from the latter to socialism, would occur just as in the evolution of species, as in the transition from monkey to man. This evolution would result from internal contradictions in the economy and not from the active and conscious intervention of the masses. In this context, the famous article "La rivoluzione contro il capitale" [The revolution against capital] of December 1917 captures with surprising lucidity the most apparent data on the first "assault on the heavens" of the twentieth century. This article, often classified as naive, idealistic and representative of a still "very immature" Gramsci, is in many ways a manifesto of the Gramscian conception of revolution:

> [The Bolsheviks] have not used the Master's work to compile an outside doctrine based on dogmatic and indisputable claims. They are living out Marxist thought, the now undying Marxist thought, which is the continuation of Italian and German thought and which in Marx was contaminated with positivist and naturalistic incrustations. And this thought has always identified as the most important factor in history not raw economic facts, but man, human society, created by men who come together, who forge through this contact (civilization) a collective will, who understand economic facts, assess them and adapt them to their will, until this becomes the driving force of the economy, shaping objective reality [...].[13]

The intellectual development of the young Antonio Gramsci, motivated by a markedly anti-positivist Marxism, was simultaneously nourished by the contributions of idealistic philosophy and by Leninist conceptions of revolutionary intervention. We must add to these two driving forces the Sorelian criticism of the decadence and corruption of Marxism, reduced by social democracy to the mere conventional formula which, according to the French philosopher, used revolutionary terminology to conceal a political practice far from the masses and at the exclusive service of a group of bourgeois leaders and intellectuals.

In Gramsci, the problem of the relationship between intellectuals and the masses within the labor movement is faced in the light of clear and blunt criticism of the decadent modalities of political leadership in socialism. He identifies in the instrumental nature of this relationship the reasons for a radical sociopolitical reorganization, for which the self-sufficiency

---

[13] Ibid., 150.

of the working class was a requirement that could no longer be postponed given the prospects of the socialist revolution.

> In the beginning, the Italian Socialist Party was built by the chaotic confluence of individuals from diverse social backgrounds: it has taken a long time for it to become an interpreter of the classist will of the proletariat. It has become the stage for bizarre individualities, for restless spirits; in the absence of political and economic freedoms that encourage action and continually renew the ruling classes, the Socialist Party has been the supplier of new individuals to the lazy and tedious bourgeoisie. The most quoted journalists, the most capable and active politicians of the bourgeois class, they are all deserters of the socialist movement; the Socialist Party has been the parade of wealth of Italian politics and has become the most effective sieve of Jacobin individualism.[14]

In such reflections, the influence that Georges Sorel, an outspoken critic of Marxist organizations' tendency toward disintegration, had on Gramsci is clear. According to the French philosopher, the emergence of revolutionary political parties creates a completely new and unforeseen scenario for the historical movement of social struggle, in which we no longer find ourselves before subaltern classes mobilized by instinct and necessity, but rather before educated leaders who reason the interests of the party out just as entrepreneurs do with their profits. First of all, these parties are motivated opportunistically by advantages offered by the exercise of state power; moreover, in the vast majority of cases, their leaders come from the very ruling class that the revolution would seek to overthrow:

> The fact is [Sorel writes] that these men, not having found in their own class the means to rise to power, had to recruit a loyal army among those classes whose interests are the opposite of their own families'.[15]

The emergence of parties within the revolutionary movement caused it to move away from "primitive simplicity". In the beginning, the will was based on numerical strength and therefore on the belief that it is possible

[14] Antonio Gramsci, "Dopo il Congresso", *Il Grido del Popolo*, 14 Sep 1918, in *Scritti giovanili 1914–1918*, cit., 313.

[15] Georges Sorel, "La decomposizione del marxismo", in *Scritti politici* (Turin, Unione Tipografico-Editrice Torinese, 1968), 747.

to establish a new order consistent with its requirements. However, when the masses accepted the leadership of men with interests different from their own, the instinct of revolt became the basis of "the people's state" (the political organization of the workers' movement) formed by the bourgeois eager to continue their bourgeois life, but now in the capacity of leaders of the proletariat. In Sorel's view, the possession of the state is the real object of desire of the bourgeois intellectuals made leaders of the revolutionary movement. It is because of this desire that socialist parties soon became complicated "electoral machines" unable to resist the force of attraction of power, ending up completely absorbed by it.

In Sorel, there are two central themes for Gramsci: (1) the instrumental use of the masses by bourgeois intellectuals as a springboard for the achievement of their personal aspirations; (2) the progressive co-opting of leaders of the workers' movement by the bourgeois state:

> Constantly increasing its number of employees, this state strives to form a group of intellectuals distinct from the producing proletariat; thus, the defense of the bourgeois structure against the proletarian revolution is strengthened. Experience shows that such a bourgeoisie of officials, however fragile their culture may be, is no less fond of bourgeois ideas; a great number of examples demonstrate that if any propagandist of the revolution can penetrate into governmental environments, he will easily become an excellent bourgeois.[16]

Referring to another theorist of revolutionary syndicalism, Fernand Pelloutier, Sorel found the solution to this problem in the full self-government of producers, essentially through their own institutions, such as *Bourses du travail*,[17] where the working class should educate and organize itself for the revolution, definitively overcoming any suggestion of reform of capitalism. Nevertheless, political parties, led by the intellectuals of the bourgeoisie, who are driven by electoral demands and the politics of concession, end up corrupting the instincts of the proletariat, causing revolutionary vigor to ebb away. Sorel referred to Pelloutier to affirm that producer organizations needed to deal with their own business, without "resorting to the advice of bourgeois representatives" and finding in general strikes the measure of their own self-sufficiency and independence from the educated classes and therefore the advent of the future world.

[16] Ibid., 749.
[17] French for "labor exchanges", which were mutual aid associations.

In his *Le strategie del potere in Gramsci*, Leonardo Paggi carefully analyzed the weight of *Sorelian* influence. At the same time, however, he stressed that Gramsci's response to this problem was not expressed in the denial of the revolutionary political party as such, but rather in "a strong correlation between socialism and culture in an attempt to highlight the role that the self-education of the working class could play in choosing a leading group capable of imposing barriers on the *dictatorship of intellectuals*".[18]

In the young Gramsci's view, contrary to what Sorel advocated, Marxism could and should be a new modality of participation of the subaltern classes in political life as a tool for releasing new human energies, both individual and collective, which would help overcome the historically determined division between rulers and those ruled, between intellectual and manual labor.

Opposition to the "dictatorship of intellectuals" (this is how leading political characters of a party were viewed) finds in the self-education of the working class its most consequential response, and this should occur first in the collective organizations of the working class, such as factory councils, and in their unmediated rise to productive and political leadership. "Self-education" and promotion to a leading role are, first and foremost, a means of making the masses self-sufficient in the face of leading groups and bureaucratic apparatuses that overlapped inorganically.

Gramsci emphasized the need to "lay the foundations of the revolutionary process in the intimacy of productive life" to prevent it from being reduced to a "useless appeal to the will, a nebulous myth, a fallacious Morgana".[19] Had part of the Marxism of the time conceived the revolution as a theatrical act, it would have been understood as a dialectical process of historical development, whose starting point would have been the creation of councils.

> The current task of communists is to promote the emergence and multiplication of worker and peasant councils, to determine their organization and organic systematization until national unity is achieved at a general congress, and to create powerful propaganda to win the majority. The urgency of this new expansion of powers that necessarily originates from the great working

---

[18] Leonardo Paggi, *Le strategie del potere in Gramsci* (Rome, Editori Riuniti, 1984), 308.
[19] Antonio Gramsci, *L'Ordine Nuovo 1919–1920* (Turin, Einaudi, 1954), 207.

masses will lead to the violent clash between the two classes and the consolidation of the proletarian dictatorship.[20]

According to Carlos Nelson Coutinho, in the writings of young Gramsci we can find a distinct way of conceiving not only representative democracy but also socialism, which are distinct from both "historical communism" and classical liberalism's merely formal sense of democracy:

> Gramsci's redefinition of democracy is not limited to liberal thought or the very dated conceptions of "historical communism"; it refers to the classics of political philosophy, particularly Rousseau and Hegel. I do not think I am mistaken when I say that Gramsci, insisting on the role of consensus in the enlarged state, reintroduced elements of the problem of contractualism into the framework of Marxist thought, not in its liberal (or Lockean) version, but in its democratic radical version proposed by Rousseau.[21]

[20] Antonio Gramsci, *Lo sviluppo della rivoluzione,* 13 settembre 1919, ("l'Ordine Nuovo", n. 18) em Antonio Gramsci, *L'Ordine Nuovo 1919–1920* (Turim, Einaudi, 1972), p. 30–31
[21] Ibid., 152.

CHAPTER 4

Lenin and the Topicality of Revolution

As we have seen, Gramsci's encounter with Turin was of paramount importance in his human and intellectual biography because he saw city as the material and spiritual vanguards of the progressive social forces at the national level due to its working class.

Fascinated by the new reality, he himself stressed the formidable dynamism of the "Italian Petrograd". When the capital was transferred from Turin, first to Florence and then to Rome, the Piedmontese city provided the newly unified state with all its technical and administrative personnel, losing much of its petty and middle intellectual bourgeoisie. Nonetheless, instead of leading to the resizing of the city, this change in roles produced a radical transformation and further development: in a city where small industry and commerce had been predominant, the capital of big industry would emerge, attracting the cream of the Italian working class.

Metallurgical, mainly automobile production, was predominant in Turin: 50 thousand workers and 10 thousand technicians and employees worked in the steel sector alone. According to Gramsci, its managers, most of whom were skilled workers, did not have the petty-bourgeois mentality of skilled workers in other countries, such as England. Metallurgical workers were the majority, and their disputes often spilled over into other categories and took on a political sense even when they emerged from union demands.

© The Author(s), under exclusive license to Springer Nature   47
Switzerland AG 2023
G. Fresu, *Antonio Gramsci*, Marx, Engels, and Marxisms,
https://doi.org/10.1007/978-3-031-15610-6_4

Here, after the brief youth experience with *L'Unione Sarda*, Gramsci committed himself professionally in his activity as a publicist and contributed, from 1915 on, to *L'Avanti!* and soon after to *Il Grido del Popolo*, in which he became one of the most important and prestigious journalists and distinguished himself particularly in the column *Sotto la Mole*:

> It is a new kind of journalism, in which the theme of culture and a deep ideological perspective were harmoniously combined with propaganda and popular education. Biting and appropriate polemical satire converges with theoretical maturity.[1]

It was not just a professional attempt or an instrument of militant action. As early as his youthful years in Sardinia, journalism was a great, all-encompassing passion for Gramsci. Now, in a reality so different from that of his homeland, the practice of journalism became a means of existential assertion, which enabled his personality and his intellectual abilities to find expression and impose themselves on the landscape of Turinese socialism.

In his preface to a recent anthology on journalism, Luciano Canfora highlighted the importance of Gramsci's statement during the interrogation of February 9, 1927, shortly after his arrest. It is well known that, when he was before Enrico Macis, an investigating judge, Gramsci denied the charges of conspiracy, stating his activity as a deputy and above all as a journalist was fully public. However, according to Canfora, not only that was a defensive statement; it was the assertion of a profession, "that of journalism, which Gramsci embraced as his job, leaving behind the university world, where his friendship with the linguist Matteo Bartoli also offered him a major life option".[2]

Once again, this stems from his unitary conception of the philosophy of praxis, in which ontological analysis ("being") and deontological ambition ("duty to be") are organically combined in coherence with a singular (new) integral worldview. For this reason, for Gramsci, journalism was a fundamental trench in the terrain of hegemonic struggle, in the dispute between Marxism and other philosophies. Unlike historical materialism, liberal ideology, with its multifaceted nature (philosophy, law, history,

---

[1] Eugenio Garin, *Con Gramsci* (Rome, Editori Riuniti, 1997), 7.
[2] Antonio Gramsci, *Il giornalismo, il giornalista. Scritti, articoli, lettere del fondatore de "l'Unità"* (org. Gianluca Corradi, Florence, Tessere, 2017), XIII.

economics), could have a consolidated tradition refined over the centuries, with incomparably greater means (universities, schools, newspapers, publishing houses, cultural organizations), besides a prepared intellectual contingent, which is the organic, unincidental expression of concrete interests.

Gramsci attributed not only to historical science but also to journalism an essential role in the development of subaltern groups' critical consciousness, either by masking the other class's latent, embryonic and open forms of ruling, or by shaping their own organic, coherent worldview. In this sense, in *Notebook 6*, he dealt with the need to train journalists "who have the technical preparation that enables them to understand and analyze the organic life of a big city and place within its context (without pedantry but also not superficially and without "brilliant" improvisations) every single problem as it arises and becomes topical".[3] For the Sardinian intellectual, the journalist, not only the editor-in-chief but also the news writer, should have the necessary technical training to perform other roles of political leaders as well (administrator, mayor, member of a provincial council); thus, "the functions of a newspaper should be equated with the corresponding administrative functions".[4]

Gramsci speaks of the "organic leader" as a figure of great intellectual depth, able to summarize the most general and constant aspects of the life of a city, place them at the core of journalistic activity, and move them away from the episodic elements of today. The theme of organicity in the profession of journalism was revisited in *Notebook 14*, in which this activity is presented as "an exhibition of a group that wishes, through various forms of publicization, to spread an integral conception of the world".[5] This was all systematically evidenced in the annual publications, the Almanacs, in which the group disseminated its own worldview, giving it a homogeneous and coherent form with the level of organicity assumed by

---

[3] Antonio Gramsci, *Quaderni del carcere*, trans. Joseph Buttigieg, *Prison Notebooks*, v. 3 (New York: Columbia University Press, 2007), 88.
[4] Ibid.
[5] Antonio Gramsci, *Quaderni del carcere*, cit., 1719.

the general conceptions of things.[6] "Integral journalism" should be able not only to "meet the aspirations of its audience, but also to generate these aspirations and even to generate the audience itself".[7]

Although Gramsci did not sign many of his articles, used pseudonyms or at most use his own initials, he did not take long to become well known in socialist and intellectual circles. In some of his memories, Alfonso Leonetti, who would become a prominent figure of the *L'Ordine Nuovo* group, described the meeting with Gramsci as a life-changing moment that led him to rethink all his political and theoretical development, recalling the endless editorial discussions that took place under the canopies or during walks in the hills, Gramsci's characteristic approach,[8] his intellectual rigor, his deference when they first met, in the editorial office on 12, *Corso* Siccardi (the address of the Casa del Popolo, the headquarters of the Italian Socialist Party (PSI), the Camera del Lavoro [Chamber of Labour] and the Piedmontese editorial office of *L'Avanti!*) in Turin in a hot summer morning of 1918.

> All I knew about him was what Giuseppe Scalarini—the famous cartoonist of *L'Avanti!*—and Alessandro Schiavi told me while I was in Milan: that in Turin I would meet a powerful young socialist writer named Gramsci, whom they told me to find and entrust with my initiation into the Turinese workers' movement.[9]

In his famous biography, Giuseppe Fiori thus describes Gramsci's debut in the field of journalism: "a new writer was born, totally different from

---

[6] From this perspective, the fundamental problem was, first and foremost, ideological, that is, whether the newspaper or journal met the political-intellectual needs of its audience. However, just as in the form of presentation of the publication, its editorial line required the same attention to the ideological and intellectual content since there is an inextricable link between these two elements. "A good principle (but not always) is to give an external aspect to the publication that in itself is noticed and remembered: it is a free ad, so to speak. But not always, because it depends on the psychology of the specific audience that you want to win over" (Ibid., 1742).

[7] Ibid., 1725.

[8] "Gramsci showed no apparent reaction, which did not prevent him from being close friends or sympathizing with people. Gramsci was as indulgent and patient with workers as he was severe, violent and impatient with intellectuals" (Alfonso Leonetti, "Gramsci, i Consigli Di fabbrica e il Congresso di Livorno", in Carlo Salinari, *I comunisti raccontano*, v. 1: *1919–1945*, Milan, Teti, 1975, 14).

[9] Ibid.

those familiar to readers of socialist journalists".[10] In his column, Gramsci wrote articles with a decidedly more cultivated tone than the average socialist publicist:

> These were satirical pieces, small jewels that made the young writer from Sardinia an exemplary pamphleteer, who was unique in a country where the pamphlet is an almost unknown genre [...]. In all of Gramsci's writings, from short theoretical essays to theater chronicles, a new style stood out: the transition from the proclamatory emphasis of the Rabezzana and Barberis to the taste for reasoning; the accurate language, in times of classical purity, so different from the language of the old.[11]

Il Grido del Popolo [The Cry of the People] was an important first response to the need for theoretical development and revolutionary action that the events of 1917 created in the new socialist generation. In the penultimate issue, of October 19, 1918,[12] Gramsci was able to say good-bye to his readers with a respectable assessment and the satisfaction of having left dense material, contributing to the political and cultural uplift of the socialists of Turin:

> *Il Grido* sought to become, like chronicle weeklies and evangelical propaganda ones, a small review of socialist culture, developed according to the doctrine and tactics of revolutionary socialism [...]. *Il Grido* attempted to define a precise, ideal direction, and it certainly succeeded since the opposing newspapers see it as an example of frantic (!) Bolshevism.[13]

With the effervescence resulting from the revolution of 1917, conflicts became fierce and unbridled. The popular forces retook the lead, now aware that they could play a decisive role in the fate of the nation. They expressed expectations and hopes for a now-very-near future, in which everything had to change. In this context, on May 1, 1919, *L'Ordine Nuovo: Rassegna settimanale di cultura socialista* [The New Order: Weekly review of socialist culture] was created certainly connected with the

---

[10] Giuseppe Fiori, *Vita di Antonio Gramsci* (Rome/Bari, Laterza, 1989), 118–9.

[11] Ibid.

[12] When the Turinese socialist section, owner of the weekly, decided on closing its doors to devote all its financial, organizational and intellectual efforts to the Turinese editions of *L'Avanti!*, *Il Grido del Popolo* stopped its publications.

[13] Antonio Gramsci, "*Il Grido del Popolo* (19 ottobre 1918)", in *Scritti giovanili 1914–1918* (Turim, Einaudi, 1975), p. 325.

disruptive force of events, the urgency of the moment, the need to take action in the most critical period of the revolutionary expansion of the twentieth century. But while urgency was decisive to galvanize the editorial board (composed of Ottavio Pastore, Palmiro Togliatti, Alfonso Leonetti, Leo Galetto and Antonio Gramsci himself) into action, the militant enthusiasm of the time also contributed to its acceleration even in the absence of real political-cultural homogeneity among the members of that board.

As Gramsci himself recalled, in an editorial we will mention again later, the only feeling that united the editorial board in its first phase "was that produced by a vague passion of a vague proletarian culture. We wanted to do more and more; we were anguished; we had no guidance; we were immersed in the passionate life of those post-armistice months, when the cataclysm of Italian society seemed to loom on the horizon".[14]

In the years of *L'Ordine Nuovo*, Turin was the most advanced point of Italian industrial expansion and traumatically experienced the exponential increase of the working population. It was the first city in Italy to experience the Taylorist model of production, with all it implied in terms of organization of work, production rates, and even social relations.

In Turin, more than in other Italian cities, the working class and its struggle had achieved a high degree of political subjectivity, and as early as 1913, it was able to impose the collective labor agreement. Besides making the Turinese working class—especially that linked to Fiat—something unprecedented in the national landscape, that enabled, as Franco De Felice wrote, "a strong confirmation of the old Marxist truths about the socialization of production and massification as the other face of the development of capital and the working class as a defined social subject capable of reorganizing production and society".[15] It was in this reality that Gramsci developed the idea of the close relationship between production and revolution as the antithesis of passive delegation to bureaucratic organization, combining the experience of councils with the development of class struggle in Europe.[16]

---

[14] Idem, "Il programma del *L'Ordine Nuovo* 1920", in *L'Ordine Nuovo 1919–1920* (Turin, Einaudi, 1972), 146.

[15] Franco De Felice, "Introduzione al Quaderno 22", in *Americanismo e fordismo* (Turin, Einaudi, 1978), VIII.

[16] Gianni Fresu, *Il diavolo nell'ampolla. Antonio Gramsci, gli intellettuali e il partito* (Naples, Istituto Italiano per gli Studi Filosofici/La Città del Sole, 2005), 43–54.

This need was expressed in the desire to make factory councils a first form of self-government of the working class, a prelude to future socialist society, in order to affirm, even before the revolutionary break, its unity and autonomy. Thus, self-management of production began to have a strategic goal: to help the proletariat learn a psychology of the ruling class. From the viewpoint of the Gramsci of *L'Ordine Nuovo* and also of the Gramsci of the *Notebooks*, workers and masses of people could only free themselves from their own subalternity by being fully aware of the legitimacy, rather than the historical necessity, of the state itself. As we will see, Gramsci thought of the revolutionary subject as a social bloc, within which the working class should take on, from its role in production, the task of guiding the "subaltern stratum" and hesitant intermediate social groups, so that they could disorganize the whole bourgeois state structure in the most critical phases of revolutionary radicalization.

In those years, the labor movement lacked political leadership and a strategy capable of overcoming the *parasitic psychology* of the "inevitability of revolution". In Gramsci's view, the PSI was no different from other parties and, in addition to its incendiary revolutionary declarations, it restricted its political activity to the right of institutional tribune, not facilitating efforts to win the majority of the exploited. Unable to develop a policy aimed at the middle stratum of the city and the countryside, the PSI limited itself to absorbing the issues of peasants in its program. All this explained the isolation of the working class during the "red biennium", despite the continuous pre-insurrectional mobilization of agricultural workers. Gramsci's battles and early reflections on the relationship between leading groups and the masses originated precisely from this dramatic contradiction between increased awareness of living a revolutionary historical period and the simultaneous perception of the structural inadequacy of the political party of the Italian working class.

Franco De Felice drew attention to the way Gramsci highlighted one of the essential principles of the capitalist order, which is based on the distinction between civil society and political society: the differentiation between bourgeoisie and citizen. To subvert that order—rooted in the prominence of the political moment—it was necessary "to recover, as a starting point, the relations of production, which in a capitalist society clearly show the division into classes and the fundamental contradiction of bourgeois society",[17] by making production the source of power and

---

[17] Ibid., XIII.

sovereignty, because the economy is not limited to the production of goods, but also involves the production of social relations.

In other words, according to Gramsci, so as to become the ruling class, the proletariat should match economic function and political function, that is, economic action should ensure, at least to the extent that political action does, the effective autonomy of workers. Socioeconomic self-determination was the requirement for its political action to have "real historical value". The factory council was therefore the basis where the working class should exercise its economic leadership because of its full political leadership. In this regard, the prospect of the political soviet should arise from the organic construction of factory councils:

> The factory council and the system of factory councils put to the test and reveal the new positions that the working class occupies in the field of production; they give the working class an awareness of its current value, of its real function, of its responsibility, of its becoming. The working class learns from the sum of positive experiences that each individual personally has, develops the psychology and characteristics of the ruling class, and as such organizes itself, that is, it creates the political Soviet and establishes its dictatorship.[18]

Gramsci's reflections in those years reflected the various experiences and theories about council democracy, but found in Lenin and the Soviet revolution their main source of inspiration. The transformation of factory councils into the first nucleus of future Soviet society distanced the workers' movement from ideological abstractionism, from radical and empty phraseology and from the inertia typical of the passive mentality centered on the inevitability of revolution, which was transformed into an act of faith.

Gramsci severely criticized the absolute indeterminacy of the discourse of socialist intellectuals and leaders on the Italian economic structure and on the concept of revolution in general, in which the rhetorical requirement of persuasion prevailed over any true intention to understand reality. In his criticism of *maximalist verbalism*, he condemned a whole group of leaders who stopped being concerned about studying Italian economic and social development in depth as soon as they rose to leadership:

---

[18] Antonio Gramsci, "Lo strumento di lavoro (*L'Ordine Nuovo*, anno I, n. 37, 14 febbraio 1920)", in *L'Ordine Nuovo 1919–1920*, cit., 79–80.

Reformists and opportunists avoid concrete determination. They, claiming to be custodians of political wisdom and of the flask with the devil within, no longer study the real problems of the Italian working class and the socialist becoming, having lost all physical and spiritual contact with the proletarian masses and with historical reality [...]; they prefer gambling and parliamentary intrigue to the systematic and deep study of Italian reality.[19]

According to Gramsci, in almost forty years of existence, the PSI was not able to produce a single serious book on the development of production relations in Italy. This disarmed the working class, making it easy prey to a useless revolutionary phraseology with no analytical bases, project or perspective.

Despite the limits of political and unionist leadership, Gramsci believed the working class managed to achieve a high degree of autonomy, created its representative institutions, and became aware of itself and its possibilities of self-government. Thanks to the councils, "and without the help of bourgeois intellectuals",[20] the working class was able to deeply understand the workings of the entire production and exchange apparatus, transforming the real experience of each of its members into collective property. From the elementary unity of its working group, it had become aware of its position in the economic field, educating itself in a socialist sense. This vital expansion of subjectivity succeeded in overcoming the tragic legacy of war, which had left the country torn apart, impoverished and dominated by social contradictions. A side effect of the greatest war in history was that it led to the participation of hitherto passive social groups, to the extent that it created an entirely new framework for "mass politics".

The First World War unleashed immense social forces by launching large masses into the international arena, which were sent to slaughter as "cannon fodder" in the greatest imperialist war ever seen.

The war was a terrible shock for Italy, which had been unified less than half a century before it. In Italy, it left 680 thousand dead, half a million maimed and disabled, more than one million wounded [...]. In no country did demobilization cause such serious problems. The traditional means of emigration, through which about 900 thousand workers were channeled in 1913, chiefly landless peasants, were gradually closing. Where to place those returning from the front and how long could the war industry keep the one

---

[19] Ibid., 80.
[20] Ibid.

million people who worked in it? How to transform the war industry into an industry of peace? In the midst of general disorder, persistent conflicts and renewed ambitions, how to make way for the world market, which had been battered, impoverished and occupied by ruthless competitors, who were more prepared and organized?[21]

The post-war economic and moral crisis was particularly severe in Italy, marked by a stagnation that coincided with the return of the soldiers from the *front* and with the difficulty in converting the war economy into civilian production. A few categories benefitted and profited from the war, but the vast majority of the population saw a significant deterioration in its living conditions. Inflation, mass unemployment, increased exploitation and the contraction of the purchasing power of wages reached very high levels. The war cost the country dearly in terms of lives and social wellbeing, not achieving any of the strategic objectives agreed on in the Treaty of London or those propagandized by the government to favor the general mobilization of the people.

The First World War caused a deep economic, political and cultural crisis in European society. The war was invoked as the progress and purification of humanity, but underlying the rapture of patriotic and military rhetoric was a social picture marked by deep division and explosive issues, among which were the ineffectiveness and instability of the liberal system, the impoverishment and reduction of the middle class, and the emergence in the political arena of the great masses mobilized during the conflict. Historians have already spoken of the moral and identity crisis of a bourgeoisie uneasy about the growth of the workers and peasants' movement and fearful of the example of the October Revolution of 1917. This dramatic and at the same time exciting context, in which the "old world" seemed fated to die overnight, left an indelible mark on Gramsci's life choices, which were devoted to political militancy, and on his theoretical development, which always problematically revolved around these contradictions. Italy was a flashpoint in the European civilizational crisis, and it was no accident that the conditions for the advent of fascism arose there.

Gramsci saw the war as a profound split in Europe's social relations. Forced out of their particular realities, peasants and workers found themselves thrown onto the conflict stage, in a general situation where their conditions of exploitation and civil oppression were reconnected in a way

---

[21] Angelo Tasca, *Nascita e avvento del fascismo* (Bari, Laterza, 1972), 17.

that no longer disguised the political and economic order from which they felt permanently excluded. They were summoned to fight and die in defense of that order, but now, after the conflict, those same masses erupted like magma into social and political life, no longer willing to return to the passivity of the past. The example of the October Revolution played a decisive role in this change of consciousness and become, in the collective imagination of millions of people, proof of the concrete possibility of subverting the state of affairs and thus of leading socialism to be more than mere utopia. How to shape that immense social force into a form of political integration that was strong enough and capable of building the foundations of the future socialist state? "How to amalgamate the present and the future and satisfy the urgent needs of the present while effectively working to create and anticipate the future?"[22] Between 1918 and 1922, Gramsci's reflections and political commitment revolved around these theoretical and practical questions.

In his view, this connection was already present and lay in workers' social life institutions. All they needed was a structured and organic form to indeed create a workers' democracy as opposed to the bourgeois state, so as to replace it in all its functions. Such institutions therefore represented the instrument for the masses to develop ownership and effective leadership of the revolutionary process, by strengthening and educating themselves for this role.

The proletariat could not simply get hold of the bourgeois state machine and change its direction, as if that meant nothing. Running the state administratively, economically and politically warranted a preparation and self-discipline that the bourgeoisie took centuries to refine. Since the proletariat did not have that long, it needed to seize the opportunity offered by the crisis of the old ruling classes so as not to waste the radicalization of the masses against the old order. It was the same problem Lenin faced regarding the revolutionary strategy, which Gramsci understood fully and deeply: the idea of bringing forward the construction of the socialist state, valuing the coordination of the councils and associations of the subaltern classes.

In *The state and revolution*, Lenin highlighted the ambivalence of democratic systems and their tendency to cause not only conflict between capital and labor but also contradictions between the formal dimension of equality, which pertained to the negative dimension of freedom (the

---

[22] Antonio Gramsci, *L'Ordine Nuovo 1919–1920*, cit., 87.

inviolability of the individual sphere by the state), and the reduction of popular sovereignty for the sake of "individualistic-ownership guarantees" through the institute of representation. That leads to retrogression, not to the development of the democratic sphere and to the bureaucratic deterioration of the political state. According to Lenin, the transformation of man into things and of ends into means occurs not only in the relations of production of wealth but also in the political relations arising from them. The construction of social relations distinct from bourgeois ones must start from an inversion of the relationship between man and the object produced by him, either in social and economic relations, or in political relations. According to Cerroni, in Lenin's view, the struggle must develop on both sides, with no dogmatism or shortcuts.

> In any case, it is forbidden to start on both sides at the same time: to extol the dogma of violent initiative and of the dictatorship of the proletariat as a form of state (single-party), not as a type of society (the elimination of capitalism and the bourgeoisie as a class), can mean (historically meant) that one does not start either way. That has been the case in the West, where reformism and extremism continue to fight for the truth.[23]

The problem of the state, Lenin wrote in the preface to *The state and revolution*, takes on a central role, especially at the stage of exacerbation of imperialist conflicts, not only theoretically but also politically, especially to overcome the evolutionary schemes of international social democracy, which, at a relatively peaceful stage of development, subjected itself to bourgeois interests even at the political-institutional level, to the point of asserting the impossibility of overcoming the representative forms of bourgeois parliamentary institutions. Quoting *The origin of the family, private property and the state*, Lenin resumed the idea of the state as a product of social relations founded on private property and created by the need to defend private property in the face of class conflict. In addition to idealistic representations, which describe the state as an expression of moral ideas, the ideologists of the bourgeoisie defined the state as an entity above the parties aiming to reconcile opposing and conflicting interests (the particular with the universal). But the state is not a third body: it is one side of the conflict's barricade, an organ of class rule, "the committee of the interests

---

[23] Umberto Cerroni, "Introduzione", in Vladimir Ilitch Lenin, *Stato e rivoluzione* (Rome, Newton Compton, 1975), 35.

of the bourgeoisie". Lenin wrote that the democratic republic is the best possible envelope for capitalism because it provides stability, strength and continuity for its rule, which is not shaken by the changes of people and parties controlling governments, even when elected by universal suffrage. One of the central themes of this work is the controversy with social democrats about overcoming the bourgeois state, which they present as a gradual process of extinction caused by the effects of the social reforms that put an end to its historical need. Thus, according to Lenin, the moment of revolutionary rupture, the radical and immediate suppression through the socialization of the means of production, and the distribution of the old social bases are omitted and abandoned. But this does not mean that, in the capitalist regime, one must oppose or be indifferent to the forms of the democratic republic; one simply must not have illusions about the limitations to social changes within this institutional form:

> We are in favor of a democratic republic as the best form of state for the proletariat under capitalism, but we have no right to forget that wage slavery is the fate of the people even in the most democratic bourgeois republic.[24]

Thus, for Lenin, the transition to socialism can occur only when the proletariat organizes itself as a ruling class, concentrating in the state, under its direction, all the elements of production, but this process needs to be started much earlier. He considered the peaceful submission of the minority (the ruling class) to the majority of the people a petty-bourgeois illusion. Thinking of the *Eighteenth Brumaire of Louis Bonaparte*, Lenin analyzed the process of enhancement of the branches (legislative, executive and judicial-repressive) of the bourgeois state through the various revolutions it underwent. At the base of centralized state power we find institutions that Lenin defined as parasitic: bureaucracy and the army. Through these two institutions, the great bourgeoisie manages to rule the petty and middle bourgeoisie (urban and rural), guaranteeing their employment in the state apparatus and a social status that differentiates them from the rest of the people and leading them to adhere to the social bloc itself, an issue to which Gramsci returned several times. Speaking of the "most developed countries" and of the consolidation of the state machine at the time of imperialism, Lenin stressed how the instruments of repression against class struggle became more powerful, but at the same

[24] Ibid., 56.

time he already noted the existence of other, more complex forms of control, which went beyond mere domination and would later be an object of study in Gramsci's prison notes:

> On the one hand, the development of "parliamentary power" both in republican countries (France, America, Switzerland), and in monarchies (Britain, Germany to a certain extent, Italy, Scandinavian countries, etc.); on the other hand, a struggle for power among the various bourgeois and pettybourgeois parties which distributed and redistributed the "spoils" of office, with the foundations of bourgeois society unchanged; and, lastly, the perfection and consolidation of "executive power", of its bureaucratic and military apparatus.[25]

The issue of the state and the kind of transition to socialism, a central problem in Gramsci's years at *L'Ordine Nuovo*, are at the core of Lenin's conceptions of revolution that have been expounded here. The historical event of the Paris Commune forced Marx and Engels to write an addendum to the *Manifesto of the Communist Party*, with a sentence that was emblematically included in the preface to the German edition of 1872: "The Commune has especially proven that the working class cannot simply lay hold of the state machinery and wield it for its own purposes.".[26] Lenin interpreted this sentence as the need to overcome the bourgeois state, and not simply seize it gradually and peacefully; in other words, for Marx, it was necessary to destroy the bureaucratic and military state machine as "a precondition for any people's revolution". The idea of a broad, inclusive revolution, extending beyond the working class to other popular classes in a larger social bloc, would be the denial of the rigid scholastic theoretical mechanism of the Second International and of the social democratic parties whose view was restricted to the limited alternative between the bourgeois revolution and the revolution of the proletariat. In this sense, the Russian Revolution of 1905, besides producing disappointing results, was neither a bourgeois revolution, nor a proletarian revolution, but rather a "people's revolution" because it was deeply marked by the uprising of the lower social stratum. Thus, based on Marx's statement, Lenin explained his thoughts on the concept of a people's revolution, indicating a cross-class alliance perspective, which would later be fundamental to the definition of the concept of "social bloc" in Gramsci:

[25] Ibid., 68.
[26] Ibid., 73.

In Europe, in 1871, the proletariat did not constitute the majority of the people in any country on the continent. A "people's" revolution, actually sweeping the majority into the movement, could only be such if it encompassed both the proletariat and the peasants. Both classes then constituted the "people". Both classes are united by the fact that the "bureaucratic military state machine" oppresses, crushes, exploits them. Smashing this machine, destroying it, is the true interest of the "people", of its majority, of the workers and most peasants; this is "the precondition" for a free alliance between poor peasants and the proletarians, without which democracy is unstable and socialist transformation is impossible.[27]

Therefore, Marx did not speak of a "people's revolution" by mistake, but he did so very realistically because he realized the power relations on the continent in 1871, noting the common interest of workers and peasants in defeating the bourgeois state machine. The adaptation of social democrats to the traditional institutions of bourgeois society, making them assert their indissolubility, left to the anarchists the monopoly of criticism of the representative relations typical of classical parliamentarism. On the contrary, Lenin writes, Marx avoided both vague revolutionary phraseology and parliamentary deviations. Marx broke with the anarchists, "due to his inability to even make use of the 'pigsty' of bourgeois parliamentarism, especially when there was clearly no revolutionary situation, but at the same time, he knew how to subject parliamentarism to truly revolutionary proletarian criticism".[28]

Inevitably linked to the problems of socialist transition, the issue of technical-administrative leadership, another point of particular interest to Gramsci, became essential. In Lenin's view, as it was not possible to suddenly and completely eliminate bureaucracy, it was necessary to replace the old administrative machine with a new one as a starting point for a renewed state organization, built on the centrality of the working masses. The replacement, both in state administration and in enterprises, of old employees with "workers' control" was the path indicated by Lenin to a radical reorganization of society, in a socialist sense. He was convinced that once capitalism was overthrown, workers could take on all the technical functions hitherto managed by employees and by cadres of the bourgeoisie. This is probably the most utopian aspect of Lenin's thought, which, after 1917, would face a much more complex reality, in which he

[27] Ibid., 74.
[28] Ibid., 81.

would have to deal with the unpreparedness of the Russian proletariat to take on bureaucratic functions and with the problem of Russia's disorganization and technical-productive paralysis in the very difficult post-revolution phase. It turned out to be one of the most difficult goals to meet. Lenin was forced to abandon the formula of "workers' control", bringing back the old technicians to control the administrative and productive machine. This was one of the elements of greatest disappointment and regret in the last years of Lenin's life, who was always very aware of the risks of bureaucratization of the young Soviet state. Thus, not even in *The state and revolution* did Lenin imagine an ideal condition of immediate revolutionary palingenesis of the administrative machine:

> We are not utopians. We do not "dream" of dispensing with all administration, with all subordination at once; these anarchist dreams, based on incomprehension of the tasks of the proletarian dictatorship, are completely alien to Marxism and as a matter of fact serve only to postpone the socialist revolution until people are different. No, we want the socialist revolution, with people like those of now, who will not be able to pass without subordination, without control, without "administrators".[29]

The perspective of the self-education of producers, who already in the capitalist system are preparing to become the ruling class in their institutions and the associations of the working class, as well as in other self-employment cooperation efforts, is therefore an answer to the historical problem faced by the young socialist state in the first years of its life, which risked its existence before it could begin the transition from the old to the new.

---

[29] Ibid., 84.

CHAPTER 5

L'Ordine Nuovo

Inspired by that, *L'Ordine Nuovo* started being published in May 1919, with the subtitle "Review of Socialist Culture", to "indicate that the vehicle was intended for proletarians, workers, intellectuals, with a specific objective: to arm the working class with consciousness and will to build a socialist society".[1] The weekly came along on the very eve of the red biennium, "the beautiful years", as Gramsci defined them. However, at birth, *L'Ordine Nuovo* was doomed to a very short life, paralyzed by the clash of two opposing political and editorial lines, Gramsci's and Angelo Tasca's. The conflict between the two approaches arose with no chance of resolution after the Congress of the Chamber of Labor of Turin, in which Tasca intervened defending that the councils should be under the control of the unions, a stance classified by Gramsci as "reactionary", which led to significant divergence of opinion that whole year.

The editorial of June 27, 1919, "Workers' Democracy", written by Gramsci with the collaboration of Palmiro Togliatti, marked the first clear break with Angelo Tasca and represented a turning point in the life of the weekly:

---

[1] Alfonso Leonetti, "Gramsci, i Consigli di fabbrica e il congresso di Livorno", in Carlo Salinari, *I comunisti raccontano*, v. 1: *1919–1945* (Milan, Teti, 1975), 15.

G. Fresu, *Antonio Gramsci*, Marx, Engels, and Marxisms, https://doi.org/10.1007/978-3-031-15610-6_5

Togliatti and I called for an editorial coup d'état, but the problem of the internal commissions was explicitly defined in the seventh issue of the magazine; a couple of nights before I wrote this article, I explained the tone of the article to comrade Terracini, and he gave his full consent as theory and practice [...]; the problem of the development of the internal commissions took center stage and became the idea of *L'Ordine Nuovo*; it was presented as the fundamental problem of the proletarian revolution.[2]

Angelo Tasca, who came culturally and politically from trade unionism, did not accept the about-face in the editorial board. Unlike Gramsci, he did not share the idea of a workers' democracy based on the self-government of internal commissions, advocating instead a solution that would place the development of struggle of the workers' movement under the leadership of the Socialist Party's Chamber of Labor.

The about-face in the editorial board could be explained by the political maturation strongly influenced by the Russian and German revolutionary process. The issue of council democracy was closely linked to the need to solidly build a workers' institution equivalent to the soviet, on which all the energy of the *ordinovist* group was concentrated. According to Leonetti, the about-face gave rise to a new magazine, whose activity, albeit the result of collective thinking and a permanent dialogue between the editorial staff and mobilized workers, was deeply marked by Gramsci's leadership. The evolution of the Turinese weekly and the rise of the council movement were simultaneous and not by chance:

That is how the movement of factory councils is born and takes shape; that is how Turin, the city of automobiles, becomes the city of factory commissioners, the city to which journalists from all over the world flock and which everyone calls the "Mecca of Italian communism", the "Petrograd of Italy". Some called it 'the city of Gramsci'".[3]

In Gramsci's view, the soviet was not a Russian institution, but a new institutional form with a universal nature where the masses governed themselves, and the internal commission of Turinese factories was its Italian translation. This conclusion led to an imperative for *L'Ordine Nuovo*: to study internal commissions and factories not only as spaces of material production but also as a "political system, as the national territory

[2] Antonio Gramsci, *L'Ordine Nuovo 1919–1920* (Turin, Einaudi, 1978), 148.
[3] Alfonso Leonetti, "Gramsci, i Consigli di fabbrica e il congresso di Livorno", cit., 16.

of workers' self-government." The initial indetermination of the weekly's editorial line, especially regarding the definition of its intended purposes, turned it into an entity of socialist preaching for some time, which was committed to ruminating the classics of Marxism with no basis in the concrete historical situation. This limitation to preaching the "ABC of worker's thought", the devotion to the exegesis of the parables bequeathed as a legacy by the fathers of socialist thought, was a response to an outdated and frustrating notion of worker culture. Instead of restricting itself to recalling the Paris Commune, *L'Ordine Nuovo* should have positioned itself to "do as the Bolsheviks did" by using Marx's reflection on the commune not to "recall" but to understand the immediate reality so as to find in the soviet the modern translation of the historical experience of the commune.

> What was *L'Ordine Nuovo* in its first issues? It was an anthology, nothing but an anthology; it was a review, one that could have come along in Naples, in Caltanissetta, in Brindisi; it was a review of abstract culture, of abstract information, with a tendency to publish horrifying tales and well-meaning wood engravings; that was *L'Ordine Nuovo* in its first issues, a disorganism, the product of mediocre intellectualism, which sought an ideal approach and a course of action by leaps and bounds.[4]

Antonio Gramsci saw the factory council as a public institution, a form of historical association comparable to the bourgeois state, where the worker begins to participate as a producer—as a result of his role in society and in the division of labor—just like a citizen begins to participate in the state. On the contrary, the party and the trade union are "privatist" institutions joined voluntarily by workers after signing a contract that can be terminated at any time. According to Gramsci, Tasca had not understood the distinction between the party or the union, which develops "arithmetically", and the factory council, which on the contrary develops "morphologically". The system of councils intervenes in the process of capitalist production and exchange, testing the possibility of having social relations of a new kind in the concrete field of the workers' direction of production. In Gramsci's view, the party and the trade union could not absorb the multifaceted existence of the working class, nor could they identify with the state, even in Soviet society, where they would continue to be

[4] Antonio Gramsci, *L'Ordine Nuovo 1919–1920*, cit., 148.

independent from the state as driving, stimulating, harmonizing entities. The social life of the working class should go beyond the associative forms of the party and the trade union, being coordinated in institutions and activities that were the manifestation of an autonomous institutional organization. With this new line, *L'Ordine Nuovo* focused on the organization of workers' democracy through the development of the system of councils, pointing out the mistake of conducting this entire system of social coordination of the working class within organizations that had other roles and functions, such as the Chamber of Labor or the party.

> The factory council is conceived of as an absolutely original institution, which arises from the situation created in the working class in the current historical period of capitalist structure, as an institution that cannot be confused with the trade union, which cannot be coordinated by and subordinate to the trade union, which, on the contrary, with its birth and its development, determines radical changes in the structure and form of the trade union.[5]

In these reflections, Gramsci found a complicating factor that later proved to be historically central and was related to the limits to the building of the new socialist society. In the first phase of its life, the idea of Soviet democracy was coordinated at many levels—organizations such as the soviet, the party, the trade union and the state had distinct roles and functions. However, in its development, this system should have become more coordinated, not simpler, because as society develops and the systems of individual and collective needs become more complex, the forms of popular expression and participation must also necessarily become more complex and coordinated. As we know, one of the reasons for the decline of Soviet society lies precisely in the fact that, at a certain point, it underwent a process of crystallization and simplification—an objective political involution—at the same time that its society tended to become more complex and demanding. In other words, the identification of the party with the state, the impoverishment of the Soviet system, and the attendant reduction of the role of trade union organizations went in the opposite direction to the economic, social and cultural growth of the Soviet Union, ultimately becoming a straitjacket, not a system of participation capable of developing "morphologically". The issue of bureaucratization and of the

---

[5] Ibid., 130.

introduction of a new technocratic nomenclature in Soviet society, dramatically a core concern in the last stage of Lenin's life, pertains to these retrogressive dynamics. Distinguishing the roles of the council, the party, and the trade union was therefore central not only to the development of the class struggle in capitalist society but also concerning the issues of transition:

> The internal commissions are organizations of workers' democracy which must be freed from the constraints imposed by employers and which must be infused with new life and energy. Today internal commissions limit the capitalist's power in the factory and perform abitrating and disciplinary roles. In the future, it is necessary to develop and value the organizations of proletarian power that replace the capitalist in all their useful administrative and directive roles.[6]

In Gramsci's view, the proletarian revolution should be a historical process, not the arbitrary act of an organization or of a system of revolutionary organization; precisely because of its procedural nature, it could not simply be identified with the development of voluntary revolutionary organizations, such as the political party or the trade union. Sorelian influence is evident in the distinction between the productive and the political moment, and above all in the attribution of a central role to the former, a predominant role in the revolutionary process:

> Revolutionary organizations are created, in the field of bourgeois democracy, as the assertion and development of freedom and democracy in general, in a field where relations between people endure: the revolutionary process takes place in the field of manufacturing, of the factory, where there is a relationship between the oppressed and the oppressor, the exploited and the exploiter, where there is no freedom for workers, where there is no democracy; the revolutionary process takes place where the worker is nothing but must become everything, where the owner's power is unlimited, the power over the worker's life and death, over his wife, over his children.[7]

In the factory, the worker becomes a "certain instrument of production", essential in the productive and labor process; he is a cog in the wheel/division of labor, without which production and capitalist

---

[6] Ibid., 11–12.
[7] Ibid., 125.

accumulation itself cannot exist. If the worker becomes aware of this defined role and places it at the basis of a representative state institution, he lays the foundations for a radically new state structure that arises from and permanently resides in production. By developing consciousness of its organic unity and building its representative state institutions, the working class expropriates the first and most important factor in capitalist production: the working class itself. In their relations with the factory council, the political party and the trade union should be aware of that:

> They must not present themselves as the guardians of or superstructures ready for this new institution, in which the historical revolutionary process takes discernible shape; they must present themselves as agents that are aware of their freedom from the oppressive forces concentrated in the bourgeois state; they must set out to organize the general (political) external conditions in which the revolutionary process must find its full speed, a process in which the productive forces are free to find their full expansion.[8]

In Antonio Gramsci's view, historically, the principle of association and solidarity removes the worker from his individualistic condition as a subject exposed to the risks of free competition, in which the initial conditions for the struggle are not equal but determined by the private ownership of the means of production by a social minority that, from time to time, imposes its rules on the game. Through the principles of association and solidarity, the psychology and customs of workers change radically; proletarian institutions and organizations arise in accordance with these principles. However, the emergence and development of proletarian institutions do not respond to the laws of the subaltern classes. They take shape not according to internal class laws, but under the pressure of capitalist competition, in a framework in which the laws of history are dictated by the class that owns the means of production and runs the organization of the state.

Workers' associations, parties and trade unions are the fruits of capitalist concentration and the attendant concentration of the working masses; they are the answer that workers give to an unequal starting position in the relationship between capital and labor, in which the worker himself operates in the terrain of free competition as an individual citizen. In this sense, when these institutions arise, the workers' movement is solely a function

[8] Ibid., 127.

of free capitalist competition. In Gramsci's view, the mistake of *pan-unionism* consists precisely in considering trade unions organized into professional categories a permanent and exclusive fact of proletarian association, that is, a notion of association determined by "laws external to the working class".

In turn, when it emerged, the Italian Socialist Party (PSI) managed to make the movement for workers' rights aware and organized, giving it a perspective consistent with the historical development of human society; however, it also made a serious mistake. By taking on a representative role within bourgeois parliamentary institutions and giving this role an almost exclusive priority, it lost its own antithetical and critical role and was absorbed by a reality that it should have controlled. According to Gramsci, the socialists ended up passively accepting the historical reality imposed by the capitalist class, making it perpetual and fundamentally perfect, the result of "natural laws". To them, the parliamentary democratic state could be polished up here and there, but it should be kept in its essential form. "An example of this narrow-mindedly vain psychology is the adamant opinion of Filippo Turati, for whom the parliament is for the soviet what the city is for the barbarian hordes".[9]

This misconception of historical becoming, marked by the constant tendency toward concession and by the "obtusely parliamentarian tactic", led to the intention to reach socialism simply by seizing the institutions of the state and modifying the essence of its activity. But as we have seen, by referring to Lenin's *The state and revolution*, Gramsci posited that the formula of the "conquest of the state" could be understood as the creation of a new institutional apparatus, established not by the laws of free competition, as is the case of the parliamentary democratic state, but by the associative experience of the working class. The proletarian revolution had to take a procedural, molecular, organic form and be the associative experience of the working class in production sites; it could not be understood as a thaumaturgic act that would begin with the dictatorship of the sections of the PSI.

Therefore, in Gramsci's writings of this period, we also find the first reflections on the party as a pedagogical instrument through which the rupture between rulers and those ruled would be repaired by establishing different relations among its constituent parts. In this sense, it was necessary to overcome the classical pyramidal form of political organizations,

[9] Ibid., 16.

whose outline is drawn up by the intellectual intuition of the leaders and then translated into categorical imperatives that the base must confidently accept and militantly discuss. An example of this approach is the article "Il Partito e la rivoluzione" [The party and the revolution], of December 27, 1919, in which Gramsci went on to talk about the need for an organization that would not only represent workers but also be run by them: an idea of a horizontal organization characterized by the distribution of its creating and directing roles, in which activity would be the result of the simultaneous action of all its elements, not the result of a chain of command similar to the army. He used the metaphor of the barrier reef here quite effectively:

> The Party, as the cohesive and militant embodiment of an idea, influences this intimate construction of new structures, this operationality of millions and millions of social micro-organisms that prepare the red coral reef which, on a not so distant day, blooms, stops the impetus of the ocean storm, enforces peace among the waves, brings a new balance to currents and the weather; but this inflow is organic, coming from the circulation of ideas, from keeping the spiritual government apparatus intact, from the fact that millions and millions of workers found a new hierarchy and establish a new order [...].[10]

The party should have adhered plastically and organically to the productive instrument; it was necessary to conceive the revolution as the historical acknowledgement of the naturalness of this development. This means that the party cannot shape the revolutionary process in bureaucratic terms as a result of its leaders' decisions:

> Woe to the Party if, with a sectarian notion of its role in the revolution, it intends to concretize that hierarchy, if it intends to fix the government apparatus of the moving masses into mechanical forms of immediate power, to try to restrict the revolutionary process to the ways of the Party; it will drive away some of the men, it will "master" history, but the actual revolutionary process will be out of the Party's control, unconsciously transformed into an instrument of preservation.[11]

---

[10] Antonio Gramsci, "Il Partito e la rivoluzione", *L'Ordine Nuovo*, 27 dez. 1919, *L'Ordine Nuovo 1919–1920*, cit., p 69.
[11] Ibid.

Influencing, forging, strengthening the consciousness of workers, encouraging their activity aiming to extract from the bourgeoisie its historical capacity for direction, with which it manages to chain the exploited and make them accept the relation of domination. A work that is intense and carried out in the extremities, not only by the party but also by all the organizations of the proletariat (councils, commissions, trade unions), transforming factories into the seat of workers' self-government, no longer resorting to the delegated functions of representation exercised by intellectuals.

A new order, to be so, should organically adhere to the "productive instruments", and the revolution was understood as the historical acknowledgement of the "nature" of this conformation. The socialist Party "is not and cannot be conceived as the form of this process, a pliable and shapeable form at the leaders' discretion".[12]

In the article "The Communist Party", Gramsci developed some reflections on the relationship between manual activity and the intellectual autonomy of workers in the factory, anticipating a theme that would later become central in the notes on *Americanism and Fordism*. In this excerpt from 1920, Gramsci highlighted how the workers' struggle and organization were the result of a process of resistance to the purely instrumental functions of their activity and intellectual deautonomization. The result of the process of division/specialization of labor represents the denial of humanity because it transforms the worker into a robot condemned to repeat, so monotonously that it could destroy inner life and human life, the same professional gestures without knowing the hows and whys of its practical activity.

The social and political self-determination of the workers' movement is an authentic miracle, a reaffirmation of subjectivity against any brutal reduction of human complexity to a prosthesis of the machine. It is the worker's victory in his struggle for spiritual autonomy that encourages him to study, learn and improve intellectually to emancipate himself materially, a struggle that every day must prevail over tiredness, alienation and the repetition of productive functions. The revolutionary political party, through which the worker becomes a leader and the creator of a new worldview, is the synthesis of this dialectical process of human emancipation.

---

[12] Antonio Gramsci, *L'Ordine Nuovo 1919–1920*, cit., p. 68.

The worker in the factory has purely executive tasks. He does not follow the general process of work and production; he is not a point that moves to create a line; he is a pin confined to a certain place, and the line results from the succession of pins that someone else's will has arranged for its goals. The worker tends to take this way of being to all the environments of life; he easily adapts, in everything, to the craft of manual worker, of a "mass" guided by a will that is not his; he is intellectually lazy, he does not know and does not want to foresee anything beyond what is immediate, so he does not discuss the choices of his bosses and is easily deluded by promises; he wants to believe that he can accomplish without much effort on his part and without having to think much. The Communist Party is the instrument and the historical form of the process of intimate freedom, in which the worker goes from executor to initiator; from mass, he becomes head and guide; from arm, he becomes brain and will; in the conformation of the Communist Party, he can reap the seeds of freedom that will have their development and full expansion after the workers' state has organized the necessary material conditions. […] starting to be part of the Communist Party, where he is more an organizer than someone organized, where he feels that he represents a vanguard that goes beyond, carrying with himself the whole mass.[13]

In Gramsci's view, the party has a fundamental historical role: to remove the terrain of the political and social domination of the bourgeoisie from its democratic-parliamentary certainties. Its task is to favor the continuous emergence and development of this vital energy. The revolution cannot be identified with the party; it cannot be reduced to the mechanical and hierarchical constriction of this process in the form of the party. If at the same time it managed to lead a large part of the masses and "master history", the real process of revolution would be out of the party's control, which would turn the organization into an instrument of preservation.

---

[13] Idem, "Il Partito comunista", 4 set.-9 out. 1920, in *L'Ordine Nuovo 1919–1920*, cit., p. 157.

CHAPTER 6

The Origin and Defeat of the Italian Revolution

Despite its significant development, the movement of the councils faced the distrust of both the party and the trade union. In this context, *L'Ordine Nuovo* should favor the autonomy of internal commissions and turn them into workers' effective self-government institutions so as to rescue them from the bureaucratic practice in which the trade union appointed commissioners and defined the political line. This major reorganization of councils should have led to the election of commissioners by all workers, who did not need to be all unionized, and to the transformation of committees into institutions of workers' representation by productive unit and structured around department or workshop divisions.[1] The commission had to overcome the condition of an institution of generic representation of leaders and prepare for a new role: to take control of production. Thus, the system of councils would transform the concept of representation, no longer structured around territorial bases and principles, valuing the productive unit.

However, in a chaotic context such as that of the post-war period, this vital need for renewal of the institutions of the workers' movement clashed with the customs of the party, which was unable to conceive an activity beyond ordinary institutional tasks, and of the trade union, which had

[1] The proposal to reform the system of councils provided for the democratic election of commissioners, who would make up the factory council, which would in turn form the internal commission.

© The Author(s), under exclusive license to Springer Nature Switzerland AG 2023
G. Fresu, *Antonio Gramsci*, Marx, Engels, and Marxisms,
https://doi.org/10.1007/978-3-031-15610-6_6

resigned itself to the historical function of economic intermediation between capital and labor and was therefore unwilling to surrender spheres of sovereignty.

This contrast was clearly manifested at the 16th National Congress of the Italian Socialist Party (PSI) in Bologna, the apotheosis of Italian "maximalism"[2] in the period of its greatest expansion. In the documents, in the discussion and in the decision taken, all the addresses adopted a radical and optimistic approach, heralding the ever greater proximity of the moment of seizure of power, but they did not present any action plan or a modality of intervention capable of going beyond the purely theoretical rhetoric of revolutionary preparation and of traditional parliamentary practice. Giuseppe Fiori left us an exemplary portrait of what the maximalist PSI had become, divided by a very evident contradiction between the heroic lyricism of the declaration of revolutionary principles and the prose of a policy that lacked boldness and transformative potential:

> It was a party in crisis, with no vitality, albeit persistent, given its recent growth, which was quite abrupt: 300 thousand people registered in comparison to the 50 thousand before the war; two million adherents to the CGL [General Confederation of Labor] in comparison to the half a million of 1914; moreover, the group of parliamentarians has tripled, from 50 to 150 deputies. An expansion that caused euphoria and also new framing issues, which produced two consequences: a diffuse revolutionary faith based more on the presumption that the march of the proletariat would continue until it fatally led to final victory than on the consciousness and inclination of the means indispensable for this victory; doctrinally unprepared and inexperienced demagogues rose to leadership positions absolutely inadequate for their capacity.[3]

At the Congress of Bologna, the positions of *L'Ordine Nuovo* were not welcomed. On the contrary, the various opinions of the PSI, reaching no convergence, found a point of agreement precisely in the radical criticism of the experience of councils. It went from the accusation of economicist corporatism, made by Bordiga, to accusations of spontaneist anarcho-syndicalism, which were commonly made by maximalists, reformist union

---

[2] The definition of "maximalism" was created after the famous Congress of Erfurt, in 1891, when the social democratic program was approved and comprised the minimum program (reforms in capitalist society) and the maximum program (socialism). Thus, the most radical and revolutionary strand of the international socialist movement called itself "maximalist" as opposed to those who defined themselves as "reformists".

[3] Giuseppe Fiori, *Vita di Antonio Gramsci* (Rome/Bari, Laterza, 1989), 148.

leaders, who vehemently opposed the atomist vote of the "disorganized".

Nonetheless, Bordiga was the first to, as early as May 1919, forcefully and explicitly advance the topic of the split of the communists of the PSI. On July 13, he presented to the National Council of the PSI the *Program of the communist faction*, after which, on November 10, he sent a letter to the Third International concretely presenting the idea of a communist split under his leadership. According to Bordiga, the natural success of the council movement was counterrevolutionary, pertaining to trade unions' traditions of reformism and corporatism.

In his view, the communists had a single goal: to form a political party and to prepare ideologically for the moment of revolution. In this sense, for abstentionists, the workers' councils should arise only at the time of political insurrection or of the maximum crisis of the bourgeoisie; otherwise, they would turn into institutions dominated by the tactics of partial conquests and reformist practice, distracting communists from their truly revolutionary tasks. Even during the red biennium, Bordiga did not give any credit to the development of the council movement, demonstrating a constant and almost pathological distrust of workers' self-government. Instead of a phase of confrontation and social radicalization, he envisioned a long era of class collaboration, failing to understand that what loomed on the horizon was not the triumph of social democratic reformism, but the most terrible reaction. An error of assessment made even by Gramsci in 1921, albeit for a short time.

In Gramsci's view, the socialist state should be concretized through the full cooperation of mass institutions and forms of participation. In Bordiga's view, on the contrary, the associative forms of the working class were understood as simple decentralized organs of the party, transmission belts, which were subservient, in every aspect and for all purposes, to the control and direction of the party.

In the socialist landscape in Italy, *L'Ordine Nuovo* was the only group to have welcomed and "translated into Italian" the meaning of the German council movement, of the experience of soviets in Russia, of the movement of workplace representatives in England (the *Shop Stewards' Committees*), that is, it was the only group to relate creatively to the new and avant-garde experiences of the European labor movement. The frequent references to Lenin and Rosa Luxemburg during those years are no accident; rather, they express a desire to put the experience of the Turinese council movement in line with the experiences of soviets and of German councils.

Moreover, the interest in the confrontation between theoretical debates and the concrete experiences of the struggle at the international level was confirmed by the space that *L'Ordine Nuovo* devoted to the international council movement by publishing the greatest international contributions of the time. The most significant contributions of the Communist International were published, such as the interventions of Lukács, Daniel De Leon, Zinoviev, Béla Kún, Trotsky, John Reed, to name but a few.

Perhaps the true limit in the propositions of the *L'Ordine Nuovo* group, as the leaders themselves confirmed on several occasions, lay in its little inclination to fight a battle, not only of ideas, within the party and in the belief that work among the masses, by itself, could change the correlation of forces in the Italian socialist movement.

With the reissue of the publications of *L'Ordine Nuovo* in May 1924, Gramsci himself recalled that the problem of forming the independent party of the revolutionary working class coexisted with the need to work in the developing mass movement:

> In the years 1919–1920, *L'Ordine Nuovo* saw the two issues as closely con-
> nected: guiding the masses towards the revolution, leading them to the
> break with reformists and opportunists in factory councils and trade unions,
> fueling the life of the Socialist Party by discussing proletarian issues in par-
> ticular, in which simple workers were above the advocates and demagogues
> of reformism; *L'Ordine Nuovo* tended to evoke even the new party of the
> revolution as an urgent need of the ongoing situation. […] It must also be
> admitted that in some moments there was a lack of courage and resolve.
> Attacked from all sides as upstarts and careerists, we did not know how to
> despise the pettiness of the accusations: we were very young and character-
> ized by great political naivety and great formal pride. That is why, at the end
> of 1919, we did not dare to create a fraction with ramifications throughout
> the country; that is why, in 1920, we did not dare to organize an urban and
> regional center of factory councils that would shake, as an organization of all
> the workers of Piedmont, the Italian working and peasant class in particular,
> and therefore against the guidelines of the CGL and the Socialist Party.[4]

---

[4] Antonio Gramsci, "Cronache de L'Ordine Nuovo", in *La costruzione del Partito Comunista 1923–1926* (Turin, Einaudi, 1978), 161.

A letter written to Alfonso Leonetti two months earlier, in which Gramsci announced his intention to issue a retraction of the mistakes made, had the same tone:

> In 1919 and 1920, we made very serious mistakes that we have hidden so far. For fear of being called upstarts and careerists, we did not build a fraction and did not set out to organize it throughout Italy. We did not want to give Turinese factory councils an autonomous management center, which could have exercised enormous influence throughout the country, for fear of splits in the trade unions and of being expelled very prematurely from the Socialist Party. We should, or at least I should, publicly admit these mistakes which have undoubtedly caused serious repercussions. Actually, if after the April split we had taken the position that I deemed necessary, we would certainly have reached a situation different from the occupation of factories and would have brought those events to a more favorable situation.[5]

During the whole year of 1919, the periodical focused on the construction of the Turinese workers' movement and on work among the masses. Party issues took a back seat. That same year, the political-social scenario was characterized by increasing tension. The summer was marked by unrest against famine, with demonstrations and strikes throughout national territory (316 in May, 276 in June), which led to the looting of food stocks. To illustrate the not merely economic nature of the unrest, it suffices to recall that the trade union, on June 20 and 21, declared a general strike in solidarity with the revolutionary processes in Russia and Hungary. Tumult also marked the whole of fall, leading to the reaction of the most conservative environments, until the declaration of a new general strike on December 2 and 3 in response to nationalists' attacks against socialist deputies. However, as far as Turin was concerned, the shocks were not particularly severe yet. The real change occurred during the first months of 1920, when the Turin group took advantage of the political work aimed at the election of the internal commissions to spread among workers the practical reasons for an idea of council struggle, showing them both the immediate role, that is, the possibility of leading to a direct confrontation with employers, and the prospects, which would make the system of councils the basis of a broader system of government of the working

[5] Idem, "Lettera ad Alfonso Leonetti, 28 gennaio 1924", em Palmiro Togliatti, *La formazione del gruppo dirigente del Partito Comunista Italiano (1923–1924)* (Rome, Editori Riuniti, 1984), 181.

class. In March, all those elected to the internal commissions in Turin were linked to the *L'Ordine Nuovo* platform.

Thus, in a climate of general mobilization of the working class, in the Mazzonis cotton mills of Sestri Ponente, the first occupations of the establishments took place, and they quickly spread to the other factories, mixing with the struggle and land occupations of agricultural workers. Aware of the hostility of the PSI's union leadership, the *L'Ordine Nuovo* group soon realized the risk of isolation, with the unified movement of the restoration offensive led by the government and industrialists. The only way to avoid a similar situation would be broadening the general political perspectives for that movement, uniting the demands of all the fighting forces in a single political domain: for this reason, the periodical introduced the idea of a national congress of councils.

The situation deteriorated when the representatives of the Industrial League, Agnelli, Olivetti and De Benedetti, announced to the mayor their intention to proceed with the general closure of the establishments and have the army preside over the factories. As a result, on March 29, the climate created quickly increased the level of confrontation between workers and employers. In the constituent congress of Confindustria, on March 20, the secretary-general of employers' organizations expressed the need to eliminate the coexistence of two powers in factories. It is common knowledge that the pretext for the closure was the strike against the introduction of standard time.[6]

> In Turin, the internal commission of the Metallurgical Industry workshop—owned by Fiat—shows the clock hands at standard time. This is not by chance. It is an assertion of worker power in the factory and at the same time a protest against everything reminiscent of war.[7]

The confrontation quickly spread from the Turin factories to the rest of the country, reaching railway, port and agricultural workers. The mobilization lasted a whole month: on the one hand, Confindustria, supported by the government and the army; on the other, a movement soon abandoned to its fate by the party and the unions. On April 13, a bitter general strike began, which intended to last until April 24, and ended with the signing of an agreement that decreed the rollback of the system of

---

[6] Standard time would be the corresponding Italian daylight saving time.

[7] Cesare Pillon, *I comunisti nella storia d'Italia*, (Rome, Edizioni del Calendario, 1967), 89.

commissars, a reduction in the powers of internal commissions and, therefore, defeat. It was called "the crushing defeat".

Faced with the general isolation of the movement, Gramsci realized how naive it was not to organize a political fraction on the Turin group's platform, capable of facing the leadership of the PSI. Exactly from that moment on, Gramsci's order of priorities changed, and the reflection on the party took center stage in his political activity and conceptions. In Gramsci's view, that movement represented a great event in the history of the working class all over the world because it had developed from a position of strength, not caused by hunger or unemployment. The workers had claimed the direction of production, waging a battle that soon spread to the reaches of the factories concerned and stirred up four million people, among industrial and agricultural workers, technicians and employees. This struggle was consolidating, despite a double counter pressure: on the one hand, industrialists and the state had adopted all coercive means at their disposal to suppress and stifle this movement; on the other hand, the leadership of the Socialist Party and the trade union had hindered, in every way, the development and possibility of radicalization in other parts of Italy and among the rest of the subaltern classes.

According to the line adopted by *L'Ordine Nuovo*, the organization of factory councils should take place on the representative bases of each industry; each of them should be subdivided into departments and these departments into groups by occupation, within which elected workers' mandates should be imperative and conditional. The assembly of these representatives formed the council, within which an executive committee was elected; the representatives of the various executives then formed the urban committee. This system of self-government, in Gramsci's intentions, should be articulated horizontally and vertically so as to accommodate the peasant masses and other exploited classes, thus constituting, indeed, the fundamental structure of revolution in Italy, just like soviets in the Russian Revolution.

The work to transform the institutions of workers' association and representation, to remove it from the guardianship of unions and to indeed provide social and political expression of life in the factory to the candidates of internal committees, gained the adherence of metalworkers to the point of, within a short period of time, taking the direction of the Chamber of Labor of Turin from the hands of the reformist trade union central.

In September 1919, the first factory council was formed at Fiat-Brevetti, followed by the election of the Fiat-Centro council and, soon afterwards, about thirty establishments were created, with 50 thousand metallurgical workers represented. However, as we have already seen, despite the growing interest of the Turin labor movement in the stances taken by *L'Ordine Nuovo*, and despite the increasing weight of the council movement, the ordinovists were a completely isolated minority in the party:

> The movement met stubborn resistance from union officials, the leadership of the Socialist Party and *l'Avanti!*. The controversy among these people was based on the difference between the concept of factory council and that of Soviet. Their conclusions were purely theoretical, abstract, bureaucratic. Their dissonant statements concealed the desire to avoid the direct participation of the working masses in the revolutionary struggle, to preserve trade union organizations' guardianship of the masses. The components of the party leadership always refused to take the initiative of revolutionary action without previously drawing up a coordinated action plan, but they did nothing to devise this plan.[8]

---

[8] Antonio Gramsci, *L'Ordine Nuovo 1919–1920* (Turin, Einaudi, 1978), 185.

CHAPTER 7

The Party Problem

The 1919–1920 biennium was marked by the shock of huge internal and international contradictions, the economic crisis and monetary devaluation. Inflation, mass unemployment, increased labor exploitation and the contraction of the purchasing power of wages reached very critical levels. Faced with the increasingly evident rise in social tensions that the old castes of notable liberals were no longer able to manage given the technical exhaustion of Giolittian social control,[1] increasingly broader categories of workers came to believe that they were faced with a crucial historical moment that would inevitably lead to the socialist revolution or to a more conservative and violent reaction. Gramsci was fully aware of that and in 1920 he wrote that the counteroffensive of the ruling classes, in addition to eliminating workers' institutions of political struggle, intended to absorb exploited classes' institutions of economic and social association into the bourgeois state:

> The current phase of the class struggle in Italy is the phase that precedes either the conquest of political power by the revolutionary proletariat through the transition to the new mode of production and distribution, which enables a resumption of productivity, or a tremendous reaction on the part of the owning class and the ruling caste. No violence will be neglected

---

[1] Reference to the reformist and clientelist policy of Giovanni Giolitti (1842–1928), president of the Council of Ministers of Italy in five different terms.

to subject the industrial and agricultural proletariat to servile labor: the destruction of the working class's institutions of political struggle (Socialist Party) will be sought, as well as the incorporation of the institutions of economic resistance (unions and cooperatives) into the cogwheels of the bourgeois state.[2]

The Sardinian intellectual was the first to identify this danger, and when most saw fascism only as a folk phenomenon of a handful of stragglers, he sensed the danger, not adhering, not even in his youthful writings, to the idea of an undifferentiated bourgeois front behind fascism. Gramsci soon realized that, in the economic, social and moral disaster produced by war, the greatest risks of reactionary subversion would come first of all from the middle classes, as well as from the possible alliance between their interests with the interests of a capital that was large and enriched, but in deep crisis at the sociopolitical level. The context of economic crisis and nationalist ideological fervor that preceded and followed the Second World War was the perfect environment for the creation of the social, political and cultural conditions necessary for the emergence of fascism.[3]

After the elections of November 1919, marked by the great success of the Socialist Party (which won 158 seats), the radicalization of the conflict led the strikes to spill over into the whole country at an increasingly pressing and overwhelming pace, involving several categories of workers: from peasants to postal and telegraph workers, from railway to industrial workers. The struggle largely developed almost spontaneously, not counting on a unifying platform or on forms of coordination at the base. In some cases, strikes resulted from economic issues, such as adjusting wages to the cost of living; in others, they developed from the state of exasperation due to the conditions of exploitation, such as in the aforementioned strike of April 1920 in Turin, which stemmed from the workers' refusal to accept the introduction of standard time.

However, in its development, the conflict tended to take on more and more political significance. This was the case of the strikes of railway workers, who decided to stop the railways that were used to carry weapons and ammunition intended for the "white armies" in the war against Soviet Russia, besides boycotting the trains used to transport troops bound for

---

[2] Antonio Gramsci, *L'Ordine Nuovo 1919–1920* (Turin, Einaudi, 1978), 117.

[3] Gianni Fresu and Aldo Accardo, *Oltre la parentesi. Fascismo e storia d'Italia nell'interpretazione gramsciana* (Rome, Carocci, 2009), 75–86.

the centers where social conflicts were developing.[4] Another example was the Ancona uprising, with the refusal of soldiers to embark for Albania and the insurgency of entire blocks (particularly the families of shipyard workers) against repression. After February 1st, strikes, occupations and demonstrations shook the entire country, from the textile sector in the North to the extractive sulfur industry in Sicily, from the entire category of metallurgists (Dalmine, Ansaldo, Ilva) to that of loggers. The convulsion of the industrial world was followed by that of the agricultural sector in Lombardy, Tuscany, Emilia-Romagna, Veneto, Piedmont, until the occupation of plantations in the *Mezzogiorno*.

But the most characteristic battle of the "red biennium" was the struggle for the recognition of councils and internal commissions, which, between August and September 1920, led to the armed occupation of factories against the repressive instrument of lockout. As we have seen, between March and August 1920, the employer forces organized themselves, creating the General Confederation of Industry and the General Confederation of Agriculture. After an initial dispersal, the industrialists oriented direct opposition toward the demands of the labor world, organizing an offensive strategy aimed at restoring the primacy of the business order in production sites. The victory won in April over strikers was the first concrete result of this action. Entrepreneurs' newfound determination and producers' growing combativeness transformed 1920 into a breeding ground, like a barrel accumulating gunpowder and about to explode. The detonation occurred in September, shortly after employers rejected the wage claims made by the Italian Federation of Metallurgical Workers (Fiom).[5] In September 1920, the council movement spread, becoming the model of direct management of the factory in the various realities of the working world:

> For the standard worker of the workshops, the factory council became a real experience and a natural expression of their form of management. Day after

[4] In April, railway workers blocked the circulation of trains in Emilia-Romagna and Tuscany, refusing to transport the troops of soldiers and carabinieri mobilized for repression. In May, in Brescia, a train carrying cannons, machine guns and ammunition coming directly from Poland was stopped, which was intended to supply the anti-Soviet front line. The same happened to railway workers in Trieste, while in Genoa port workers refused to carry out their activities in support of the boarding operations of a ship flying the tsarist flag.

[5] Fiom is the organization of the category of metallurgical workers within the Italian Trade Union Centre (Italian General Confederation of Labour; CGIL, acronym in Italian).

day, and not only among metal workers, but also among many other workers who adopted the factory council in this revolutionary wave, factory councils were created and structured, playing a directive role in production, discipline, armed surveillance.[6]

While the long and patient effort of Turinese workers for the recognition of councils did not change the correlation of forces within the Italian Socialist Party (PSI), at least it made the council a reality, a decisive factor in the struggles of the working class. A year later, even *l'Avanti!*, after considering the *ordinovist* platform utopian and literary, was forced to reconsider its statements and recognize the explosive power and revolutionary potential of a movement capable of going ahead with production under the sole leadership of technicians and employees, with limited availability of stocks of raw materials.

However, the isolation of the movement did not stop the opposing forces from making it return to its contract-based origins and, thus, the agreement signed on September 27 and 28 between unions and industrialists was reached. Even though the agreement produced considerable wage and regulatory gains, it still represented a crushing defeat for the labor movement, causing a deep split that destroyed not only the credibility of the PSI but also the hopes brought by that revolutionary era. The defeat definitely paved the way for the emergence of a new party:

> The occupation of the metallurgical factories is the origin of the split of Livorno with as many as 21 points of the Communist International: it accelerates and radicalizes the process that had already started in Moscow, in a situation that demonstrates the ebbing of the red wave and marks the beginning of a long phase of decline and withdrawal of the Italian workers' movement, of defeat even.[7]

The signing of the agreement paved the way for the blindest reaction of an impoverished bourgeoisie that at the same time was tormented by the still present danger. The advent of the fascist regime was predicated on the failure of the red biennium, the disillusionment that spread among the working and peasant masses. This tragic end was certainly facilitated by the irresponsible behavior of maximalist leaders, who were only able to

---

[6] Paolo Spriano, *L'Ordine Nuovo e i Consigli di fabbrica* (Turin, Einaudi, 1971), 120.

[7] Ibid., *Storia del Partito Comunista Italiano*, v. 1: *Da Bordiga a Gramsci* (Turin, Einaudi, 1967), 78.

entice the masses with slogans of insurrection and proletarian revolution without acting to make those prospects real. As Angelo Tasca himself wrote:

> The leadership of the party spent months preaching the revolution; it did not foresee anything or prepare anything [...]; the Italian working class, in turn, believed it was on the threshold of power, left the old hiding places and, instead, saw the usual horizon, open for a moment but closing again right in front of it.[8]

After the revolutionary rhetorical torpor of the Congress of Bologna, the PSI was effectively reduced to a parliamentary party, incapable of any activity except the right to speak guaranteed by parliamentary democracy.

It was based on this confluence of factors that Gramsci, with the article "Primo: rinnovare il Partito" [First: renew the party], written in January 1920, began to address, with absolute priority, the issues related to the Socialist Party. In the historical reckoning, the organization had managed to bring to itself and to its program, along its development, the attention of Italian workers, raising awareness and calling for mobilization. Over time, however, it proved unable to carry out the essential part of its historical task. The progress expected ultimately determined its political inertia and lethargy, causing it to distance itself from the great moving masses and to dissolve, on the one hand, in revolutionary phraseology, and on the other, in the futility of opportunism. "The party that had become the greatest historical energy in the Italian nation fell into a crisis of political infantilism and today is the greatest weakness of the Italian nation".[9]

The PSI had to renew itself so as not to be annihilated by events and not to thwart the revolutionary possibility, but this renewal should be led by the organization of the workers without mediation. Once again, the dual relationship between rulers and those ruled was pointed out as the main cause of the degeneration of the party; it was therefore necessary to reconcile the renewal of the PSI with the organization of the masses to be the ruling class:

> The organized masses must become masters of their struggle organizations; they must organize themselves as a ruling class, first and foremost, in their own institutions; they must have ties to the Socialist Party. Communist

[8] Angelo Tasca, *Nascita e avvento del fascismo* (Bari, Laterza, 1972), 172.
[9] Antonio Gramsci, *L'Ordine Nuovo 1919–1920*, cit., 389–390.

workers, the revolutionaries aware of the enormous responsibility of the current period, must renew the party, give it a precise outline and a precise direction; they must prevent petty-bourgeois opportunists from reducing it to the level of so many other parties in the Country of Pulcinella.[10][11]

In the context of this debate, Gramsci wrote, in May 1920, the motion "Per un rinnovamento del Partito Socialista" [For a renewal of the Socialist Party], approved in the Turin section of the PSI. This motion, taken to the analysis of the Second Congress of the Communist International, held in Petrograd in July, was approved as fully corresponding to the principles of the International, both due to the criticism of the direction of the PSI, and due to the political proposal presented, to the point of being explicitly mentioned in Lenin's congressional theses on the 17th point:

> With regard to the PSI, the Congress of the Third International considers the criticism of the party and the practical proposals substantially fair, which were published as proposals to the National Council of the PSI, on behalf of the Turin section of the party itself, in the issue of *L'Ordine Nuovo* of May 8, 1920, which fully correspond to all the fundamental principles of the Third International.[12]

At this stage, Gramsci's insights on the party were combined with those on the associative institutions of the working-class movement, aiming to promote the coordination of and an organic relation between the two realities; the development of the council movement clashed not only against the limitations of the political leadership of the Socialist Party but also, and above all, against the intention of the trade unions (whose central was in reformists' hands) of managing the movement bureaucratically and militaristically. The union was committed to preventing the growth of new forms of association of workers independent from its control and direction. Thus, in addition to the party problem, another issue to be solved was the union problem.

---

[10] Pulcinella is a burlesque character of Neapolitan origin, characterized by a usually black mask and a prominent nose. Its origin is lost in time. The designation of Italy as the "Country of Pulcinella" highlights above all the fact that it is a country that does not take itself and is not taken seriously.

[11] Antonio Gramsci, *L'Ordine Nuovo 1919–1920*, cit., 392.

[12] Vladimir Ilitch Lenin, "Tesi sui compiti fondamentali del II Congresso dell'IC", in *Opere complete* (Rome, Editori Riuniti, 1955–1970), v. 25, 324.

In Gramsci's view, the union is the form historically taken by labor as a commodity in the capitalist regime, as a way to tilt the balance between capital and labor in favor of the most fragile side. It arises thanks to the concentration and organization of the workforce. The trend toward the development of trade unions tends to marshal growing masses of workers into the organization and to concentrate the power, strength and discipline of the workers' movement in the trade union central. Precisely due to the concentration of the workforce in a central office, which assumes, in its direction, a stability and discipline taken from the whims and volubility of the spontaneity of the disorganized masses, the union is positioned to make commitments and to negotiate legally with employers to obtain results that can improve the living and working conditions of the masses it represents. The assertion of this "industrial legality" and of the contractual force of the world of work was a great historical achievement, which ended workers' previous atomistic and disaggregated condition of isolation and ushered in an extraordinary period for their growth and emancipation. However, "industrial legality" was not, in Gramsci's view, the last and definitive achievement of the working class, but only a form of concession that was necessary when power relations were not tilted in its favor.

If the union tends to reinforce, universalize and perpetuate the "industrial reality", the factory council, arising from the servile and tyrannical condition of labor, universalizes the forms of rebellion against exploitation, making the working class a source of industrial power. It therefore tends to destroy the condition of "industrial legality". Thus, if the union tries to lead the class conflict to extract favorable results from it, the council, through its revolutionary spontaneity, tends to encourage and develop the conflict. The relation between these two labor movement institutions must reconcile two opposing trends: the union must prevent any whim or impulse of the council from resulting in regression in terms of workers' conditions; the council, in turn, must accept and embrace the discipline of the union, but at the same time, with its revolutionary nature, it must encourage it and push it constantly so it can overcome its natural tendency to bureaucratize itself based on the technicism of unions.

It was precisely the need for this balanced relationship that led Gramsci, in contrast to Angelo Tasca, to reject a relationship of mere "hierarchical dependence" between the two institutions:

> If the conception that makes the council a mere instrument of trade union struggle is materialized in bureaucratic discipline and in the union's capacity

for direct control over the council, the council is exhausted as revolutionary expansion [...]. Since the council emerges from the ground that the working class has been gaining in the field of industrial production, the attempt to subordinate it hierarchically to the union would sooner or later lead to the clash between the two institutions. The strength of the council lies in the fact that it adheres to the consciousness of the working mass, the very same consciousness of the working mass that wishes to emancipate itself autonomously, that wishes to assert its freedom of initiative in the creation of history.[13]

In the 1920s, events sparked theoretical debate, which made political discussions and development happen at a faster pace and led to improvised convergences and harsh polemics. The crisis of the socialist movement in all its components—the party, the union and the various factions—translated into ever-increasing atomization, an incommunicability that led each component to independently follow its own path.

Day after day, the problematic relationship between the Third International and the PSI became an increasingly explosive issue,[14] while the subject of renewal tended to increasingly become a discussion about whether or not to found an autonomous communist party in Italy. Although at that time Gramsci did not have the split in mind yet, he reflected on the constituent elements of communist action and what should be understood as a communist party, which had elements distinctively different from the abstentionist component of Bordiga, who already intended to work for the communist split within the PSI.

Intervening in this debate, Gramsci moved away from "doctrinal and academic discussions" on the construction of a "truly communist" party and, more vehemently, moved away from the "aberrant" simplifications of electoral abstentionism, defined as "particularistic hallucinations".[15] In his view, the task of the communists was not to get lost in useless discussions but to work out the conditions of the masses for the organic development of the revolution. A communist party should be an action party, work

---

[13] Antonio Gramsci, *L'Ordine Nuovo 1919–1920*, cit., 133–134.

[14] For a deeper understanding of the topic, refer to Vladimir Ilyich Lenin, *Sul movimento operaio italiano* (org. Felice Platone and Paolo Spriano, Rome, Editori Riuniti, 1970).

[15] According to Gramsci, the Communist Party cannot refrain from participating in elections to bourgeois representative institutions because it must organize all oppressed classes around the working class and become the governing party, "in a democratic sense", of these classes.

among the masses, and rise dialectically from the "historical initiative" of "industrial autonomy" of the masses, not from the intellectual intuitions of thinkers and politicians who have a *good* opinion and say *good* things about communism. These reflections constituted a clear distance from the conception of the communist party as an institution separate from the masses—which made its leaders and intellectuals the priestly guardians of communist revolutionary purity—and constituted an important anticipation of the major topics related to the party, which characterized Gramsci's writing in the *Lyon Theses*.

The party should emerge from the oppressed classes and be in permanent contact with them, being structured by an organic relation with the autonomy of producers in the industrial field, which had a specific shape in factory councils. For the communists, the revolution was not only an abstract scheme produced by the monotonous repetition of the certainties of historical materialism but also a dialectical process in which political power enabled industrial power, and industrial power enabled political power. For this reason, the communists should not cling to discussions of an abstract thought, but live reality and understand it as it is and live the struggle to transform it into instigation so as to organize and positively shape the degree of spiritual autonomy and the spirit of initiative that industrial development itself determined among the masses:

> It is necessary to promote the organic constitution of a communist party, which is not an agglomeration of doctrinaires or latter-day Machiavellis, but a party of revolutionary communist action [...] which is perhaps the party of the masses that will free themselves by their own means, autonomously, from political and industrial slavery through the organization of the social economy and not through a party that uses the masses to attempt heroic imitations of the French Jacobins.[16]

In these reflections, three fundamental aspects of Antonio Gramsci's political thought already stand out: (1) the issue of the dual relationship between rulers and those ruled in the workers' movement; (2) the centrality and autonomy of producers, that is, the idea of a party that emerges from its concrete experience of association and of struggle in production; (3) the denial of a mechanical and deterministic conception of historical materialism and revolution.

[16] Antonio Gramsci, *L'Ordine Nuovo 1919–1920*, cit., 139–140.

In Gramsci's view, the PSI was not able to drive history, governing and coordinating the mass initiative of its own members. His ill-fated pronouncement on the agitations in favor of the revision of the collective contract of metallurgists in the summer of 1920 confirmed that. Indeed, the experience of councils and of occupation of factories had represented a profound change in the labor movement's method of struggle because until then, when workers tried to improve their economic situation or their working conditions, they limited themselves to adopting the instrument of strike due to the trust placed in their leaders. By occupying the factory and directing production on their own, the workers started to have a different shape and meaning: "Union leaders can no longer lead; union leaders have faded into the vastness of the landscape; the mass must solve the problems of the factory on its own, with its own means, with its own men".[17]

It was this profound change in the method of struggle and in the very psychology of the masses that led Gramsci to consider the old understandings about party and the union outdated and inadequate in view of the new consciousness of the masses. Trade unions and socialist parties, which emerged within the framework of the Second International, played a fundamental role in the early history of the workers' movement, when the masses still had no voice. The First World War, the October Revolution and the western proletariat's concrete experience of the struggle stirred among the masses an unprecedented spirit of initiative and an unrelenting aspiration to be the leaders of their own emancipation. Those events brought a vitality and richness to subaltern classes' lives and to their forms of participation that they could no longer fit into the classical schemes of traditional unionism and that notion of socialist party. The masses no longer wanted to be "cannon fodder", inert matter in the hands of social groups that controlled their fate at will. This was, for Antonio Gramsci, the greatest of all the lessons that could be learned from the experience of factory councils, and any proposal for the renewal of workers' organizations should stem from that lesson.

In a capitalist regime, the factory was a small state, controlled by a tyrannical lord, where the worker was reduced to a purely instrumental function with no choice. The occupation of factories had ousted this tyrannical power, making the productive unit an illegal state, a proletarian republic. The first problem that this state faced was military defense, and

---

[17] Ibid., 164.

this was already completely unprecedented since, in the bourgeois state, the army is built on three social orders: the popular masses, which constitute the military mass; the high bourgeoisie and the aristocracy, which represent the highest officer ranks; and the petty bourgeoisie, which is the command of the subaltern army. In this army, one finds the same form of hierarchy that, in both cases, relegates the subaltern classes to a passive condition of mass of maneuver. In the factory republic, the army consists in a single class, at the same time mass and leadership, where the forms of factory hierarchy and the bourgeois state do not have the same value. The same hierarchical modality of the factory and of the bourgeois army shapes the political and institutional organization of bourgeois society: in both cases, the emergence of a new power with industrial and administrative bases completely destroys the modality of social hierarchy between rulers and those ruled.

The political parties that emerged from the bourgeois revolution decay until they become mere personal collusion, and the socialist party, sticking to the field of parliamentary activity and reproducing within itself the same modalities of differentiation between rulers and those ruled, also participates in this process of decay.[18] Gramsci believed the communist party should emerge from the core of the socialist party, from the repudiation of this decay in all its forms and expressions.

In his view, within the PSI there was already a communist party; it only lacked explicit organization. It encompassed all those groups of "conscious communists" who, in the sections, in the factories, in the villages, worked against socialist decay and the complete defeat of the subaltern classes. Now Gramsci understood that the task of all communists, considering the National Congress, initially planned to take place in Florence, was to create an organized and centralized fraction. However, in September 1920, that is, four months before the Congress of Livorno, Gramsci,

---

[18] "In fact, the Italian Socialist Party, due to the historical origin of the various currents that constituted it, [...] due to the unlimited autonomy given to the parliamentary group, is revolutionary only in the general statements of its program. It is a conglomerate of political parties; it moves and can only move lazily and slowly; it continually exposes itself to becoming the terrain for adventurers, careerists, ambitious people who lack integrity and political capacity; given its heterogeneity, given the high friction between its cogs, it is worn or has been sabotaged by brownnosers; it is no longer in a position to assume for itself the weight of and responsibility for the initiatives and revolutionary action that events required. This explains the historical paradox that in Italy it is the masses that push and educate the party of the working class and it is not the party that guides and educates the masses" (Ibid., 161).

unlike Bordiga, still did not explicitly speak of a split. His goal continued to be the transformation of the PSI into the communist party and the dissolution of all ambiguities regarding the platform for adherence to the Third International.

Nonetheless, only a month later, the communist fraction was created in Milan and, in November, the various communist components of the Socialist Party were unified, including the Bordigist fraction, which, at the meeting in Milan on October 1, 1920, renounced the abstentionist theses, conforming to the directives of the Third International. The agreement between the three primary founders of the Communist Party of Italy (PCd'I)—Bordigists, ordinovists and left-wing maximalists—based on the change of the name of the party, the expulsion of reformers, and the acceptance of the platform for adherence to the Third Communist International, led to the establishment of the interim committee of the communist fraction of the PSI, made up by Bordiga, Repossi, Fortichiari, Gramsci, Terracini, Bombacci and Misiano, and at the election of the Executive Committee were Bordiga, Fortichiari, and the left-wing maximalist Bombacci.

In fact, the starting point of the progressive unification of the left of the PSI, which led to the emergence of the PCd'I, was the meeting that took place three years before, precisely on November 18, 1917, a few days after the seizure of the Winter Palace. It was a secret meeting held in Florence between twenty socialist delegates of the maximalist wing, organized to discuss the events in Russia and the revolutionary prospects in Italy. This meeting was attended not only by maximalist leaders, such as Serrati and Lazzari, but also by two young revolutionaries: one from Turin, aged only twenty-six, and the other from Naples, aged twenty-eight. They were Antonio Gramsci and Amadeo Bordiga. According to the recollections of the latter, the differentiation of communist-leaning maximalists and their progressive organization on a different strategic basis started in this meeting, in which both Gramsci and Bordiga showed the pressing need to learn from the Russian revolutionary experience, while most maximalists insisted on the traditional approach of revolutionary waiting, reaffirming the tactic of neither entering nor sabotaging the war.

In this fraction, either at the Milan conference, or at the Imola Conference of November 30 and December 1, 1920, as in the first phase of the PCd'I, Gramsci's group still had a subaltern and unorganized role, which was even overwhelmed by some internal confusion (especially concerning the relationship with Angelo Tasca), while the components of the

Naples soviet, thanks above all to the organizational talents of Amadeo Bordiga, constituted the major group. Gramsci himself mentioned this fact in a letter he wrote to Palmiro Togliatti on May 18, 1923.

> We, an old Turin group, had made many mistakes in this field. We avoided taking the ideal and practical disagreements that we had with Angelo [Tasca] to the extreme, we did not elucidate the situation and now we have come to this point: a small fraction of comrades explore on their own the tradition and the strength that we built in Turin, which is proof against ourselves. In the general field, because we rejected the idea of creating a fraction in 1919–1920, we ended up isolated, simple individuals or almost, while in the other group, which was abstentionist, the tradition of fractions and collective work left deep marks that until now have very considerable ideal and practical reflections for the life of the party.[19]

[19] Antonio Gramsci, "Lettera a Palmiro Togliatti del 18 maggio 1923", in Palmiro Togliatti, *La formazione del gruppo dirigente del Partito Comunista Italiano (1923–24)* (Rome, Editori Riuniti, 1984), 63.

CHAPTER 8

Revolutionary Reflux and Reactionary Offensive

Gramsci's political biography between 1917 and 1926 was marked by the dramatic failure of revolutionary attempts in the West and the beginning of a phase of reflux that facilitated the radical reactionary rise. The main question that Gramsci asks himself in the *Notebooks* is why, despite the deep economic crisis and the hegemony of the ruling class, in an objectively revolutionary context, was it not possible to repeat, in Italy and Europe, the victorious experience of the Russian Bolsheviks?

As pointed out, among the various re-readings of the work and the political biography of Antonio Gramsci, over time, a tendency centered on the presumption of discontinuity between the reflections before and after 1926 gained ground. Fascism itself is one of the conceptual areas in which the thesis of pre- and post-prison rupture proves weak and shows, on the contrary, deep continuity and analytical organicity, which began right after the war, in the relation between "organic crisis" and "subversivism of the ruling classes". The very category of "reactionary subversivism", continuously employed by Gramsci, is one of the examples that explain the reasons for Gramsci's international success, as it is used, for example, in Latin America to explain the cyclical tendency toward coups d'etat and the historical origin of an endless series of bloodthirsty dictatorships on the continent.

According to Gramsci, when the ruling classes, due to their inherent limits and to how the process of national unification and the construction of the new state were shaped, are faced with phases of hegemony crisis,

© The Author(s), under exclusive license to Springer Nature
Switzerland AG 2023
G. Fresu, *Antonio Gramsci*, Marx, Engels, and Marxisms,
https://doi.org/10.1007/978-3-031-15610-6_8

they tend to seek subversive and authoritarian shortcuts. More precisely, in the phases of historical crisis, these ruling classes are willing to subvert even the liberal institutions created by them to ensure the old balance. When it was a little more than sixty years old, the young Italian state witnessed at least five twists and turns: with Crispi, during the "crisis of the end of the century"; in the extraparliamentary solution that led it to the First World War, against the position of the chamber of deputies; with the rise of Mussolini to power after the "March on Rome"; and, finally, with the introduction of the "most fascist laws" after the "Matteotti crisis".

Antonio Gramsci's reflections on fascism escape rigid historiographical classifications.[1] In the Gramscian interpretation, the starting point is certainly historical materialism, which leads to the characterization of a general plot that has as its initial factor socioeconomic elements; however, even the factors considered subjective, such as the moral crisis of the bourgeoisie, have a decisive and central role. Gramsci also interpreted fascism as a reaction to a phase of profound social upheaval connected to the First World War and, above all, to the October Revolution, but he did not think of the bourgeoisie and its mode of production as a single and homogeneous bloc.

He identified, within the dominant social bloc, differences and contradictions that were precisely related to the birth and advent of fascism. He analyzed the attempt to focus bourgeois interests on fascism, but considered it a phenomenon that occurred socially among the petty and middle urban bourgeoisie, precisely for historical reasons, and which developed due to the support of the ruralists and also, although not always in a linear and harmonious way, of great industrial capital. In sum, Gramsci was not content with the reading of Fascism as a simple anti-proletarian reaction, having always even countered the essentiality of this factor.

In short, the Sardinian intellectual historically interpreted fascism in relation to the weakness of the Italian ruling classes and the limits of the process of political unification and economic modernization in the history of Italy, but he did not see it as an inevitable result of that process. He only understood it as historically determined, *in Hegelian terms*, so to speak, as a phenomenon that was rational while it was real and vice versa, unlike Croce who, paradoxically, as he was an idealistic philosopher, was content

---

[1] Gianni Fresu, "Antonio Gramsci, fascismo e classi dirigenti nella Storia d'Italia", *NAE: Trimestrale di Cultura*, Cagliari, Cuec, n. 21, ano 6, 2008, 29–35.

with the irrational, and therefore unreal, idea of fascism as an unexpected pathology in a healthy body.

In the political sphere, Gramsci wrote, fascism proved to be influenced by Corradini's nationalism[2] especially with regard to the concept of struggle between a "proletarian nation" and a "capitalist nation", which would lead the "young nation" to replace the "decrepit nation" in the development of humanity. This concept was adapted, in a distorted way, from Marx's theory of class conflict and translated into the sphere of international politics from a nationalist perspective. During the First World War, the still young Gramsci (who was then twenty-five years old) did not ignore the danger of this theoretical procedure (in the article "Lotta di classe e uerra", published in *L'Avanti!*, Piedmontese edition, August 19, 1916), which would be the central premise of the category of "living space", which expresses the political struggle through war, the conquest of markets, the "economic and military subordination of all nations to a single one, that which, through the sacrifice of blood and of immediate well-being, has proved to be the chosen one, the one that is worthy".[3]

Culturally, fascism was influenced by Marinetti's irrationalism and futurism, with which it shared the same "self-proclaimed innovative" nihilism that actually contained a confusingly reactionary idea of society. For Gramsci, the political manifesto of Filippo Tommaso Marinetti was nothing but a bland liberal program. He saw in futurism the convulsion of a disguised and disoriented bourgeoisie, but the distance between this disguised form of liberalism and the political stature of a figure like Cavour became enormous:

The descendants of Cavour forgot the teachings and doctrines of their ancestor. The liberal program seems so extraordinarily foolish that futurists have taken it for themselves, convinced that they are very original and most advanced. It is the most heinous mockery of the ruling classes. Cavour was unable to have in Italy other disciples and followers besides F. T. Marinetti and his noisy group of apes.[4]

[2] Enrico Corradini (1865–1931) was the founder of the Italian Nationalist Association in 1910, which merged into Mussolini's National Fascist Party (PNF) in 1923.
[3] Antonio Gramsci, *Scritti giovanili 1914–1918* (Turin, Einaudi, 1975), 41.
[4] Ibid., 49.

In terms of economic doctrine, fascist corporatism had its precursors among nationalist economists such as Filippo Carli,[5] for whom, through enterprise planning, it would be possible to overcome social conflicts and political prejudices for the sake of higher national interests. But the abandonment of the conflict would inevitably require the forced regimentation of the working class, its complete renunciation of the economic and, above all, political struggle. Carli spoke of the need to promote the cooperation of the proletariat with the bourgeoisie, to educate the former in an intensive culture so that it would know the social objectives of production and of "national life". Under the guise of expressions such as "social collaboration" and "national education", the true goal of nationalist revolutionism took shape: "the consolidation and perpetuation of the privileges of an economic category, today's industrialists, and of a political category, which is made up of its own self-proclaimed innovative people".[6]

Carli's passion, as well as that of many exponents of the Italian liberal world, for the German economic system and the exaltation of state capitalism combined with an aggressive policy of conquest were evidence of the backwardness of the Italian bourgeoisie.

> Even in Germany, the bourgeoisie was fatally undergoing its liberal evolution, destroying its corporations: war was the ultimate attempt to preserve an uneconomic system of production, the attempt to integrate social deficit into the spoils of war.[7]

In Gramsci, the "national convulsions" of the Italian bourgeoisie seemed to be the result of economic weakness and particular forms of national unification. This topic, then systematically developed in the *Notebooks*, had already been addressed by him in January 1918 in the article "Funzione sociale del Partito nazionalista" [Social function of the nationalist Party].

The economic and social weakness corresponded to political-institutional backwardness, which the Sardinian intellectual did not hesitate to call "the Pasha regime". In Italy, the liberal political cooperation was not uniformly organized nationwide, corresponding to the ruling classes; there was no national bourgeoisie with widespread common

---

[5] Filippo Carli (1876–1939), a sociology and economic history scholar, was one of the leading theorists of corporatism and nationalism before and after fascism.

[6] Antonio Gramsci, *Scritti giovanili 1914–1918*, cit., 51.

[7] Ibid., 147.

interests. Instead, there were "factions, cliques, a local clientele that engage in conservative activities not to promote the general bourgeois interest, but to promote the particular interests of local business clients".[8]

Despite the limitations, the Italian bourgeois regime represented the conquest of a more technically advanced form in the systems of production and exchange, an advance of the whole society. But now, due to the contradictions arising with the war, this very bourgeoisie remained a disturbing element of national life, capable of sabotaging and destroying the very economic apparatus that it built. The fascination of a part of the Italian bourgeoisie for D'Annunzio's rhetorical and extremist nationalism sought to indeed contrast the legal discipline of the central government with the irregular armed organization of Fiume's government. These were the first signs of this reactionary subversion behind which Gramsci could already foresee the civil war.

> The civil war was triggered precisely by the bourgeois class that strongly condemned it with words. Because civil war means precisely the clash of the two powers that vie for state government, a clash that occurs not in an open field between two very distinct armies, regularly aligned, but within society itself, as a clash of groups, as a chaotic multiplicity of armed conflicts in which it is not possible, for the great mass of citizens, to articulate, in which individual and patrimonial security disappears and is succeeded by terror, by disorder, by "anarchy".[9]

A few months later, the warning signs of this civil war became concrete. On December 2 and 3, 1919, worker riots and strikes spontaneously spread against the aggression suffered by socialist deputies in the hands of nationalists and monarchists. In Gramsci's view, this was an important episode of the struggle between the classes, but not of the struggle between capitalists and the proletariat, but rather between the latter and the petty/middle bourgeoisie. With the war, the petty bourgeoisie suddenly found itself in a prominent role in the chain of command, taking on a central role in the military reorganization of national civil, military and economic life.

---

[8] Antonio Gramsci, "L'unità nazionale", *L'Ordine Nuovo*, 4 out. 1919, in *L'Ordine Nuovo 1919–1920* (Turin, Einaudi, 1972), 277.
[9] Ibid., 276.

With no previous cultural and spiritual preparation, tens of thousands of people have been led to emerge from the bottom of the villages and suburbs of the south, from the gardens of their fathers' shops, from the tables that are heated to no avail in secondary and higher education, from the editorial office of blackmailing newspapers, from the junkyards in the suburbs of the city, from all of the ghettos where the laziness, cowardice and pride of the social fragments and debris deposited after centuries of servility and foreign domination decay; they were not given an indispensable and irreplaceable salary, and they have been entrusted with the government of the masses of men in factories, in towns, in barracks, in trenches at the front.[10]

Demobilization, the rhetoric of "mutilated victory", the economic crisis, the double pressure of capital and labor, and therefore the phenomenon of the proletarianization of the middle classes would have been the main concerns of the small and middle bourgeoisie during the post-war period. Here lies the origin of the "reactionary subversion" that found in Mussolini's nationalism, in D'Annunzio and, finally, in fascism the reason for its own social revolution. Salvatorelli made that perfectly clear after the "March on Rome": historically, the petty bourgeoisie always aspired to its own autonomous and radical revolution; however, not being a real social class, but an agglomeration that lives on the margins of the production process that is fundamental to capitalist civilization, its horizon can never go beyond revolt and demagogy.[11]

The reason for this situation was attributed to industrial capital's domination over the composition of the dominant groups in power and over the fundamental choices of economic policy. The need to protect the interests of industrialism was detrimental to the more general interests of the country and those of the petty bourgeoisie in particular. The war did nothing but intensify all the negative features of the liberal historical bloc, and Gramsci already saw on the horizon a change in the administrative personnel leading the country, even with no change in social relations. In particular, he saw in the People's Party, not in the fascist movement yet, the first party of the petty bourgeoisie; however, in addition to this serious error of judgment, it is interesting to note how the process of "decay" of the liberal system had already begun with the rise of this class.

---

[10] Antonio Gramsci, "Gli avvenimenti del 2–3 dicembre", *L'Ordine Nuovo*, 6–13 dez. 1919, in *L'Ordine Nuovo 1919–1920*, cit., 62.

[11] Luigi Salvatorelli e Giovanni Mira, *Storia d'Italia nel periodo fascista* (Turin, Einaudi, 1964).

The historical parties of the Italian bourgeoisie were destroyed by this suffocating and destructive hegemony that politically went by the name of Giovanni Giolitti and was exercised with the most blatant violence. War and its consequences revealed and developed new forces that tend towards a new arrangement of economic and political bases. The whole internal structure of the Italian state underwent, and continues to undergo, an intense process of organic transformation, the normal results of which are not yet exactly predictable and will change the administrative staff; state power will entirely fall into different hands from the traditional ones, from... Giolittian ones.[12]

In other capitalist countries, such as England, a balance was sought between industrial capital and land capital through the organization of the democratic state, thus promoting the interests of the working masses; they even introduced free trade and eliminated customs barriers against cereals. In Italy, on the contrary, the state as such was created by industrial capital, the leader and aim of all fundamental political and economic choices, including customs ones. The policy of industrial incentive had developed to the detriment of the rest of society and against the interests of the nation.[13]

In the *Notebooks*, this theme was revisited and extensively developed. Gramsci specifically identified Francesco Crispi as the main source of industrial and protectionist change:

The government of the moderates from 1861 to 1876 had only somewhat allowed for the external conditions of economic development—arrangements related to the state apparatus, roads, railways, telegraphs—and organized the finances burdened by the debts of the Risorgimento; the government of the left tried to overcome the hatred stirred among the people by the fiscalism of the right, but could not go beyond this: being a safety valve; it was right-wing politics conducted by left-wing men and sentences. Crispi, in turn, dealt a real blow to Italian society; he was the real man of the new bourgeoisie.[14]

Crispi was closely connected with large southern landowners, as a more unitary class, and at the same time worked to strengthen industrialism in the country. The hallmark of this commitment was the policy of customs

---

[12] Antonio Gramsci, *L'Ordine Nuovo 1919–1920*, cit., 410.

[13] Gianni Fresu, *Nas trincheiras do Ocidente: lições sobre fascismo e antifascismo* (Ponta Grossa, Editora UEPG, 2017), 115 and 136.

[14] Antonio Gramsci, *Quaderni del carcere* (Turin, Einaudi, 1977), 45.

protectionism and the denunciation of trade treaties with France. As for the programs, Crispi was for Gramsci a "pure moderate" and at the same time a passionate man who was obsessively conditioned by the issue of the political and territorial unity of the country, to which he had also subordinated the demands of colonial expansion. If the immense masses of landless peasants of the *Mezzogiorno* aspired to land, Crispi managed to draw these hopes and divert them, nonetheless, into the mirage of colonies. In this sense, Crispi's imperialism was also "rhetorical-passionate" and had no economic-financial basis. While imperialism was characterized by the export of capital and the search for cheap labor to obtain new forms of remuneration from it, Italy had no capital to export; in fact, it had to turn to foreigners for development in its own territory and, instead of seeking cheap labor to exploit, it intended to export its labor to colonies.

> Italian imperialism lacked a [real] basis, and this was replaced with the passionate sentiment: castles-in-the-air-imperialism, which was hindered by the same capitalists who would have willingly wished to invest in Italy the huge sums spent in Africa. But Crispi was popular in the Mezzogiorno thanks to the mirage of land.[15]

Between 1920 and 1921, Gramsci interpreted fascism as a symptom of an international crisis arising from capitalism's inability to dominate productive forces.[16] The petty bourgeoisie had the leading role in this new script, after being the mouthpiece of the abstract and bombastic war ideology. The war turned out to be just one part of a much larger process of dividing the world into hegemonic spheres that, in spite of everything, ended up crushing that same social class. Fascism was a new opportunity to get out of the crossroads through its armament and the introduction of "military methods of assault and surprise" in the class struggle. A significant example of an analysis of the social basis of fascism is contained in the

---

[15] Ibid., 46.

[16] In the article "Italy and Spain" of March 11, 1921, he wrote: "What is fascism, observed on an international scale? It is the attempt to solve the problems of production and exchange by means of machine guns and revolvers. The productive forces were ruined by the imperialist war. [...] a unity and simultaneity of national crises were created and they make the general crisis extremely bitter and permanent. But there is a stratum of the population in all countries—the petty and middle bourgeoisie—that believes that it can solve these problems with machine guns and fire, and this stratum feeds fascism by providing effectives to fascism" (Antonio Gramsci, *L'Ordine Nuovo 1919–1920*, cit., 101).

article "Il popolo delle scimmie "[The ape people], published in *L'Ordine Nuovo*, on January 2, 1921:

> Fascism was the last show put on by the urban petty bourgeoisie in the theater of Italian political life. The miserable end of the Fiume adventure is the last scene of the show. It can be considered the most important episode in the process of intimate dissolution of this class of the population. [17]

In this article, Gramsci told the parable of the Italian petty bourgeoisie from the rise of the "left" to power to the emergence of the fascist movement. With the development, concentration and centralization of financial capitalism, the petty bourgeoisie had lost its productive function, becoming a "pure political class" specializing in "parliamentary cretinism". This phenomenon took on different shapes, finding expression in the governments of the "historical left", in Giolittism, in socialist reformism. This degeneration of the petty bourgeoisie corresponded to the degeneration of parliament, which became "a shop of rumors and scandals, [...] a means of parasitism", a parliament corrupt to the core, which gradually lost prestige among the popular masses. Distrust of the parliamentary institution led the popular masses to identify the only instrument of control and pressure in the direct action of the social opposition, the only way to assert their sovereignty against the arbiters of power. Gramsci interpreted the red week of June 1914 in this sense. Through interventionism, fascism and D'Annunzio's adventurism, the petty bourgeoisie "imitates the working class and takes to the streets".

> This new tactic is implemented in the ways and forms allowed to a class of chatty, skeptical and corrupt people: the events that were called the radiant days of May, with all their journalistic, rhetorical, theatrical and demagogic repercussions during the war, seem like the projection into reality of Kipling's jungle story: the novel of Bandar-Log, the monkey people, which considers itself superior to all the other peoples of the jungle, possessor of all intelligence, of all historical intuition, of all revolutionary spirit, of all the wisdom of government, etc. etc. And this happened: the petty bourgeoisie, subject to government power through parliamentary corruption, changed its way of acting, became anti-parliamentary and tried to corrupt the streets.[18]

---

[17] Idem, *Socialismo e fascismo* (Turin, Einaudi, 1978), 9.
[18] Ibid., 10.

The decay of parliament reached its peak during the war, when the petty bourgeoisie tried to consolidate its new position as a barricade builder through an ideological mixture of nationalist imperialism and revolutionary syndicalism. In its anti-parliamentary position, the petty bourgeoisie tried to organize itself around the richest employers, finding a foothold between agrarians and industrialists. Thus, even if the Fiume adventure remained the "sentimental reason" for this strong initiative, the true center of the organization lay in the defense of industrial and agrarian property, against the claims of the lower classes and their growing agitation. In turn, the owning class had made the mistake of believing that it could better defend itself from the attacks of the labor and peasant movement by abandoning the institutions of its state and following "the hysterical leaders of the petty bourgeoisie".

The origin of the fascist movement was in the various groups of former interventionists, who were daring and simple latecomers, and anti-Bolshevik groups, around which the social categories that were most affected by the structural crisis that hit the country gathered. Among them, on March 23, 1919, the first *Fascio* was founded in Milan, which gradually structured itself as a movement, until it absorbed the various groups of the nationalist right that emerged in those years.

Behind the squads, Gramsci saw a very precise direction and at the same time an atomized intensification devoid of discipline and driven by blind and gratuitous violence, the result of the decay and absence of moral cohesion in the state and society. Fascism was the emblematic mirror of all this. The anti-political accusation of fascism eventually unleashed "unstoppable elementary forces in the bourgeois system of economic and political governance".

> Fascism presented itself as anti-partisan, opened the doors to all candidates, gave way, with its promise of impunity, to a displaced crowd to cover with a veneer of vague and nebulous political idealism the wild flood of passions, hatreds, desires. Thus, fascism became a fact of custom, identified with the barbaric and antisocial psychology of some strata of the Italian people, not yet modified by a new tradition, by school, by coexistence in a well-ordered and well-governed state.[19]

[19] Ibid., 150.

Gramsci identified in the background of Italian society fierce and barbaric traits that also largely explained the intensity of its class conflict: this was the country where murders and exterminations predominated, "where mothers educate their children with a helmet on their head",[20] where there are fewer forms of respect and protection for the younger generations, a country where in some regions winegrowers were gagged so that they did not eat grapes during harvest. For Gramsci, cruelty and lack of empathy were peculiar characteristics of the Italian people, "who go from youthful feeling to the most brutal and bloody ferocity, from passionate anger to the cold witnessing of the misfortune of others". Faced with these conditions, the emergence of the Italian state had been defective, as it was weak and unsteady, also due to the weakness and delinquency of its own ruling classes.

The inherent weakness of the Italian bourgeoisie forced its ruling classes to commit themselves continuously to remain in power; in Italy, unlike the rest of Europe, there was no struggle between industrial entrepreneurs and landowners: on the contrary, there was a conciliation whose cost was paid by the whole country and mainly by the *Mezzogiorno*, forced into underdevelopment and a condition of colonial regime. Even the lack of definition of true political parties of the ruling classes, which actually alternated according to a liberal or conservative perspective, was a consequence of this social dynamic. Hence the indistinct and swampy nature of liberal factions and of established transformist practices. The only mortar in the country was a bureaucratic apparatus led by groups with no objective basis in society. As will be explained in the two subsequent chapters, according to Gramsci, the fragile political and territorial unity of the country was also threatened by three pressing issues: the subversive attitude of the Vatican and the Church; the southern question; the emergence of a proletariat with increasingly revolutionary connotations. The first of these issues led to a lack of communication between the Church and the state, at least until the Church identified an enemy considered to be more dangerous: socialism; the second emerged from the condition of poverty and exploitation of the masses in the south, which were subject to a social and political domination that kept their feudal nature unchanged and subject to an endemic rebellion with no coordination or political perspectives; and the third one was the biggest threat to the existing state of things, in spite of the persistent political and organizational inefficiency of the anarchist and

[20] Ibid.

socialist perspectives adopted by the working-class movement in Italy at the turn of the twentieth century. The emergence of this new social-political reality was faced by the new state, at least until 1900, in a way that was completely analogous to what was later done by fascism, that is, with states of siege, courts martial, suspension of individual and collective freedoms characteristic of a liberal state.

But the systematic and violent repression of popular unrest turned out to be completely ineffective in quelling it, and it posed a risk to the entire institutional system, which was several times on the verge of terrible authoritarian retrogression. After the climax of the conflict, reached during the Milan massacre (6–8 May 1898) and the assassination of Umberto I (29 July 1900), the new century began with the creation of a new governmental line represented by Giovanni Giolitti, who attempted to insert the popular parties, cleared of any subversive impulse, into the new balance. The period that followed, the so-called Giolittian era, was marked by remarkable economic development and a major modernization of the country that, however, left behind all the *Mezzogiorno*. Therefore, it was a modernization unable to overcome some of the fundamental contradictions of the country. Moreover, the new line of inclusion in government areas, which concerned only limited segments of the socialist movement of the north (reformist) and later of the Catholic world, was not organically and politically clear, but rather involved a branched system of political corruption, a consolidated practice of transformism and the use of violence in the South. But not even this government system managed to prevent the development of social conflict in the country.

PART II

The Political Leader

CHAPTER 9

The New Party

In the history of the twentieth century, the events related to the Italian Communist Party (PCI) were addressed in research and monographs only as a part of studies that aimed to understand fascism, surely the most studied Italian historical-political phenomenon. And yet, as has already been pointed out by Franco Livorsi, amid this colossal work of historical reconstruction there are some "gray areas", among which what certainly stands out is the lack of or insufficient historicization of the current of Amadeo Bordiga, the main architect and protagonist of the emergence of the PCd'I. The tendency to consider Gramsci the founder of the new party results from an instrumental representation of the facts, which met the demands of the political struggle inside that organization in the phase after his arrest. However, while the historical background and the dialectical needs that determined this tendency changed, this view is still widespread in the PCI today, of a "Gramsci founding father of the party". In fact, without a realistic assessment of the role of Bordiga at the time the organization was created and during its first years, that is, without knowing the main aspects of its political conception, it is hard even to fully understand both Gramsci's process of intellectual development and the analytical categories that he developed during one of the greatest periods of his theoretical work: the years when he was a prominent political leader in the Comintern of the PCd'I.

© The Author(s), under exclusive license to Springer Nature   109
Switzerland AG 2023
G. Fresu, *Antonio Gramsci*, Marx, Engels, and Marxisms,
https://doi.org/10.1007/978-3-031-15610-6_9

Two essential reference points in the ideological conception of Amadeo Bordiga can be identified in the constant interaction between "economic determinism" and "revolutionary faith".[1] Despite having nothing to do with the cultural matrices of old socialist positivism, Bordiga shared with them a conception of subjective intervention strongly linked to the *iron laws* of economic transformation processes. The most emblematic confirmation of this approach in Bordiga's stances since the 1950s (the so-called formula of *attendismo*[2]) led the surviving Bordigist fractions to withdraw from active politics in anticipation of the great final crisis of capitalism, which, in Bordiga's predictions, should have hit in 1975. According to Ernesto Ragionieri, undoubtedly one of the great Italian scholars in the field of the history of the labor movement, "the fate of Bordigism can only be reconstituted considering the context of crisis of Italian society, of which he is an expression. His inability to offer an explanation of what was happening in Italy and, at the same time, his tendency to see through Italian lenses the problems of world revolution, the inflexibility of his thought and his tactical understanding constituted the measure of the passive condition that explains, at the same time, his success and his eclipse".[3]

Regarding the centrality that "revolutionary faith" has in the "purist" conception of the cadre party—which would be moderate and not corruptible by reformist contaminations—it is attributed not only to Bordiga's uncompromising nature but also, and above all, to the deeply degenerate context of Neapolitan socialism in which he developed his ideas.[4]

The PSI of Naples, which Bordiga joined at the age of twenty-one in 1910, was a very particular reality where the most heterogeneous positions were present: from the reformists to the anarcho-syndicalists, from the "uncompromising" to the Masons. In this jumble, marked by angry confrontations and divisive principles, Bordiga further developed his

---

[1] Gianni Fresu, *Il diavolo nell'ampolla. Antonio Gramsci, gli intellettuali e il Partito* (Naples, Istituto Italiano per gli Studi Filosofici/La Città del Sole, 2005), 93–120.

[2] *Attendismo* refers to waiting for objective conditions favorable to revolutionary action.

[3] Ernesto Ragionieri, *Palmiro Togliatti* (Rome, Editori Riuniti, 1976), 69.

[4] In this regard, most scholars who have studied Amadeo Bordiga, including Paolo Spriano, agree: "since he advocated the need to *create a movement of strong anti-bourgeois inspiration*, he recognized this obsession with purity—so well defined like a Jacobin-Robespierrean accent—which not only responded to his own temperament, but was also a natural reaction to the environment of Neapolitan socialism, prone to stubborn transformations, to clientelist corruption, which collides with his enthusiasm as an undefeated neophyte" (Paolo Spriano, *Storia del Partito Comunista Italiano*, v. 1: *Da Bordiga a Gramsci*, Turin, Einaudi, 1967, 12).

rejection of electoral decay and any tactics focused on a positive policy of alliances.

The spontaneous aversion to clientelist affairs, into which the increasingly transformative politics of the party in Naples sank, found its natural outlet in the turn to the left that occurred in the Congress of Reggio Emilia of 1912, followed by the establishment of the "uncompromising fraction" at national level. In the Congress of Reggio Emilia, the ultra-reformist group led by Bonomi and Bissolati was expelled, in which other illustrious exponents of socialism, such as Cabrini, Podrecca and Ferri, participated. The group was in favor of convergence with the "Giolittian bloc", supporting the colonial aggression against Libya. The expulsion was decreed, with the "uncompromising" delegates showing enthusiasm, and followed by an angry, violent anti-militarist demonstration on the part of Benito Mussolini, who became the director of *L'Avanti!* in that congress. Bordiga, a delegate of the Socialist Youth Federation, then became a contributor to the *PSI* newspaper and a close collaborator with its director, taking anti-parliamentary stances and opposing any collaboration with reformists, both at the political and at the union level.[5]

In his studies, Franco Livorsi drew attention to the fact that during this period, in Bordiga's theoretical formulations, whose conceptions were based on the refusal of any mixture of Marxist materialism and philosophical idealism, Marxism was presented simply as an "anti-philosophy" centered on the absolute primacy of practice over ideas. In this conception, the influence of some kind of "Rousseaunian utilitarianism" could be identified, besides Giovanni Gentile's theorization, which was present in his work of 1899, *The philosophy of Marx*.

> In this rough, incisive and suggestive position, anticulturalism seems to become an anticulture. Here, the proletariat is the gravedigger of, not the heir to bourgeois civilization. This is an inconceivable [...] position in Gramsci or Togliatti.[6]

Bordiga played an important role in the radicalization of the positions of socialist youth. As early as September 1911, he delivered a rousing speech against Italy's military expansion plans. The declaration of war on

---

[5] In Bordiga's view, in fact, union corporatism and egoisms were the germs responsible for socialist decay, as pernicious as parliamentary arrivism.

[6] Franco Livorsi, *Amadeo Bordiga. Il pensiero e l'azione politica 1912–1970* (Rome, Editori Riuniti, 1976), 35.

Turkey on September 25, 1911 provoked an immediate and spontaneous popular reaction of hostility. However, within the PSI, only the left led a battle without barracks against the military campaign, and in the midst of this situation, Bordiga stood out for his emphasis on the fundamental incompatibility between socialism and patriotism.

The battle fought by Bordiga and his closest collaborators against Mussolini's interventionist about-face in 1914 was particularly important. Bordiga was probably the most efficient in exposing Mussolini's *sparafuci-lism*[7] and in ridiculing his positions so as to effectively target the only sector of the PSI in which Mussolini, with his positions, had followers, that is, the Federation of Socialist Youth. It was Bordiga who led the decisive confrontation against Lido Cajani, the secretary-general of the pro-Mussolini Youth Federation, which resulted in his expulsion.

Bordiga wrote memorable anti-war articles, opposing the ambiguous distinctions between offensive and defensive warfare and between the imperialist forces involved in the conflict. He realized, early on and until the end, the dangers inherent in the "distinctions" made by Mussolini and, despite having been bound to him by a long relationship of collaboration, esteem and friendship, declared war on him.

According to Andreina De Clementi, Bordiga's course of political development between 1913 and 1919 ended up coinciding with a process of progressive awareness of the strangeness of the PSI when it came to the essential aspects of Marxist theory in the face of a reality that quickly moved toward a revolutionary solution to contradictions. Nonetheless, according to Clementi, this awareness was not the result of a process of intellectual development, but rather of Bordiga's multiple political initiatives:

> Bordiga's approach to the history and experience of the workers' movement lies not so much in the theoretical level, but rather in the political use of some fundamental modules of Marxist doctrine, in his ability to use them as an instrument for measuring not only historical reality but also the interpretative criteria and their respective solutions, which were adopted by workers' organizations at various stages.[8]

---

[7] Formed by the verb *sparare* (shoot) and the noun *fucile* (rifle), this neologism humorously and sarcastically denotes the current of opinion that was in favor of armed violence and war.

[8] Andreina De Clementi, *Amadeo Bordiga* (Turin, Einaudi, 1971), 24–5.

Analyzed from a national and international perspective of the topicality of revolution, even electoral abstentionism, according to Franco Livorsi, had a particular Neapolitan origin; it was a reaction to the failure of the electoral bloc in the administrative election in Naples, in which Bordiga identified unacceptable levels of degeneration in the PSI. To this origin, the influence of Mussolinian and maximalist anti-parliamentarism was added, which Bordiga turned into a strong belief in the incompatibility between democracy and socialism, to the point of denying even a tactical role to socialist participation in bourgeois institutions.[9]

This background approach remained unchanged even in the turbulent environment of the split of Livorno and in the first years of the new party. This is not the place to fill the void, or the "gray zones" that Livorsi spoke of, and these issues cannot be discussed in-depth here; however, in addition to the positions taken and to the battles that led to the phases before and after the split, the interventions and the articles written in this phase by the first secretary of the Communist Party of Italy are very useful to understand the political views of this new organization and therefore the dialectics in which Antonio Gramsci's critical intervention is inserted. For instance, in "Mosca e la questione italiana " [Moscow and the Italian question], an article written five months after the Congress of Livorno, Bordiga responded to reformists' accusations that communists had caused an artificial split under Russian guidance. It is an essential document to understand the historical genesis of the PCd'I from the perspective of its main founder, in which Bordiga associated the historical need for the split with a phase well before the Russian Revolution. The PSI had already experienced processes of division in Reggio Emilia and Ancona, but did not definitively overcome the problems of coexistence between two conceptions of socialism that were so different as to be antithetical. The events determined by the "red week" uprisings in 1914 confirmed the internal contradictions of the party, an organization that had a revolutionary vocation but was in fact inert and harmless, despite comprising millions of workers. According to Bordiga, the reasons for the split, already

[9] Bordiga's abstentionist position, however, was not always absolute: in the elections of 1913, he spoke out against anarchists' abstentionist tendencies. The turn to the left of the PSI, which in that election supported positions that Bordiga defined as "sincerely revolutionary", and more generally the belief that the harshest criticism of the reformist and parliamentary degeneration of the party should not be linked to anarchism and unionism led Bordiga to write an article against what he himself classified as the abstentionist threat and the anti-election boycott attempts made by the PSI.

unavoidable at the time, had little to do with Moscow; they were much more connected with the problems of the PSI itself.

In his view, even in the troubled years of the war, the neutralist unity of the socialists was only apparent because the right wing of the PSI maintained a hostile stance on any active opposition to the war, fighting fiercely against the chances of a general strike, which were discussed then.

The Battle of Caporetto, between October 24 and November 9, 1917, with the "irredentist war", suddenly transformed into defensive war, ended up further taming the socialist leadership, which feared being seen as an anti-national force, and that increased the gulf between the revolutionary wing and the reformist wing of the Socialist Party. As can be seen, the position of Italian socialism was one of the softest, while the other socialist organizations in Europe allowed themselves to be absorbed in the turmoil of war to the point of Lenin calling them "social-chauvinism". The "taking responsibility before the nation" and misinterpreted patriotism, unable to see the material interests behind the conflict, were the basis for the capitulation of the Second Workers International at the outbreak of the First World War. The concept of fatherland (understood in socially neutral terms) overlapped that of socialism, and the notion of people replaced the notion of class, so European socialist parties not only voted, in parliaments, in favor of war credits (urging the "proletarians of all countries" to kill each other rather than unite) but even held ministerial positions in warring governments.

In the face of this international disaster, the option of "neither entering nor sabotaging" helped to keep the PSI united until the end of the conflict in an attempt to at least spare parliamentary opposition to the war; however, the reasons for the split were already there.

Notice that I do not mind being identified as a precursor of the events, so much so that I stress that awareness of the split was not only mine, but everyone's. If I may refer to the critical notes of *L'Avanti!*, I will demonstrate how it was aligned with that issue: we will tolerate the right, but once the war is over, we will set things straight. Serrati had our support, but not that of the majority of the party leadership. He was convinced that the split would take place and subsequently admitted that to us. But that is not all. Turati himself sensed this unavoidable event, and at the war congress of 1918 [...] he ended his speech by saying: when the war ends, we must maintain the unity of the party. Everyone felt that an abyss was opening up between us.[10]

---

[10] Amadeo Bordiga, *Selected Writings* (Milan, Feltrinelli, 1975), 119.

The mistakes of the Bologna Congress of 1919 and above all the socialist electoral victory artificially prolonged the fictitious and ambiguous unity of the maximalist leadership of Serrati, who intended to bring together in the PSI its exact antithesis, condemning it to inertia in a historical phase of radicalization of the masses and of deep crisis of the old liberal institutions.

The greatest mistake of that congress was the illusion of a new revolutionary and communist leadership, which could lead to a profound political change capable of marginalizing, if not eliminating, the opposition of the reformists. However, in Bordiga's view, the maximalists were no revolutionaries. On the contrary, their line was the result of great theoretical inconsistency (both tactical and strategic), based on gross misconceptions and political mistakes. Thus, statements in favor of the Russian Revolution, the Third International and the Soviet system were based on rhetorical enthusiasm devoid of any concrete effect on the party's choices. In the Congress of Bologna, it was possible to "deliberate on the revolution" for the following Sunday and to vote on the constitution of soviets in Italy without knowing well what that was all about:

> The party did not even show signs of preparation. What did most people in Bologna know about principled positions and the tactics of the Communist International? Less than nothing. Most did not distinguish the concept of conquest of power from that of capitalist expropriation and had no idea of the problem of union action or of any other issue. The imminence of the electoral struggle prevailed over everything and stifled the original development of the divergence that grew under the surface of the tactics adopted during the war. Then it was possible to form the Serratian bloc, which had no homogeneity and which would inhibit the diffusion of communist consciousness, including the painful experiences of the field of action.[11]

The mistake of the communist minority was therefore to believe that the PSI was overwhelmingly revolutionary, a misconception fueled by an objectively revolutionary context and the strong belief in an imminent break with the ailing old order. The outbreak of social conflict and growing popular participation in the struggle led the left to confuse reality with hopes by naively believing that the development of the revolutionary movement had led the most advanced positions to defeat the reformists and put the party in the foreground.

[11] Ibid.

The fact that events unfolded quickly and the immediate demand for action prevailed over the need for enlightenment, the contradictions born of the conflict were neglected, and things happened on their own as no one knew for sure what was going on.[12]

The day after the split, within the communist ruling group, the major group was constituted by Bordiga's area of influence; the maximalists themselves continued being somewhat representative, while the *L'Ordine Nuovo* group was still scattered and underrepresented. Thus, in the Central Committee were present eight abstentionist communists, Bordiga, Fortichiari, Grieco, Parodi, Polano, Repossi, Sessa and Tarsia; five maximalists, Bombacci, Belloni, Gennari, Marabini and Misiano; and only two representatives of the Turin group, Terracini and Gramsci (who faced resistance due to accusations that he had been an interventionist in his youth). Thus, the Executive, attended by, in addition to Secretary Amadeo Bordiga, three exponents of the *Soviet* magazine (Fortichiari, Grieco and Repossi), in addition to Terracini, was safeguarded.

Bordiga was the first to build a strong and radical communist faction in the PSI and, with his uncompromising intransigence ahead of the socialist leadership, he won the admiration and respect of several cadres of the revolutionary left in this field. He was undoubtedly the protagonist of the split and of the foundation of the PCd'I, a leader endowed with great skills in organization and in political leadership, but above all with charisma. In short, the Neapolitan revolutionary had that political cunning that the ordinovist group lacked, and at the time of the split he managed to achieve a consensus among all communist components.

In a traumatic phase such as that of the split, Bordiga was the leader the organization needed, the only one able to guide it properly even in the most difficult situations. Due to his charismatic influence and his organizational skills, it was natural that the leading group (from the Executive to the Federation) should be formed around him, with cadres organically linked to their positions.

However, such an unbalanced composition within the ruling group did not lead to a severe dialectic, to a critical position, let alone to the creation

---

[12] The thesis that, right after the war, the force of events would have prevailed over the need for political enlightenment is also confirmed in several reflections of Gramsci; among them is the editorial of August 14, 1920 "Il programma de *L'Ordine Nuovo*", in which he explains the confusing emergence of the "ordinovist" editorial board, which arose precisely from the wish to take action at a time considered revolutionary.

of fractions on the part of the ordinovist group. This attitude, according to Palmiro Togliatti, was the consequence of a new spirit, shared by both simple members and party cadres.[13] After the foundation, the internal dynamics of the party were inspired by the principle of discipline and unity, since the PSI's opportunism and its inability to take on a revolutionary role were attributed to the current structure itself. Any difference should therefore be considered overcome. Such attitude may seem to be the result of an obstinate naivety of the Turin group, but in reality, according to Togliatti, it reflected a motivation dictated by trust in the collective and the wish to give the party a new character, no longer reproducing in it the fragmentations and lacerations of the old Socialist Party.

Only in 1922, with the full unfolding of the reactionary reflux and the exhaustion of the sectarian limits of the organization, did the constitution of a new group within the PCd'I become an unavoidable political necessity in the face of the collapse or even the lack of effectiveness of the party born in Livorno.[14]

The lack of solution to contradictions inherent in the PCd'I led it, as early as its first two years of existence, to massive imbalances and to a hardly sustainable contradiction between the potential and the effective capacity to act on real processes through some daily action able to align the immediate issues with the *ultimate end.*

Under Amadeo Bordiga's leadership, the messianic inertia and *attendismo* typical of maximalism and of the Second International approach, which were fought against and should have been eliminated with the split of Livorno, achieved an unexpected, peremptory posthumous victory, which killed the seed that germinated in January 1922. In Togliatti's view, the most negative and destructive aspects of Bordiga's leadership were related to his conception of party:

> To solve these problems, he did not start from the working class, of which the Communist Party is a part, from examining the real situation in which the class finds itself and moves, and therefore from setting concrete objectives that correspond to each situation. He started from abstract principles derived from an intellectual process, which should be applicable to any time

[13] Palmiro Togliatti, *La formazione del gruppo dirigente del Partito Comunista Italiano (1923–24)* (Rome, Editori Riuniti, 1984), 17.

[14] At the end of 1922, the Communist Party was practically beheaded by police-like reaction, and its political leadership was unfit and unable to respond to the changing national and international context.

and situation. Considering the ultimate goal was the conquest of power, the range of intermediate positions and their dialectical connection disappeared, the value of the democratic political movement and of progress in the field of democracy was denied, class antagonisms were perceived as rigid and schematic, the opponents were seen as one and the same, and it was not even possible to make allies; form and words prevailed over content, coherence became stubbornness, and party action was stifled, reduced to a mere exercise in propaganda and polemics. [15]

It was an approach extremely distant from the experience and conceptions of the Turin group; however, Togliatti, Terracini and many of the other ordinovists ended up capitulating before Bordiga, "letting themselves be seduced by his mathematical logic". For some time, Gramsci himself limited his criticism to private and informal discussions, refraining from publicly disclosing his divergence in the party's political leadership organs.[16] A letter from Togliatti to Gramsci of 1924 is indicative of this situation; in the text, Togliatti looked in hindsight at that period, accusing the Sardinian intellectual of being excessively tactical:

> I won't hide my opinion that you should have said well before many of the things you say to me now, not in private conversations and not indirectly, but before the party. In the section established in Livorno, you represented the group that followed a different orientation from that of Bordiga, the group that should be credited for leading the party to the only and greatest adherence of the masses that it has ever had. I, for instance, only began to know and to be able to assess the way the party was led and organized after the Congress of Rome, and even now in an incomplete way.[17]

According to Togliatti, in the PCd'I under Bordiga, the guiding principles were intended for "external discipline", which was created by a

---

[15] Palmiro Togliatti, *La formazione del gruppo dirigente del Partito Comunista Italiano (1923–24)*, cit., 20.

[16] In 1923, especially when the issue of the merger with the PSI led to a crisis between the line of the secretary-general of the PCd'I and the Communist International—in June, the enlarged Executive imposed a new Executive Committee of the Italian Party, indeed intervening—Togliatti strengthened his relations with Bordiga "until he made his presence in the governing bodies an absolutely harmful condition" (Ernesto Ragionieri, *Palmiro Togliatti*, cit., 107).

[17] "Lettera di Togliatti a Gramsci del 23 febbraio 1924", in Palmiro Togliatti, *La formazione del gruppo dirigente del Partito Comunista Italiano (1923–24)*, cit., 213.

purely hierarchical relationship between the top and the rest of the party, more generally between the party and the masses, and in the party the role of militants and cadres should only be that of executors of the isolated orders coming from the Executive. In Bordiga's view, the autonomy of action given to intermediate cadres and to the basic structures of the party should be avoided so that mistakes are not made, but above all so that they do not fall prey to opportunism. Only by executing the orders of a conscious and prepared leadership would this not happen:

> The party vision was the same as that of a military-type organization, more than a political one; but of an ancient military organization, devoid of a soul, based on mere obedience and above all on the nearly superhuman skills of a leader or of a small ruling group to cope with everything, to deal with each contingency by providing appropriate guidance, to timely give all the necessary directives and orders. What was the point of transforming it into a school, where one could develop knowledge not only of Marxist doctrine, but also, through the study of real situations and experiences, of geography, history, the economic structure of the country, of helping the comrades to develop for themselves the capacity for autonomous judgment about the concrete determination of political and organizational tasks?[18]

The way of understanding and leading the revolutionary organization, under Gramsci's harsh criticism, was fully theorized as early as the first months of 1921 in two articles by Bordiga ("Partito e classe" [Party and class], of April 15, and "Partito e Accione Di classe" [Party and class action], of May 31, both published in *Rassegna Comunista*), which proved extremely important to understand how he intended to guide and characterize the party from the beginning. In the former, all the fundamental aspects of his conception of party, its relationship with the masses, the avant-garde idea of organization were already present. In his conception, which was profoundly different from Gramsci's, the Communist Party should not encompass the whole class, not even its majority, but only the most conscious part of it. In his view, there is no class without a party, in the sense that one cannot even speak of class in the absence of a minority tending to organize itself into a party. Economic and social conditions do not suffice to define a class, nor do the positions of a certain group on relations of production, because Marxism does not analyze classes as a statistical entity, as *naturalists* do; on the contrary, it considers humanity

[18] Ibid., 21.

dynamically and dialectically in its continuous historical becoming, trying to find the definition of class in the singular aspects of this becoming. To establish a class and its action within a certain historical context, it is *not* enough to know the exact number of individuals that make it up; it is necessary to analyze the entire historical period attempting to find a social and political movement that expresses the interests common to those who share the same position with regard to the mode of production. In Bordiga's view, this method would make the analysis superior to mere statistical deduction.

Once a movement that pursues an objective related to the interests of a particular social group is defined, one can then speak of class in the true sense of the word. The class party is based on two elements, doctrine and method, simultaneously being a school of political thought and an organization of the struggle due to the interconnection between consciousness and will. But the process of developing consciousness and will is restricted to a small group that identifies a goal linked to the general interests of the class and that attracts the greater mass toward that direction. Bordiga saw this limited group as the class party and when it reaches a certain degree of development, one can speak of class in action:

> Including only a part of the class, only the party can give the class unity of action and movement, for the party amalgamates those elements, overcoming the limits of categories and localities, which are sensitive to the class and represent it. This explains the meaning of the fundamental truth: the party is only a part of the class.[19]

In Bordiga's view, the rest of the mass of individuals, still devoid of conscience and will, is moved by a selfish spirit, category interests, and local or national belonging. To guide the mass toward general objectives, which are connected to the historical movement, an organization emerges in a position to shape and unite it. Such organization is the party, the essential core of the class, which would not be organic without social assemblage; in short, it could not be defined as a class.

> The class presupposes the party because to exist and to act in history, the class must have a critical doctrine of history and an aim to attain. The true

---

[19] Amadeo Bordiga, *Scritti scelti*, cit., 126.

and only revolutionary conception of class action lies in the delegation of class leadership to the party.[20]

The categories and concepts present in "Party and class" were further developed in the latter article, "Party and class action". Class government, related to the theme of transition to socialism, is only understood as "party government"; likewise, revolutionary action is only party action. If the party is to be a fraction of the class, the most important issue is the size of the organization and how the masses fit into it. In Bordiga's view, a "voluntarist" mistake, one of "anti-Marxist opportunism", would be to try to establish a priori a number for that fraction, above or below some proportion between the fraction and the mass itself. By presenting the theoretical perspective in favor of a small, pure party as a principle and by asserting the need to guide ever-larger parts of the mass, the solution presented to the problem is definitely marked by classical determinism.

In Bordiga's view, the intention of changing the numerical constitution of the organization[21] should be considered "voluntarist" because the organization's size would be determined objectively, in each historical period, by the specific conditions of development of productive forces and revolutionary confrontation. Indeed, in his view, when revolutionary confrontation is still not fully developed and the revolutionary perspective is distant, the class party should be established by small groups of "forerunners" able to understand in advance the prospects of historical development. Only when the relations of bourgeois production are fully in contradiction and the revolutionary conflict occurs can the party increase its ranks and develop greater presence among the proletariat:

> If the present period is a revolutionary one, as all communists firmly believe, then it follows that we must have large parties exerting strong influence on broad sections of the proletariat in every country. But wherever this has not yet been accomplished, despite undeniable proof of the severity of the crisis and the imminence of its outbreak, the causes of this deficiency are so complex that it is urgent to conclude that when the party is too small and has little influence, it must be artificially increased by fusing into it other parties or fractions of parties whose members are supposedly linked to the masses.[22]

---

[20] Ibid.

[21] That is, the intention to build a party of masses.

[22] Amadeo Bordiga, "Partito e azione di classe", *Rassegna Comunista*, I, n. 4, 31 May 1921.

When the conditions are not objectively revolutionary, "taking the party to the masses" means mischaracterizing it as the consciousness of being a vanguard able to influence the masses and guide them is lost:

> Once the Communist Party is solidly based on the result derived from the doctrine and from historical experience with the specific characteristics of the revolutionary process [...], its organizational physiognomy is defined and it must be understood that its ability to attract and empower the masses will result from its adherence to strict discipline with regard to the program and its internal organization. As the Communist Party has theoretical consciousness [...], even if the masses turn away from it in some phases of its life, it is guaranteed to have them back when they face revolutionary problems whose only solution is within the party's program. When the exigencies of action necessitate a centralized, disciplined leading organization, the Communist Party, whose constitution was inspired in these principles, will lead the moving masses.[23]

Therefore, these criteria do not consist in the party's capacity for intervention and action in society and among the masses, but only in strict internal discipline, in adherence to the theoretical bases of its program, in absolute intransigence before like-minded parties, in "being the first to say" how the final process of the struggle between classes takes place. Only by acting decisively based on these criteria will the party be able, when the revolutionary crisis is acute, to attract the still hesitant members to its sphere of influence. If on the contrary the revolutionary prospects are not immediate, the party should not risk moving away from the context of radical preparation, distracting itself with circumstantial problems or deviating tactically from its target, that is, changing its strategy in order to adapt it to reality. This strict understanding of the relationship between subjective intervention and objective context, as well as the rather simplified way of conceiving the "early consciousness of intellectuals", had many points of contact with Kautsky's early conceptions of party and revolution, to the same extent that it had no connection with Lenin's thought. Just as Kautsky stated that the task of the Marxists was not to organize the revolution, but to organize themselves for the revolution, not to make the revolution, but to use it, in Bordiga's view, "neither parties nor revolutions can be created. Parties and the revolutions are led, by unifying all useful international revolutionary experiences, so as to secure the greatest

---

[23] Ibid.

chances of victory of the proletariat in the battle which is the inevitable outcome of the historical period in which we live".[24]

The explosion of contradictions within the Italian party was favored by the Communist International's new tactical framework, called the formula of the "united front", when the difficulties of the young Soviet state, the defeat of the revolutions in Europe, the beginning of a new backward phase in the movement, and the reactionary offensive of rising fascism led Lenin to a profound shift so as to overcome the crisis, which indicated an unprecedented modality of collaborative organization, political action, and attainment of hegemony among civil society. This episode is clearly explained by Paolo Spriano in his introduction to a selection of texts written by Lenin on the Italian labor movement, published by Editori Riuniti between the 1960s and 1970s:

> The years of 1921–1922 confirm the severity of the crisis of leadership of the labor movement. Old and new pathologies were added to the crisis, making its defeat definitive: the inaction of maximalism, the true and peculiar capitulations of reformism [...] were joined by an extremely sectarian conduct in which the PCd'I is isolated. What affects the most this last issue is the type of propaganda, of polemic, of action entirely dominated—between 1921 and 1922—by the obsession with a "Nittian reformist" perspective, which is expected to provide a solution to Italian politics. The prevalence of Bordigist leadership, of its working methods, of the strictness of its "uncompromising" formulas come along with the almost complete underestimation of the fascist phenomenon, the refusal to seek a common platform of workers' and popular resistance against expanding paramilitarism.[25]

As we know, this underestimation led Lenin to polemically comment on the mistakes of the Italian communists, stating that fascism taught them a hard lesson and demonstrated the poor education and inadequate political preparation of the ruling group. In fact, Lenin had already severely criticized Bordiga's stances, expressing support, in contrast, for the ideas of the *L'Ordine Nuovo* group. In addition, against the abstentionist positions of the Neapolitan leader and the "exasperated leftism" of a part of the international movement, Lenin wrote the famous *"Left-wing" communism: an infantile disorder* in 1920.

---

[24] Ibid.
[25] Vladimir Ilitch Lenin, *Sul movimento operaio italiano* (Rome, Editori Riuniti, 1970), 42.

Further discussing this complex dialectic, which opposed the first ruling group of the PCd'I to the Executive of the Comintern, can be overwhelming; however, it is essential to explain its nature in order to understand the political evolution of the Sardinian intellectual, at least for two reasons: (1) because the dissemination of criticism of the Italian party led Gramsci to break the silence and to distinguish himself publicly from Bordiga's political line; (2) because the "united front" about-face was for Gramsci a fundamental theoretical (not just tactical) change which would later be the premise of his reflections on the concept of "hegemony".

CHAPTER 10

The Comintern and the "Italian case"

At the beginning of 1921, the Soviet state was in a very complicated situation, compounded by the destruction caused by the First World War and the civil war. Against this background, in the 10th Congress of the Russian Communist Party, Lenin first alluded to the need for the country to make a profound shift in its economic policy. Reality had dramatically shown how insufficient it was to seize the state machine to change society's direction and enable a transition. Many of the perspectives considered before the revolution, especially that of "workers' control", clashed against a reality much more complex than that of Lenin's political predictions. The internal difficulties were compounded by international ones, with the beginning of a phase of revolutionary reflux and reactionary offensive after the failure of the various insurrectional attempts in the West. All this necessitated a thorough revision of the line, from a perspective in which the solutions adopted for the two levels, domestic and international, should be inextricably linked.

Thus, at the assembly of secretaries of the Moscow party cells (April 9, 1921), Lenin stated that the New Economic Policy (NEP) was an urgent and inevitable exigency to overcome absolute misery and the limits of "war communism", a phase imposed by the state of need, not by a theoretical choice. The terms of this profound shift were explained by Lenin in the essay "The tax in kind", of May 1921, in which he exposes the contradictions in the transition from capitalism to socialism in a society in which

G. Fresu, *Antonio Gramsci*, Marx, Engels, and Marxisms, https://doi.org/10.1007/978-3-031-15610-6_10

the patriarchal economy, petty commodity production, private capitalism, state capitalism and socialism still coexisted.

Lenin presented the NEP as a new stage of the class struggle, and the government adopted urgent measures that had a disruptive effect on international communism:

(1) the abolition of forced requisitions and their replacement with taxes in kind; (2) reintroduction, with some limitations, of freedom of trade; (3) authorization of the existence of private enterprises; (4) return of enterprises with fewer than ten employees to their former owners; (5) a new regime of wage incentives corresponding to the activities developed; (6) authorization for Soviet citizens to own commercial enterprises, enter into contracts, own property, choose occupations; (7) approval (October 30, 1922) of the land code, which allowed peasants to use market laws and granted them the right of ownership of everything that enabled the improvement of crops, obviously with no right to sell or mortgage the land because it was state domain; (8) abolition of the gratuitousness of public services, elimination of equal pay and compulsory labor. Along with all that, the program of electrification of the country was organized, which was a fundamental operation for the transition, according to Lenin, and made his formula "communism = Soviet power + electrification"[1] famous.

In the 10th Congress, Lenin incited the cadres to self-criticism. It was necessary to abandon all forms of abstract utopianism. "War communism", that is, the management of the dramatic emergency faced by the Soviet state, could not be considered, let alone presented as the historical materialization of communist society, unless a "caricature" was intended. In the following months, the revolutionary strove to make the measures adopted immediately come into effect, not sparing harsh criticism against those who attached themselves to a romantic and bookish vision of socialist transition. In his words, the greatest risk came from left-wing infantilism and the intention to resolve any contradiction with an act of will, a concept that was accurately synthesized in a sentence that would later become eternal: "There is nothing more harmful or fatal for communism than communist boasting—we'll manage on our own".[2]

The collapse of the rural economy, typical of war communism, was at the core of one of the most important problems identified by Lenin in his critical notes on the Soviet state, bureaucratic practices:

---

[1] Jean Ellenstein, *Storia dell'URSS*, v. I: *1917–1936* (Rome, Editori Riuniti, 1976), 166.
[2] V. I. Lenin, *Lenin Collected Works* (Moscow, Progress Publishers, 1973), v. 45, 133.

In our country bureaucratic practices have different economic roots, namely, the atomised and scattered state of the small producer with his poverty, illiteracy, lack of culture, the absence of roads and exchange between agriculture and industry, the absence of connection and interaction between them. This is largely the result of the Civil War. [...] We must learn to admit an evil fearlessly in order to combat it the more firmly, in order to start from scratch again and again; we shall have to do this many a time in every sphere of our activity, finish what was left undone and choose different approaches to the problem. In view of the obvious delay in the restoration of large-scale industry, the "locking up" of exchange between industry and agriculture has become intolerable. Consequently, we must concentrate on what we can do: restoring small industry, helping things from that end, propping up the side of the structure that has been half-demolished by the war and blockade. We must do everything possible to develop trade at all costs, without being afraid of capitalism, because the limits we have put to it (the expropriation of the landowners and of the bourgeoisie in the economy, the rule of the workers and peasants in politics) are sufficiently narrow and "moderate". This is the fundamental idea and economic significance of the tax in kind.[3]

Thus, taxes in kind were an essential measure to correct mistakes, avoiding the disasters of misery and famine, and to restore small industry, which did not require large investments in machinery or large reserves of raw materials and fuel, thus providing vital aid to the peasant economy. All this, in Lenin's intentions, would inevitably restore the petty bourgeoisie's freedom of trade at the local level, a condition considered a necessary evil in such a disastrous situation. To that end, he urged the leadership of the Bolshevik Party to concentrate their efforts on favoring the development of the economy toward state capitalism, rather than wasting them on attempts to prevent the resurgence of bourgeois social relations. In this sense, taxes in kind represented the passage from the extraordinary condition of war communism to the ordinary condition of regulating the socialist exchanges of products between city and countryside, which was necessary to combat the scattering of small producers and bureaucratic practices, even if that meant taking lessons in modernization from the bourgeoisie:

We must not be afraid of Communists "learning" from bourgeois experts, including merchants, petty capitalist co-operators and capitalists, in the

---

[3] Ibid., v. 32, 351–2.

same way as we learned from the military experts, though in a different form. The results of the "learning" must be tested only by practical experience and by doing things better than the bourgeois experts at your side; try in every way to secure an improvement in agriculture and industry, and to develop exchange between them. Do not grudge them the "tuition" fee: none will be too high, provided we learn something. Do everything to help the masses of working people, to come closer to them, and to promote from their ranks hundreds and thousands of non-Party people for the work of economic administration.[4]

Lenin considered the NEP essential also in relation to the new international political situation; not by chance this turn and that of the "united front" were the essential topics of discussion between the Third and Fourth Congress of the Communist International. As we know, according to Lenin, all the subjective conditions for the socialist revolution were present in Russia in 1917, while the development of productive forces was completely insufficient; in Germany, on the contrary, the optimal objective conditions were present, but there were great difficulties with the revolutionary initiative. Lenin's conviction (which later proved to be mistaken) was that the viability of the Russian revolutionary process would spread from "Petrograd to Berlin"—and then to the rest of Europe—thus uniting all the conditions for a complete socialist revolution into a single whole.

With the end of the first world conflict, these conditions seemed closer and closer to being fulfilled, thanks not only to German revolutionary prospects but also to the emergence of the Hungarian Republic from workers' and peasants' councils. Although this experience was interrupted in 1919 by the intervention of the counterrevolutionary forces under Admiral Horthy, hopes for a world revolution seemed about to materialize at the beginning of 1920 due to the advance of the Red Army over Warsaw, the beginning of the "red biennium" in Italy, and above all the growing turmoil in neighboring Germany.[5] As we know, between the fall of 1920 and March of 1921, all these prospects were ruined with the resolution of the conflicts brought to an end by the international revolutionary movement, together with the growing difficulties of Soviet Russia, which, despite having won the civil war against the "white armies", was in an

---

[4] Ibid., 365.

[5] For further study, see Miloš Hájek, "La discussione sul fronte unico e la rivoluzione mancata in Germania", in Eric Hobsbawm (org), *Storia del marxismo*, v. 3: *Il marxismo nell'età della III Internazionale* (Turin, Einaudi, 1980), 442–63.

economic and social situation on the verge of collapse, which was made even more dramatic by the advance of famine in the countryside. In such context, characterized by immense difficulties, the Third Congress of the Communist International began between June and July 1921, properly considered an essential tactical turning point in the history of the world communist movement.[6]

In the congress, the reasons for the about-face were listed in three fundamental reports: *Theses on the international situation and the immediate tasks of the Comintern*, submitted by Trotsky; *Report on the tactics*, written by Lenin, and *Theses on the tactics*, presented by Karl Radek.

In his report, Trotsky pointed out how the new situation was characterized by signs that were very contradictory and difficult to understand; in fact, during the year between the Second and the Third Congress of the Comintern, a whole series of uprisings and battles of the working class ended with a "partial defeat": the advance of the Red Army over Warsaw in August 1920, the movement of the Italian proletariat in September 1920; the uprising of German workers in 1921. All in all, the phase of uprisings that erupted spontaneously with the end of the war seemed to have come to an end, and the bourgeoisie, after reorganizing and gaining confidence, launched the offensive against the workers of all countries, both on the political and on the economic front. That led Trotsky to ask himself a series of questions about how stable the new balance achieved by the bourgeoisie could be considered and how long the capitalist restoration would last. In 1919, a new phase of organic development of capitalism began, and it managed to absorb the demobilized workforce and boost the confidence of the bourgeoisie in the face of the possibility of easing the social tensions that had arisen. However, this economic renewal did not mean the viability of economic reconstruction after the war; rather, it constituted an artificial extension of the illusions of prosperity created by the war. In Trotsky's view, the nature of this so-called renewal was fictitious:

> The bourgeois governments, acting in alliance with banks and industrial monopolies, at the expense of a following organic disorganization of the economic system [...], managed to contain the outbreak of the political crisis caused by demobilization and the first post-war settling of accounts. Managing to achieve a remarkable period of truce, the bourgeoisie imagined

---

[6] Gianni Fresu, *Lénin leitor de Marx: dialética e determinismo na história do movimento operário* (trans. Rita Matos Coitinho, São Paulo, Anita Garibaldi, 2016), 153–70.

that the danger of a crisis was definitely gone. It became optimistic. It seemed that the need for reconstruction had ushered in a lasting era of industrial and commercial prosperity and, above all, financial speculation. The year of 1920 crushed those hopes.[7]

The crisis of 1920 did not fit into the routine of economic cycles, but was above all a reaction to the artificial nature of that wartime prosperity, which was faced with the collapse of the last seven years of European production. The renewal was therefore ephemeral because, in a general trend of underproduction, it was the result of an economy numbed by financial speculation.

The unstable nature of the new balance lay in the colossal imbalances of production, trade, and credit in the world market; in this context, Germany faced unsustainable public indebtedness, which along with monetary devaluation and rising prices, led the working class to considerable deterioration in living and working conditions. England had emerged victorious from the conflict, keeping all its possessions and taking new ones; however, the contradiction between its predominance in the world and its economic decline was increasingly evident, which would lead it either to confront the new rising power, the United States, or to become a second-class power. With the conflict, the United States, in turn, emerged from the status of a debtor country to a creditor country of the whole world, absorbing half of all the world's gold reserves and transforming itself, above all, from a country exporting agricultural products and raw materials to a country exporting mainly industrial products. This led the dollar to replace the British pound as the main currency in international transactions, but despite this, even the United States was experiencing great imbalances largely due to the disastrous situation in Europe, which was unable to deal with not only the enormous productive growth of the US but also the inflating of the speculative bubble, which would later lead to the crisis of 1929.

Europe, up to its neck in debt, was facing productive decline, from which no possibility of success was expected; it needed American products, but found an insurmountable obstacle in the devaluation of its main currency; the world market was totally disorganized, characterized by the

---

[7] L. Trotsky, "Le tesi sulla situazione mondiale e sui compiti del Comintern adottate dal III Congresso", em Jane Degras (org.), *Storia dell'Internazionale comunista attraverso i documenti ufficiali*, t. 1: *1919–1922* (Milan, Feltrinelli, 1975), 250.

oscillation between European dumping and American protectionism and by the sudden and devastating speculative storms in the financial system, which led capitalist production to lose all of its usual reference points. That was compounded by the phenomenon of the proletarization of the petty and middle European bourgeoisie and the escalation of social tensions. Thus, if on the one hand, the destruction of productive forces had led Europe to lag behind decades in its availability of material resources, on the other, the level of class confrontation increased exponentially.

In such situation, the reconstruction of the productive system destroyed by the war and the effective renewal of economic development required huge amounts of capital, which made the European proletariat work harder and for lower wages. Two opposing trends derived from this state of affairs: the struggle of workers to improve their own living and working conditions, in contrast to the effective possibilities of capitalism; the reactionary offensive of the ruling classes to break the resistance of the world of work.

> Ultimately, the question of restoring capitalism to its former foundations can be thus summarized: in today's incomparably more difficult situation, is the working class willing to make the necessary sacrifices to return to the conditions of stability for its servitude, which is harsher and crueler than those existing before the war? [...] Capitalism can only be restored with infinitely greater exploitation, with the loss of millions of lives, with the lowering of the standard of living of millions of people to a minimum, with perpetual uncertainty, and this leads to continuous clashes and uprisings.[8]

It is clear that at a stage like this, in which capitalism had managed to restore a provisional and precarious balance, in a situation that remained revolutionary, both the proletariat's defensive struggles and the communists' ability to guide such struggles and give them an organic character took on a decisive role in Trotsky's view.

In his report, Lenin started from Russia's internal situation in 1921, from the hostility in its confrontation with western powers, but also from the failure of all attempts at military intervention made against it. In the first years of socialist Russia, there was a stage of open struggle (combat) of the international bourgeoisie against it, which eventually brought it to the center of international political issues.

---

[8] Ibid., p. 256–7.

Now Russia's situation on the world stage was characterized by a new phase of unstable and relative balance because both in capitalist countries and in those subjected to colonial rule there was so much flammable material that insurrections, conflicts and revolutions could suddenly and unexpectedly break out anytime, anywhere. The task of the communists at this stage was to know how to take advantage of the truce and adapt their own tactics to the new situation.

In Lenin's view, this new situation represented an inadmissible need of a hegemonic nature, mentioned by Gramsci in the famous notes of *Notebook 7*, in the passage on the "war of movement and war of position":

> We must now thoroughly prepare for revolution and make a deep study of its concrete development in the advanced capitalist countries. [...]; we must take advantage of this brief respite in order to adapt our tactics to this zigzag line of history.[9]

The central issue in this unprecedented phase was again winning over the majority:

> The more organised the proletariat is in a capitalistically developed country, the greater thoroughness does history demand of us in preparing for revolution, and the more thoroughly must we win over the majority of the working class.[10]

In this context, the colonial issue became absolutely central for Lenin. A large part of the members of the Second International had developed a sentimental attachment to and merely moralistic sympathy for oppressed colonial and semi-colonial peoples, but were largely indifferent to anti-colonial movements, considering them irrelevant to the purpose of the general struggle for socialism. The communists, on the other hand, should realize that at the beginning of the twentieth century hundreds of millions of individuals were acting as "active autonomous revolutionary factors". In the future battles for world revolution, anti-colonial struggles—initially aiming for national liberation, but inevitably destined to clash with imperialism—would take on a more important revolutionary role than might have been expected. This consciousness led the Communist International to invest resources and energy in anti-colonial struggles, providing

---

[9] V. I. Lenin, *Lenin Collected Works* cit. v. 32, 481.
[10] Ibid.

fundamental political, economic and organizational support for the mobilization of the peoples subject to the domination of the West and for their historical process of emancipation.

According to Domenico Losurdo, the Russian Revolution, among its multiple meanings, represented a turning point in world history precisely because of its content and anti-colonial commitment, and therein lies the distinction between eastern Marxism and western Marxism after Marx.[11] From the Second International to Toni Negri, Michael Hardt and Žižek, including so many "critical" intellectuals associated with the left (Adorno, Arendt, Foucault and Marcuse, to name but a few), incomprehension, undervaluation and paternalism in the face of the colonial issue produced contradictory readings that shed light on much of the ideological subalternity, inoperativeness and marginality of the left in countries marked by advanced capitalism. The complete inability to face the drama of new colonial wars, and therefore the inability to become (unambiguously) the active and propelling center of an anti-imperialist movement is proof of the limits of contemporary western Marxism and of many of its post-ideological ramifications that are in vogue today.

Lenin, anticipating Gramsci's categories[12] and referring to the NEP, described a world divided into two spheres: the capitalist and developed West and the colonial East, explored and dominated by the former.[13] Continuing the reflections in *Imperialism, the higher stage of capitalism*, his most effective synthesis, Lenin repeatedly highlighted in those years

---

[11] Domenico Losurdo, *Il marxismo occidentale. Come nacque, come morì, come può rinascere* (Bari/Rome, Laterza, 2017).

[12] Gramsci defines the concepts of East and West as the result of a historical-cultural convention, a historical fact produced by the development of civilization, but even if it is a construction, it is not simply a purely arbitrary and rationalist construct. In the absence of man, it would not make sense to think in terms of East and West, or North and South, because these are real relations that are difficult to understand without man, without the development of civilization and, above all, without hegemonic relations between rulers and those ruled: "it is evident that East and West are arbitrary, conventional, that is, historical constructions because, outside real history, every point of the Earth is East and West at the same time. This is clearly evidenced by the fact that these terms became consolidated not from the point of view of a hypothetical and melancholic man in general, but from the point of view of European cultured classes which, through their world hegemony, made them accepted everywhere. [...] Thus, through the historical content that combines with the geographical term, the expressions East and West end up indicating certain relations between complexes of different civilizations" (Antonio Gramsci, *Prison Notebooks*, Turin, Einaudi, 1977, 1419–20).

[13] Vladimir Ilitch Lenin, *Opere complete* (Rome, Editori Riuniti, 1955–1970), v. 33, 455.

the close and permanent relationship between the struggle for emancipation from the colonial rule of the "eastern" countries and the survival of the socialist state, placing the two realities on the same battlefront and in the same counterhegemonic sphere, in a context dominated by the collapse of revolutions in the West:

> The system of international relationships which has now taken shape is one in which a European state, Germany, is enslaved by the victor countries. [...] At the same time, as a result of the last imperialist war, a number of countries of the East, India, China, etc., have been completely jolted out of the rut. Their development has definitely shifted to general European capitalist lines. The general European ferment has begun to affect them, and it is now clear to the whole world that they have been drawn into a process of development that must lead to a crisis in the whole of world capitalism. Thus, at the present time we are confronted with the question—shall we be able to hold on with our small and very small peasant production, and in our present state of ruin, until the West-European capitalist countries consummate their development towards socialism? But they are consummating it not as we formerly expected. They are not consummating it through the gradual "maturing" of socialism, but through the exploitation of some countries by others, through the exploitation of the first of the countries vanquished in the imperialist war combined with the exploitation of the whole of the East. The East, on the other hand, definitely entered the revolutionary movement precisely after this first imperialist war, and was permanently dragged into the general maelstrom of the world revolution. [...] The outcome of the struggle ultimately depends on the fact that Russia, India, China, etc. they constitute the vast majority of the population. And it is precisely this majority that in recent years, with a speed never seen before, has entered the struggle for its own liberation.[14]

International dynamics would force these two spheres into a new imperialist war, with the aim of further dominating colonial peoples and destroying the Soviet state.

In Russia, according to Lenin, important changes were taking place regarding the old, expropriated ruling classes, with the establishment of a political front of the exiled bourgeoisie capable of mobilizing the newspapers and parties of the large landowners and the petty bourgeoisie, thanks to the financing provided by the foreign bourgeoisie, which was necessary to preserve all the means and tools to fight the Soviet Revolution.

[14] V. I. Lenin, Lenin Collected Works, cit., v. 33, 498–499.

If at the time of the seizure of power, in the revolution of 1917, the bourgeoisie was disorganized and not politically developed, as it did not exercise any real hegemony in society, after four years it had managed to reach the level of consciousness and political development of the bourgeoisie of the West. In other words, the Russian bourgeoisie suffered a terrible defeat, but according to Lenin, it learned the lesson from history and reorganized itself accordingly. All of that made the process of transition to socialism more complicated due to the persistence of a hard class struggle even after the seizure of power by the proletariat.

By mentioning the need for a different attitude on the part of the Russian proletariat toward the high bourgeoisie and the old class of landowners, on the one hand, and the petty bourgeoisie, on the other, Lenin outlined the new tactical framework of the Russian communists on the basis of the NEP. If when confronting the high bourgeoisie and the old class of landowners the only possible relationship was indeed the clearest and most open class struggle, the petty bourgeoisie, after the years of "war communism", required another kind of relationship.

In western countries, the small estate constituted a social group that ranged from 30% to 50% of the total population, while in Russia the peasant mass constituted the vast majority of the population. For this reason, because of this class, relations should be based on a very close alliance, capable of making the hegemony of the proletariat take the place of the hegemony that the great bourgeoisie exercised over it.

> We have concluded an alliance with the peasants that we will defend in this way: the proletariat frees the peasant from exploitation by the bourgeoisie, from its direction and influence and conquers him for his cause of defeating the Explorers together.[15]

During the revolution and with the land reform, the Bolsheviks knew how to exert this direction and influence, which is confirmed by the loyalty of the peasant masses during the civil war. In the new situation, given the unprecedented organizational skills of the Russian bourgeoisie, the simple military alliance was no longer enough and it was necessary to form an economic alliance.

Seven years of uninterrupted war, the state of exception and a policy dictated by the civil war led the mass of peasants to deprivations that now

---

[15] Ibid., v. 32, 485.

became intolerable and necessitated profound transformations. In the spring of 1921, the entire Russian economy was paralyzed, which included poor harvests, fodder shortage and lack of fuel.

> We had to show the broad masses of the peasants immediately that we were prepared to change our policy, without in any way deviating from our revolutionary path, so that they could say, "The Bolsheviks want to improve our intolerable condition immediately, and at all costs." [...] we changed our economic policy, yielding to exclusively practical considerations, and impelled by necessity.[16]

The disastrous productive situation therefore required a change in economic policy that was all the more necessary as the alliance relation between the proletariat and the peasantry risked being compromised, which threatened the preservation of Soviet state power and the leading role of the proletariat. It was necessary to move away from the mere "military alliance"—like the one that secured victory over the white armies—toward an "economic alliance". In a country like Russia, with its high level of productive backwardness, and particularly where the peasant masses constituted the majority of the population, only the constitution of this social bloc could enable the consolidation the Soviet state.

In this completely different framework of the Third Congress, Lenin and the ruling group of the PCd'I clashed violently. "The Italian question" provoked less of an outcry than the conflict between the Executive of the Third International and some German communists, but its solution assumed strategic importance for the assertion of the new line.

Umberto Terracini, representing the Italian party, spoke in favor of the so-called offensive theory, which considered any action aimed at conquering the majority of the proletariat superfluous, as a premise of effective revolutionary action. According to this theory, the offensive of small revolutionary groups would indeed lead the necessary forces to success. Taking this stance, which amounted to the faithful application of Bordiga's theses, the PCd'I was situated within the scope of left-wing opposition to the Executive of the Third International, which was particularly supported by German communists. Lenin's retort to Terracini was very sharp:

[16] Ibid., 487–488.

Comrades! I deeply regret that I must confine myself to self-defence. I say deeply regret, because after acquainting myself with Comrade Terracini's speech and the amendments introduced by three delegations, I should very much like to take the offensive, for, properly speaking, offensive operations are essential against the views defended by Terracini and these three delegations. If the Congress is not going to wage a vigorous offensive against such errors, against such "Leftist" stupidities, the whole movement is doomed.[17]

In Lenin's view, the PCd'I made several mistakes that were the result of a superficial and schematic analysis and a general conception dominated by "unconscious adventurism", which reduced all the action of the communists to the struggle against the centrists and reformists, recasting it as a proposal in a decidedly inappropriate context.[18]

Terracini, in defense of his theory, used the very example of the Russian Revolution, in which the Bolsheviks would have prevailed despite the fact that the Bolshevik Party was small and did not devote itself to winning over the majority. Contrary to what Terracini maintained, Lenin asserted, in Russia victory was possible because the revolution was prepared during the war, when the Bolsheviks were sought to win over the majority not only of the working class but also of all those exploited, starting with the peasant mass, through the slogan of peace at all cost and the acceptance of the agrarian program of the revolutionary socialists:

We were victorious in Russia not only because the undisputed majority of the working class was on our side [...], but also because half the army, immediately after our seizure of power, and nine-tenths of the peasants, in the course of some weeks, came over to our side; we were victorious because we adopted the agrarian programme of the Socialist-Revolutionaries instead of our own, and put it into effect.[19]

The international difficulties and the complexity of the revolutionary processes in the West prompted the Executive of the Communist International to launch, in the Second and Fourth Congress, the slogan of the conquest of the majority of the subaltern classes and the unity of the

[17] Ibid., 468.

[18] "We in Russia have already had adequate political experience in the struggle against the Centrists" (ibid., 472) was Lenin's reply, but that is not enough if work is not done to win over the majority of those exploited.

[19] Ibid.

working class through the tactic of the "united front", which was essential, as we will see, for Gramsci's definition of hegemony. In his retort to Terracini, Lenin discussed at length the concept of masses, the changes that it undergoes in each context and the nature of the struggle:

> At the beginning of the war, a few thousand effectively revolutionary workers are enough to speak of a mass. If the Party manages to bring into the struggle not only its members and reaches even those without a party, this is already the principle of the conquest of the masses [...]. When the revolution is already sufficiently prepared, the concept of mass is another: a few thousand workers no longer constitute a mass.[20]

According to the Russian revolutionary, the minority tendencies implicit in Terracini's intervention pointed to a certain "fear of the masses". Thoroughly preparing the revolution, "winning over the great masses", "obtaining the sympathy of the masses", was necessary if the aspiration was not only to start a revolution but also above all to win it and stay in power:

> Will comrade Terracini address, even if only with words, the issue of food products? Because the workers demand that the supply of food be ensured, even though they can really bear the suffering caused by hunger, as we once saw in Russia. We need to attract. We need to attract to ourselves not only the majority of the working class, but also the majority of the working and exploited peasants.[21]

The thesis on the tactics presented by Radek, strongly contested by the German left and by Bordiga, dealt with the general ebb of the revolutionary wave. The seizure of power in western countries was becoming more distant, and that required new tactics, which should be more suitable to the changing context. Capitalism had managed to conquer lost positions by making a truce, and in Radek's view, at that stage, the Comintern should devote itself not so much to preparing for civil war but rather to working on organization, on taking root and on agitation. The several degrees of the worsening of capitalist contradictions, the differences in social cooperation and in the organizational skills of the bourgeoisie in many countries, and the still severe limitations in proletarian organizations

---

[20] Idem, *Sul movimento operaio italiano* (Rome, Editori Riuniti, 1970), 232.
[21] Ibid., 233.

had not led to the immediate victory of the world revolution soon after the end of the war. At the time of imperialism, the process of social revolution was not understood as a straight line, but as a long series of civil wars in the capitalist state, of war between the great powers, on the one hand, and the colonial peoples, on the other. In Radek's view, the revolutionary process in the rest of Europe proved to be much longer than what had been previously predicted. This led to a difficult phase in which even the probability of the European communist movement's defeat had to be taken into account. Thus, Radek and the entire Executive of the International launched the slogan of the conquest of the great working masses to make European communist parties no longer small vanguard groups, but "great armies of the world proletariat". This shift reached the core of Bordiga's political and organizational conceptions for the party.

In *Theses on tactics*, the most serious problem faced by the International was indeed that of exerting predominant influence on the majority of the working class and, more broadly, the exploited classes:

> As soon as it was established, the Communist International clearly and unequivocally stated that its goal was not to form small communist sects limited to trying to impose their own influence on the masses of workers through propaganda and agitation, but rather to take part in the struggle of the masses of workers, to lead this struggle in the spirit of communism and, during the struggle, to create mass communist parties.[22]

In the disputes of the PCd'I, the reasons for the fight against the reformists and centrists, who were held responsible for the defeat in the struggles of 1919–1920, and the fairness of the Livorno split were highlighted. However, the priority of the Comintern was now the effort to make the party a mass force "able to associate with the masses in trade unions, in strikes, in the fight against the fascist counterrevolutionary movement, to seize and transform the spontaneous actions of workers into a carefully prepared struggle".[23]

In Radek's view, the organic connection between the mass and the party should happen first of all at the union level, but this objective should not translate into the mechanical and external subordination of the union to the party, the surrender of the autonomy necessary for its activity. The

---

[22] Karl Radek, "Tesi sulla tattica del III Congresso del Comintern", em Jane Degras (org.), *Storia dell'Internazionale comunista attraverso i documenti ufficiali*, cit., 262.

[23] Ibid., 264.

task of the communist party should be, above all, to act in such a way that its union leaders guide union action consistently considering the general interests of the proletariat in its struggle for the seizure of power. The communist party's goals should be derived from the proletariat's concrete struggle, fighting opportunism, sectarianism, and revolutionary phraseology, which did not contribute to a clear perception of the real correlations of force and led to ignorance of the difficulties of the struggle. The communist party should put itself at the forefront of all the struggles and partial demands of the workers to expand and radicalize them aiming to include them in the general struggles of the working class. Each slogan originating from the concrete needs of the subaltern classes should converge into the struggle for production control and be connected to factory councils and to other institutions led by the working class. This passage specifically criticizes the way of conceiving the relationship between the party and masses that is characteristic of Bordiga and the newly created PCd'I:

> Every objection to the advancement of such partial claims, every accusation of reformism for this purpose, is the product of the same inability to understand the indispensable conditions of revolutionary action, which is expressed in the hostility of certain communist groups to participation in trade unions, to the use of parliament.[24]

The policy launched in the Third Congress created growing contradictions between the line of the International and that followed by the PCd'I. However, the leadership of the latter did not inform its militants of the terms of this dialectic. The existence of such contrasts was ignored not only by the militant body but also by a significant part of the middle cadres. The Lombard communist Carlo Venegnani, a delegate of the PCd'I in the Fifth Congress of the International in June 1924, mentioned that in his memoirs. Venegnani recalled that only on that occasion did he become aware of the existence, within the Italian party, of three tendencies (left, center and right) opposing one another.

> I had served in the party since its foundation, convinced that this was a monolithic bloc with an undisputed leader: Amadeo Bordiga. [...] Only in

---

[24] Ibid., 269.

Moscow did I learn about the profound changes that had taken place a few months earlier in our party.[25]

The consensus achieved by Bordiga was predicated upon his being the representative of the line of the International, in which communist militants experienced a greater sense of belonging than that fostered by their own party.[26]

There was a new opportunity for confrontation in the Second Congress of the Italian Communist Party, in March 1922 in Rome. In the conference, Bordiga's classical approach was reiterated, and all theses focused on the unscrupulous struggle against the socialists—"the bourgeois left"—offering an incredibly superficial analysis of the Italian situation. Just to illustrate how abstract they were, these theses did not consider the possibility of a fascist coup, and more generally they overlooked the danger of Mussolini's movement. According to the theses, in a period of crisis such as that of 1921–1922, the greatest risk for a revolutionary organization was not reaction, but the reformist degeneration of the party, the loss of the unitary character of its initiatives toward the ultimate goals of the revolution, the tactical decline toward the achievement of contingent results, the reforms in the bourgeois regime, the betrayal manifested in the doctrine and the program. This reference to the problem of the "deforming revision" in a period of revolutionary reflux was not new in Bordiga's thought; rather, it was his most characteristic obsession. However, after recent deliberations on the tactics adopted by the Third International, it took on a new sense of radical political dissent. Some years later, in a 1925 article, Bordiga recalled the disagreements with the International between 1921 and the beginning of 1922, vigorously standing for the choice made in opposition to the tactical shift.

Faced with the formula of the workers' government, we strongly asserted that it was not only an inadequate and underperforming tactical solution,

[25] Carlo Salinari, *I comunisti raccontano*, v. 1: *1919–1945* (Milan, Teti, 1975), 85.

[26] The Third Congress of the Comintern was also important to the PCd'I because, in parallel work sessions, the problems concerning relations with Serratian maximalists, who formally continued to adhere to the Communist International, were dealt with. I cannot dwell on all these topics because priority must be given to the subject under study. For further research, refer to the documents that I studied: Partito Comunista d'Italia, *La Questione italiana al Terzo Congresso della Internazionale Comunista* (Rome, Libreria Editrice del Partito Comunista d'italia, 1921).

but a real contradiction with our Marxist and Leninist doctrine, and precisely with the conception of the process of liberation of the proletariat, the illusory possibility of solutions, even if partially peaceful and democratic, was introduced.[27]

Precisely with regard to these theses, Gramsci publicly revealed his divergence from Bordiga's line, first in the Turin Congress, then in the political committee of the Rome Congress, in which the Sardinian intellectual intervened to eliminate considerations about fascism. This is what Gramsci himself recalled in a 1924 letter:

> In 1921–22, the party had this official conception: that the advent of a fascist or military dictatorship was impossible; to a large extent, I managed to prevent this idea from being registered in the documents, fundamentally changing theses 51 and 52 on tactics.[28]

However, those times were not ripe yet, and Gramsci decided not to intensify the clash, not openly mentioning the divergence in the plenary session and, more broadly, in the debate that followed the congress. Before the assembly, the *Theses* were examined by Executive Committee of the Comintern, more precisely by Trotsky and Radek, drawing harsh criticism and even receiving a formal rejection proposal. The Italian party was accused of "sectarian and infantile radicalism", while more specifically the complete contrast between the *Theses* and what had been deliberated in the Third Congress of the International was revealed. For the Executive Committee, if the PCd'I did not want to break the discipline of the International and therefore be left outside it, the party would have to change its attitude toward the tactics of the "united front" and the goal of winning over the majority of the Italian proletariat.

This intervention of the Comintern led to conciliation: although the *Theses* were voted, they ended up taking on a merely consultative role in the preparation for the Fourth Congress of the Comintern, but all the disagreements remained, so much so that Kolarov, an envoy of the International, reiterated them in the rostrum of the congress in two speeches, openly criticizing the superficiality of the *Theses*.

---

[27] Amadeo Bordiga, "Il pericolo opportunista e l'Internazionale", *l'Unità*, 30 Sep. 1925.

[28] Antonio Gramsci, "Lettera a Togliatti e Terracini del 9 febbraio 1924", in Palmiro Togliatti, *La formazione del gruppo dirigente del Partito Comunista Italiano (1923–24)* (Rome, Editori Riuniti, 1984), 199.

The rejection of the International in the midst of the works of the congress left many delegates disoriented; Togliatti was convinced of this, to the point of believing that if an alternative platform aligned with the Comintern had been offered, it would have won. Nonetheless, Gramsci, fearing a split of the main group of the party, which was still convinced of Bordiga's indispensable role in the leadership of the organization and, above all, eager not to be confused with Tasca's right, "a heterogeneous minority alien to the split of Livorno", preferred to vote on the *Theses* and reforge, as in the days of the first congress, the alliance with Bordiga:

> In Rome, we accepted Amadeo's theses because they were presented as an opinion for the Fourth Congress, not as a guideline for action. We believed that we would thus keep the party united around its fundamental core; we thought that this concession could be made to Amadeo due to the importance he had in the organization of the party: we do not regret that; politically, it would be impossible to lead the party without the active participation of Amadeo and his group in the work.[29]

In the congress, Gramsci was tasked with representing the PCd'I in the Comintern Executive in Moscow. According to Giuseppe Fiori, this result was possible due to the convergence of two factors: Gramsci's reservations about the consistency of the *Theses*, which helped him win the goodwill of the International, and Bordiga's wish not to have him as an enemy. To these factors we can add the concern of not having him as a competitor for the position of leader of the PCd'I.

In May 1922, after fifteen years, Gramsci left Turin and the leadership of *L'Ordine Nuovo* to have a new experience, which was destined to shape him politically. In Moscow, where he would remain until December 1923, the Sardinian intellectual lived a third moment of existential transformation, after Cagliari and Turin, with very important implications for the sphere of affection and life choices.

On the eve of the Fourth Congress of the International, Bordiga published (in the September 1922 issue of *Rassegna Comunista*) an article, "The relations of social and political forces in Italy", very representative of the distance between their positions—those of the International and Gramsci's—with regard to the role of the communists in the midst of the crisis of fascist reaction.

[29] Ibid.

After analyzing the conditions of capitalist development and the bourgeois-democratic revolution in general terms, Bordiga asserted the absolute modernity of the liberal process in Italy. In his view, the historical genesis of the Italian state fully embodied the characteristics typical of bourgeois democratic regimes.

The prevalence of the industrial and commercial bourgeoisie over the social relations of feudal production was grafted onto the capitalist economic structure only embryonically. According to Bordiga, the Italian *Risorgimento*, despite being characterized by an intense process of economic modernization, proved to be far behind if compared to other advanced capitalist countries. In spite of that, the process of political democratization lagged behind that of England, France and the United States only partially, and even the Italian bourgeois revolution ended up faithfully coinciding with the emergence of the liberal democratic regime in much of Europe. Although in the nineteenth century industrial development was far behind in Italy, Italian commercial and industrial capitalism was much older.

For the leader of the communist left, all the political-ideological themes of the *Risorgimento* in Italy were perfectly combined with those of the liberal revolution, based, in both cases, on the struggle for national independence and against the privileges of the old regime, that is, on the assertion of the parliamentary constitution and of freedom of worship, of the press and of association. Thus, the governments that promoted the emergence of the new state—both the historical right and the left—were in all respects liberal, while the parties linked to the old regime ("absolutists, temporalists, Bourbon supporters, Austrians and reactionaries in general") disappeared from the new institutional scenario.

Bordiga considered the thesis on the incomplete nature of the bourgeois-democratic revolution in Italy superficial. In his view, it was a mistake to believe in the governmental balance of the unitary state based on the dichotomy between a bourgeois ruling class in the North and a feudal landlord in the South. Firstly, because most of the members elected in the electoral colleges of the South belonged to the "left" while the industrial bourgeoisie of the North belonged to the classical right; secondly, because in the South feudal power would not have developed sufficiently to be able to resist the bourgeois revolution. In Bordiga's view, the predominant social class in the South was linked to the medium-sized land property and it adapted effortlessly to the new institutional political system, accommodating itself to the new power in government and in parliament, which was built upon the clientelist and criminal forms typical of southern administration.

At the level of constitutional structures, the Italian state had all the typical features of bourgeois modernity and did not contradict it, even in the most brutal and systematic police repression used against the subaltern classes, especially at the turn of the century, because democracy would actually be only a perfect class instrument for the protection of the interests of the ruling class by any means, including the use of the most brutal and reactionary force:

> A state of the bourgeois class, the Italian regime historically acts as a representative of bourgeois interests. In other countries, the means are more precise and more powerful, but from our viewpoint, in Italy the special conditions provide a fuller experience of the class functions of the bourgeois state up until the recent events of the post-war period which, in our humble opinion and as we now see, are not a return to the past, but an early example of how the political struggle will be shaped in the advanced stages of the evolution of the world capitalist system.[30]

In Bordiga's view, the most modern form of the bourgeois regime is not expressed in the greatest degree of freedom and democracy of its institutions, but in a way the true face of modernity would have found its most characteristic manifestation in the brutal and overtly reactionary nature of the methods of government. By "liberal model", according to Bordiga, one should not understand the "democratic model", the ideal universe of the declaration of human and citizen rights, but rather the evolution of the domination systems characteristic of imperialist monopolism, which were typical of the phase before the First World War.

In this context, social democracy not only seemed functional but also was an organic part of the scheme of bourgeois government based on social reconciliation and repression. In Bordiga's view, the perfect model of "democratic left" politics was Giolittism, which on the one hand began to weave social reconciliation with the proletariat's political and trade union leaders, but on the other did not cease to violently quash the lower classes' attempts at rebellion:

> The double-dealing of social democratic politics had emerged from this contrast as well. Just as Minister Giolitti simultaneous granted reformist laws

---

[30] Amadeo Bordiga, *Scritti scelti* (Milan, Feltrinelli, 1975), 157.

and police machine guns, in the political field he also worked on the great suffrage reform while triggering the Libyan war, an authentically imperialist action from the point of view of the politics of the Italian state [...] and in the international field, a prelude to imperialism's great orgy of blood triggered by Turkey's defeat in the Balkan wars.[31]

To consider this contradiction the symptom of a delay in democratic development meant relying on democratic politics as a rational process aimed at peaceful coexistence between classes and peoples domestically and internationally. In fact, the two aspects of the politics of democratic governments were inseparable; it was no coincidence that the First World War had its first manifestations in contexts of advanced democracy and political and social reformism, which are characteristic of all the imperialist powers involved. The distance between the positions of the secretary of the Communist Party of Italy and Gramsci's reached its peak in the considerations on the relationship between democracy and fascism. According to Bordiga, there were no real contradictions and distinctions between fascism and democracy; on the contrary, fascism appeared as a social-democratic perspective expressed by new and "ceremonial" forms. Communists should therefore be disinterested in the democratic issue, not opt for one or another form of bourgeois government, and resolutely end any possibility of collaboration with the other democratic and even social-democratic forces opposing fascism:

> In fascism and in today's bourgeois counteroffensive in general, we do not see a change in the policy of the Italian state, but the natural continuation of the method applied, before and after the war, by democracy. We will not believe in the antithesis between democracy and fascism more than we believed in the antithesis between democracy and militarism. We will no longer give credit, in this latter situation, to the maintenance of the natural supporter of democracy: social-democratic reformism.[32]

In November 1922, the Fourth Congress of the Communist International began, during which the conflict between the Italian party and the Executive of the Comintern reached its peak. This congress, also due to the confluence of several other factors, created the conditions for

---

[31] Ibid., 159.
[32] Ibid., 162.

the creation of a new leadership group in the PCd'I, whose undisputed leader was Gramsci.

The Fourth Congress was held in an increasingly difficult international context: just a few weeks before the fascists came to power in Italy, a moment when it seemed that the long shadow of reaction was about to be cast throughout Europe. In Lenin's view, the change in the world scenario created the need for the various communist parties to know how to tactically deal with the new situation and also prepare for a "strategic retreat" to avoid being cornered and destroyed for several years.

> We should not only know how to act when we launch an offensive and when we win. In a revolutionary period, this is not so difficult or even so important; at least it is not the most decisive thing. In a period of revolution, there are always times when the opponent loses his head, and if we attack him in one of those moments, we can easily win. But this still does not mean anything because our opponent, if he has enough self-control, can then gather strength again etc. And then he can easily provoke and attack us, leading us to a retreat of many years. For this reason, I believe that the idea of preparing for a withdrawal is of great importance, not only from a theoretical point of view. Even from a practical point of view, all parties that, planning for the near future, are preparing for the offensive against capitalism should now also think about how to ensure their withdrawal.[33]

As we have explained, the "united front" and the NEP were two sides of the same policy and, according to Lenin, the prospect of "state capitalism" also represented a possible line of retreat to hold positions in a difficult phase. One of the most important political meanings of the economic alliance launched with the NEP was the attempt to overcome the use of coercive state means to impose socialism on the peasant masses. After the end of the phase marked by "war communism", through the NEP, an attempt was made to follow a different path in order to lead the majority of peasants to be voluntarily convinced of the superiority of cooperative production or of the large state enterprise over small land property. The goal was to lead peasants to socialism voluntarily and without administrative methods.

Because of the way the Congress of Rome ended and the unresolved issues in the relationship between the Executive of the Comintern and the Italian Communist Party on the issue of the "united front", a conflict

---

[33] Ibid., 387.

between these two levels seemed inevitable. The *Theses on the tactics* mediated between the positions in favor of the "united front from above" and those only in favor of the "united front from below": the former represented the line of Karl Radek and the German [communist] right; the latter represented that of Zinoviev himself and the German [communist] left. The analysis of the international situation made the option for the "united front" and the slogan of the Third Congress ("toward the masses") even more urgent; therefore, the Comintern demanded a quick alignment of all the adherent parties, albeit with variations in each country. The "united front" tactic amounted to taking on the daily struggles of the great working masses in defense of their most vital interests, even if that meant reaching an agreement with social democracy, but not understanding that as an organizational merger of the workers' parties or translating that into mere electoral alliances for simple parliamentary purposes:

> The tactic of the united front is the offer of a joint struggle of the communists with all the workers belonging to other parties and groups, and with the workers without a party, in defense of the fundamental interests of the working class against the bourgeoisie.[34]

Communists should not limit their activity to agitation and propaganda; they should carry out great work of taking root in workplaces, factories, councils, supervisory committees composed of workers. The "united front" should therefore emerge from below, from the innermost conditions of the associative life of the masses; however, this impulse should not lead the communists to preclude the possibility of summit agreements with other workers' parties.

The next step in the tactic of the "united front" would therefore be the watchword "workers' government", which assumed its greatest importance in countries marked by the political instability of the bourgeoisie, where the immediate problem of forming a government representative of the class interests of the proletariat arose. If in these countries social democracy came to the rescue of liberal institutions through the implementation of agreements with bourgeois forces, the communists should, on the contrary, propose the government of united workers through the coalition of workers' governments at the political and economic levels.

---

[34] Gueórgui Zinoviev, "Le tesi sulla tattica al IV Congresso del Comintern", em Jane Degras (org.), *Storia dell'Internazionale attraverso i documenti*, cit., 449.

Control over the state machine by the workers' government should be associated with workers' control over production.

> The prime objectives of the workers' government should be to arm the proletariat and disarm the bourgeoisie and counterrevolutionary organizations, introduce production control, transfer much of the tax burden to the rich, and break the resistance of the counterrevolutionary bourgeoisie.[35]

Two risks, however, were lurking: triggering the bourgeoisie's rash and violent reaction—of which fascism was an example—and being dragged into a political dynamic alien to the communists' conceptions. For these reasons, the first condition for the materialization of the workers' government should be the guarantee of the greatest autonomy of the communist party, the complete preservation of its own identity and freedom of agitation.

Another fundamental point that set the *Theses* of the Fourth Congress apart from Amadeo Bordiga's party conception was related to the need for the party to take root in the workplace through the creation of communist cells. A serious and well-organized mass communist party could not be regarded as such without this rooting, and a movement was not authentically proletarian if it were not able to create a system of factory councils. At this point, maximum distance was reached from Bordiga's leading group while great convergence was found with the classical approach of the ordinovists and Gramsci in particular.

Immediately after the introductory report of the president of the International, Zinoviev, the first to intervene was precisely Bordiga, who sharply criticized the tactics of the "united front" but above all challenged the formula of the "workers' government" proposed by Zinoviev in at least three cases: Germany, Czechoslovakia and England.

In Bordiga's view, this "ambiguous formula" would deceive and disarm the working class, diverting it from the only viable path to the conquest of power, the violent path of armed revolution. There were no alternatives or intermediate degrees between the dictatorship of the proletariat and the dictatorship of the bourgeoisie. Consequently, it would be misleading and harmful to imagine a transitional phase in the bourgeois regime in which the communist party would have to assume a government function, especially in coalition with the social democrats.

---

[35] Ibid., 450.

After Bordiga, Antonio Graziadei, who stood on the right wing of the PCd'I, intervened in favor of the immediate merger with the PSI. He attacked the secretary of the PCd'I head-on in all its lines, particularly focusing on the sectarian attitude taken by the majority toward the socialists and toward the issue of the "workers' government". For the first time in the international assembly, a leader of the PCd'I openly challenged the political direction of his party.

However, in this congress, it was Angelo Tasca who would really take the leadership of the right-wing minority as he was politically more prepared than Graziadei and had more mobility. As we have already seen, at this stage Gramsci feared above all the right wing of the party because, in his view, almost everything could fit into its composition. Although the left was very far from the positions of the old Turin group, with Bordiga there was still a very important road to go. Gramsci did not consider it possible to wage a centrist battle on two fronts, against both Bordiga and Tasca, without tearing the party apart and favoring the right.

The real clash occurred in a committee specifically set up to deal with the issue of relations with the socialists and the possibility of merger. In this regard, Spriano wrote:

> In it, which had Zinoviev and Radek as presidents, Trotsky, Rákosi, the secretary, and many others representing various communist parties, including Klara Zetkin and the Bulgarian Kabakčiev were present. The majority of the PCI was seen as defendants; the minority (with the presence of Graziadei, Tasca, Bombacci, Presutti and Vota), as prosecution witnesses.[36]

Gramsci was torn about what to do, hesitating, uncertain both because of the potential effects of the split and because of the pressure exerted by the International to lead the opposition to Bordiga and become the new leader of the party in Italy. Gramsci's mood and indecisiveness were also affected by his declining health, which led to his admission to the Sieriebriani Bor sanatorium on the outskirts of Moscow on the eve of the Fourth Congress, where he met the Schucht sisters and, in particular, Julca.

Nothing is as representative of the meaning of Gramsci's work as his own words in a letter addressed to Scoccimarro and Togliatti, in which he mentions the pressure he suffered, first from the IC envoy, Chiarini,[37] in

---

[36] Paolo Spriano, *Storia del Partito Comunista Italiano*, v. 1: *Da Bordiga a Gramsci* (Turin, Einaudi, 1967), 249.

[37] Chiarini, whose real name was Cain Haller, was the representative of the Communist International in Italy from 1920 to 1921.

1921, and then from Rákosi, "the Penguin", whom he certainly did not hold in high esteem:

I must say on this issue that Palmi [Togliatti] underestimates my attitude in the past. I will only say that in the Rome Congress I was aware of the most serious issues of the party and that this took place in a way that made it impossible for any judgement to be made. Again: in 1921 I was sent to Rome by Chiarini, who, without explaining much, invited me to join the Executive to offset Amadeo's influence and take his place. I replied that I did not want to devote myself to intrigues of this nature, that if we wanted a different direction, the issue should be put in political terms. Chiarini, who had never taken a stand, pretended to be on Bordiga's side in Rome, while in Moscow he sent reports against the party; he neither insisted nor explained to me in more detail what it was all about. [...]. In the Fourth Congress, I had just returned from the sanatorium [...]; generally, exhaustion and the impossibility of working due to amnesia and insomnia persisted. The Penguin [Rákosi], with his distinguishing diplomatic courtesy, took me by surprise and again proposed that I become the leader of the party, eliminating Amadeo, who would be excluded from the Comintern if he continued with that line. I said that I would do everything possible to help the Executive of the International to solve the Italian question, but I did not believe that it was possible (let alone for me) to replace Amadeo without previously providing guidelines for the party. I was walking on eggshells, and this was not the most suitable work for my condition of chronic weakness. I realized that most of the delegation had no adequate guidance [...]. If the Penguin, instead of being a fool, had so much as a shred of political intelligence, the party would have made a terrible impression because the majority, at least in the congressional delegation, would have turned out to be a ghost with no consistency. [...] What would have happened if I had not dragged my feet, as unfortunately I had to do? The majority of the delegation would be with me, [...] and there would have been a remote crisis in the party without prior agreement with you: Urbani [Terracini], Bruno [Bruno Fortichiari], Luigino [Luigi Repossi], Ruggero [Grieco], Amadeo [Bordiga] would have fallen; unaccustomed to working, the CC would have dissipated, and the minority, even less prepared than it later became, would have achieved... nothing at all! Perhaps I was too pessimistic? Maybe, given my condition. But I don't think so.[38]

[38] Antonio Gramsci, "Lettera a Scoccimarro e Togliatti del 1o marzo 1924", in Palmiro Togliatti, *La formazione del gruppo dirigente del Partito Comunista (1923–24)*, cit., 218–30.

At first, on November 13 and 14, Gramsci stood by Bordiga, the majority of the delegation remained united in their anti-merger positions, and the conflict between the PCd'I and the International therefore seemed inevitable. The situation remained unchanged until November 24, when a letter of the CC of the Russian Communist Party, signed among others by Lenin, Trotsky, Zinoviev and Bukharin, effectively imposed the beginning of a negotiation on the merger with Serrati's maximalists, at the risk of leaving the International. At this point, the Italian delegation ended up capitulating, except for Bordiga, who remained adamant in his aversion, as he was convinced that the reasons for the punishment would not be enough to make him change his mind, and ready to continue the fight elsewhere.

The split of the majority born in Livorno began to take place at this moment, when Scoccimarro and Gramsci decided to take the initiative and discuss the conditions of the merger, also to avoid the predominance of the right-wing minority and Serrati's maximalists in the leadership of the party. The majority of the Italian delegation aligned with them, while Bordiga continued to adamantly oppose any negotiation, steadfast in his opposition, to the point of rejecting the proposal, put forward by Zinoviev, to join the inter-party commission in charge of conducting the operation. To speed things up, the International decided to send Gramsci to Italy. Initially, apparently with Serrati's consent, the Executive had decided to give Gramsci the role of co-director in the preparation of *L'Avanti!* and the same powers over the editorial line of the newspaper that the maximalist leader had. The failure of the operation was attributed to Serrati and his typical indecisiveness;[39] the maximalist leader actually claimed to have voted the resolution by mistake due to an incorrect translation:

> Last night something unprecedented happened. Serrati stated that he understood that I would become co-director of *L'Avanti!* after the merger congress, not immediately, and argued that keeping such a deliberation would mean losing the majority of the Socialist Party, losing "*L'Avanti!*" etc. etc. The news that Serrati received from Italy about the state of mind of his party must be very serious if it led him to make such a ridiculous excuse as that of stating that he approved such deliberations, so sensitive and

---

[39] At the time, the notorious indecisiveness typical of Serrati earned him several humorous epithets used by Gramsci in his polemical studies, among which the most frequent was "Stenterello". [Besides referring to the mask of the Florentine theater of the nineteenth century, the word also means a very thin person, or one who expresses oneself with an affected and artificial prose.]

important, due to Comrade Bukharin's poor French, without understanding what they really meant![40]

Besides Serrati's notorious indecisiveness, however, the merger did not occur due to the consolidation of an anti-merger majority in the PSI Congress (held in Milan in April 1923) and the strong resistance of the communists to this hypothesis. To oppose the merger agreed between Serrati and the International, Pietro Nenni and other socialist leaders in Milan formed the Socialist Defense Committee, occupying in January 1923 the editorial office of *L'Avanti!* to forcefully assume its editorial direction. The same happened in the parliamentary group, in which Deputy Francesco Buffoni, in favor of the merger, was first placed in the minority and then removed by the party leadership, where he represented the group of deputies. There was talk of "a real coup d'etat".[41] Nonetheless, the major blow to the merger process came from the arrests that occurred on March 2, 1923, a day after Serrati's return from Moscow, right before the socialist congress convened in April. This clash, unprecedented in the experience of the young party, resulted in an effort that led the entire Executive to resign with a harsh letter from Ruggiero Grieco. The whole situation took place amid the violent repression of the fascist regime, with the arrest of numerous leaders and militants, including Bordiga (arrested in February 1923) and Grieco, the destruction and end of the entire socialist, communist and opposition press, and the establishment of an increasingly difficult and dangerous political climate.

The following period, which ended with the Como Conference in May 1924 and the rise of Gramsci to the General Secretariat of the party, was well defined by Spriano as a "phase of interregnum", a period of general repositioning of the party in Italy, of conflicting and uncertain dynamics within the former majority, still owing to Brodiga's strong influence. The now former leader of the party was increasingly determined to go on a head-on collision with the Comintern, even if that meant parting ways with it definitively.[42]

[40] Antonio Gramsci, "Lettera a Julca, Mosca 10 gennaio 1923", in Giuseppe Fiori, *Antonio Gramsci. Vita attraverso le lettere* (Turin, Einaudi, 1994), 27.

[41] Cesare Pillon, *I comunisti nella storia d'Italia* (Rome, Edizioni del Calendario, 1967), v. I, 192.

[42] Gianni Fresu, *Il diavolo nell'ampolla. Antonio Gramsci, gli intellettuali e il partito* (Naples, Istituto Italiano per gli Studi Filosofici/La Città del Sole, 2005), 120–52.

CHAPTER 11

Toward a New Majority

The clash occurred in the spring of 1923. Amadeo Bordiga's line did not admit setbacks; the old majority should resort directly to the entire PCd'I and to the proletariat to openly express their opposition to the Executive of the Communist International. Bordiga aspired to rebuild the old majority and organize left-wing opposition within the Comintern. These intentions took shape in the so-called *Bordiga's Manifesto*, written in prison in the summer of 1923, as an act of denunciation of the deep crisis between the administration of the PCd'I and that of the International.

Still in Moscow, Gramsci learned of Bordiga's intentions thanks to a letter from Togliatti written on May 1, 1923. Although Togliatti did not fully agree with the arguments of the Manifesto—because he was frightened by the prospect of a break with the International—he, still very attached to Bordiga, was undoubtedly fascinated by the "mathematical logic of Bordiga", to the point of confessing his indecision as to what to do.

> He [Bordiga] wants the political group that until then led the PCI to address the proletariat with a manifesto. [...] The merit of what Amadeo proposes is that it conforms to an overly strict logic, and I will not hide from you that his proposal should therefore hold great attraction for the most intelligent comrades, especially if we consider the weight of his personal influence. In practice, given the current conditions, doing what Amadeo says will mean openly fighting against the Communist International, being outside of it, being deprived of a powerful material and moral apparatus, reduced to a very

© The Author(s), under exclusive license to Springer Nature Switzerland AG 2023
G. Fresu, *Antonio Gramsci*, Marx, Engels, and Marxisms,
https://doi.org/10.1007/978-3-031-15610-6_11

small group united almost exclusively by personal bonds, and soon being doomed, if not to completely disperse, certainly to lose any real, immediate influence on the development of the political struggle in Italy. Would this immediate practical damage be offset by the value of an absolute and uncompromising statement of principles like the one Amadeo would like to make? I confess that I am still a little puzzled to be able to provide an answer.[1]

In Togliatti's view, breaking with the International meant disappearing; on the other hand, abandoning the line adopted in Livorno would probably also produce the same result: "What will happen is that little by little we will disperse, either in an organization that will not be the one that the moment necessitates or outside it. The fruits of three years of work, criticism, organization and struggle will be lost".[2] This statement was followed by a rhetorical question in which Bordiga's influence on the future leader of the Italian communists and his initial indecision were evident: "If we have already predicted that we will thus disappear, would it not be better to adhere to what Amadeo says, that is, to at least support, to the end, the personality and political will that encouraged us from the start?".[3]

Ragionieri pointed out that the period of greater adherence to Togliatti's pro-Bordiga theses coincided with the most complicated phase and, if we go back in the history of the party, that occurred amid the advent of fascism in power and increasingly in contradiction with the line adopted by the International. Therefore—this is the reasoning of the historian—Togliatti's adherence to Bordiga's positions "cannot be considered only the consequence of the personal influence of the leader, with whom he remained for many months in prolonged direct contact, but also an immediate reaction to a situation in which no way out could be seen".[4] In those years, Togliatti's biased indecision was a consequence of the state of siege experienced by the party and the fear of breaking, at this stage, with his only stable point of reference. Moreover, as we have already seen, even Gramsci, for the same reasons until the Fourth Congress, was forced to delay things[5] and avoid beginning a public dispute with the secretary of

---

[1] Palmiro Togliatti, "Lettera ad Antonio Gramsci del 1o maggio 1923", in *La formazione del gruppo dirigente del Partito Comunista Italiano (1923–24)* (Rome, Editori Riuniti, 1984), 54–5.

[2] Ibid., 58.

[3] Ibid.

[4] Ernesto Ragionieri, *Palmiro Togliatti* (Rome, Editori Riuniti, 1976), 79.

[5] Antonio Gramsci, "Lettera a Scoccimarro e Togliatti del 1° marzo 1924", in Palmiro Togliatti, *La formazione del gruppo dirigente del Partito Comunista Italiano (1923–24)*, cit., 218–30.

the PCd'I. Bordiga was still considered, and would be so at least until the Congress of Lyon, the main protagonist of the split in Livorno and the important architect of the foundation of the party, for which his authority still seemed unassailable.

However, and under pressure from the Comintern, Gramsci realized that it was no longer possible to postpone the process of questioning the secretary's line and decided to declare war on him. Thus, Gramsci's response to Togliatti of May 18 already contained all the themes of the battle against Bordiga and the foreshadowing of a new majority in the party. The break with the "boss" was now inevitable, because the differences with him did not boil down to the position on the "united front" or relations with the socialists; they were rather related to the political action of the Italian communists. Gramsci, addressing the old comrades of the Turin group, showed in unambiguous terms the need for a new leadership group, far from both Bordiga's sectarianism and Tasca's confusing right-wing maximalism. He knew how dispersed the old Turin group was in the new party; however, he saw no other way:

> During the Fourth Congress, I had some conversations with Amadeo that led me to believe that an open and definitive discussion among us is necessary on some issues that today seem, or may seem, like intellectual battles, but in my view they lead to the revolutionary development of the Italian situation as they are a reason for internal decomposition and crisis. The fundamental issue today is the following: we must create a core within the party, which is not a fraction, made up of comrades who have maximum ideological homogeneity and are thus able to give practical action the maximum unity of direction.[6]

Meanwhile, in June 1923, the Executive Committee of the Comintern intervened with the creation of a specific commission to solve the "Italian question". The International reproached the entire majority of the PCd'I, including Gramsci, accused by Zinoviev of duplicity, and decided to override the party, imposing a new leadership group aligned by conviction, not

[6] Antonio Gramsci, "Lettera a Palmiro Togliatti del 18 maggio 1923", in Palmiro Togliatti, *La formazione del gruppo dirigente del Partito Comunista Italiano (1923–24)*, cit., 64.

by discipline.[7] A new executive was proposed: three members of the old majority, Fortichiari, Scoccimarro and Togliatti, and two of the minority, Tasca and Vota.

Although Gramsci appeared as a "co-defendant of the great majority"[8] in this "trial", the work of this commission led him to take on a leading role and gain confidence until he was finally emancipated from Bordiga to become the man of the International, the catalyst for the new course of the party.

Immediately after the work of the commission ended, the great majority gathered and decided to turn into a fraction, in which Amadeo Bordiga was appointed. Terracini, Fortichiari, Leonetti, Ravera and Togliatti were present at the meeting. Fortichiari had already stated that he refused to take up the post in the new Executive Committee of the Party. Terracini proposed the formal acceptance of the deliberations of the International, but at the same time he declared himself in favor of a working fraction to safeguard power relations on behalf of the former majority. Togliatti's intervention was marked by even greater strictness:

Palmiro does not want it to be considered a question of technical organization, but rather a political one. He believes that if the political position of the majority group is not defined with a series of direct acts, acceptance will be impossible, even if followed by a group agreement in the sense mentioned by Umberto [Terracini]. Acceptance of these conditions would put us on the same level as the minority, that is, it would be the beginning of the transformation of our political group into a personal coterie that would be

---

[7] The resolution of the Third Plenary of the Executive of the Comintern on the Italian question read: "To some extent, the failure [of the merger with the PSI] is also due to the wrong tactics followed by the majority of the CC of the PCI. Hypnotized by the previous struggle against Serrati's group, and suffering from extreme dogmatism, the majority of the CC completely failed to take into account that in the trade union movement the situation had changed radically [...]. Not only did it not work for the merger with the PSI, but it even prevented the implementation of the guidelines issued by the Fourth World Congress. The enlarged Executive decided: 1. The International demands from the CC of the PCI not only formal recognition, but also practical execution of this decision. 2. The PCI must use the tactic of the united front, adapting it to Italian conditions, that is, it must present proposals to the leaders of the PSI in a manner consistent with the decisions of the CI. 3. The composition of the PCI Executive must ensure the execution of these measures" (Jane Degras, org., *Storia dell'Internazionale comunista attraverso i documenti ufficiali*, t. II: *1923/1928*, Milan, Feltrinelli, 1975, 60).

[8] Paolo Spriano, *Storia del Partito Comunista Italiano*, v. 1: *Da Bordiga a Gramsci* (Turin, Einaudi, 1967), 285.

ignored or whose existence and positions would not be understood by the masses, and which sooner or later would be doomed to dispersion. [...] We made the mistake of not taking a controversial position with the International in front of the whole party and the working masses. No organizational expedient [organizing into a fraction] will be able to appropriately position us before the party and the masses if we do not get to a public controversy.[9]

Bordiga's reaction to the International's decisions was uncompromising, as had always been the case since his arrest at Regina Coeli. He rejected the post of member of the *Presidium* of the International proposed by Zinoviev; he resigned from the CC of the party; he invited Scoccimarro, Togliatti and Fortichiari to do the same, and urged them to take the confrontation against the "degenerative drift" of the International to extremes. The only one to follow Bordiga to the end was Fortichiari. On July 16, Togliatti wrote a letter to Gramsci and Scoccimarro in which he repeated many of Bordiga's arguments, confirming his indecision:

As for the resolutions adopted by the Enlarged Executive Committee [of the International], I would like you to know that I have not yet decided whether I will accept to be part of the new governing body of the party or not. For now, I am more inclined to refuse than to accept, even if that meant committing a disciplinary infraction.[10]

The stance taken by Gramsci, Scoccimarro, and Montagnana was very different because they deemed it a priority not to leave room for Tasca, refusing a position on the Executive, even if for different reasons: Montagnana was the first to mention major differences in the traditions of the ordinovist group and those of abstentionists; Scoccimarro still believed that the old majority of Livorno and Rome could be restored; Gramsci was the most resolute in his decision to break up with Bordiga and his political culture, while the International was still trying to win back the former leader of Italian communism by offering him a position of prestige since the old majority of the PCd'I was still strongly influenced by him. At this stage, unlike all his old comrades, Gramsci reached a point of no

---

[9] "Tratto dal verbale della riunione di frazione del 12 luglio 1923", in Palmiro Togliatti, *La formazione del gruppo dirigente del Partito Comunista Italiano (1923–24)*, cit., 89.
[10] Palmiro Togliatti, "Lettera a Scoccimarro e Gramsci del 16 luglio 1923", in *La formazione del gruppo dirigente del Partito Comunista Italiano (1923–24)*, cit., 91–7.

return in the relationship with Bordiga. Thus, his replica to Togliatti had a particularly harsh tone:

> Your letter deeply impressed me and hurt me: now I understand better how it was possible to create the paradoxical situation that involves us, a minority that does not objectively exist, which was created by our mistakes and our passivity and which, should your perspective prevail, will lead the Party; a majority that does not know exactly what it is, whether it has a program, whether it is worth remaining at its post at the terrible moment the Italian proletariat is experiencing today. Excuse me for my harsh words, but I confess that I consider it absolutely incomprehensible that revolutionaries who are convinced of their program abandon their post, which today, given the general situation, is a barricade, and not only as far as the enemies ahead of us are concerned.[11]

In August, when Terracini left for Moscow to become the new Italian representative in the *Presidium* of the IC, the operational core of the party which had escaped from prisons formally requested Gramsci to be put in charge of the organization's reconstruction. As we know, Gramsci could not return to Italy yet because an arrest warrant for him was still outstanding; thus, the Comintern Executive Committee sent him to Vienna to be the head of the Liaison Office between the PCd'I and the other communist parties. He stayed there for six months, starting December 3, 1923, redoing his journalistic work, organizing and editing the reissue of *L'Ordine Nuovo*, creating a complex network of contacts aimed at repositioning Bordiga. As we will see, the third edition of *L'Ordine Nuovo*, entirely curated by Gramsci, would be decisive for the establishment, in the spring of 1924, of the core group intended to manage the transition to the Congress of Lyon.

Bordiga's line was now incompatible with that of the Comintern; the Executive was preparing to wage a battle in this regard. To fight it more effectively, the direction of the International approved, in September 1923, the proposal to create a "workers' newspaper" capable of shaping the strategic objective of uniting the Italian subaltern classes, the working masses in the North and in the rural areas of southern Italy. Precisely for

---

[11] The passage of this letter from Gramsci to Togliatti of August 1923 was published by Rinascita in 1966, and in the first volume of Spriano's *Storia del Partito Comunista Italiano*, which was mentioned in previous pages.

this reason, in a letter to the Executive of the PCd'I of September 12, 1923, Gramsci proposed the title *l'Unità*:

> I propose the title *l'Unità*, plain and simple, which will be meaningful for the workers and will have a more general meaning because I believe that, following the decision of the enlarged Executive on the workers' and peasants' government, we must attach importance particularly to the southern question, that is, the question in which the relationship between the workers and peasants emerges not just as a question of class relations, but also, and particularly, as a territorial question, which is one of the key aspects of the national question.[12]

In this letter, Gramsci proposed not only the name but also the role and the editorial line of the newspaper. Given the context, marked by the rise of fascism to power, a newspaper that could legally resist as long as possible was necessary. Gramsci did not intend it to be a party organ, but rather to make sure it had a "legal platform", that is, continuous and systematic connection among the greater masses:

> Thus, the newspaper will not only need to have some indication of the Party, but it will have to be written so that its actual dependence on our party does not show very clearly. It must be a left-wing newspaper, of the workers' left, faithful to the program and tactics of the class struggle, which will publish the acts and discussions of our Party, as well as possibly the acts and discussions of anarchists, republicans, unionists, and make its judgment in a disinterested tone, as if it had a superior position in the struggle and positioned itself from a "scientific" point of view.[13]

Between 1923 and 1924, the differences between Gramsci and his former comrades of the Turin group increased with the publication of *Bordiga's Manifesto*, announced in the spring and now submitted to the adherence of the entire former majority. The Manifesto, the subject of two successive editorials precisely to obtain Gramsci's consent, was signed by Togliatti, Terracini and Scoccimarro.

In the Manifesto, the Italian party's dissent from the Comintern was even more evident. In addition to the tactical inflection point, the deeper

---

[12] Antonio Gramsci, "Lettera all'Esecutivo del PCd'I, 12 settembre 1923", im Antonio Gramsci, *Epistolario*, volume 2, gennaio novembre 1926, Istituto della Enciclopedia Italiana Treccani, Roma, 2011, p. 127.

[13] Ibid., 45.

strategic revision was contested, which was considered contrary to the program and to the fundamental organizational rules of communist parties, a theoretical betrayal so serious that it affected the constitution and the very nature of the Party in Italy. The disagreement with the Comintern had already been expressed in the Third Congress, although the revelation of the break with the Italian political line was postponed. However, when the meaning of the slogans "united front" and "workers' government" became clear, to the point of predicting the hypothesis of merger with the detested maximalist socialists, Bordiga decided to make the confrontation with the International explicit in Italy too. The international communist movement faced a deep crisis dominated by "opportunistic danger", and that legitimized it to propose a critical platform opposing the line of the Comintern, bringing together the Italian cadres. For Bordiga, there was no longer room for discussion; the old majority of the Italian party would have to refuse any task in the International that denounced the "right-wing revision" introduced by the inflection point of the "united front".

Gramsci, now absolutely convinced of the need for a new direction in the party, refused to sign the Manifesto, declaring himself ready to lead, even if alone, the battle against Bordiga and those who supported him.

On December 25, 1923, Scoccimarro wrote to Gramsci to present him the Manifesto, proposing the possibility of reconstituting the old majority around this battle. In subsequent letters, Togliatti and Terracini spoke of the need to sign the Manifesto. Although Togliatti, in particular, criticized the "historical" and "sterile" nature of that document for being totally attached to past issues, he still considered it a basis for clarification indispensable for resuming work. Terracini, who had attempted at mediation by proposing altering the Manifesto, did not hide all his resentment at Gramsci's complete unavailability.

Masci's [Gramsci's] decision not to sign the common Manifesto reaches the basis of action we had agreed on and initiated with the difficult achievement of an agreement with Amadeo. Indeed, the main reasons that moved us were the preservation of the ties we had established with the comrades of the majority because we thought that the preservation of unity should prevail over all other objectives. The reservations that Masci had expressed at the end of the EE [Enlarged Executive] era were not about the need for a common document, but rather about its content. In fact, he accepted the criterion of preserving our unity, although he defended the prerogative to give it a particular basis. We have to note that he only refrained from actively intervening in this issue at the last moment, although he had already known about the events for about two months and, speaking to me personally, he never mentioned the slightest possibility of adopting such an extreme stance.[14]

Realizing the failed attempt at mediation, Terracini proposed that Togliatti and Scoccimarro proceed autonomously with respect to Gramsci and sign the document proposed by Bordiga. "We must not hide from ourselves that Negri, Palmi, I, etc., in this case, as in all the past life of the party, built the bridge between Amadeo and Masci; without a beach, I wonder what the bridge is for."[15]

Gramsci replied with two letters: the first, dated January 5, addressed to Scoccimarro; the second, written on the 13th of the same month, addressed to Terracini. In the first letter, perhaps the most important of that period, he explained in detail why he would never have signed the Manifesto and why he now considered any agreement with Bordiga impossible. Criticism of the document involved form and substance: according to the Manifesto, history ended with the Third Congress, as if the Fourth Congress did not exist, as if the Enlarged Executive of the IC had not met, as if a new Executive had not been established in the party. Such position might seem plausible if adopted by a single comrade, but it became completely illogical if promoted by the faction that had been leading the party and had been ahead of it since the Third Congress. With regard to form, Gramsci challenged the complete lack of discipline of the Italian leadership group, which was to blame, from the formal point of view, for making a public proclamation of adherence to the principles of democratic centralism only to disregard and challenge, in the concrete work, all the deliberations of the International. Gramsci reminded his comrades of the existence of the article of the Statutes of the Comintern, approved and supported by all, that required the effective implementation of the Executive's deliberations by the adhering parties:

> Given the concept of party that derives from the Manifesto, exclusion [from the Comintern] should be mandatory. If one of our federations did only half of what the majority of the party wants to do in relation to the Comintern,

---

[14] "Lettera di Umberto Terracini a Gramsci e Scoccimarro del 2 gennaio 1924", in Palmiro Togliatti, *La formazione del gruppo dirigente del Partito Comunista Italiano (1923–24)*, cit., 144–7.
[15] Ibid.

its dissolution would be immediate. I don't want to, by signing this manifesto, look like a total clown.[16]

Gramsci challenged the Manifesto also in its content, distancing himself from its postulations with arguments that anticipate themes characteristic of the subsequent struggle against Bordiga's left:

> I have another conception of the party, of its function, of the relations that must be established between it and the masses without a party, between it and the population in general; I do not believe at all that the tactic developed from the enlarged Executive and the Fourth Congress is mistaken. Neither in the general postulations nor in the small details. I believe that is also the case for you and for Palmi, and I cannot understand how, having such a light heart, you were able to embark on such a risky course. I am under the impression that you are in the same state of mind that I was in during the Congress of Rome. Perhaps because in the meantime I was away from the internal work of the party, this state of mind has changed. In fact, it has changed for other reasons as well. And one of the most important is that one absolutely cannot make agreements with Amadeo. He has such a strong personality and such a deep conviction that he is right that the thought of making him commit himself to something is absurd. He will keep on fighting and going back to his theses on all occasions.[17]

The struggle on both fronts was now a major, urgent requirement, and Gramsci again declared himself willing to lead it, even if alone. In order to more successfully persuade his old comrades and make it clear that his position was not dangerous, but only dictated by objective needs, he recalled an episode from the past, when in 1920 he parted company with Terracini and Togliatti to come closer to the abstentionists' position while they both reached an agreement with Tasca.

---

[16] In the letter to Scoccimarro, dated January 5, 1924, in order to confirm the thesis about how ill-timed it was to break with the Comintern and to leave Tasca the title of representative of the International, Gramsci accused the Party of meaning too little to its militants due to its great weakness since, to their mind, the power and prestige of the International were quite different: "Actually, I am convinced that the party comrades are mainly attracted by the prestige and the appeal of the International, not the ties that any specific action of the Party may have established, and it was precisely in this respect that we created a minority. And this minority boasts of the status of true representative of the International in Italy" (Palmiro Togliatti, *La formazione del gruppo dirigente del Partito Comunista Italiano (1923–24)*, cit., 151).

[17] Ibid., 150.

Today, the opposite seems to be happening. But in reality, the situation is not very different from what happened in the Socialist Party, when it was necessary to rely on the abstentionists to create the fundamental core of the future party; today we must fight extremists if we want the party to develop and stop being just an external fraction of the Socialist Party. Indeed, both forms of extremism, in the right and in the left, having encapsulated the party exclusively in the discussion of relations with the Socialist Party, reduced it to a secondary role.[18]

It is clear that Gramsci took for himself the Leninist theme of the battle on two fronts (against opportunism and against sectarianism), which was discussed by the Bolshevik leader throughout his existence. Precisely during this big controversy, on the night of January 21 to 22, 1924, news of Lenin's death came, and the bitter dispute over his succession was already underway.

Among the letters of this period from Gramsci to Alfonso Leonetti, that of January 28 is particularly important. Leonetti, very close to Antonio Gramsci, not only politically but also humanly, had written to him eight days earlier, totally agreeing with his positions. Leonetti also thought that the Manifesto expressed wrong and unacceptable positions. He proposed the construction of a new group linked to the ordinovist experience, which could represent the line of the International and combat both Tasca's right-wing positions and Bordiga's sectarianism. However, according to Gramsci, insisting too much on the Turin tradition would simply rekindle old personal controversies and bring the new group more problems than consensus; moreover, the positions of some figures, such as Togliatti and Terracini, regarding the Manifesto made this hypothesis impractical:

Togliatti can't make up his mind, as usual; Amadeo's strong personality has strongly affected him and keeps him halfway, in an indecision that seeks justifications in purely legal discussions. I believe that Umberto is fundamentally even more extremist than Amadeo because he has absorbed the conception, but does not have the intellectual power, practical sense and organizational skills. How could our group be restored then? It would look like just a clique clustered around me for bureaucratic reasons.[19]

---

[18] Ibid.
[19] Antonio Gramsci, "Lettera ad Alfonso Leonetti del 28 gennaio 1924", in Palmiro Togliatti, *La formazione del gruppo dirigente del Partito Comunista Italiano (1923–24)*, cit., 183.

The real problem underlying the battle was the notion of party, its function, its relationship with the masses. These themes were constantly present in the political biography of Antonio Gramsci and developed over time continuously:

> The same fundamental ideas that characterize the activity of ON [*L'Ordine Nuovo*] today are or will be anachronistic. Apparently, at least today, issues take the form of organizational problems, particularly party organization ones. I say apparently because in fact the problem is always the same: that of relations between the ruling center and the mass of the party, and between the party and the classes of the working population.[20]

In the dense correspondence of this period, the letter of February 9 must be taken into account, which Gramsci addressed to Togliatti and Terracini and explained all the points of his position, expressing it for the first time in an organic and coherent way. From a political point of view, this letter assumed paramount importance in Gramsci's attempts to persuade Terracini and Togliatti.

Acceptance of the Manifesto would have meant departure from the Comintern because, in Bordiga's intention, this was the beginning of an open battle against the International, aimed at the tactical review developed after the Third Congress, whose premises, in turn, were completely claimed by Gramsci. Contrary to what the Manifesto stated, for him that line did not really represent the tradition of the organization; rather, it was the expression of the traditions and conceptions of a single group: Bordiga's. The PCd'I was created in Livorno not in line with a common concept that later continued to exist, but on the basis of a contingent situation: the existence of the struggle against the reformists and the acceptance of the 21 points established in the Second Congress of the International. Bordiga, ahead of the party, especially with the *Theses of Rome*, had ensured the prominence of his conceptions. Regarding this attempt, Gramsci reiterated his opposition, which was expressed in the federal Congress of Turin. On every occasion the PCd'I should have developed an intense activity among the masses, with a serious work of agitation and propaganda, on every occasion the organization should have guided the masses, it actually demonstrated all its inability and distance from the masses. This was Gramsci's clear opinion:

[20] Ibid.

Every occasion, every local, national or world event should have served to stir the masses through the communist cells, promoting the voting of motions, the dissemination of manifestos […]. The Communist Party opposed the creation of factory cells. Any participation of the masses in the activity and internal life of the party, except for special occasions and following a formal order from the center, was seen as a danger to unity and centralization. The Party was not conceived as a result of a dialectical process to which the spontaneous movement of the revolutionary masses and the organizational and leading will of the center converge, but only as something ethereal, which develops by itself and which the masses will achieve when the situation is favorable and the revolutionary wave reaches its peak, or when the center of the party believes that it should launch an offensive and reach the masses to encourage them and galvanize them into action.[21]

In Gramsci's view, Bordiga led with great wit and coherence a battle to win over not only the center of the PCd'I but also the leadership of the International since he considered his tactic mistaken for reflecting only the Russian situation, that is, a tactic created within a backward and primitive mode of production. With the victory of a revolution in the West, this was the conviction of the leader of the left, power relations would change, which would put an end to the primacy of the Russian Party. According to Bordiga, in Russia, given the absence of the social and production relations developed by capitalism, only with an extreme effort of will would it be possible to accomplish a victorious revolutionary activity, whereas in the West the revolution would begin simply by monitoring and safeguarding the ideological purity of the party because in western countries the "historical mechanism works according to all Marxist crises" and there are objective conditions that make tactics useless or superfluous. In addition to the divergence, Gramsci's answer is particularly important, as it already contains some of the essential elements of his future writings on the difference in context between East and West, civil society and hegemony.

The political conception of the Russian communists was developed on the international not on the national ground […]; in central and western Europe, the development of capitalism determined not only the emergence of broad popular strata, but also the creation of the upper stratum, the

---

[21] Antonio Gramsci, "Lettera a Terracini e Togliatti del 9 febbraio 1924", in Palmiro Togliatti, *La formazione del gruppo dirigente del Partito Comunista Italiano (1923–24)*, cit., 195.

workers' aristocracy, with trade union bureaucracy and social-democratic groups as accessories. The determination, which in Russia was straightforward and launched the masses on the path of revolutionary assault, in central and western Europe is more complex because of all these political superstructures created by the great development of capitalism, which makes the action of the masses slower and more prudent and therefore requires from the revolutionary party much more complex and lasting tactics and strategies than those that were necessary for the Bolsheviks between March and November 1917. That Amadeo has this conception and seeks to make it triumph not only on a national but also on an international scale is one thing [...], but that we, who are not convinced of the historicity of this conception, politically continue to support it and thus give it international value, is quite another. Amadeo is aligned with the point of view of the international minority. We must stand on the side of the point of view of the national majority.[22]

At the end of this complex dialectic, between February and March, Gramsci managed to win his battle, convincing the old comrades to align themselves with his positions. The positive result of the process was influenced by the release of the new series of *L'Ordine Nuovo*, on March 1, 1924. Gramsci involved the entire PCd'I leadership group in the editorial project, including Tasca and Bordiga, but above all strengthened the ties that were essential to the establishment of a new majority. Meanwhile, in the political elections of April 6, Gramsci was elected deputy in the Electoral College of Veneto. Thanks to parliamentary immunity, he finally managed to leave Vienna and return to Italy on May 12.

[22] Ibid., 197.

CHAPTER 12

Gramsci Leading the Party

The Central Committee of April 18 was the first meeting in which the "new direction" presented itself united and won the majority. The debate was very limited, except for a critical intervention by Angelo Tasca about the direction of the party from 1921 to 1924. He accused the new group led by Gramsci of insincerity, duplicity and transformism, stating that the conversion of the centrists was not by conviction and simply concealed the intention to incorporate part of the left into more orthodox positions so as to better lead the fight against the right, the only component, in his opinion, that was loyal and consciously aligned with the International.

At this meeting, three different motions were put forward, representative of the three factions that were being formed in the party. The majority's motion was structured in seven points, with several limits in terms of approach, and tended to justify the past by omission, showing that it was possible to have the left involved again while creating an insurmountable barrier against the right-wing minority. This was clearly a maneuver designed to undermine Bordiga's consensus; not by chance, in the first point, the continuity of the leading group created in Livorno was demanded, but in general it insisted in controversy with the left. All that contradicted the (demanded) revision process initiated in the Fourth Congress of the International and the full implementation of its line. Even though the merits of the *Theses of Rome* were not criticized, their merely guiding role and advisory value regarding tactics were consolidated so as to prevent a traumatic split in the leadership and the bulk of the

© The Author(s), under exclusive license to Springer Nature Switzerland AG 2023
G. Fresu, *Antonio Gramsci*, Marx, Engels, and Marxisms,
https://doi.org/10.1007/978-3-031-15610-6_12

PCd'I. Different assessments of these theses were perhaps the only significant divergence with the left. For these reasons, the majority's motion led by Gramsci was generally contradictory and lacked a driving force since it did not highlight past mistakes and responsibilities and, at the same time, it did not adequately explain what the guiding lines of the new political proposal should be. The new leadership group's ties with Bordiga were still strong, and Gramsci did not intervene much to change this direction, although he did not agree with some positions.[1] The motion put forward by the left, personally written by Bordiga, seemed more logic and, besides vigorously following the Livorno line of August 1922, it fully supported the principles formulated in the *Theses* on the tactics of the Congress of Rome, completely refuting the positions consolidated in the Fourth Congress of the Comintern. This document definitively explained the true intentions of Bordiga, who was interested in creating a leftist opposition within the International. Only if this line prevailed in the ruling bodies of the Comintern would the exponents of the left be willing to take on responsibilities in the Comintern and in the party.

After the meeting in April, the National Conference of Como was held in May 1924 (it was basically a central committee extended to the secretaries of the federation and to the representative of the youth federation, with an advisory role regarding the political line of the party) in view of the planned National Congress after the Fifth Congress of the Comintern. The clandestine conference took place in the valleys surrounding the center of Lombardy; the delegates, Gramsci himself told Julca Schucht in a letter of July 21, pretended to be employees of a company in Milan: "Discussions all day about trends, tactics and, during meals, in a retreat house full of excursionists, fascist speeches, hymns to Mussolini, a masquerade not to raise suspicions or be disturbed in the meetings held in the beautiful valleys of daffodils".[2] The conference was attended by sixty-seven delegates: eleven from the CC, forty-six from the federations, five from

---

[1] This ambiguity was precisely what led the minority to request supplementary discussion and analysis of the political direction of the party between 1921 and 1924 to be able to identify those accountable for the "artificial" disagreement with the International and, more broadly, for the sense of unease and unpreparedness of the organization. According to the document presented by Tasca, the responsibility was indeed fully attributed to those who had led the party since 1921, and one could therefore not exempt even the part of the majority that was now critical of the *Theses of Rome*, but which had actually led and continued to lead the party based on them.

[2] Antonio Gramsci, "Lettera a Julca Schucht, 21 luglio 1924", in Giuseppe Fiori, *Antonio Gramsci. Vita attraverso le lettere* (Turin, Einaudi, 1994), 84.

the inter-regional committees, four representatives of the technical team and the head of the youth federation.

The meeting was preceded by the publication, in *Lo Stato Operaio*, of the three schemes of the *Theses* outlined in the Central Committee of April; however, if on that occasion the center group had managed to win the majority, in this circumstance it was a minority, obtaining even fewer votes than the right-wing minority. Two simultaneous factors influenced this result: the new leadership group had not been able to coordinate the new line in the territories yet; the secretaries of the federation were all cadres trained according to Bordiga's political-organizational principles and continued to see in him the effective leadership of the party.

The majority's document presented in Como was structured in fifty-seven points demanding the shift toward the "united front" and the necessary discipline within a single world party, not a federation of autonomous parties. The tactic of the "united front" was not a revision with regard to the process of founding autonomous communist parties of socialist groups. The "workers' government" slogan did not mean abandoning the revolutionary path and adopting the parliamentary and governmental path under the bourgeois regime. The "workers' government" was only a possibility whose tactical reasons lay in the difficult world situation of the communists, which resulted from the failure of revolutions in western countries. Regarding the Italian party, the value of the split of Livorno was fully upheld despite the limits—in an objectively difficult, forced context—revealed in the functioning of the organization: the yawning gap between the main groups of the party and the masses, the military and sectarian conception of the party.

> Therefore, the absence of a generalized critical spirit, even among the most capable members of the party; the military nature that prevailed as a the result of our internal organization, often at the expense of its ability to serve as a tool in the work among the masses; and finally, the so-called sectarianism, which was the target of criticism and no more than an angry reaction to the habits of carelessness and corruption that prevailed in the political practice of the PSI and of the Italian proletarian organizations.[3]

---

[3] "Schema di tesi sulla tattica e sulla situazione interna del PCI, presentato dalla maggioranza alla Conferenza nazionale di Como", in Ugo Pecchioli (org.), *Da Gramsci a Berlinguer. La via italiana al socialismo attraverso i Congressi del Partito Comunista Italiano*, v. 1: *1921–1943* (Venice, Marsilio/Edizioni del Calendario, 1985), 177.

The document formalized Gramsci's criticism of the *Theses of Rome* expressed in his correspondence with comrades: "They tended to conceive the development of the party regardless of the development of real situations and movements that, propelled by it, are carried out by the working mass".[4] It also made the causes of the increasingly explicit distance between the party and popular masses evident. This notion of party should be eliminated if the majority of the exploited masses were expected to be won over, according to the orientations of the Third and Fourth Congresses of the Comintern.

Just as in the meeting of the Central Committee, the minority led by Tasca accused the entire leadership of the PCd'I since its creation. The Livorno split had few repercussions among the working masses because the only point of understanding at its basis, between the two main components of the party, was a "generic awareness" of the need to break with the reformists in order to found "a true revolutionary party". Since none of the profound differences between the two groups were addressed, the PCd'I emerged after the mere mechanical acceptance of the twenty-one points of adherence to the International, with no explanation at all of the experiences of 1919–1920 and of the tactics to be adopted. The split took place far to the left, keeping in the former PSI a considerable number of "honestly third-internationalist proletarians", which prevented the Communist Party from becoming the effective guide of the subaltern classes in Italy. Subsequently, the leadership group followed a line of systematic indiscipline regarding the deliberations of the International about coordination with the PSI and the "winning of the majority of those exploited". However, for two years this leading group concealed the dissent of the militant body of the International in order to prevent Lenin's controversial intervention in the Third Congress from reaching the party press and prevent the tactic of the "united front" from being mentioned by the party speakers in their interventions. In Tasca's view, Gramsci and the "center" group should once again be held accountable together, along with Bordiga.

The notion of party in the *Theses of Rome*, an organization intended as a vanguard outside the class, had nothing to do with the orientations of Lenin and the International:

[4] Ibid.

If the party is conceived as an organ of the working class (of its most advanced part) and not as part of the class, and there is a difference in nature between the two elements, then we have perfect identity. The organicity of the party is the organicity of the part of the working class that constitutes it (as such); in the aforementioned formulation, we have the organ, the most advanced part of the proletarian class and the remaining proletariat: thus, the process remains inevitably interrupted, and no reconstruction is capable of restoring the natural and organic continuity between party and mass inherent in the concept we endorse.[5]

For the minority document, the practical consequence of such conception was contained in the *Theses of Rome*—"it cannot be required that, at a certain time or right before general action, the party meet the conditions to bring the majority of the proletariat under its leadership or to lead it to join its ranks".[6] In the *Theses*, the Comintern's orientation to create large mass parties was not only disregarded but totally reversed.

The Bordiga report in Como presented once again the *Theses of Rome* and what had been said at the meeting and in the CC in April, supporting the accuracy of the party line from Livorno to the enlarged Executive, not adding new arguments to those already traditionally supported by the left.

Only a month after the Como Conference (June 17 to July 8, 1924), the Fifth Congress of the Communist International was held, an event of considerable importance since the new ruling group led by Gramsci, besides being officially acknowledged by the Comintern, also recorded Tasca's convergence.

Paradoxically, it was precisely the congress marked by the most decisive shift toward the left of the International, with positions in many respects similar to those of the left of the PCd'I, that led to the definitive exclusion of the Bordigists from the governing bodies of the party and to the beginning of an increasingly fierce battle against fractionation both in the international party and in Italy.

In the congress,[7] the first without Lenin's leadership, there was a reversal of line in relation to the German question, around which the tactical

---

[5] "Schema di tesi della minoranza alla Conferenza nazionale di Como", in Ugo Pecchioli (org.), *Da Gramsci a Berlinguer*, cit., 199.

[6] Ibid.

[7] Although Gramsci was particularly keen on attending the congress, also to meet again, after six months, his partner Julca, who was pregnant, he was detained in Rome due to the outbreak of the Matteotti crisis, not being able to reach Moscow.

themes of the western communists revolved. The change of line elevated the left of the KPD again and put in the dock Karl Radek, who was challenged above all by Zinoviev, the protagonist of this change. In a context marked by the increasingly bitter clashes over Lenin's succession, Zinoviev seemed to assume a role of greater importance and prestige than the other leaders of the old guard.

According to Zinoviev, in the new *Theses* on the tactics of the International, the world politics of the bourgeoisie was going through a "democratic-pacifist" phase that would bring the parties of the Second International to the leadership of many western countries, and that inevitably created, among the popular masses, multiple "illusions" about the possibility of reforming capitalism. However, it was not the beginning of a true democratization of western societies. In Zinoviev's view, this new phase was only the masking of a power that would manifest itself in an increasingly cruel and reactionary way at the international level. Confirmation came from concrete examples. Thus, the victory of the democratic forces in France and England, both nations led by socialists and labor activists, did not halt, in any way, the arms race, the massive looting and exploitation of colonial and semi-colonial peoples, nor did it affect the inter-imperialist contradictions, which on the contrary were increasingly more serious. It was precisely in this regard that the growing antagonism between the United States and Japan clearly revealed the outbreak of a new imperialist world war.

In this context, Zinoviev saw social democracy as the best disguise by, on the one hand, confusing the masses with talk of a general strike against the war, but on the other continuing to support the imperialists from home, helping to isolate the Soviet Union and supporting preparations for the military invasion of Russia. Two tendencies in the bourgeoisie's world politics were competing for influence: one was more reactionary and authoritarian, eager for an open confrontation without mediation with the revolutionary forces; the other was democratic-reformist, interested in improving power relations in its favor thanks to the corruption of the working masses encouraged by the "policy of small concessions". The bourgeoisie was no longer able to rule with its traditional methods; therefore, it alternated between fascism and social democracy. In both cases, for the Bolshevik leader, the goal was the same: to mask the capitalist nature of its rule.

For several years now, social democracy has been undergoing a metamor-
phosis: from the right wing of the trade union movement, it tends to turn
into the left wing of the bourgeois side, sometimes even into the fascist
wing. That is why it is historically inaccurate to speak of the victory of fascism over social democracy. As far as the ruling strata are concerned, fascism
and social democracy are only the right hand and the left hand of modern
capitalism [...].[8]

These statements paved the way for one of the most nefarious formulations in the history of communism for the fate of the world workers'
movement and others: "social fascism", for which, in general terms, it is
not possible to find gradations of diversity between democratic, social
democratic and fascist parties, between authoritarian and democratic
forms of bourgeois government. Amadeo Bordiga can be considered a
forerunner of the theory of social fascism, and he not only never changed
his position, even after the disaster of 1933, but later went so far as to say
that the worst fruit of fascism had been precisely anti-fascism.

Although they are in absolute contradiction with the previous line, the
Theses formally reaffirmed the premises of the Third and Fourth Congresses:
the winning of the majority of those exploited through the creation of factory cells, of communist fractions in the unions, and of structured movements in the system of factory committees, as well as the strategic
development of the peasant and national question.

If the theses on tactics advanced by the Fourth Congress mediated
between the two opposite interpretations (left and right) of the "united
front" and the workers' government, in the Fifth Congress all mediation
imploded, with a clear predominance of the positions supported by the
left. Karl Radek was accused of opportunism, responsible for completely
distorting the meaning and prospects of the tactics decided by the
Comintern. According to Zinoviev, the notion of "united front" and a
government of workers and peasants should not be interpreted as "a petty
political alliance, an organic coalition of all workers' parties, a political alliance of communists with social democracy";[9] on the contrary, it pointed
to a resolute struggle to "unmask social democracy" before the workers
and limit its influence. The contradiction between these theses with what
had been approved in the two previous congresses, and especially with

[8] Jane Degras (org.), *Storia dell'Internazionale comunista attraverso i documenti ufficiali*,
t. 2: *1923–1928* (Milan, Feltrinelli, 1975), 168.
[9] Ibid., 172.

what Lenin stated in his speeches, is all too evident. For the theses of the Third and Fourth Congresses, approved and signed by Lenin, the task of creating mass parties and materializing the "united front", actually more open to alliance solutions, should not be reduced to a mere work of agitation and propaganda and to the idea of a "united front from below", while for the *Theses* of the Fifth Congress, "the tactic of the united front is only a method of revolutionary agitation and mobilization of the masses in a certain period".[10] In the Fourth Congress, the slogan of the workers' and peasants' government had led to intermediate solutions to the collaboration of the communists with social democratic and even democratic forces. The solutions of the Fifth Congress were completely different:

> The opportunistic members of the Comintern also tried to distort this slogan, interpreting it in the sense of government, within the bourgeois-democratic structure and the political alliance with social democracy. The Fifth World Congress of the Comintern solemnly rejected this interpretation. For the Comintern, the watchword of the workers' and peasants' government is the watchword of the dictatorship of the proletariat [...]; it is nothing more and can only be a method of agitation and mobilization of the masses through the revolutionary overthrowing of the bourgeoisie [...], which can only be achieved by an armed revolt of the proletariat with the support of the best part of the peasants, only by the workers in a civil war. [...] For the communists, the watchword of the workers' and peasants' government can never be the tactic of parliamentary agreements and coalitions with social democracy. On the contrary: the activity of the communists in Parliament should aim to reveal the counterrevolutionary role of social democracy and show to the working masses the treacherous nature and mystifying character of the so-called labor activists, who owe their existence to the bourgeoisie and take part in liberal and bourgeois governments.[11]

Zinoviev did not dare to reject the deliberations of the Third and Fourth Congresses, supported by Lenin's authority, but condemned without reservation Karl Radek's positions, instead rehabilitating the positions of the German left led by Ruth Fisher, against which Lenin and Radek led a fierce political battle. It was a major revision of the previous line, after which, however, the continuity of the new positions was confirmed. Being at odds with Lenin would have been risky even for the rising star of the

---

[10] Ibid.
[11] Ibid., 173–4.

Russian Party, Zinoviev. The practice of revision within the formal scope and within the continuity scope will be repeated several times in the history of the Third International, giving rise to a strand of political exegesis and to the training of specialized intellectuals whose main function was practically very similar, in some respects, to that exercised by the *ulama* in positive Islamic law: to ensure, in the transition from principle to implementation, respect for some formal rules in order to legitimize a result, even if it is in contradiction with the principle on which it was based, and to institutionalize some procedures aimed at legalizing any discrepancy between theory and practice.[12] Nonetheless, taking completely different positions, Bordiga and Radek were resourceful in showing the limits of this supposed continuity: the former observed with satisfaction the change of line that occurred, now calling for serious self-criticism on the part of the Comintern regarding the deliberations of the Third and Fourth Congress; the latter, starting from a reflexive position, reframed the theses of these two congresses with coherence and logic, highlighting the severe discrepancy of the new theses advanced by Zinoviev.

Not going into detail about a debate that is nevertheless full of interesting points at the historical and theoretical level, the most important political information regarding this congress was the decisive shift toward the left of the International, exactly when the new majority of the PCd'I was trying to align the organization with the *Theses* of the Third and Fourth Congress. As part of the work, a new composition was formed in the main organs of the Italian party, the Central Committee and its Executive, the majority of which remained with the center and the groups associated with Tasca, who in the meantime was publicly separated from the well-known exponents of the maximalist right, such as Bombacci, a future fascist, and Graziadei, the revisionist of Marx's value theory.

The left, in turn, still clearly reluctant to assume any responsibility in the governing bodies, for the first time was also absent from the CC. During the congress, Zinoviev and the Executive of the International sought to no avail a dialogue with Bordiga, also offering him the vice-presidency of the International. The next phase, until the Congress of Lyon, was characterized by the consolidation of the new majority around Gramsci, the new secretary-general of the party, and the intensification of Bordiga's fraction and opposition activities.

---

[12] Biancamaria Scarcia Amoretti, *Il mondo musulmano. Quindici secoli di storia* (Rome, Carocci, 1998), 29.

CHAPTER 13

Theoretical Maturity between 1925 and 1926

Gramsci engaged in parliamentary activity precisely at the most dramatic moment of transition from the liberal system to the fascist regime, which began with the Matteotti case and ended with the authoritarian enactment of the *most fascist laws*, a prelude to the arrest of the Sardinian intellectual.

The political crisis linked to the murder of Giacomo Matteotti[1] caused a reaction to fascism by important members of the country's ruling classes, both in the economic and in the banking sector—which proposed a national reconstruction government—and, in particular, by important members of the small and middle bourgeoisie, the main social basis of fascism. Faced with the crisis, the parties of the constitutional opposition,

---

[1] Giacomo Matteotti (1885–1924) is one of the most important figures of Italian antifascism. A socialist deputy and journalist, he was a staunch opponent of Mussolini who denounced the electoral fraud, the violence and even the corruption of the fascist movement. For this reason, he was kidnapped and murdered by a gang of Mussolini's trusted men. The Matteotti case, which involved fascism in a scandal that triggered government crisis (because Mussolini's responsibility was soon evident), has incredible features in common with Marielle Franco's murder.

© The Author(s), under exclusive license to Springer Nature Switzerland AG 2023
G. Fresu, *Antonio Gramsci, Marx, Engels, and Marxisms*,
https://doi.org/10.1007/978-3-031-15610-6_13

which attracted public opinion's interest,[2] were characterized by "wrong and insufficient action".[3] These forces believed they could defeat fascism through parliamentary action, but the Mussolini government, despite attempts to find constitutional ground for its militia, was above all an armed dictatorship, and the Aventine parties[4] cleverly underestimated that.

Among the most significant and representative contributions of Gramsci's theoretical development is certainly his only intervention in Parliament, made in the Chamber of Deputies on May 16, 1925, against the Mussolini-Rocco bill on the *Origins and aims of the law on secret associations*.[5] There are many testimonies to the fascists' attention to Gramsci's intervention, in addition to the account in the letter to Julca of May 25:

> Regarding this law, I made my debut in Parliament. The fascists did me a favor because, from a revolutionary point of view, I started with a failure. As I speak softly, they gathered around me to hear me and allowed me to say what I wanted, constantly interrupting me just to divert the thread of the speech, no sabotage intended. It was amusing to listen to what they said, but I couldn't stop answering and ended up playing their game because I got

---

[2] In a letter to Julca of November 26, 1924, Gramsci reported the new climate in the country, under a seemingly ailing regime: "We have become very strong: we have managed to hold public rallies in front of factories in the presence of four thousand workers who cheered the party and the International. Fascism no longer stirs so much fear [...]. The bourgeoisie is confused: it no longer knows how to provide a trusted government: it must cling to fascism desperately; the opposition is weakening and actually only works for Mussolini to comply with legal practices" (Giuseppe Fiori, *Antonio Gramsci. Vita attraverso le lettere*, Turin, Einaudi, 1994, 99–100).

[3] Antonio Gramsci, *La costruzione del Partito Comunista 1923–1926* (Turin, Einaudi, 1978), 27.

[4] The so-called Aventine secession was an act of rebellion on the part of anti-fascists in parliament (socialists, republicans, Catholics, liberal democrats) who, after the abduction of the socialist deputy Giacomo Matteotti (June 10, 1924), decided (as of June 26) to no longer engage in the work of the Chamber of Deputies until the resolution of the case and the clarification of the Mussolini government's responsibility. The name Aventine evoked was the so-called *secessio plebis*, which occurred in ancient Rome between the fourth and third centuries BC, when the plebeians rebelled against the nobles' malfeasance and retreated to the Aventine Hill (one of Rome's seven hills) after having abandoned the city en masse. That paralyzed all military, productive and commercial activities carried out by the people, which demanded equal rights with the "patricians".

[5] Gianni Fresu, "Antonio Gramsci, fascismo e classi dirigenti nella Storia d'Italia", *NAE: Trimestrale di Cultura*, Cagliari, Cuec, n. 21, ano 6, 2008, 33–4.

tired and could no longer stick to the approach I had intended to take in my speech.[6]

In Gramsci's intellectual biography, this intervention has taken on particular importance for three reasons: because it is a fundamental link between the pre- and post-prison stance on the theme of fascism/ruling classes; because it anticipates many themes of the analytical turn of the Congress of Lyon; and finally because it definitively shows the distance, now irreversible, between Gramsci's and Bordiga's theoretical-political approach.

In his speech, which was interrupted repeatedly by the intemperance of fascist deputies, Gramsci made one basic point clear above all: the real target of the law was not Freemasonry, with which fascism would later make an agreement, but anti-fascist opposition. Overall, the bill on secret associations was an opportunity to suppress freedom of association; it stated the need to target Freemasonry, but actually intended to interfere with other democratic freedoms.

This bill was fascism's first organic attempt to assert its own "revolution" and, faced with such aim, Gramsci claimed that the communists had always taken the fascist danger very seriously, even when the other forces underestimated it by considering it mere "war psychosis" and a superficial and temporary phenomenon. As early as November 1920, Gramsci recalled that he had predicted Mussolini's movement would rise to power if the working class did not oppose its rise with arms.

In Gramsci's view, Freemasonry was the only true party of the Italian bourgeoisie from the *Risorgimento* to the "March on Rome". After unification, Freemasonry was the main tool for this class to advocate the creation of a unitary and liberal state from the threats of its main enemies: the Vatican and its armed wing, the Jesuits, with the organ *Civiltà Cattolica*, behind which were the "old semi-feudal classes of Bourbon tendency in the South and the Austrians in Veneto-Lombardy". The Vatican never concealed the goal of sabotaging the unitary state, resorting to parliamentary abstention and preventing in every way the creation of a liberal order capable of questioning or destroying the old order. In 1871, with the creation of a "rural reserve army", the Jesuits undertook to block the path of the urban proletariat, both on the revolutionary ground and at the level

---

[6] Antonio Gramsci, *Vita attraverso le lettere*, (org.) Giuseppe Fiori, Einaudi, Torino, 1994, p. 108–109.

of democratic achievements. Freemasonry was the organization and at the same time the official ideology of the Italian bourgeoisie; therefore, declaring oneself contrary to its tradition meant being against the political history of the Italian bourgeoisie, liberalism and the *Risorgimento* itself. These very rural classes, previously represented by the Vatican, were now mainly associated with fascism, which took on the historical function of the Jesuits: to put the progressive classes under the control of the backward classes. With the war-induced crisis, the industrial bourgeoisie, unable to control the urban proletariat and the increasingly restless peasant masses, found its only answer in the slogan of fascism. This crisis, which was not a purely Italian phenomenon, but European and global, had its own physiognomy for three reasons: the absence of raw material and therefore the strong limitation of industrial development in the country potentially capable of developing and absorbing surplus labor; the absence of colonial possessions capable of generating the necessary profits for a working-class aristocracy permanently allied with the bourgeoisie; the southern question understood as a peasant question closely linked to mass emigration. Imperialism, Gramsci noted, is characterized by the export of capital; Italy, instead, exported only labor used to remunerate foreign capital, which drained the country's most active and productive part. Thus, "Italy has only been a means of expanding non-Italian financial capital".[7]

The liberal parties of the Italian bourgeoisie and Freemasonry followed two directions corresponding to well-defined social blocs: (1) Giolittism aimed to form an alliance with the socialists to create an industrial-bourgeois aristocracy and subjugate the peasant masses of the *Mezzogiorno* as well as the industrial proletariat. That materialized in the North with parliamentary collaboration, the policy of public works and the policy of cooperatives; in the South, with the corruption of the intellectual classes and domination over the masses through "inciters"; (2) the *Corriere della Sera* newspaper, however, supported southern politicians such as Antonio Salandra, Vittorio Emanuele Orlando, Francesco Saverio Nitti and Giovanni Amendola and was in favor of an alliance between northern industrialists and southern rural democracy in the field of *free trade*. Both solutions, despite being affected by internal distortions and contradictions, tended to broaden the base of the Italian state and consolidate the achievements of the *Risorgimento*.

[7] Antonio Gramsci, *La costruzione del Partito Comunista*, cit., 78.

Fascism stated its wish to seize the state. Actually, that law under discussion suggested a much more nefarious goal: to replace Freemasonry, the only organized and efficient force of the Italian bourgeoisie, in the occupation of the administrative-institutional apparatus. Therefore, when Mussolini interrupted Gramsci claiming every revolution had the right to replace the ruling class, the perfect Gramsci merely replied: "only the revolution based on a new class is the revolution. Fascism is not based on any class that was not yet in power…".[8]

Regarding Freemasonry, fascism employed the same tactics it had used with other sectors of the bourgeoisie, but failed to fully absorb the organization. First, it tried to infiltrate into the core, and then used the terrorist methods of paramilitarism to reduce resistance; now it intervened in legislative action to definitively make the influential personalities of state bureaucracies and high banking compliant. Fascism would have sought conciliation with Freemasonry, but in the way it is usually done with a stronger enemy: "first you break their legs, then you get an agreement in conditions of superiority".[9] Freemasonry would have adhered to fascism, constituting a trend. However, fascism represented a solution that was not only retrogressive but was also affected by an inherent weakness stemming from the fact that all its power was based on the use of force.

> When the Italian bourgeoisie achieved unification, it was a minority of the population, but since it represented the interests of the majority, even if the majority did not follow it, it managed to remain in power. You [Mussolini] won by arms, but you have no program; you do not represent anything new and progressive.[10]

In Gramsci's view, fascism would not have been able to resolve the fundamental contradictions of Italian society, starting with the southern question; in fact, it would have further exacerbated them, adding other elements to those already accumulated by the development of capitalist society. The law against Freemasonry was precisely the attempt to circumvent the fundamental contradictions of the Italian mode of social production, seeking additional support for maintaining power through the police state and the systematic repression of all freedoms. In this intervention, he

---

[8] Ibid.
[9] Ibid.
[10] Ibid., 82.

anticipated some of the most important themes of the *Theses of Lyon*, exposing the need for a less schematic and crude analysis of the Italian ruling classes. For Gramsci, it was inconceivable to assert the absence of differences between a democratic regime and a fascist one, and it was equally hard for him to believe that there was a monolithic bloc of the Italian ruling classes behind fascism. There were, on the contrary, great contradictions that had to be revealed to enable its destruction.

After the wave of indignation at Matteotti's murder and Mussolini's accusation of political and moral responsibility for this murder, the Aventine opposition demonstrated its ineffectiveness and political inertia. The communist parliamentary group assumed its stance before the Opposition Committee in a letter later published by *l'Unità*. In the political situation of fascist crisis, which was determined by Matteotti's murder, parliamentary activity was not considered enough, except as a reflection of a strong movement of social opposition to fascism capable of involving the great working masses. In addition, the communist group led by Gramsci proposed to the "Opposition Committee" the constitution of an antifascist parliamentary assembly, separate from and in opposition to the fascist parliament, which was elected on the basis of violence, fraud and malfeasance. The communist group intended the "Antiparlamento" to transfer Matteotti's murder from the legal to the political field, galvanizing the great working masses to demand better living and working conditions and to physically resist fascist violence; besides, it was necessary to reach out to veterans and the army through the slogan of tax strike and by establishing workers' and peasants' committees to overthrow the fascist regime. In response to the repeated refusals by opposition parliamentary groups, the communist group reiterated its proposal for an anti-fascist parliament. Isolating from the masses and standing among the forces that supported fascism would only lead to the strengthening of fascism and the complete defeat of the opposition. The fascist regime was preparing to launch the system of the *most fascist laws* with which it would definitively suppress parliamentary institutions and individual and collective freedoms, building the totalitarian state.

In the article "Elementi della situazione" [Elements of the situation] (*l'Unità*, November 24, 1925),[11] Gramsci wrote that the predictable and expected deterioration of the Constitutional Committee of the opposition had given fascism a strong new impetus. Having escaped danger, the

[11] Ibid., 85.

regime now moved in two directions: first, aiming for the organic unification, under its direction, of all the forces of the bourgeoisie so as to concentrate all conservative and reactionary groups around a single political center. This happened with the molecular absorption of political groupings, or by an increasingly tough fight against all the former leading groups that had not yet surrendered. The law against Freemasonry served exactly this purpose. Aiming to become the only central direction of the bourgeoisie, on the economic front, fascism implemented a number of measures (restoration of customs duties, unification of the banking system, changes in the commercial code) so as to ensure the supremacy of the industrial-agricultural oligarchy, which was entrusted with the keys to the entire national economy.

The second fundamental direction of fascist politics targeted the world of labor aiming to suppress its political and social subjectivity. In essence, the goal was to deal with all possibilities of workers' autonomous organization by limiting their participation in political life and thwarting their ambition to make their fundamental choices. This was the purpose of the trade union policy of fascism (with the fascist trade union law), the law of associations already passed by the Senate, the reform of the administrative system with the institution of the *Podestà*[12] for the municipalities of the countryside and the creation, by corporations, of advisory organs, which would exclude those considered "subversive".

The institutional structure built by the fascist regime found an essential point in the regulation of all economic and social organs of the world of labor. The network of fascist syndicalism did not arise because of a plan made by the regime, but in Gramsci's view it was the consequence of a failure resulting from the March on Rome: the absence of agreement with traditional unions.

Before having a monopoly on the fascist unions, Mussolini relied on collaboration with the CGdL [General Confederation of Labor] and met several times with the socialist leaders. There was a meeting in particular with D'Aragona and Buozzi where the leader of fascism asked the union to take the leadership of the Ministry of the National Economy and accept the merger with the fascist corporations. This perspective failed, not so

---

[12] With this reform, the democratic institutions of the municipalities were abolished and the mayors were replaced with a new figure appointed directly by the central government, the *Podestà*.

much because of the opposition of trade unionists, but because of the unavailability of the great bourgeoisie.

Collaboration with the reformists failed, despite some mutual sympathy, because as a result of the departure of the workers of the small and middle bourgeoisie from the CGdL after the incursions of the fascist squads, the organization found itself increasingly dominated by the communists. Thus, the adherence of the reformists to the fascist union led the CGdL to fall into the hands of the most radical members of the labor movement. The failure of this attempt led to legislative provisions that, between 1924 and 1926, suppressed trade union freedoms, along with individual and collective freedoms, with the consolidation of corporatism and the creation of a single trade union.

The law enacted on June 2, 1926, in particular, gave the fascist union the exclusive right to negotiate labor contracts after the agreement of the leaders of the CGdL reform. At the end of the year, the union leaders closed the organization—with a document signed by Ludovico D'Aragona, Rinaldo Rigola, Giovanni Battista Maglione, Ettore Rena and Emilio Colombino—declaring that they identified with fascism's union policy. A capitulation, perceived as a betrayal, not recognized by significant part of the union, which reorganized clandestinely in the congress of February 1927.

CHAPTER 14

The Congress of Lyon

The PCd'I, the Italian section of the Third International, was created in Livorno on January 21, 1921. To further emphasize its national roots, after the dissolution of the Communist International, it took the name of Italian Communist Party on May 15, 1943. However, the choice for a clearer national contextualization of the organization was made well before 1943, with the first change in its political direction between 1925 and 1926. The *Theses* of the Congress of Lyon, in 1926, are considered the pivot of the turn in the history of the communists in Italy, regarding both the conception of party and the analysis of society. In both cases, Bordiga's *Theses* for the Congress of Rome were completely overcome after the great change in the political direction of the party under Antonio Gramsci.[1]

It is well known that after the end of the 1930s and especially in the struggle for national liberation, the Communist Party became a political subject able to attract students, workers, artists, intellectuals, university professors. From a small cadre party, and its presence restricted to certain realities of the country, it became the main political organization of the Resistance until it unexpectedly became the main party of the Italian left and the largest communist party in the West. Such transformation seemed impossible, taking into account the marginal condition and minority

---

[1] Gianni Fresu, *Eugenio Curiel. Il lungo viaggio contro il fascismo* (Rome, Odradek, 2013), 103.

© The Author(s), under exclusive license to Springer Nature Switzerland AG 2023
G. Fresu, *Antonio Gramsci*, Marx, Engels, and Marxisms,
https://doi.org/10.1007/978-3-031-15610-6_14

culture of this organization at the time of its creation, during the years of fascist growth. A first explanation for this fact should be sought in the perseverance of the PCd'I, even in the harshest years of fascist repression, in striving to maintain a clandestine and active structure in Italy, rather than confining itself to transferring its entire organization abroad.

Notwithstanding the repressive waves that from time to time beheaded its vanguard, the party always continued its clandestine activity thanks to the influx of new affiliates, especially young people. Between 1926 and 1943, out of the 4,671 people convicted by the fascist special court, 4,030 were members of the Communist Party; out of the total 28,671 years in prison, almost 24,000 were served by its leaders and militants.[2] However, albeit important, the stubborn presence of the communists in the country, by itself, does not explain this phenomenon of exponential growth. It was probably also influenced by the evolution of its line, which abandoned its original sectarian and minority approaches and more flexibly embraced national conditions to become a mass party, in many respects as an heir to the organizational and social tradition of old socialism.

First, during and after the Congress of Lyon, two radically opposed notions of party were confronted and clashed, thus summarized:

(1) the party understood as part of the class, that is, an organization with mass ambitions, organized in factory cells and committed to the permanent development of all its cadres;

(2) the party understood as an organ outside the class, that is, an organization restricted to revolutionary leaders, moderate and incorruptible, capable of seeing in the economic and social landscape the fundamental contradictions that would lead, at the right time, to the sparks of the revolution.

In the first case, we have the notion of a party eager to organically adhere to the productive structure—which is based on a molecular and procedural conception of revolution, methodologically adverse to any messianism—and which intends to plastically adapt its activity to the daily action of the workers, the so-called economic struggle. In the second case, the notion considers the struggle for the improvement of living and working conditions, as well as the political struggle for daily taking positions of strength in society, as a vehicle for corporate mentality and for the corruption of revolutionary purity. In this interpretation, the connection between

---

[2] Arturo Colombi, *Nelle mani del nemico* (Rome, Editori Riuniti, 1971).

party and masses would only happen at the specific moment of class conflict.

The period between the beginning of 1925 and the congress of January 1926 was crucial for the evolution of Gramsci's thought concerning the party, its relationship with the masses and the roles performed by intellectuals in it; it was a period when his experience of political direction and guidance from 1923 onwards reached maturity. A phase in which his analysis developed seeking to question what role is played by intellectuals in Italian society and what the fabric that connects the ruling classes is. In these analyses, the redefinition of the concept of state that anticipated the hegemonic category was already present. Gramsci's reflections in this phase are the essential basis of the theory on intellectuals developed in *The southern question* and in his prison reflections. At the same time, his prison reflections are the point of arrival of his *Notebooks* reflections and, on the whole, have their roots in the ordinovist experience.

The leftist congressional platform, published in *l'Unità* on July 7, 1925, based the positions already stated several times by its leader Amadeo Bordiga on three fundamental grounds: (1) the party should be understood as a class organ that synthesizes and unites individual desires, differentiating itself from the particularism of category and attracting elements from the proletariat in several categories, the peasants, the deserters of the bourgeois class; (2) the rejection of "Bolshevization"—which started in the Fifth Congress and was reasserted by the "centrist group" led by Gramsci—that is, the organizational division of the party into cells at the bases of the factories; (3) the refusal to struggle against the fractions determined by the Comintern.

This stance was manifest in the writing of the *Theses* for the congress. According to Bordiga, it was impossible to change the essence of objective situations arising from the more general framework of social relations of production by means of an organizational form. An immediate organization of all workers on economic bases would end up constantly dominated by the impulses of several professional categories to satisfy their own economic interests determined by capitalist exploitation. Hence the deep distrust, already expressed at the time of the councils, of the commitment of the organization to workers' disputes in the union. In the same issue of *l'Unità*, on July 7, Gramsci set out to give him an important reply. In this reply, the continuity of his thinking in the years of *L'Ordine Nuovo* on the topic of the autonomy of producers was entirely clear, and the idea of the "organic intellectual" was first approached by stating that each worker, upon joining the Communist Party, became a leader and therefore an intellectual. The left conceived the party as a synthesis of the individual members, not as a mass and class movement, and this was the basis of Bordiga's party theory:

> In this conception there is a shade of marked pessimism over the capacity of the workers as such, since only the intellectuals could be political men. Workers are workers and can only be so while capitalism oppresses them: under capitalist oppression, the worker cannot fully develop, cannot escape the spirit typical of his category. Then what is the party? It is restricted only to the group of leaders who reflect and synthesize the general interests and aspirations of the mass, even within the party. Leninist doctrine asserts and demonstrates that this is a false and extremely dangerous conception; it led, among other problems, to the phenomenon of union mandarinism. [...] The workers join the Communist Party not only as workers (metalworkers, joiners, builders etc.), but as communist workers, as political men, that is, as theorists of socialism, therefore not as mere rebels; and in the party, through discussions, readings, the party school, they develop continuously, they become leaders. Only in the union is the worker in his capacity as a worker, not as a politician who follows a certain theory.[3]

According to Gramsci, Bordiga's conception was attached to the first phase of capitalist development. In 1848 it was still possible to affirm that "the party is the organ that synthesizes and unites the individual and collective desires motivated by the class struggle", but in the phase of greater capitalist development (imperialism), the proletariat was deeply revolutionary and was already taking on a leading role in society. In that same period, Gramsci wrote an introduction to the first course of the internal school to the PCd'I, whose objective of ideologically and politically strengthening the cadres and militants was seen as the main objective of a party that intended to become a mass party. Schooling was a way of turning the communist worker into a leader and not leaving the ideological struggle exclusively in the hands of bourgeois intellectuals.

> Theoretical activity, struggle on the ideological front, has always been neglected in the Italian workers' movement. In Italy, Marxism has been studied more by bourgeois intellectuals, in order to pervert it and make it serve the purposes of bourgeois politics, than by revolutionaries. It seasoned the most indigestible sauces that the most reckless adventurers could put on

---

[3] Antonio Gramsci, "Il Partito si rafforza combattendo le deviazioni antileniniste", *l'Unità*, 5 Jul. 1925.

sale. Marxists of this ilk included Enrico Ferri, Guglielmo Ferrero, Achille Loria, Paolo Orano, Benito Mussolini...[4]

In this introduction, Gramsci explicitly challenged the party conceptions exposed in the *Theses* on the tactics of the Congress of Rome:

> [In the theses] centralization and unity were understood too mechanically: the central committee and the executive committee amounted to the entire party, instead of representing and leading it. Had this conception been applied permanently, the party would have lost its distinctive political features and become, at best, an army (and a bourgeois kind of army), losing its power of attraction and being separated from the masses. In order for the party to live and be in contact with the masses, every member must be an active political element, a leader. [...] Ideological mass preparation is thus a necessity of the revolutionary struggle, and one of the indispensable conditions for victory.[5]

For Gramsci, the task of building factory cells was an occasion for the self-education of the working class; the cells, as a simple organizational instrument, became the main organ in the education of the "organic intellectuals" of the working class, being able to contribute to autonomy in the face of the external bourgeois contribution:

> The cell turns every member of the party into an active militant, giving each one practical and systematic work. Through this work, a new class of proletarian leaders is created, linked to the factory, controlled by their fellow workers, so that they cannot turn into officials and mandarins, a phenomenon that occurs on a large scale in all parties that have maintained the old structure of the socialist parties.[6]

In his report to the meeting of the Political Committee for the congress, Gramsci compared the points of divergence between "the center of the party" and the "extreme left" on three levels of relationship: between the party's ruling group and other members; between the ruling group and the working class; between the working class and the rest of the subaltern classes:

[4] Idem, "Introduzione al primo corso della scuola interna di Partito", em *La costruzione del Partito Comunista 1923–1926* (Turin, Einaudi, 1978), 50–1.
[5] Ibid., 56–7.
[6] Ibid.

Our position derives from the conclusion that maximum emphasis should be placed on the fact that the party is united with the class not only by ideological ties, but also by physical ones. [...] According to the extreme left, the process of party establishment is synthetic; for us, it is a process of historical and political nature, closely linked to the development of capitalist society. This difference in understanding leads to a distinct determination of the roles and tasks of the party. Due to the misconceptions of the extreme left, all the work that the party must do to raise the political level of the masses, to convince them and bring them to the terrain of the revolutionary class struggle has been depreciated and hindered due to the initial separation that has been created between the party and the working class.[7]

The theoretical question of organization in cells highlighted the need for "physical links" between party and class as a whole, while in the affirmation of a necessary ruling "guardianship" by the specialized group Bordiga presented the risk of corporatism among the workers as a central problem. In Gramsci's view, this showed a paternalistic conception that substantially depreciated the leadership capacity of the working class by reducing it to a minor subject, incapable of political self-determination.

In the debate that preceded the Congress of Lyon, and to a greater extent in the event itself, Gramsci presented the theory on the leftist party in continuity with the entire intellectual history of Italy, with Croce's philosophy and the elitist and oligarchic tradition of idealistic and liberal political philosophy. Such concept would later be revisited in the *Notebooks*, in which Gramsci equated the intellectual behavior of Bordiga's "pure intellectual" with that of Croce:

What matters to Croce is that intellectuals do not descend to the level of the mass, that they understand that one thing is ideology, a practical instrument for ruling, and another thing is philosophy and religion, which should not be prostituted in the consciousness of the same priests. Intellectuals must be rulers, not those ruled, producers of ideologies to rule others, not charlatans who allow themselves to be poisoned and bitten by their own vipers. [...] The position of "pure intellectual" is a truly deteriorated form of "Jacobinism" and, in this sense, albeit different in stature, Amadeo can be compared to Croce.[8]

---

[7] Ibid., 482.
[8] Antonio Gramsci, *Quaderni del carcere* (Turin, Einaudi, 1975), 1.213.

Upon addressing the relationship between the working class and the rest of those exploited and making it the basis of the congressional theses, Gramsci emphasized the strategic value that Lenin attributed to the peasant question and the policy of alliances.[9] In Lenin's view, if the aspiration was not only to start a revolution, but above all to win it and hold onto power, it was necessary to fully prepare for the revolution, "to win over the great masses", "to gain the sympathy of the masses". "To attract to us not only the majority of the working class, but also the majority of the working and exploited population of the fields".[10]

This was a fundamental theme for a country like Italy, where the proletariat was a minority with no national character. More precisely, Gramsci tried to contextualize for Italy the great theme debated between the Third and Fourth Congress of the Communist International. As has already been thoroughly explained, on that occasion, noticing the international difficulties and the complexity of the revolutionary processes in the West, Lenin and the Comintern Executive launched the slogan of winning over the majority of the subaltern classes and of the unity of the working class through the tactic of the "united front", which is essential for the definition of the categories of hegemony in Gramsci.

In the Congress of Lyon, three kinds of problem were presented that eventually became the backbone of the famous essay of 1926 on the peculiar condition of the South in the Italian national balance: the southern question, understood as the peasant question; the theme of the political party of the peasant class; and the Vatican's reactionary role.

The attitude toward fascism in the *Theses of Rome* and more broadly Bordiga's theoretical approach, his tendency to underestimate the difference between the democratic and reactionary framework, were for Gramsci clear examples of a wrong way of conceiving the tactics. As already mentioned in the beginning of this chapter, the *Theses of Lyon* also marked a complete change in the analysis of Italian society, anticipating multiple aspects of Gramsci's prison thinking and the more mature assessment of the PCd'I ruling group that was consolidating in the mid-1930s.

In the period of crisis that followed the crime against Matteotti, it was not enough to conduct a campaign of ideological criticism of the regime and of the opposition and to be limited to a propaganda capable only of treating the two subjects equally; it was necessary to galvanize the

---

[9] Vladímir Ilitch Lènin, *Opere complete* (Rome, Editori Riuniti, 1955–1970), v. 32, 457.
[10] Idem, *Sul movimento operaio italiano* (Rome, Editori Riuniti, 1970), 233.

opposition into overthrowing fascism as the initial premise of any other action of the communists. The *Theses* clearly refuted any simplistic equivalence between the democratic framework and fascism, such as the ideas supported by Bordiga and defended in the Comintern between 1928 and 1930. Incidentally, such clear words would only be found after the Seventh Congress of the Communist International of 1935:

> It is absurd to say that there is no difference between a democratic situation and a reactionary situation and that in a democratic situation it is more difficult to work to win over the masses. The truth is that today, in a reactionary situation, one struggles to organize the party, while in a democratic situation one would struggle to organize the insurrection.[11]

When fascism was emerging and developing, according to Gramsci, the PCd'I simply considered it a "fighting organ of the bourgeoisie", not a social movement. Hence, the PCd'I was not positioned to control its advance and oppose its rise to power through appropriate political action; that also led it to work against the "Arditi del Popolo",[12] a mass movement coming from below that the PCd'I should have helped and eventually led.

The very goal of defeating fascism was related to the problem of the hegemony of the working class before the peasant masses:

> The Italian situation is characterized by the fact that the bourgeoisie is organically weaker than in other countries and remains in power only as long as it manages to control and dominate the peasants. The proletariat must fight to remove the peasants from the influence of the bourgeoisie and put them under its political direction. This is the central point of the political problems that the party is expected to solve in the near future.[13]

According to the *Theses*, the predominant element of Italian society was a particular form of capitalism combining an industrialism that was still fragile and unable to absorb the majority of the population and an agriculture that still constituted the economic base of the country, which was

---

[11] Antonio Gramsci, *La costruzione del Partito Comunista*, cit., 487.

[12] Literally, "the daring of the people", an anti-fascist organization inspired by unions, created in Italy in 1921 by a group of veterans of the First World War aiming to stand up for the workers. *Ardito* he was the soldier of the Italian combat group in the First World War.

[13] Antonio Gramsci, *La costruzione del Partito Comunista*, cit., 487.

marked by the predominance of poor strata (agricultural wage earners, itinerant rural workers) that were very close to the conditions of the proletariat and therefore potentially sensitive to its influence.

Between the two ruling classes—industrial and agrarian—an extensive petty and middle urban bourgeoisie was a connecting element. The feebleness of the mode of production in Italy—devoid of raw materials—pushed industry to various forms of economic conciliation with large landowners, which were based on a "solidarity of interests between privileged strata to the detriment of the more general productive requirements". The very process of *Risorgimento* reflected this feebleness because the national state was constructed thanks to the exploitation of particular factors of international politics, and its consolidation necessitated the social conciliation that rendered inoperative, in Italy, the economic struggle between industrialists and landowners and the change of the ruling group, which was typical of other capitalist countries. This conciliation based on parasitic exploitation by the ruling classes caused a polarization between the accumulation of immense wealth in restricted social groups and the extreme poverty of the rest of the population, leading to trade balance deficit and the limitation of economic development to certain areas of the country, which made it difficult to modernize the country's economic system in a harmonious and balanced way considering national characteristics.

Both the disaster at the beginning of the First World War and the very advent of fascism are analyzed in the *Theses* in light of this feebleness originating in Italy, which anticipates a fundamental interpretative pattern in the reflections in the *Notebooks* concerning the *Risorgimento*. The conciliation between industrialists and landowners attributed to the working masses of the *Mezzogiorno* the same position of the colonial populations; in this conciliation, the industrialized North was like the capitalist mother country for the colony; the ruling classes of the South (large landowners and the middle bourgeoisie) performed the same role as the social categories of the colonies allied with the colonizers to keep the mass of the people subject to exploitation. However, from a historical perspective, this system of conciliation proved ineffective because it became an obstacle to the development of the industrial and agricultural economy. At various times, this led to critical levels of struggle between the classes and, therefore, to increasingly intense and authoritarian pressure of the state on the masses.

The period of greatest weakness of the Italian state was identified by Gramsci in the 1870s–1890s, mainly due to the Vatican's action as a catalyst for the anti-state reactionary bloc consisting of members of the aristocracy, landowners, rural populations that owned land, and the parishes. The Vatican had stated its intention to act on two fronts: on the one hand, explicitly against the unitary and liberal bourgeois state; on the other, trying to constitute, through the peasants, a kind of reserve army to bar the advance of the socialist workers' movement.

The unstable balance of the new state, a theme present in the *Theses*, is also one of the fundamental lines of inquiry in the *Prison Notebooks*. We can think of the notes in which Gramsci delves into the rhetorical formula (idealized by the clerics) that tended to contrast a real Italy, composed of the Catholic majority averse to the new unitary state, and a legal Italy consisting of a minority of ardent patriots devoted to the national cause and the liberal ideology. Although the formula arose in a political editorial context of a "foolish defamatory pamphlet from the sacristy", it was, for Gramsci, very effective from the point of view of controversy because it was a clear sign of the existing separation between the state and civil society. Obviously, the whole of civil society could not be understood as having a clerical feature because it was largely heterogeneous and shapeless. And it was precisely because of this disaggregated nature that the state had no difficulty in controlling it, overcoming the contradictions and conflicts that erupted sporadically and locally, with no coordination at the national level or tendency toward some end.

Thus, besides an objective situation of separation between state and society, clericalism itself could not be considered a real expression of civil society, over which it demonstrated difficulty in exercising real and effective control. The Church actually feared the very masses of people it controlled with the promise of salvation. In Gramsci's view, even the formula of *not expedit*[14] was a display of this dread and political incapacity: after all, it foreshadowed an attempt to boycott the new state that turned out to be objectively subversive. That explains why, with the crisis of the end of the century and the events of 1898, the state reacted both against the first initiatives of socialist organization and against clerical organizations. The Vatican's abandonment of the policy expressed by the formula "neither

---

[14] With the so-called *not expedit*, in 1868, Pope Pius X declared that Italian Catholics should not participate in the elections of the Kingdom of Italy. This provision formally took effect until the 1919 elections. However, five years earlier, a pact was made between the liberal Giovanni Giolitti and the Catholic Ottorino Gentiloni to stop the parliamentary advance of the Socialist Party, which made it possible for the faithful to participate in the elections of 1913.

voters, nor elected officials", which led first to the Gentiloni Pact and then to the birth of the Popular Party, was a result of the realization of that failure.

Gramsci saw an actual split between the real country and the legal country in the facts that divided Italy at the beginning of the Matteotti crisis and led to the *most fascist laws*, when this split was overcome through the suppression of political parties and of individual and collective freedoms and the integration of civil society into a single political organization that made state and party coincide.

The period from 1890 to 1900 was the first in which the bourgeoisie was faced with the problem of organizing dictatorship itself. It was a period marked by a series of protectionist political and legislative interventions—favoring large industrial production (particularly the mechanical industry) and agriculture based on large estates (grains, rice, corn)—which led to the denunciation of trade treaties with France and Italy's falling within the orbit of the Triple Alliance led by Germany. In this phase, the alliance between industrialists and landowners was subsequently forged, subtracting the rural strata from the control of the Vatican in an antiunitarian perspective.

The progress of the workers' organizations and the rebellion of the peasant masses therefore correspond to the alignment of the agroindustrial bloc.

But it is in the definition of fascism that the *Theses* reach their highest level of analysis and conceptualization, introducing a new interpretative model of the phenomenon that would later gain widespread acceptance in historiography, and not only within the Marxist field.

Fascism totally fit into the traditional framework of the Italian ruling classes, taking the form of armed reaction with the precise goal of disaggregating the ranks of the organizations of the subaltern classes and thus ensuring the supremacy of the ruling classes. For this reason, it was favored and indistinctly protected by all the old ruling groups, among which it was above all the large landowners who financed and supported the fascist squads against the peasant movement. The social basis of fascism, however, was composed of the urban petty bourgeoisie and the new agrarian bourgeoisie.

Fascism achieved ideological and organizational unity in the paramilitary organizations that inherited the tradition of arditism and applied it to the guerrilla against the workers' organizations. Through the *Theses*, fascism put into practice its plan to conquer the state with a "mentality of

nascent capitalism" that could provide nonconformist ideological homogeneity to the petty bourgeoisie in opposition to the old ruling groups and
socialism.

> In content, fascism changes the program of conservation and reaction that
> had always dominated Italian politics only through a distinct way of conceiv-
> ing the process of unification of reactionary forces. The tactics of agree-
> ments and concessions is contrasted with the purpose of achieving an organic
> unity of all the forces of the bourgeoisie in a single political organization
> under the control of a single central that should also rule the party, the gov-
> ernment and the state. This purpose corresponds to the will to strongly
> resist any revolutionary attack, which allows fascism to gain the adherence of
> the most decidedly reactionary part of the industrial and agrarian
> bourgeoisie.[15]

Nonetheless, the fascist method of defense of order, property and the
state did not immediately and completely lead to this level of centralization of the bourgeoisie with the seizure of power. Thus, the political and
economic translation of its purposes produced various forms of resistance
within the ruling classes themselves. The two traditional inclinations of the
Italian liberal bourgeoisie—the one that dated back to Giolittism and the
one that related to the *Corriere della Sera* [newspaper]—were not completely absorbed or subdued after Mussolini's seizure of power. This
explains the struggle against the remaining groups of the bourgeoisie and
against Freemasonry, that is, against its main center of attraction and organization that was at the base of the state.

In the economic field, fascism worked completely in favor of large
industrial and agrarian oligarchies, neglecting the aspirations of its own
social base, the petty bourgeoisie, which hoped to achieve a breakthrough
in social and economic conditions with it. That occurred in terms of trade
policies, with the increase in customs protectionism; in the financial sector,
with the centralization of the credit system for the benefit of the big industry; and in the production sector, with the increase in working hours and
the decrease in wages. But the real goal of fascism was related to foreign
policy and its imperialist aspirations; in this regard, the *Theses* put forward
an idea that would come to fruition fourteen years later.

---

[15] Antonio Gramsci, *La costruzione del Partito Comunista*, cit., 495.

The crowning of all ideological propaganda, of the political and economic action of fascism is its inclination toward imperialism. This inclination is the expression of the need felt by the industrial and agrarian ruling classes to find, outside the national field, the elements for the resolution of the political crisis of Italian society. These are the seeds of a war that will apparently be waged for Italian expansion, but in which fascist Italy will actually be an instrument in the hands of an imperialist group that seeks world domination.[16]

The instruction provided by the Congress of the International for building the mass parties rooted in workplaces through factory cells (the so-called Bolshevization) was resumed and developed by the old ordinovist group by revisiting the themes that emerged in the "red biennium", from the experience of the council movement, which was explicitly mentioned in the *Theses*:

The practice of the factory movement (1919–1920) demonstrated that only an organization adhering to the place and system of production allows the establishment of contact between the upper and lower strata of the working mass and the creation of bonds of solidarity that nip in the bud any phenomenon related to the formation of a working aristocracy. Organization by cells leads to the formation, within the party, of a vast stratum of organizational members (cell secretaries, members of cell committees, etc.), who are part of the mass and keep having directive roles in it, unlike the territorial section secretaries, who were necessarily elements detached from the working masses.[17]

In this definition, the theme of the relationship between rulers and those ruled, between intellectuals and the mass, according to the classical terms of Gramscian thought, is fully and completely developed. In Gramsci's view, in the internal clash with the PCd'I, the distinction between the two different ways of understanding the revolution was clear: on one side, the masses were considered mass of maneuver, an instrument of the revolution; on the other, they were understood as the main, conscious subject of the revolution. In the *Notebooks*, this theme was largely developed from reflections on the political party, the instrument by which the relationship of representation should overcome its condition of passive delegation, which is characteristic of bourgeois society. In reality, the

[16] Ibid., 497.
[17] Ibid., 505.

parties and the representations ended up becoming a space for oligarchic occupation and management of the centers of power and for the exclusive perpetuation of their directive functions. In Gramsci's view, the relationship between rulers and those ruled derives from the division of labor, the distinction between intellectual and manual functions. For him, "every man is a philosopher"; it is technical organization that makes him ruled and no longer a ruler. Therefore, the main object of a party consists in preparing leaders, and its starting point must lie in not considering that distinction natural and immutable.

Thus, the problem of the absence of an organic relationship of representation in politics concerned not only the parties of the elite in a liberal tradition, in which the leadership role was exercised unilaterally by men of culture, but also the parties of the workers' movement. If, in a party, the only role of the masses is that of military loyalty to the ruling groups, the dualistic relationship is exactly the same.

The *Theses of Lyon* represent an important watershed, surely the highest point of connection between Gramsci's theoretical perspective and political direction. In Gramsci's biography, they represent a point of continuity between the battles before 1926 and the prison reflections, the most powerful testimony to how impossible it is to separate the political and militant Gramsci from the Gramsci that is "disinterested" or a "man of culture". The *Theses of Lyon* are the confirmation of the "new course" of the PCI and, within the party, of the leading group led by Gramsci, which emerged around *L'Ordine Nuovo* in the tumultuous years of the post-war period; in this group, the new perspective and the political and intellectual path of the old Turin group are reconciled. The Lyon turn is the essential premise to understand the historical role assumed by the PCI both in the Resistance and in the post-liberation phase; it is the most meaningful antecedent of the profound change in the initiative of the communists between the Seventh Congress and the "turn of Salerno" of 1944.

PART III

The Theoretician

CHAPTER 15

From Sardinia's Contradictions to the Southern Question

The southern question is systematically present throughout Gramsci's political thinking and analysis of Italian society, a problematic issue involving the contradictions of the national unification process and the distorted modality of economic and social development of the country. Going deep into the topic, with reflections that took years, Gramsci was able to define some of his most important and most studied categories worldwide, such as hegemony, intellectuals and subaltern groups, today considered essential to decipher international relations of colonial rule.

As stated in Part One, Gramsci's thought is based on the centrality of this problem, being deeply marked by his direct knowledge of distorted forms of modernization and of the colonial submission of his land, Sardinia. The nineteenth century was emblematic of the history of Italy, not only due to the political processes that prepared and led to an event as complex and difficult as the Unification but also because this century saw significant dialectical tensions (economic-social, political-institutional, cultural ones) related to modernization, which would later have important consequences for the history of the twentieth century itself, starting with the history of Sardinia. In the course of the nineteenth century, there were reform processes that, regardless of the assessment of their merits and of the results obtained, meant an epic moment of changes regarding

G. Fresu, *Antonio Gramsci*, Marx, Engels, and Marxisms, https://doi.org/10.1007/978-3-031-15610-6_15

modernization.[1] The problem of the constitution of an original capital and of a consequent bourgeoisie with modern characteristics, the changes in the land regime and in the modalities of production and accumulation in the fields, the issue of the institutional arrangements of the island in relation to the very complex changes in the peninsula, these are all topics of fundamental historical importance that, in the past, were the object of in-depth monographs in the economic, legal and historical fields.[2] In Sardinia, the town-country dialectic tradition acquires a particular connotation as a cross-dialectic between the urban bourgeoisie and pastoral communities and, at the same time, between sedentary and nomadic agriculture. All economic, cultural and political problems related to the reforms on "perfect property"[3] and the subversion of the old feudal regime, as well as the most critical phases of social discomfort manifested in the waves of banditry, are directly associated with this dialectic. This is confirmed by the numerous research and analysis materials related to the several parliamentary investigations carried out in Sardinia after an investigation, which was particularly important, led by Agostino Depretis between 1868 and 1871,[4] and the documents of the Kingdom of Sardinia dating back to the years of reform in the land regime kept in the State Archive of Turin and Cagliari. The attempts at reform in the institutional, economic and social field and their social repercussions—starting with the measures that produce the perfect fusion in the constitutional framework

---

[1] The insights on this topic derive from my study on social banditry and the transformations that occurred in Sardinia in the nineteenth century. Part of this study resulted in a monograph, and many of the considerations present in this chapter derive from it. Gianni Fresu, *La prima bardana. Modernizzazione e conflitto nella Sardegna dell'Ottocento* (Cagliari, Cuec, 2011), 115–25.

[2] Among so many, we highlight the works by Italo Birocchi: "Considerazioni sulla privatizzazione della terra in Sardegna dopo le leggi abolitive del feudalesimo", *Archivio Sardo del Movimento Operaio, Contadino e Autonomistico*, n. 11/13, 1980; *Per la storia della proprietà perfetta in Sardegna. Provvedimenti normativi, orientamenti di governo e ruolo delle forze sociali dal 1839 al 1851* (Milan, Giuffrè, 1982); "La questione autonomistica dalla 'fusione perfetta' al primo dopoguerra", in *La Sardegna* (Turin, Einaudi, 1998); "Il *Regnum Sardiniae* dalla cessione ai Savoia alla 'fusione perfetta'", in *Storia dei Sardi e della Sardegna. L'Età contemporanea. Dal governo Piemontese agli anni Sessanta del nostro secolo* (Milan, Jaca Book, 1990).

[3] The privatization of the land that had been subject to common civic uses and the rules of the feudal regime.

[4] Francesco Manconi (org.), *Le inchieste parlamentari sulla Sardegna dell'Ottocento. L'Inchiesta Depretis* (Cagliari, Edizioni della Torre, 1984).

of the Albertine Statute—allow us to have an overview of the history of the ruling and subaltern classes in Sardinia.

In the same years when the phenomenon of crime in the South acquired mass connotation, social banditry in Sardinia reached extreme levels of intensity. The particularity and, if we wish, the element of greatest scientific interest, is that in Sardinia there was an anticipation of some essential features in the forms of hegemony and domination of the Savoy governments, which would also end up characterizing the subsequent takeover of the southern regions after Unification. The administrative and modern conception of the Piedmontese state, permeated by physiocratic illustration and confidence in the possibilities of normative transition to modernity, revealed, in the clash with Sardinia's reality, a certain political rigidity that, even in the liberal era, prevented the deep understanding of the true causes of its discomfort. Everything integrated the same practices of military confrontation and legislative intervention aimed at erasing the anomalies of Sardinia's pastoral civilization with a land regime that threatened its survival. "The Piedmontese followed a more specific and rigorous colonization plan than the Spanish, a project that required careful control over the entire territory of the island."[5] The state of latent anarchy, marked among other things by four hundred murders a year, in a modest population,[6] was intolerable even for the Piedmontese ruling classes, and suddenly the illusory intention to militarily conquer the zone of discomfort and normalize it definitively was expressed. This strategy was pursued and systematically employed since the very harsh repressive expeditions between 1735 and 1738. Modern Sardinian banditry, with its known and constant characteristics until relatively recent times, exploded due to the clash between this intention and the resistance that it met. The contemporary history of Sardinia shows its own historical paradigm in the face of the advent of the modern state and the transition processes of the modes of production, in a situation therefore marked by political contradictions and by the weakness of the new social classes in the process of consolidation.[7]

In Antonio Gramsci's view, the agrarian class remained the central issue in the political processes between the eighteenth and nineteenth centuries,

---

[5] Manlio Brigaglia, *Sardegna perché banditi* (Milan, Carte Segrete, 1971), 60.

[6] In the middle of the twentieth century, Sardinia had 600,000 inhabitants. Today it has 1.5 million inhabitants. It is the region with the lowest population density in Italy.

[7] Eric J. Hobsbawm, *I banditi. Il banditismo sociale nell'età moderna* (Turin, Einaudi, 2002), 107.

and the lack of solution in a progressive sense[8] left a very specific mark even on the history of Italian *Risorgimento*:

> Any shaping of popular national collective will is impossible if the large masses of peasants do not simultaneously enter political life. [...] The whole history from 1815 onwards shows the effort of the traditional classes to prevent the shaping of a collective will of this kind, to keep "economic-corporate" power in an international system of passive balance.[9]

The process of fusion and absorption involving Sardinia and Piedmont also took place through a "passive balance", which would later have a negative weight in Sardinian ruling classes' bargaining power and ability to affect the national balance; however, it brought along the consolidation of a conservative sociopolitical bloc that would last long. Regardless of value judgments, this remains the main political fact.[10]

As Birocchi—perhaps the scholar who dealt with these issues with greatest scientific rigor and method—put it well, "the triumph of property in Sardinia coincided with the emergence of a bourgeoisie not only lacking the universalist horizons that led it to the leadership of the reform movement elsewhere, but also related to clientelist mentalities and practices arising from extremely narrow interests".[11]

In the last thirty years of the nineteenth century, therefore also in Gramsci's childhood, Sardinia was hit by a series of contradictory signs: new aspects of economic and social modernization that coexisted with extreme backwardness and a growing state of misery in the vast majority of its population. For several reasons—such as excessive division of property, the excessive weight of land taxes, lack of capital for investments, insufficient credit—the reforms did not lead to the expected changes in terms of modernization of agricultural production, lifestyles and social relations. However, with its unresolved contradictions, Sardinia was moving toward a capitalist transformation in its social relations and toward its

---

[8] In Gramscian terminology the use of "progressive"—which should not be referred to as "progressist"—refers to the changes that lead not only to modernization, but also to democratization: the expansion of the social base of the state, the inclusion of previously excluded social strata as citizens.

[9] Antonio Gramsci, *Quaderni del carcere* (Turin, Einaudi, 1977), 1560.

[10] Gianni Fresu, *La prima bardana*, cit., 109–137.

[11] Italo Birocchi, *Per la storia della proprietà perfetta in Sardegna*, cit., 446–7.

insertion into a broader circuit of the national and European market, and that also happened with the expulsion of increasingly larger segments of the population engaged in rural activities, mainly small landowners, from their land. That happened without Piedmontese rule, in the first place, and the unification of Italy, subsequently, having resolved the contradictions or minimally changed the structural backwardness of the economy.

The terms of this uneven development and Sardinia's intrinsic weakness during the transition to modernity would persist even in the new century. Paradoxically, one of the strongest signs of unity that led Sardinia to be recognized as an integral part of national reality is related not to the history of the ruling classes, but to that of its exploited masses: the launching of the first national general strike in the history of Italy, in 1904, ensued by the Buggerru massacre.[12] In 1919, in an article entitled "I dolori della Sardegna" [The pains of Sardinia], Antonio Gramsci expressed himself in these terms:

> Why should it be forbidden for *L'Avanti!* to recall that the administrative councils of the Sardinian railways and of some mining companies were located in Turin? [...] Why should not we remember that the miners of Sardinia receive starvation wages while the shareholders in Turin keep their portfolios with dividends reaped with the blood of the miners of Sardinia, who often live on roots so as not to starve to death? Why should it be forbidden to recall that two thirds of the inhabitants of Sardinia walk barefoot in winter and summer because the price of fur is raised to prohibitive levels by the protectionist taxes that enrich leather industrialists in Turin, one of whom is president of the Chamber of Commerce? Why is it forbidden to recall that in the Italian state, in Sardinia, peasants, shepherds and artisans are treated worse than the colony of Eritrea since the state "invests" in Eritrea while it explores Sardinia, charging it imperial taxes?[13]

---

[12] The massacre in Buggerru (a small town in southern Sardinia) is one of the most notorious episodes in the history of class struggle in Italy. It was the repression of the army, which during the strike of September 4, 1904 shot at miners who demonstrated for a reduction in the levels of exploitation, increasing wages and labor protection measures in the mines. This event led to the first general strike called by the union in the history of Italy.

[13] Antonio Gramsci, "I dolori della Sardegna", Piedmontese edition of *L'Avanti!*, 16 abr. 1919, in *Scritti 1915–1925* (Milan, Moizzi, 1976), 177.

In his study *Rapporti di produzione e cultura subalterna* [Relations of production and subaltern culture], on a concrete socioeconomic system such as Sardinia's rural system, the anthropologist Giulio Angioni analyzed the profound differences between the subaltern strata and the corresponding levels of social consciousness in relation to the different forms of appropriation of wealth. This social stratification, with the consequent differentiation of "disorganized ideologies or patched pieces of ideologies", is subject to nonlinear forms of exploitation and domination according to modalities that, in many cases, can be equated with "pre-capitalist or non-capitalist" realities.

> In areas of unevenness, such as the so-called "internal zones" of Sardinia, agricultural and pastoral communities may be the object of such exploitation and subjected to such a repressive regime that some have compared these situations to a process of colonial or semi-colonial plunder, while in other cases we can speak of the system's easy absorption and "functionalization" of local particularities and possible resistance.[14]

In Angioni's view, the notion of underdevelopment and backwardness must be added to that of dependence and subordination, which is particularly important in a peripheral region of Europe such as Sardinia, which has remained until relatively recent times outside the processes of industrialization. The economic backwardness and the weak development of productive forces certainly influenced the "primordial and gelatinous" configuration of civil society, the limited expansion of this set of private initiatives that, in Gramsci's view, create the apparatus of political and cultural hegemony of the ruling classes. According to Angioni, the transformation of the land regime during the nineteenth century, in a way that was "more functional for the development of the continental regions of the Kingdom", constitutes an "early case of internal colonialism" that, in several aspects, anticipates the characteristics of the uneven development typical of the southern question after Unification:

---

[14] Giulio Angioni, *Relations of production and subordinate culture. Contadini in Sardegna* (Cagliari, Edes, 1982), 55–6.

With some precision, it can be said that Sardinia was, in a way, a small test of the process of discrimination that developed macroscopically later in the context of the Italian national state, which was run by the industrial and financial bourgeoisie of the northern regions and, secondarily, by the landowners and other classes of parasites of the South.[15]

Understanding Gramsci in depth without being aware of how such background influenced him seems unrealistic or, at the very least, partial. It was not only in adulthood that Gramsci developed the vision of class conflict and revolution as the objectification of a social bloc that brought together the claims of the northern working class and those of the subaltern groups of the *Mezzogiorno*. As we mentioned at the beginning of this volume, due to its importance, in Gramsci the peasant question did not arise only from the reading of Lenin, but had its roots in the concreteness of Sardinian social development, in the set of life experiences and the careful observation of his world, with all its contradictions. This matrix reemerged in the years of socialist militancy, when the centrality of the unequal relations of development between the North and the South in the defense of passive national social balances became increasingly clear to Gramsci.

In an article of April 1916, Gramsci found in the southern question a mix of paradigmatic contradictions in the limits of the national unification process, with the choice for the centralist model, which was inadequate for Italian reality and significantly different from what Cavour had in mind. After more than a thousand years, two parts of the peninsula, until then characterized by completely different forms of historical, economic and even institutional development, were reunified. "Brutal centralization", wrote young Gramsci, conceived the South as a colonial market of the North, which misjudged or ignored the real needs of the *Mezzogiorno*. The only alternative to absolute misery was found in the biblical exodus of mass emigration, while the reaction to this state of affairs was manifested in the episodic and inorganic forms of peasant rebellion or banditry. In Gramsci's view, protectionism was the instrument that made the southern question organic and structural; not by chance, in 1913 the still very young Gramsci joined the Antiprotectionist League of Sardinia of Attilio

[15] Ibid., 70.

Deffenu,[16] a figure that greatly influenced him, but who is still little known among his scholars. Protectionism was the bargaining chip of the histori-cal bloc that united the northern industrial bourgeoisie and the parasitic classes of southern estates, whose bills were paid by the southern grass roots:

> Industrial protectionism raised the cost of living of the Calabrian peasant, and agricultural protectionism, useless for producers, [...] did not manage to restore the balance. The foreign policy of the last thirty years has ren-dered the benefits of emigration almost worthless. The Eritrean wars in Libya led to the provision of internal loans, which absorbed emigrants' sav-ings. It is customary to speak of a lack of initiative among the southerners. That's an unfair charge. The fact is that capital always looks for the safest and most profitable forms of employment, and the government offered the five-year allowances very insistently. In places where a factory already exists, it continues to develop in order to save, but in places where every form of capitalism is uncertain and random, hard-earned savings accumulated with effort are not trusting and will seek investment where there is tangible profit. Thus, large estates, which at some time tended to be divided among the returning rich Americans, will continue to exist for a while thanks to the scourge of the Italian economy, while the industrial enterprises of the North find in war a source of huge profits, and the entire national productive potential for the war industry is even more limited to Piedmont, Lombardy,

---

[16] One of the most representative figures of political renewal in the new century was Attilio Deffenu, born in Nuoro in 1890, and killed in the Battle of the Piave River on June 16, 1918, at the age of only twenty-seven. The son of the president of the workers' society of Nuoro (Giuseppe), he had the opportunity to live these years intensely and provide a new perspective to Sardinia's traditional claims. While studying law in Pisa, Deffenu came into contact with socialists and anarchists, associating with the orientations of intellectuals such as Georges Sorel and trade unionists such as Arturo Labriola. He collaborated with the anar-chist magazine *Il Pensiero* and with *Il Giornale d' Italia* and founded, in 1914, the magazine *Sardenha*. Deffenu was especially associated with the southern thought of Gaetano Salvemini; in this sense, he joined the anti-protectionist movement, wrote a manifesto about it and published, in his magazine, a really novel and profound debate, even though he devoted only four issues of the publication to *The Sardinian question*. Instead of focusing on the mistakes and indifference of national policy toward Sardinia, a topic that is certainly not neglected, Deffenu preferred to concretely analyze the economic and social themes of uneven develop-ment, proposing the establishment of a united front of the (southern) regions that suffered the most from the unbalanced process of building the national state and identifying the true origin of all its evils in the clientelism and the parasitic nature of the ruling classes in Sardinia.

Emilia and Liguria, which makes the little life that existed in the southern regions disappear.[17]

In an article published on July 7 of the same year, in the Piedmontese edition of *L'Avanti!*, Gramsci returned to this theme. In Italy, protectionism was consolidated by skillfully exploiting the antagonistic interests of the city and the countryside, thus contrasting one part of the country with the other and ensuring the consensus of the regionally established ruling classes. In these dynamics, the price of wheat became a way to ensure the survival of unproductive and parasitic sectors, rather than being an instrument for favoring rural development.

> The protectionist wheat tax led many from the countryside to sow on semi-sterile lands, with the guarantee of a tiny profit artificially guaranteed by the state, at the usual ratio of the increase in national products. The monopoly situation created by the war, which raised wheat prices from 29 francs to more than 40 francs, serves to create the illusion that, even sowing in the sand, there is always enough to be earned. However, the farmers of the Padana Plains, who did not sow in the sand, but in the fertile and irrigated lands of Lombardy and Emilia in particular, made a tremendous profit, which were matched only by the industrial super-profits of war. It is very convenient for these gentlemen to exploit the fait accompli of harvesting wheat from unproductive lands to insinuate that the maximum price must be set to ensure poor farmers a fair income, but at the expense of taking seemingly unpleasant and hateful attitudes, it is the proletariat, especially in cities, that must react against these biased campaigns.[18]

Still under the impact of what had occurred in Russia in 1917, Gramsci returned to this theme in *L'Ordine Nuovo* on August 2, 1919, advancing the idea of an alliance between workers and peasants to overcome the antagonistic relationship between the city and the countryside. In the article, Gramsci described the process of concentration and centralization from a monopolistic perspective during the war and the definitive triumph of the imperialist form of development of Italian capitalism. This text is particularly interesting also because it contains the first elements of his

[17] Antonio Gramsci, "Il Mezzogiorno e la guerra", *Il Grido del Popolo*, XXII, n. 610, 1o abr. 1916, *Scritti* (1910–1926), volume I (1910–1916), Istituto della Enciclopedia Italiana, Treccani, Roma, 2019, p. 278–279.

[18] Idem, "Clericali ed agrari", Piedmontese edition of *L'Avanti!*, XX, n. 187, 7 jul. 1916, in *Scritti* (1910–1926), volume I (1910–1916), cit., p. 42–3.

reading of the subaltern groups, which would later be central to the *Notebooks*. The backward and parasitic forms in feudal social relations (in Russia, Italy, France and Spain) correspond to certain psychology, in which economic and political institutions are not historical categories, but natural and, as such, perpetual categories. In reality, according to Gramsci, large estates were perpetuated as such only because they were protected from free competition. Here the mindset of peasants also remained the same as that of the "serf of the soil", who tended to periodically rebel against the "lords" but were unable to think of themselves as part of a class that acts collectively toward a certain end and based on historical consciousness itself. Although these passages of the article do not directly mention Sardinia, they make clear reference to its social reality:

> The psychology of the peasants was, in these conditions, uncontrollable; the real feelings remained hidden, encompassed and mixed up in a system of defense against exploitation, which was purely selfish, had no logical continuity, and was largely characterized by stealth and false servility. The class struggle was mixed up with criminality, blackmail, forest arson, cattle theft, the kidnapping of children and women; with attacks on the municipality: it was a form of elementary terrorism, with no stable and effective consequences. Thus, the psychology of peasants was objectively reduced to a very small amount of primordial feelings, which depended on the social conditions created by the parliamentary democratic state: peasants were completely at the mercy of the owners and their flatterers and corrupt public officials, and the greatest concern in their life was to defend themselves physically from the traps of elementary nature, from abuse and from the vile barbarism of the owners and of government officials. Peasants always lived outside the rule of law, having no legal personality, no moral individuality: they remained anarchic elements, the independent atoms of a chaotic turmoil, only restrained by fear of the police and of the devil. They did not understand organization, they did not understand the state, they did not understand discipline; they were patient and tenacious in the individual effort to pluck scarce and meager fruits from nature, capable of unprecedented sacrifices in family life, impatient and brutally violent in the class struggle, unable to establish a general goal and pursue it with perseverance and systematic struggle.[19]

---

[19] Idem, "Operai e contadini", *L'Ordine Nuovo*, 2 ago. 1919, in *Scritti politici* (Rome, Editori Riuniti, 1969), v. I, 227.

However, according to Gramsci, the war and the sacrifices of the trenches radically changed this psychology, favoring the outburst in the political landscape of the hitherto silent social strata and categories, which became protagonists of the Soviet revolution within a broad social bloc with the working class. It is precisely based on this vision that Gramsci develops an idea of revolution that is not found in the rest of the Italian socialist movement. Such concepts were embraced and developed in a column of *L'Ordine Nuovo* on January 3, 1920, in which, among other things, the notion of the South as an exploitation colony within the passive modalities of national conservative modernization can be found more explicitly.

Even the creation of the *l'Unità* newspaper, which has already been mentioned, was closely linked to this perspective, which became more urgent given the consolidation of fascism as the consolidation of this passive balance between dynamic and parasitic or unproductive parts of Italian society. The newspaper was created in the midst of the crisis of fascist reaction and in a phase of deep crisis of the newly created Communist Party, which was paralyzed by a deeply sectarian conception both of the organization and of the class alliances to be pursued. To oppose it more effectively, the administration of the International approved the proposal to start a "workers' newspaper" capable of consolidating the strategic objective of uniting the Italian subaltern classes, the working masses of the North and the rural working masses of the *Mezzogiorno*.

The famous essay *Alcuni temi della questione meridionale* [Some themes of the southern question] was written in October 1926, a difficult month which, in several respects, was crucial for Antonio Gramsci's life: on the 14th, he wrote the famous letter to the CC of the Russian Communist Party (RCP) criticizing the methods used to eliminate opposition to Stalin, while claiming to identify with the positions supported by the majority. Regarding the debate, Gramsci reflected on issues of merit, clearly distancing himself from the method used by the group led by Stalin and calling on the Soviet party for the necessary unity that was indispensable to the international communist movement, especially in such phase of reflux. As is now well known, Togliatti, then a representative of the party in Moscow, refused to forward the letter, not sharing its content and causing a divergence, about which more than enough has already been said and written, often also irrelevantly, and we do not intend to delve into it. A month earlier, Gramsci had had a major controversy with Alfonso Leonetti, director of *l'Unità*, which gave rise to a series of furious letters[20] between the secretary-general and the editorial staff, until his arrest.

In the essay on the southern question, Gramsci returned to some of the main themes of the *Theses of Lyon* aiming to further explore them and provide them with an organic form, to the point of developing an analysis tool useful for better understanding the historical origins of fascism and finding the most appropriate tools to defeat it. Gramsci was aware of the importance of this task and the weight of his responsibility, so much so that he wrote very slowly, reflecting on the effect of each word and fearing not being able to express his thoughts clearly. According to several statements in this regard, especially Ruggiero Grieco's, already mentioned several times here, this concern led Gramsci to suffer from insomnia and anxiety and prompted him to submit the drafts to the scrutiny of all the comrades who sought him. As we know, the last document before his imprisonment had not been finished because of his arrest, on November 8. After a meeting of the communist parliamentary group to discuss the attitude to be taken toward the agenda in the Chamber of Deputies session, which was scheduled for the following day (reinstatement of the death penalty and revocation of the parliamentary seat of the Aventinian deputies), Gramsci was returning home, on Morgagni Street, at 10.30 pm, when he was arrested. Taken to the Regina Coeli detention center, he was subjected to solitary confinement for seventeen days, before starting the journey through several prison centers in the country.

"La questione meridionale" [The southern question] was recovered in Gramsci's home immediately after his arrest by Camilla Ravera and was published by Palmiro Togliatti on the party magazine, *Lo Stato Operaio*, which was printed in Paris in 1930. On June 6, 1932, Gramsci wrote Tania Schucht a very important letter to situate "the southern question" in its correct dimension and to understand how, after this article, Gramsci embarked on an analysis of "transformism", which was understood not as a simple phenomenon of bad political custom, but as a precise process of formation of the Italian ruling classes through enticement. This phenomenon necessarily implied a redefinition of the notion of state, which should be extended to the different gradations found in political domination in Italian society.

---

[20] For more details, refer to Giuseppe Fiori, *Antonio Gramsci. Vita attraverso le lettere* (Turin, Einaudi, 1994), 121–4.

If you study the entire history of Italy from 1815, you will see that a small leading group managed to methodically absorb into its circle the entire political contingent that the mass movements, of subversive origin, created. From 1860 to 1876, the Action Party was absorbed by monarchy, leaving insignificant remnants that continued to live as the Republican Party, but its significance was more folkloric than historical-political. The phenomenon was called transformism, but it was not an isolated phenomenon; it was an organic process that replaced, in the formation of the ruling class, what had happened in the revolution with Napoleon in France and with Cromwell in England. In fact, even after 1876, the process goes on, molecularly. It grows to a remarkable extent after the war, when it seems that the traditional ruling group is not able to assimilate and guide the new forces arising from the events. But this leading group is more harmful and capable than one might think: the absorption is difficult and heavy, but it nonetheless occurs in several ways and through different methods. Croce's activity is one of these forms and methods; his teaching produces the greatest amount of "gastric juices" suitable for digestive functions. Placed in a historical perspective, of Italian history of course, Croce's diligence appears as the most powerful machine to reconcile the new vital forces that the dominant group has today.[21]

As Gramsci himself made clear in the beginning, the writing of the essay was inspired by the publication, in the *Quarto Stato* magazine, of an article in which Guido Dorso's book *La rivoluzione meridionale* [The southern revolution] was analyzed. Indeed, in this article, a specific accusation was made against the ordinovist group: to have treated the southern question with a demagogic attitude entirely focused on the "magic formula" of the subdivision of large estates among the rural proletarians. Contrary to this thesis, confirmed by an article in *L'Ordine Nuovo* on January 3, 1920, which was quoted in the essay, Gramsci claimed that the communists of Turin should be credited for taking the southern question beyond an indistinct intellectual scope and presenting it to the working class as a central problem for the national politics of the proletariat. The southern question was taken from the monopoly of the great "gurus" of the academic and intellectual world mentioned by the editors of the *Quarto Stato*, and at the same time there was now room for the anti-meridional approach, which verged on racism—typical of the Italian socialist tradition. For the positivist intelligentsia of the PSI, and at an elementary level

[21] Antonio Gramsci, *Lettere dal carcere* (Turin, Einaudi, 1975), 232.

for the masses of the North, the backwardness of the *Mezzogiorno* had no historical reasons of a social and economic nature, but genetic, biological ones.

> The Mezzogiorno is the ball and chain that prevent Italy's civil development from progressing more rapidly; the southerners are biologically inferior beings, semi-barbarians or total barbarians, by natural destiny; if the Mezzogiorno is backward, the fault does not lie in the capitalist system or in any other historical reason, but in Nature, which has made the southerners lazy, inept, criminal and barbaric—only tempering this terrible fate with the purely individual explosion of great geniuses, who are isolated palm trees in an arid, barren desert. [...] the Socialist Party gave its blessing to all the southern literature of the clique of writers in the so-called positive school, such as the [Enrico] Ferris, the [Giuseppe] Sergis, the [Alfredo] Niceforos, the [Paolo] Oranos, who in articles, short stories, novels, impressions and memoirs, in several ways, repeated the same refrain; once again, science was aimed at crushing the poor and exploited, but this time it was dressed in socialist colors and pretended to be the science of the proletariat.[22]

For Gramsci, the Turin communists had already put the southern question in the terms of a "hegemonic" conquest of the northern proletariat in the face of the disaggregated masses of the South:

> The Turin communists had concretely posed the question of the hegemony of the proletariat, that is to say, of the social basis of the dictatorship of the proletariat and of the workers' state. The proletariat can become a ruling and dominant class insofar as it can create a system of class alliances that enables it to mobilize the majority of the working population against capitalism and the bourgeois state, which means, in Italy, in the real class relations existing in Italy, insofar as it can achieve consensus about the great peasant masses.[23]

The specific development conditions of Italian society, its history and tradition made the peasant question take on two typical and peculiar forms: the southern question and the Vatican question. Establishing the historical goal of winning over the majority of those exploited by the proletariat means socially acknowledging these issues and absorbing them,

---

[22] Idem, *La questione meridionale* (Rome, Editori Riuniti, 1991), 9–10.
[23] Ibid., 8.

that is, incorporating the class needs of the peasant masses, both in the immediate demands and in the revolutionary program for the transition.[24]

According to Gramsci, to fulfill its historical role as a "general class", the proletariat would have to take a leading role in relation to the peasants and some semi-proletarian categories of the city, that is, to abandon any residual corporate and trade union mentality. Its members should present themselves and think as members of a class capable of directing both peasants and intellectuals. This was the only way for the proletariat, still a minority of the Italian population, to start a revolutionary process. In the absence of this leadership role, those oscillating social strata, potentially sensitive to radicalization, would remain under the hegemony of the bourgeoisie, helping to reinforce its dominance.

The abandonment of a purely corporate mentality was therefore the condition to perform a leadership role and avoid the absorption of the working class, precisely because of its corporate interests, by the dominant social bloc. Gramsci explained this phenomenon by referring to some concrete historical experiences of the Italian working class. In particular, the proposal for the direct management of the company in a cooperative manner, presented by Fiat to the workers occupying the plant, was interpreted in the light of these considerations. Based on the interests of the category, affected by the imminence of a new economic crisis and the need to safeguard jobs in danger, the reformist leaders of the Socialist Party and the Confederazione Generale del Lavoro (GCL) pronounced in favor of this solution. Gramsci's socialist section intervened, asking the workers to reject it.

A large company like Fiat can only be taken over by the workers if they are determined to enter the system of bourgeois political forces that governs Italy today. The bourgeoisie, even before the war, could no longer govern quietly. [...] After the bloody decade of 1890–1900, the bourgeoisie had to renounce a very exclusive, violent and open dictatorship: the southern peasants and the northern workers rose against it simultaneously, though lacking coordination. In the new century, the ruling class ushered in a new policy of

---

[24] This is probably the passage in which the creative reintroduction of the concepts developed by Lenin at the Third Congress of the Comintern and their application to the concrete Italian reality emerged more clearly. Just as, in that congress, Lenin stressed the need for the hegemonic conquest of most of the exploited, citing as an example the Bolsheviks, who incorporated the agrarian program of the revolutionary socialists and in a short time won the support of the peasants in several Soviets, Gramsci also posed the problem of incorporating the southern and peasant question into the revolutionary program of the Italian communists.

class alliances, of class political blocs, that is, of bourgeois democracy. It had to choose: either a rural democracy, that is, an alliance with the southern peasants, […] or a capitalist-worker industrial bloc, without universal suffrage, in favor of tariff barriers, of the maintenance of a highly centralized state (the expression of bourgeois dominion over the peasants, especially in the Mezzogiorno and the islands), and of a reformist policy on wages and trade union freedoms. It was not by chance that it chose this latter solution; Giolitti embodied bourgeois rule; the Socialist Party became the instrument of Giolitti's policies.[25]

In the course of the 1920s, Giolitti tried again the same strategy, seeking to include the northern working class in his power bloc; achieving this objective would represent the total subordination of the working class and its division:

What will happen if Fiat's workforce accepts the board's proposals? The existing industrial supplies will become debentures, that is to say, the cooperative will have to pay debenture holders a fixed dividend, whatever the turnover may be. The Fiat company will be sliced in every way by credit institutions, which remain in the hands of the bourgeoisie, which is interested in downsizing the workforce at its discretion. The workers will necessarily have to bind themselves to the state, which will help them with the work of workers' deputies, with the subordination of the workers' political party to the dynamics of government. That is Giolitti's plan as fully implemented. The Turin proletariat will no longer exist as an independent class, but only as an appendage of the bourgeois state. Class corporatism will have triumphed, but the proletariat will have lost its position and its function of leader and guide; it will seem privileged to the masses of the poorest workers; it will seem like an explorer to the peasants, just like the bourgeoisie. [26]

Organic inclusion in Giolitti's bloc would have led the disaggregated masses of the south to oppose the working class, rather than favor the establishment of a new social bloc as opposed to the "historical" one. Therefore, the corporate mentality (along with trade unionism) was for Gramsci one of the main vehicles for the bourgeoisie's implementation of its inclusive and transformist processes toward worker aristocracies, making them stand out from all subordinate classes, decapitating the workers'

---

[25] Antonio Gramsci, *La questione meridionale*, cit., 20.
[26] Ibid., 24.

movement and ultimately nullifying any possibility of revolutionary radicalization.

As we will see in more detail, in Gramsci's view, "every social organism has its own optimal principle of defined proportions", and that of the southern agrarian bloc reached its maximum degree of centralization in the ideological field. According to Paggi, in Gramsci's view, this is in keeping with the belief that the whole of the Italian philosophy of idealism is in some way related to the notion of autonomy and of the unbroken continuity of the intellectual class, which ends up establishing a correspondence between the "theoretical concealment of social contrasts, which is typical of this philosophy" and the hegemonic role that it plays, and this happened precisely through the achievement of the highest level of centralization in the field of ideology, by giving intellectuals a special status as a class.[27]

Gramsci defined the *Mezzogiorno* as "a great social disaggregation", in which the peasants are not a coherent group. The peasant masses, who made up the majority of the population of the South, ceased to give "centralized expression" to their aspirations and materialized their permanent leaven through a state of endemic rebellion with no prospects. Above these masses, the domination apparatus of the agrarian bloc was structured, which was able, through its "defined proportions", to permanently maintain the peasant masses in their "amorphous and disaggregated" condition, and that prevented any form of cohesion for this permanent state of fermentation.

> The middle stratum of intellectuals receives the impulses for its political and ideological activity from the peasant base. The large owners in the political field and the great intellectuals in the ideological field centralize and ultimately dominate this whole set of manifestations. Naturally, it is in the ideological sphere that centralization is most effective and precise: Giustino Fortunato and Benedetto Croce thus represent the cornerstones of the southern system and, in a sense, are the two key figures of Italian reaction.[28]

In the southern system, therefore, the role of intermediate intellectuals gained great importance because they created the connection between the large landowner and the farmer. This type of intellectual, coming from the

---

[27] Leonardo Paggi, *Le strategie del potere in Gramsci* (Rome, Editori Riuniti, 1984), 334.
[28] Antonio Gramsci, *La questione meridionale*, cit., 28.

small and middle agrarian bourgeoisie, who generally lived on the rental fees of their rented or shared properties, was a form of survival of old society, which was later replaced in industrial societies by the organizing, technical intellectual, an expert in applied sciences. This parasitic stratification, typical of southern society, was later analyzed in detail in the notes on *Americanism and Fordism* in the *Notebooks*, precisely in order to understand some of the fundamental economic and social reasons of fascism.[29]

In Gramsci's view, fascism and Americanism-Fordism are the two answers, which are profoundly different from the answer that bourgeois civilization provided at the beginning of the twentieth century: the former solution is highly regressive; it is an angry defense of the traditional established order, of the system of privileges and of stratification of the parasitic tenants who, over the course of the centuries, stacked up in European society; on the other hand, the latter is a programmatic perspective on the abandonment of old economic individualism—therefore progressive and rational—although it is also marked by inner contradictions. As Alberto Burgio points out in one of the most interesting works on the Sardinian intellectual, "the American attempt contains, in Gramsci's view, elements of undoubted rationality, potentially capable of determining the overcoming of this old economic individualism whose defense constituted, on the contrary, a constitutive objective of fascism, as we know".[30]

The phenomenon was also studied in relation to the "tendency of the rate of profit to fall", as an attempt to overcome its persistence. Therefore, everything, from the improvement of machines and production techniques, through the construction of a new worker image, to the reduction of waste and the use of by-products, was aimed at moving from a phase of increased costs to another of decreasing costs, but with constant increase in capital.

Americanism-Fordism and its effort to build a programmatic economy characterized the replacement of the old plutocratic classes by creating a new system of accumulation and distribution of financial capital, which was founded immediately on industrial production and purged of all intermediation processes typical of European civilization. Not by chance, in Europe, attempts to introduce these elements of the programmatic

---

[29] Gianni Fresu, "Americanismo e fordismo: l'uomo filosofo e il gorilla ammaestrato", *NAE: Trimestrale di Cultura*, Cuec, Cagliari, n. 21, ano 6, 2008, 54 and 58.

[30] Alberto Burgio, *Gramsci storico. Una lettura dei Quaderni del Carcere* (Bari, Laterza, 2003), 212.

economy were met with great "intellectual and moral" resistance, but above all they gave rise to the fallacious attempt to reconcile Fordism with the anachronistic sociodemographic structure of the old continent. In Gramsci's words:

> Europe would like to have the full bottle and the drunken wife, all the benefits that Fordism produces regarding the ability to compete, keeping its army of parasites that devour large masses of surplus value, increase upfront costs and reduce the power of the competition in the international market.[31]

It is in this contradiction that one must seek the true origin of the "organic crisis" that struck the great European nations in the postwar period.

For Americanism to concretely materialize, it requires an initial condition of "rational demographic composition", that is, the inexistence of large classes that have no essential role in the productive world, "parasitic classes". On the contrary, European civilization, especially southern civilization, was characterized by the proliferation of similar classes created by the richness and complexity of past history, which left behind a heap of passive sediments produced by the phenomenon of the saturation and fossilization of state officials and intellectuals, the clergy and land ownership, piratical commerce and the army. In *Notebook 7*, Gramsci comments on Alfredo Rocco's article of 1931, in which the different economic capacities of France and Italy are analyzed. Gramsci raises again the main question, which is the fact that in Italy there are much larger parasitic classes than in France, among which the most important is the rural bourgeoisie.[32]

The older the history of a country, the more extensive and harmful are these "sedimentations of idle and useless masses that live on the 'patrimony' of 'grandparents', of these pensioners of economic history".[33] It was evident that this reality was present in the Italian system of "one

---

[31] Antonio Gramsci, *Quaderni del carcere*, cit., 2141.
[32] Ibid., 807.
[33] Ibid., 2141.

hundred cities",[34] a result of that apparatus of "non-productive diligence" that characterizes the "mystery of Naples": "For a large population of this type of city, one can quote the popular proverb: when a horse defecates, a hundred sparrows have breakfast".[35] In this sense, the system of annuity payments guaranteed to southern land, through the system of lease or of primitive sharing, led to one of the most terrible and harmful forms of accumulation of capital because it was based on the usurious exploitation of agrarian poverty and because such lease was extremely expensive, since, in order to maintain the high standard of living of the families of those "landlords", who were used to living like parasites on the income of large estates, it was necessary to have ever greater amounts, and that hindered the accumulation of savings—let alone any sort of productive investment of rural income.

Precisely because it protected this "absolute parasitism", fascism arose, by nature, in deep contradiction with the attempts of Fordist rationalization.

The occasion to explain the reasons was in the commentary notes of some writings by Massimo Fovel,[36] in which corporatism is interpreted as a key premise of the Taylorist modernization of Italian production, capable of overcoming the semi-feudal economic persistence that removes portions of surplus value stolen from accumulation and the economy. In reality, according to Gramsci, corporatism did not emerge with the intention of reorganizing the country's production structures, but rather for mere reasons of "economic policing".

In Italy, the working class never opposed technical innovations aimed at reducing costs and rationalizing work; on the contrary, analyzing without bias the phase before 1922 and also the year 1926, it seemed that the

---

[34] The phrase *cento città* [one hundred cities] refers to the historical fragmentation of Italy which, in a limited territory, led to the proliferation of cities with very different systems, uses and customs from each other. The existence of these systems demonstrated, according to Gramsci, the lack of a process of national unification and the emergence of a modern state capable of overcoming the "municipal corporatism" of Italy between the fifteenth and twentieth centuries. However, this fragmentation also produced the great cultural richness that translates, for example, into the gastronomic variety of the country, which is also marked by huge differences in terms of language and traditions in a very concentrated area. After the unification of Italy, and particularly after 1887, the publisher Sonzogno published *Le cento città d'Italia illustrate*, installments that introduced the Italians themselves to all this variety and its features.

[35] Antonio Gramsci, *Quaderni del carcere*, cit., 2143.

[36] N. Massimo Fovel, *Economia e corporativismo* (Ferrara, S.A.T.E., 1929).

workers' movement itself started to make such demands. In corporatism, the negative reasons of "economic policing" prevailed over any positive element of the true renewal of economic policy. Americanism demanded as a condition the existence of a certain economic and state environment of a liberal type, characterized by free initiative and economic individualism, reaching "with its own means, as a civil society, the regime of industrial concentration and monopoly".[37]

Contrary to what Fovel argued, corporatism did not lead to overcoming parasitic and semi-feudal encrustations that subtracted surplus value quotas, but rather protected them. Precisely there lay, on a purely economic level, the decidedly more regressive nature of fascism in comparison with Americanism, as well as the clear predominance of these elements of "economic policing":

> The [fascist] state creates new rentiers, that is, it promotes the old forms of parasitic accumulation of savings and tends to create closed social frameworks. In reality, until now, the corporate orientation has worked to support dangerous middle-class positions, not to eliminate them, and due to the vested interests of the old base, it is increasingly becoming a machine of preservation of the existing as it is, not a driving force. Why? Because corporate policy also depends on unemployment: it guarantees employees a certain minimum of life that, if competition were free, would collapse, causing serious social unrest; and it creates occupations of a new kind, organizational and unproductive, for the unemployed of the middle classes.[38]

Unlike Italy, the United States was not burdened with the "historical basis" of the parasitic classes, which also explained its extraordinary ability to accumulate capital, even in the presence of a clearly higher standard of living than that of the European working classes. The absence of such sedimentation provided a healthy basis to industry and trade, allowing a significant reduction in many intermediate phases between the production and marketing of goods. This inevitably had positive effects on accumulation, investment capacity and the distribution of the wealth produced. These preconditions therefore made the process of rationalization between production and labor relatively easy through the combination of social coercion (the destruction of labor unionism) and consensus (high wages, social benefits, ideological and political propaganda). Americanism

---

[37] Antonio Gramsci, *Quaderni del carcere*, cit., 2157.
[38] Ibid.

consisted in concentrating the whole life of the country on production: "Hegemony is born in the factory and, to be exercised, it requires no more than a minimum number of professional intermediaries in politics and ideology".[39]

In southern Italy, on the other hand, social control was guaranteed precisely by intellectuals whose main political role was, in Gramsci's view, to prevent the establishment of autonomous and independent mass organizations, of peasants able to choose peasant cadres of peasant origin. When rural workers managed to enter the institutional structures of the state, such as local administrations or Parliament, this always happened through "compositions and decompositions of local parties, whose leadership is made up of intellectuals, but who are controlled by the great owners and their trusted men, such as [Antonio] Salandra, [Vittorio Emanuele] Orlando, Antonio Colonna Di Cesarò".[40] Intellectuals established the agrarian bloc, the "intermediary and supervisor" of parasitic capitalism in the North:

> Above the agrarian bloc, in the Mezzogiorno there is an intellectual bloc that has practically served so far to prevent the fissures of the agrarian bloc from becoming too dangerous and causing snowslides. The exponents of this intellectual bloc are Giustino Fortunato and Benedetto Croce, who can therefore be considered the most diligent reactionaries of the peninsula.[41]

The great social disintegration of the *Mezzogiorno* was related not only to the peasant masses but also to the intellectuals themselves. Thus, in the South, along with large estates, there were large cultural and intelligence accumulations on the part of autonomous individuals or of small groups of large intellectuals, while they were completely absent in any form of organization of middle culture. In the *Mezzogiorno*, there were important publishing houses, such as Laterza, academies and cultural enterprises of great importance, but at the same time there were no small and medium-sized magazines, no publishing houses around which groups of average southern intellectuals could organize themselves. For this reason, the intellectuals who managed to face the southern question in radical terms, emancipating themselves from the agrarian bloc, could conduct this

---

[39] Ibid., 2146.
[40] Antonio Gramsci, *La questione meridionale*, cit., 37.
[41] Ibid.

process only in publishers outside the *Mezzogiorno*. In this context, Benedetto Croce and Giustino Fortunato performed a very specific role: "supreme political and intellectual moderators" committed to preventing a revolutionary qualitative leap in the way of dealing with southern problems. Croce and Fortunato were defined by Gramsci as "men of great culture and intelligence", associated with European and world culture and yet rooted in their original southern cultural terrain, true instruments of cultural and political training capable of co-opting, into the bloc of national power, the intellectuals who emerged in the southern cultural terrain:

> They had all the necessary skills to satisfy the intellectual needs of the most sincere representatives of the cultured youth in the South, to indulge their restless impulse to revolt against existing conditions; [...]. In this sense, Benedetto Croce performed an extremely important national function: he separated the radical intellectuals of the Mezzogiorno from the peasant masses, forcing them to take part in national and European culture, and through this culture, he guaranteed their absorption by the national bourgeoisie and therefore by the agrarian bloc.[42]

In Gramsci's view, the detailed analysis of the intellectual bloc of the *Mezzogiorno*, "the pliant but very resistant armor of the agrarian bloc", was not intended only for selfless knowledge. In his conception of revolution in Italy, among the tasks of the communists was, above all, the disintegration of this bloc. This goal was pursued with two lines of action: based on an accurate work of political direction, promoting the organization of ever wider masses of poor peasants being formed autonomously and independently from dominant social structures; causing a split of organic nature within the mass of intellectuals, producing among them a left tendency favorable to the leading function of the working class.

Collaboration with Piero Gobetti and other members of the Rivoluzione Liberale group, part of *L'Ordine Nuovo*, responded precisely to this need. Gobetti and his group, despite not being communists, indeed cast the urban proletariat as the modern protagonist of Italian history and of the southern question; they served as intermediaries between the proletariat and some intellectual strata, working for this split in the ranks of southern intellectuals. Therefore, collaboration with Gobetti played a double role

---

[42] Ibid., 39.

for Gramsci: firstly, in connecting the working class with intellectuals born in the terrain of capitalist technique who had adopted a left-wing position during the "red biennium" period; secondly, in connecting the working class with the southern intellectuals who placed the southern question outside the traditional standards of the intellectual bloc hegemonized by Benedetto Croce, introducing the northern proletariat. In this way, it would have contributed even more to destroy the remnants of the corporate mentality of the working class, placing it ahead of those intellectuals and the peasant masses made autonomous by the agrarian bloc and by the semi-proletarian masses of the cities, and creating, in short, a new revolutionary social bloc.

This essay was written in the midst of Mussolini's second coup d'état, when the regime finally eliminated what was left of the statutory protections for democratic plurality and legally destroyed the individual and collective freedoms already violated. The *most fascist laws* led the Great Council of fascism to the top of the state. It was assigned most of the powers previously belonging to Parliament. The Special Court for the Defense of the State was established, the death penalty was reinstated, the paramilitary militia of the Fascist Party—now called the Voluntary Militia for National Security—was institutionalized, and the civil and criminal procedure codes were fascistized. Along with parties and organizations, all trade unions except fascist ones were suppressed. The confrontation came to blows with the failed attack on Mussolini on October 31, 1926; however, in August, Gramsci had predicted that the PCd'I would be outlawed, indicating the need to prepare an efficient clandestine structure more quickly. In a few weeks, the repressive apparatus came crashing down, legally prepared in the previous months and perfecting the tools and apparatus of legal persecution of the opposition, starting with the cancellation of all foreign passports. For the communist organization, as for all other anti-fascist forces, the abyss of an even more manifest police dictatorship opened up, an authentic "manhunt"[43] street by street: fascist teams, now fully supported by the law, destroyed parties, unions and newsrooms, using terror indiscriminately. The leaders of the Communist Party, starting with Gramsci, were arrested, and their ordeal began in the special courts between imprisonment and forced confinement. Repressive action was

---

[43] The expression was coined by Velio Spano (1905–1964), a renowned Sardinian leader in the Italian Communist Party between 1923 and 1946 and a prominent figure of anti-fascism.

extremely effective, and by December 1926 a third of its members were in prison. These events cannot be discussed in detail here, but they are extensively described in several publications of historiographic reconstruction and memoirs. Suffice it to recall the point of no return, which began between 1926 and 1927, to understand the climate that led to the escape of the antifascists[44] who broke out of prison and the great difficulties of living in hiding faced by the imprudent who had the courage to challenge fascism at all cost, remaining in their homeland to combat it.[45] In this climate, a woman was the protagonist of the immediate reconstitution of a clandestine secretarial office: Camilla Ravera, who thus recalled the beginning of clandestine life in her memoirs:

> In a small country house near Genoa, in Sturla, in November 1926, I organized the clandestine secretariat of the Communist Party: a stony and narrow road led to it, between thick hedges and strong walls; [...] I chose it precisely because of that garden that isolated it and mixed it up with similar ones scattered in that field. [...] Apparently, there were always three of us in that house: me, Giuseppe Amoretti and Anna Bessone. To make our life look normal, similar to that of the families living there, we hired a profoundly deaf old local woman, who came to tidy the rooms occupied on the ground floor every morning; the rooms on the upper floor were uninhabited. [...] In the evening the meetings began, the discussions between us from the center with the comrades who came from other places. Discussions often lasted until late at night, and the visiting comrades had to be accommodated upstairs and depart the following day on tiptoe, leaving no trace. Ignazio Silone named our headquarters Hostel of the Poor.[46]

Concurrently, thousands of kilometers away, the struggle for Lenin's succession reached its peak, leading to a dramatic and unprecedented confrontation within the leadership of the Bolshevik Communist Party that

[44] In December the external center of the PCd'I was established in Paris, with Grieco, Togliatti and Tasca.

[45] "In Italy, Camilla Ravera, Paolo Ravazzoli, Alfonso Leonetti, Ignazio Silone, Luigi Ceriana, Carlo Venegoni, Pietro Tresso and Teresa Recchia continue working. Camilla Ravera, who takes on the task of reorganizing the internal center of the party, takes a number of important measures. Genoa is chosen as the headquarters of the secretariat office and other offices, while the union office, headed by Ravazzoli, is established in Milan" (Paolo Spriano, *Storia del Partito Comunista Italiano*, v. 2: *Gli anni della clandestinità*, Rome, Editori Riuniti, 1969, 96).

[46] Camilla Ravera, in Cesare Pillon, *I comunisti nella storia d'Italia* (Rome, Edizioni del Calendario, 1967).

would adversely affect the fate and the line of the Comintern and its national sections. Among them, the Italian one was the most subject to fluctuations and therefore to pressure from Moscow due to its serious political-organizational situation resulting from the dictatorship and from the arrest of its main leader. Precisely between November and December 1926, at the height of repression in Italy, the Seventh Plenary Session of the Communist International was held in Moscow, where the dramatic confrontation at the summit of the Russian Party occurred with the division between the supporters of the vision of "socialism in one country", supported by Stalin and Bukharin, and those of Trotsky's "permanent revolution", supported by Zinoviev and Kamenev. It is well known that the three main leaders of the Russian Party, who clashed with Stalin, ended up being definitively liquidated at the end of this confrontation. We will not delve on this issue either as it suffices to recall it in order to illustrate the real political-organizational disaster faced by Italian communists in the transition between 1926 and 1930, not to mention to the dramatic shock experienced by the main party of the International, which was so serious that it led Gramsci to invite all to a sense of accountability in the famous letter to the Central Committee of the Bolshevik Communist Party, written less than a month before his arrest. The protagonists were the first to recognize the shock, which was then corroborated by the merciless data provided by historical research: in all respects, 1927 was the *annus horribilis* of communist history in Italy. Chief of Police Arturo Bocchini established the highly efficient special inspection in Milan against political dissidents, Organizzazione per la Vigilanza e la Repressione Dell'antifascismo (Ovra) [Organization for the surveillance and repression of anti-fascism], which was then structured and operationalized throughout national territory. According to Spriano, the ratio between repressors and those repressed is one to one:

> If 100 thousand are enlisted [into the Communist Party], there is at least the same number of police officers (from the investigative services agents of the PS and the MVSN,[47] through the carabinieri, through the officers of the ministries on special duty, to the soldiers of the border, the port, the railway) who are mainly assigned or work exclusively to increase surveillance and

[47] In 1925 an autonomous organ of *Pubblica Sicurezza* (PS) [Public Security] was created, which gave rise to the *polizia* [police]. MVSN stands for *Milizia Volontaria per la Sicurezza Nazionale* [Voluntary militia for national security], that is, the old fascist paramilitary squadrons were legalized and incorporated into the state.

political repression. Judging by the examination of the documents related to the opposition, at least three quarters of the work carried out by this actual army was aimed at the communist conspiracy.[48]

On March 13, 1927, the great trials of the Special Court began in Rome, initially dealing with the communist prisoners before the turn of 1926, particularly the thirty-nine members of the Florence organization arrested in 1925. From that moment on, the Special Court and prisons would work at full capacity for the continuous waves of arrests, thanks to Ovra's skillful use of informants and spies introduced into "subversive" environments, certainly the most effective tool in the hands of the structure created by Bocchini.

Thanks to the denunciations, several attacks were launched: in March, against the newly reestablished Milan steering committee; in April, against the Roman organization; in June, still against the structure in Milan, but also in Varese, then in Naples, Emilia-Romana, Tuscany, Umbria; in July, the target was the historical bulwark of the workers' movement, Turin, and so on, without respite. All surviving leaders of the organization who were still in the country were arrested in 1927; afterwards, repressive action intensified again after the attack on Victor Emmanuel III at the Milan fair on April 12, 1928. The bomb did not reach its target; twenty dead and many wounded lay on the ground, but the action was never explained: in the ranks of the anti-fascist opposition, it was not known who had planted the bomb and—the mystery deepens—there was the hypothesis that those responsible for the attack should be sought among the most uncompromising components of fascism, eager to get rid of the complicated figure of the king so as to more decisively advance toward the stage of revolution.[49] Although those who ordered and executed the attack were never found, it was an opportunity to unleash terrorism against anti-fascism again: there were almost six hundred arrests immediately, and torture was systematically used to extract confessions. Once again, the communist organization suffered most arrests—important leaders were caught by the police, such as Girolamo Li Causi, Edoardo d'Onofrio, Giuseppe Amoretti and Anna Bessone, the general staff of the reconstituted internal center. It was the prelude to the trial against the communist

---

[48] Paolo Spriano, *Storia del Partito Comunista Italiano*, v. 2: *Gli anni della clandestinità*, cit., 91–2.

[49] This hypothesis was subsequently disclosed by Minister Luigi Federzoni.

ruling group: on May 28, 1928, twenty-three defendants appeared before the Special Court of Rome, including Antonio Gramsci, who was accused of conspiracy, propaganda, incitement to armed class struggle, outrage, contempt and the creation of a revolutionary army with the specific aim of overthrowing the established order.

CHAPTER 16

The *Notebooks*: The Difficult Beginnings of a "Disinterested" Work

In the Turi prison (in the region of Puglia), on February 8, 1929, two years after his arrest, Gramsci began writing the *Notebooks*. In prison, studying is a method of resistance to intellectual brutalization, an instrument of physical and political survival. As Valentino Gerratana wrote, the tension between these two needs gave rise to the *Notebooks*, a work composed of notes and reflections that were intended to be better defined later, but still extraordinarily rich, to the point of being considered indispensable for many different scientific fields: from literary criticism to linguistics, from history to political science, from pedagogy to theater. This work is the object of in-depth scientific studies in the United States, England, Japan, India, Brazil and Mexico, as well as Italy.

According to Carlos Nelson Coutinho, the widespread international diffusion of Gramsci and his importance for different disciplines in the field of humanities and social sciences confirm how appropriate it is to define his work as "classic". However, Coutinho also argues that this statement requires additional clarification, because behind "classical monumentalization" there is always the risk of intellectual mummification and because there is a difference between Gramsci and other "classics", that is, authors capable of interpreting time itself, of remaining relevant for subsequent periods. If works such as *The Prince*, by Machiavelli, or *Leviathan*, by Thomas Hobbes, can be considered "classics" that exhibit strong modern features, in the sense they provide useful insights to analyze the

G. Fresu, *Antonio Gramsci*, Marx, Engels, and Marxisms, https://doi.org/10.1007/978-3-031-15610-6_16

contemporary world, Gramsci's work is of current interest in a different sense: "he interpreted a world that, in essence, remains our world today".[1]

The *Notebooks* give rise to the political rigor and, at the same time, the unwavering concreteness underlying the Sardinian intellectual's explanation for the collapse of the liberal system in Italy and thus the crushing of the workers' movement and its political field. This historical drama led Gramsci to investigate, with no indulgence, the limits, errors and abstractions of the entire opposition front against Mussolini. Based on this requirement, a *corpus* was assembled from notes and it subjected the facts of men and of ideas to Gramscian reflection, which were exposed with a careful and critical prose that often does not shy away from grasping the ironic side of things. The non-dogmatic nature of Gramsci's work allowed him to escape from rigid classifications, go beyond the crisis and collapse of his own political-ideological field, and cross the temporal and political boundary of the twentieth century. The *Prison Notebooks* are an essential tool for reading current events, providing to our days useful guidance on the contradictions of modernity, and it is no coincidence that scientific studies of different disciplines give them today, more than before, an absolute prominent place at an international level among the great thinkers in the history of humanity.

The prison regime proved extremely difficult, especially at the beginning of the study, since it made it impossible to have a dialogic relationship with other individuals, which was necessary to avoid a work that is too self-reflective.

In addition to the subjective condition, it was very hard to obtain the means to study continuously and write following a rational order. The discomfort resulting from the first disordered readings led Gramsci to doubt the real possibility of success of the project. Thus, in a letter to Tania on May 23, 1927, he announced that he wanted to devote himself to two activities with a therapeutic goal, namely physical exercises and translations from foreign languages:

> I believe that actual and appropriate study is impossible for me for many reasons, not only psychological ones, but also technical ones; it is very difficult to completely abandon myself to a topic or subject and immerse myself only in it, as one does when studying something seriously in order to understand all possible relationships and connect them harmoniously. Something

---

[1] Carlos Nelson Coutinho, *Il pensiero politico di Gramsci* (Milan, Unicopli, 2006), 146.

in this sense may begin to happen for the study of languages, [...] now I am reading the tales by the Brothers Grimm. I am truly keen to make language study my main activity.[2]

In addition to the "therapeutic" aspect, these translations are also important within the biographical scope. In a letter to his sister Teresina, of January 18, 1932, Gramsci wrote that he wanted to make a small contribution to the development of her children's imagination by copying and sending them the translations of the Brothers Grimm, "a series of folk tales like those we loved dearly when we were children. They are a bit old-fashioned, rustic, but modern life, with radio, planes, sound films, Carnera[3] etc., has not yet penetrated Ghilarza enough for children's preferences to be very different now from our preferences".[4] Despite originating in German tradition, the stories, set in dense, dark forests inhabited by spirits, witches and goblins, were not too far from the oral tradition of Sardinian folk fantasy and seemed to fit perfectly into the atmosphere both of their land and of Ghilarza in particular, a place "where there will always be old-fashioned types like 'aunt Adelina' and 'Corroncu',[5] and the stories will always have a suitable environment". The world of these fairy tales brought to his memory the childhood outings in the valleys of Sardinia, between Ghilarza and Abbasanta, when, inspired by adventure stories, he never left home without grains of wheat and matches wrapped in tarpaulin in his pocket, just in case he ended up on a desert island.

Gramsci's interest in linguistics dates back to the troubled years of university studies in Greater Turin, which were marked by health problems and an economic hardship verging on absolute poverty. The young Sardinian immediately attracted the attention of one of the most important glottology scholars at the time, Matteo Bartoli, and strengthened relations with literature professor Umberto Cosmo, who previously taught at Liceo Dettori in Cagliari. Bartoli, in particular, encouraged him to study Sardinian linguistics. Therefore, it is not uncommon to find letters to relatives on this subject. In one of them, addressed to his father, dated January 3, 1912, he asked when, in the Fonni[6] dialect, the *s* "is pronounced

---

[2] Antonio Gramsci, *Lettere dal carcere* (Turim, Einaudi, 2020), p. 110–11.
[3] Primo Carnera (1906–1967), world heavyweight champion between 1933 and 1934, was a very famous Italian boxer and wrestler in the first half of the twentieth century.
[4] Antonio Gramsci, *Lettere dal carcere*, cit., 560.
[5] Ghilarza personalities quoted in the letter.
[6] A small mountain town located in the inner zone of Barbagia, in the interior of Sardinia.

softly, like *rosa* in Italian" and "when [it is pronounced] strongly as in *sole*". In other letters addressed to his sister, he asked for information about some peculiarities of Logudorese and Campidanese:[7] terms, pronunciations, varieties.

It is therefore not a surprise that in the *Notebooks* he pays close attention to glottology and linguistics in general. After years of militancy and intense theoretical-political activity, the translation of these first prison notes had a preparatory and therapeutic value, which was necessary at the beginning of a "disinterested" work not favored by material conditions.

We must also mention a letter to Tania, dated December 15, 1930, in which personal and study considerations are mixed:

> Perhaps because all my intellectual training has been of a controversial nature, even disinterested thinking is difficult for me, that is, studying for the sake of studying. Only sometimes, but rarely, do I forget a certain order of reflections and, as it were, find in things themselves the interest to devote myself to their analysis. I usually need to ask myself from a dialogic or dialectical point of view; otherwise, I feel no intellectual stimulus.[8]

In addition to this self-critical assessment, a characteristic feature of Gramsci's personality, translations and linguistic studies were conducted with a certain philological rigor, intellectual curiosity and a method that today is analyzed with great attention by experts in the field. In a letter, upon expressing the desire to devote himself to a systematic study of comparative linguistics, he confessed to his sister-in-law Tania that one of his greatest intellectual regrets was the disappointment of Professor Bartoli, of the University of Turin, who envisioned for Gramsci a great future among the "neogrammarians". But the events of the "great, terrible and complicated world", which preceded and followed the war, led the young Sardinian intellectual, like many in his generation, to find in political commitment a new reason for existence which made risking everything, including life, worth it.

The third translation notebook, besides continuing the study on the linguistic lines of Franz Nikolaus Finck, contains the translation of Eckermann's *Conversations* with Goethe. The *Conversations* gather the

---

[7] Logudorese is the dialect of Logudoro, a region located in the inner and central part of northern Sardinia, while Campidanese is the dialect spoken in Campidano, a floodplain that extends from the South to the center of the island.

[8] Antonio Gramsci, *Lettere dal carcere*, cit., p. 590.

memories of the great German poet and writer through conversations with his secretary Johann Peter Eckermann. Goethe was defined as a universal genius due to the versatility of his talent manifested in different fields of knowledge, poetry, literature, science, philosophy. With the memoirs, Eckermann reconstructs the ideal universe, the world and values, and he sketches a biographical fresco deemed one of the greatest works of western literature, so much so that Nietzsche defined it as the best German book ever written. Goethe is a figure systematically present in the *Notebooks* and on the letters. In Gramsci's view, every nation has a writer who somehow symbolizes its intellectual glory: Shakespeare in England, Cervantes in Spain, Dante in Italy and Goethe in Germany.[9] However, only Shakespeare and Goethe can be considered intellectual figures who also fit into the contemporary era; they are authors of topical interest due to their ability to "teach, as philosophers, what we should believe, as poets, what we have to intuit (feel), as men, what we should do".[10] In Goethe, Gramsci sees a political-cultural force capable of going beyond its time and imposing itself in the present: "Only Goethe is always of certain relevance because he expresses in a serene and classical fashion what in Leopardi is still murky romanticism",[11] which represents confidence in man's creative activity in a nature that is not seen as an enemy and an antagonist.

The reading of *Conversations with Goethe*, in his condition of detention, connected Gramsci's experience to that of a great French literary critic who lived in the same years, Jacques Rivière. In *Notebook 1*, Gramsci reported some excerpts from "Impressioni di prigionia" [Impressions of captivity], written by the historical editor of the *Nouvelle Revue Française*.[12] In these excerpts, Rivière recounted the harassment experienced while imprisoned in the First World War, in particular the humiliation to which he was subjected during a search in his cell, when the few things in his possession were taken away, among which the only book he had with him,

---

[9] Idem, *Quaderni del carcere* (Turin, Einaudi, 1975), 1026.

[10] Ibid., 1187.

[11] Ibid.

[12] The work *L'Allemand: Souvenirs et réflexions d'un prisonnier de guerre* [On German nature: memories and reflections of a prisoner of war] was published by Éditions de la Nouvelle Revue Française in 1918, but it is likely that Gramsci read the excerpts published in *La Fiera Letteraria. Giornale Settimanale di Lettere, Scienze ed Arti* (founded in Milan in 1925 by Unitas publishing, under the direction of the writer Umberto Fracchia), in the April 1928 issue, three years after the death of Jacques Rivière, as he himself notes in paragraph 70 of *Notebook 1* ("Impressioni di prigionia", *Quaderni del carcere*, Turin, Einaudi, 1977, 79).

precisely *Conversations with Goethe*. Gramsci transcribed the Frenchman's feelings of despair and anguish over the brutal and uncertain state of captivity, experienced as an inevitable "pang in my heart", in which he was constantly exposed to all kinds of harassment and the condition of physical and mental oppression became unbearable. This anguish—present in all the correspondence—was shared by the Sardinian intellectual who, naturally, concluded these notes by reporting the crying in prison, "when the idea of death presents itself for the first time and you suddenly grow old".[13]

In these years, Gramsci experienced another moment of great political anguish, as he had no part in the change in the international communist movement between 1928 and 1930; such anguish became even greater due to his isolation among the communist prisoners themselves. The orientations provided by the Tenth Plenum and the Seventh Congress of the International, which led to the consolidation of the theory on social fascism, caused a deep crisis in the ruling group of the PCd'I, with Togliatti himself accused of "ambiguity" due to the political line subject to deep revision, and also due to his previous relationship with Tasca. This crisis was marked by outright expulsions (Pietro Tresso, Paolo Ravazzoli, Mario Bavassano, Francesco Leonetti, Angelo Tasca, Ignazio Silone), by bitter controversies and harsh accusations, in a general context of weakening of the clandestine organization, which was now almost completely ruined in the countryside. In a letter addressed to the ruling group of the PCd'I, Umberto Terracini expressed his criticism against the expulsions and the revision of the political line, starting a divergence that would drag on for twelve years, until his banishment in the period of exile in Ventotene.[14] In this letter, the future president of the Constituent Assembly, besides expressing his reservations regarding disciplinary procedures, offered specific criticism of the "social-fascism" theses, rightly accusing the leadership of the organization of adopting the positions previously expressed by Amadeo Bordiga on the equivalence between fascism and democracy. Precisely in this letter, which is the object of several analyses and studies, Terracini clarified the positions expressed by Gramsci and Scoccimaro in the discussions of the group in the Regina Coeli prison. According to the imprisoned secretary-general, with the defeat of fascism, it would be necessary to go through a democratic phase, with the creation of a republican Constituent Assembly, exactly when first the International then the Italian

---

[13] Ibid., 80.

[14] Ventotene was one of the islands where the antifascists were kept.

party began to condemn this position as "opportunistic deviation". Several accounts, among them that of Athos Lisa, confirmed the adoption of the slogan of the Constituent Assembly and the demand for a united offensive of the communists with other anti-fascist parties on the part of Gramsci: the exhortation "not to be afraid of making politics" and to abandon what was left of maximalist mentality. Gramsci's non-alignment with the new positions of the International and of the party was the reason for great dissension within the group of detainees in Turi. Such dissension led to the isolation of the Sardinian, who was bitterly forced to shut himself away, in silence and studying:

> Probably at that moment, a certain climate of suspicion was created in the Turi prison; a certain accusation of being outside the party line, of adherence to social-democratic positions, which weighed heavily on Gramsci's state of mind and increased his isolation, was combined with the petty accusations of being too far apart, of wanting to be excessively legal in relation to the prison regime, of being individualistic simply because he wanted to guarantee the minimum conditions to be able to continue studying.[15]

[15] Paolo Spriano, *Storia del Partito Comunista Italiano*, v. 2: *Gli anni della clandestinità* (Turin, Einaudi, 1969), 286.

CHAPTER 17

Hegemonic Relations, Productive Relations and the Subaltern

I am convinced of this idea: it is necessary to do something *für ewig*, according to Goethe's complex conception, which I remember tormenting our [Giovanni] Pascoli a lot. In short, according to a pre-established plan, I will deal intensely and systematically with some topic capable of absorbing me and centralizing my inner life. Do you remember the shallow and superficial text I wrote about southern Italy and the importance of B. Croce? Well, I will return to the theses I outlined there, from a disinterested point of view, *für ewig*.[1]

This excerpt, extracted from the famous letter written to Tania Schucht on March 19, 1927 in the Milan prison, constitutes a bridge between the analysis of the *southern question* and of the *Notebooks*, in which the theme of relations between the North and the South, in the light of the antagonistic polarization between city and country, is absolutely central and approached from a historical perspective that goes to the heart of the dynamics of the Italian *Risorgimento* and the role of intellectuals as a class.

In recent decades, the notes on the *southern question* and research into subaltern groups have drawn great attention within the framework of *postcolonial studies* and *Subaltern Studies*,[2] although it is necessary to make a

---

[1] Antonio Gramsci, *Lettere dal carcere* (Turim, Einaudi, 2020), p. 75.

[2] In August 2011, a major international congress on this topic took place at the Marilia campus of Sao Paulo State University (UNESP). The proceedings of the event are published in Marcos del Roio (org.), *Gramsci: periferia e subalternidade* (São Paulo, Edusp, 2017).

© The Author(s), under exclusive license to Springer Nature Switzerland AG 2023
G. Fresu, *Antonio Gramsci*, Marx, Engels, and Marxisms,
https://doi.org/10.1007/978-3-031-15610-6_17

timely distinction between the two branches. Iain Chambers spoke of the great leap in western critical thought made by Gramsci (and reworked by Edward Said), according to whom the political and cultural struggle would not be based on the relationship between tradition and modernity, but rather on the dialectic between the subaltern and the hegemonic part of the world.[3] Therein lies the conviction that culture plays a decisive role in the definition of ruling structures and in the construction of the historical-social bloc.[4] Owing to this awareness and to the definition of the concept of subaltern, Gramsci is present in *postcolonial studies* often imprecisely and incoherently, through the transposition of his categories, of the Italian historical and territorial dimension, of the global dimension concerning the North-South relationship, and especially of the subaltern condition imposed on the South by the West.[5]

For some of the most renowned authors in this line of research, the profound global transformations in the relations of exploitation made the concept of subalternity undergo an evolution that went beyond the conceptual framework of "orthodox Marxism".[6] Thus, the issue went from a context marked by the capital/labor conflict to a dimension of race, ethnicity and territory, as well as gender.[7] The importance of the spatial dimension of relations of domination and hegemony, that is, the geographical and territorial characterization of the concept of subalternity, was already present in Gramsci in the definition of the common ground between the peasant mass of the *Mezzogiorno* and the proletariat of the North, just as it is present in the East/West relationship. Some incoherent uses of Gramscian categories, supported not only by lack of philological accuracy but also by interpretations based on second-hand or third-hand readings, are often the result of painful decontextualization. In our humble opinion, it is not possible to understand Gramsci's legacy well and

---

[3] Iain Chambers (org.), *Esercizi di potere. Gramsci, Said e il postcoloniale* (Rome, Universale Meltemi, 2006).

[4] Edward W. Said, *Cultura e imperialismo* (Rome, Gamberetti, 1998); idem, *Orientalismo* (Turin, Bollati e Boringhieri, 1991).

[5] Incidentally, the International Congress "Gramsci in Asia and Africa", held at the University of Cagliari, on February 12 and 13, 2009, was particularly interesting, and the lectures were published by Annamaria Baldussi and Patrizia Manduchi, *Gramsci in Asia e in Africa* (Cagliari, Aipsa, 2009).

[6] Iain Chambers e Lidia Curti (orgs.), *La questione postcoloniale* (Naples, Liguori, 1997).

[7] Gayatri Chakravorty Spivak, *Critica della ragione postcoloniale. Verso una storia del presente in dissolvenza* (Rome, Meltemi, 2004).

truly without the theoretical debate that nourished it and the political discussion surrounding Gramsci throughout his existence.

Once these critical clarifications have been provided, the need to strengthen the conceptual categories, to contextualize them in the face of the determining historical reality, is entirely consistent with the spirit of Gramsci's work and with his desire to avoid the narrow-mindedness and generality of ideological statements. In his several works, Peter Thomas has shown countless times how, converted into the singular, the category of subalterns favored the development of an entire field of academic studies, the *Subaltern Studies*, which allows a major expansion of its possible areas of application. Peter Thomas himself drew attention to the ambivalence of the feelings evoked by this expansion in the community of the most traditional and "orthodox" scholars: on the one hand, satisfaction with the widespread diffusion of their categories; on the other, bewilderment, if not disappointment, due to some excessively injudicious uses of such categories.[8] In addition to these conflicting feelings, the creative and heterodox expansion of Gramsci's theoretical legacy, in fields of application so diverse and not always coherent, there is the study of the characteristic elements of each specific cultural setting, linked at the same time to the major conceptual question of the "translatability" of philosophical languages, of development dynamics and of social relations. Starting from the concept of "historically determined" and from what can be defined, in Hegelian terms, as "second nature", Gramsci repeatedly used classical analytical categories of geography in his analysis of hegemonic processes and of relations of domination at the international level.

In this sense, the Sardinian intellectual defined the concepts of East and West as consequences of a historical-cultural convention, which refer to a historical fact produced by civilizational development. However, although it is a construction, it is not just a purely arbitrary and rational artifice. In the absence of human beings, it would not make sense to think in terms of East and West, or North and South, because these are real relations hardly intelligible in the absence of humans, of the development of their civilizations and above all of the hegemonic relations between rulers and those ruled.

---

[8] Peter D. Thomas, "Cosa rimane dei subalterni alla luce dello Stato integrale?", *International Gramsci Journal*, v. 2, n. 4, 2015, 82–92.

It is evident that East and West are arbitrary, conventional, that is, historical constructions, because outside of real history any point on Earth is East and West at the same time. This can be seen most clearly due to the fact that these terms were consolidated not from the point of view of a hypothetical and melancholic man in general, but from the point of view of the European cultured classes which, through their world hegemony, made them accepted everywhere. [...] Thus, through the historical content that was attached to the geographical term, the expressions East and West ended up indicating certain relationships between different sets of civilizations.[9]

For this reason, Gramsci wrote, Japan is the Far East for both the Californians and the Japanese themselves who, through the mediation of English political culture, consider Egypt the Near East, while the Italians see Morocco as an Eastern country, part of Arab and Muslim civilization. In this sense, in Gramsci's definition, the concept of *West* is essentially related to the reality characterized by a major development of the productive forces and of the hegemonic apparatus, while that of *East* refers to the reality characterized by a civil society still "primordial" and "gelatinous" in which power is essentially exercised by relations of domination proper to political society. It is a historical characterization, obviously not static nor definitive, that must be observed in its concreteness, taking into account the real processes of development typical of each socioeconomic setting.

In Gramsci, the North/South relationship, like the East/West relationship, is inseparable from the materialist conception of history, that is, from the centrality of the social relations of production in the definition of the concepts of hegemony and domination. Dealing again with the southern question, *Notebook 1* addresses precisely this type of problem starting from a methodological consideration: the dynamics between city and countryside change profoundly in relation to the context observed and, therefore, no generalization would be scientifically appropriate. In Gramsci's view, Italy, with its own history, is the practical demonstration of the veracity of such assessment, which can be added to another: the general statement that the city is always more progressive than the countryside can only be considered valid if the city in question is "typically industrial", whereas in the absence of that condition the progressive role of the city would have to be proved. Thus, in Italy urbanization was not linked to the industrial

---

[9] Antonio Gramsci, *Prison Notebooks* (Turin, Einaudi, 1977), 1419–20.

phenomenon, and only in rare cases did the so-called "hundred cities" system manifest itself in the form of an industrial city. This is evident when we recall that the largest city was Naples, which did not have an industrial apparatus comparable to that of northern cities and, in general, was considered backward.

According to Gramsci, the North-South relationship in Italy fit well into the classical scheme of the dialectic between city and country and could be analyzed in the various forms of culture expressed by the two realities.[10] The structure of the intellectual classes differed significantly in these two contexts: in the South, the figure of the intellectual of a "bacharelesco" type still prevailed, whose job was to keep the mass of peasants in contact with that of landowners and the state; in the North, the "office technician" type prevailed, which related the worker to the capitalist class, while the connection between the working mass and the state fell within the remit of a new kind of intellectual caste: the union caste, or the caste that represented political parties.

The hegemony of the North and the South could have historically played a positive and progressive role if industrialism had aimed to broaden its base with new frameworks, incorporating—not dominating—the newly assimilated economic zones. In this sense, the hegemony of the North could have expressed a "struggle between the old and the new, between the progressive and the retrogressive, between the most productive and the least productive".[11] Such dynamics could have started or favored an economic revolution with a national character; on the contrary, hegemony did not have an inclusive character aiming to reduce that distinction, but rather a "permanent", "perpetual" one, in the sense of organizing itself around an idea of unequal development to the point that the weakness of the South became a factor—indeterminate in time—useful to the industrial growth of the North, as if the former were a colonial appendage of the latter.

In Italy, the process of national unification did not occur on the basis of an egalitarian relationship, but rather through an unequal relationship in

---

[10] Benedetto Croce and Giustino Fortunato are classified by Gramsci as leaders of a southern cultural movement that opposed the [futurist] cultural movement of the North. Within these dynamics, however, Sicily stands out from the rest of the South, and its intellectuals have a different position; thus, Francesco Crispi is the man of northern industry, while both Giovanni Gentile and Luigi Pirandello can be included—albeit with differences—in the futurist cultural movement.

[11] Antonio Gramsci, *Prison Notebooks*, cit., 131.

which the enrichment and industrial growth of the North depended largely on the growing impoverishment of the *Mezzogiorno*. The reality of semicolonial exploitation of the South was always carefully arranged among the ruling classes and, according to Gramsci, this arrangement was aided by the socialist intellectuals themselves who, instead of revealing the origin of unequal relations, explained the backwardness of the South with the idea of the organic incapacity, biological inferiority, congenital barbarism of southern man. The ancient and ingrained representations of "Neapolitan delinquency" were translated into the "pseudoscientific" doctrine by positivist sociologists and scholars in the area of criminal anthropology, many of them intellectuals of the Italian Socialist Party. Through these arguments, it became common, even among the popular masses of the North, to believe in a South free from the Bourbon yoke, fertile and rich in natural resources, and yet unable to be emancipated from misery and backwardness for reasons internal to the region itself. The image of a "ball-and-chain" South was consolidated, which prevented the North from making faster progress toward industrial modernity and economic wealth.

In Gramsci's view, this uneven development was politically promoted in the liberal programs—from the Unity of Italy to the advent of fascism—in two main lines: first, in Giolittism, whose goal was to create an urban-industrial (capitalist-worker) bloc as the social basis of a protectionist state, in which the South was supposed to play the role of a semicolonial sales market for Northern industry; second, in the program supported by *Corriere della Sera*, which was based, this time, on the alliance between northern industrialists and the southern agrarian elite.

The first of these two main lines of liberalism in Italy was oriented by the violent repression of every mass peasant movement and by a system of privileges and favors benefitting the intellectual castes of the South, which were incorporated into public service in a personal capacity. Therefore, any point of connection between these two elements of southern society was prevented, and thus "the social stratum that could have organized southern dissatisfaction becomes [on the contrary] an instrument of northern politics, its policing accessory".[12]

Within this system of power, intellectuals played the same role as non-commissioned officers and junior officers in the army, that is, they made the connection between senior officers and the troops. In *Notebook 3*, the concept of "subversive", authentically Italian in essence, is systematically

---

[12] Ibid., 36.

defined as a negative class position, not a positive one, which distinguishes both the primitive non-conformism of the peasant masses (landless rural workers) and the reactionary dissatisfaction of the rural and urban petty bourgeoisie. For instance, Gramsci speaks of the elementary and superficial aversion, on the part of the people, to the lords. This hatred reflects the old opposition between city and countryside, of a semi-feudal type, which is a manifestation of the backward condition of class consciousness, which in its primitive form is purely negative.

> Not only are they not exactly aware of their own historical personality, but they are not even aware of the historical personality and limits of their own adversary (the lower classes, being historically on the defensive, can only develop self-awareness through denial, through awareness of the adversary's personality and class limits: but this process is still uncertain, at least on a national scale).[13]

In the countryside, the expression "starved" refers to both the agricultural day laborers (rural subproletariat) and the petty bourgeois who descend from a rural bourgeoisie whose property ends up reduced to nothing by progressive fragmentation from one generation to another. Thus, even in this case, it is a starving person who, nonetheless, does not want to perform manual labor and aspires to small municipal and public jobs. In the description made by the Sardinian intellectual, the social basis of the first form of fascism is easily recognizable.

> This stratum is a disturbing element in country life, always eager for changes (elections, etc.); it is the local "subversive" and, since it is quite widespread, has some importance: it allies especially with the rural bourgeoisie and against the peasants, also organizing at its service the "starved day laborers". These strata are present in all regions and are also common in cities, where they are associated with professional delinquency and variable crime rates. Many small city employees derive socially from these strata and keep the arrogant psychology of the decadent nobleman, of the owner who is forced to toil. The "subversiveness" of these strata has two faces, left and right, but their adherence to the left is only a means of blackmail; in decisive moments they always go with the right, and their desperate "courage" always prefers to have the carabinieri as allies.[14]

---

[13] Ibid., 323–4.
[14] Ibid., 325.

These intellectuals, already defined in the aforementioned notes of *Notebook 22* as an organic expression of a caste of "pensioners of economic history", come from a petty and middle agrarian bourgeoisie, usually live off their land, intended for rental or shared ownership, and represent the survival of old society; this type of intellectual was replaced in industrial society with the organizing, technical intellectual, an expert in applied sciences.

The fact that great and middle intellectuals were barriers against the tendency of the subaltern groups to unite is present in all *Prison Notebooks*, and there is a passage of fundamental importance in *Notebook 25*. In this passage, Gramsci states that every aspect of autonomous initiative—whether political, cultural or social—on the part of the subaltern classes has "inestimable" value for the "episodic and disaggregated" nature of their history. What had been specifically made clear in the *southern question* for the understanding of Italian society here becomes a kind of historical-political norm. In their activity, the subaltern groups are constantly affected by the initiative of the dominant groups, even when they revolt and rebel. The direct consequence is that the tendency toward a coherent centralization of such activity, which is capable of changing rebellion or mere economic claims, is always dissolved and loses organicity in the face of the ruling classes' interdiction skills. The subalternality of these groups can end only with their "permanent" victory, so only with the completion of a historical cycle can it be said that the initiative of the subaltern groups was successfully implemented. More precisely, the subaltern groups can only unite if they become the state.[15]

The unity of the ruling classes, in turn, happens within the state, so it can be said that their history coincides with that of the state; however, it is not necessary to believe that everything will be solved in the legal and policial sphere of institutions, because the domination of one class is not limited to coercive methods, and the operational dimension of a state is not limited to institutional evidence. While commenting on the book by Daniel Halévy, *Decadenza della libertà*[16] [Decadence of freedom], in *Notebook 6*, Gramsci writes about how the "general concept of state is one-sided and leads to colossal mistakes"[17] simply because it is reduced only to the coercive and government apparatus, without also understanding "the

---

[15] Ibid., 2288.
[16] *Décadence de la liberté* (Paris, B. Gasset, 1931).
[17] Antonio Gramsci, *Quaderni del carcere*, cit., 801.

private apparatus of hegemony and civil society". The state is synthetically exemplified in the formula dictatorship + hegemony.

Thus, if the history of the ruling classes ends up coinciding with that of the state, the history of the subaltern classes is, on the contrary, a "disaggregated and discontinuous function" of the history of civil society and, in turn, of the history of the state. In the study of the subaltern classes, every detail takes on central importance for the "integral historian", and Gramsci indicates some essential points in such investigation, among which is the importance of the hegemonic struggle:

(1) how the subaltern groups are formed and how they develop in relation to economic production processes, their quantitative dissemination, their possible origins from pre-existing groups, including the possibility of persisting mentalities, ideologies, and goals; (2) the modalities, manifest or concealed, of adherence to the political forces of the dominant groups, the attempts to condition the programs through their own claims, the impact of such dynamics on the political history of the subaltern classes; (3) the creation of new political groups to maintain consensus and control over the subaltern classes; (4) the existence of organizations of the subaltern groups in the terrain of economic-corporative claims; (5) the existence of new settings that, on the other hand, attest to the autonomy of the subaltern groups through the persistence of the old cadres; (6) the mobilization of forces able to assert the full autonomy of the subaltern groups, that is, the ability to create their own organic intellectuals.

Research into the evolution process (from the primitive, economic-corporative dimension to the fully autonomous dimension) of the consciousness of the subaltern groups is done very attentively in the face of all the manifestations of the so-called "spirit of cleavage" and in the face of all contradiction embodied in such process as the political groups of the subaltern classes also contain elements from the ruling classes playing leading roles.

In *Notebook 3*, the fragmentary history of the subaltern classes is studied in the light of the dialectical relationship between spontaneity and conscious direction. First of all, for the Sardinian intellectual, there is no "pure spontaneity" in history and even in the most spontaneous movement there are always elements of conscious direction; the problem is that it is difficult to identify such elements, since historically verifiable documents are rare due to the limited level of consciousness that usually characterizes the subaltern classes.

> It can be said that the element of spontaneity is therefore characteristic of the "history of the subaltern classes" and, above all, of the most marginal and peripheral elements of such classes, who have not reached class consciousness "for themselves" and therefore do not even suspect that their history may be important and that it is worth documenting it.[18]

Because they are in the presence of a multiplicity of elements of conscious direction, none of them can become predominant and surpass the level of popular science and common knowledge of the subaltern classes, that is, their traditional worldview. Hence the need to study historically and actively, not sociologically or descriptively, the elements of psychology, culture, and common knowledge of the popular masses, a requirement that Gramsci finds at least implicitly in the doctrine of Ilyich (Lenin).

Even in spontaneous movements, there are primitive elements of conscious direction, as is confirmed by the existence of realities that support spontaneity as a method of action. To better explain this concept, Gramsci reflects on the experience of the "red biennium" council movement. As we have seen in the first chapter of this volume, the ordinovist group was accused—both by the reformists, such as Turati, and by the revolutionaries, such as Bordiga—of simultaneously being "spontaneist" and "voluntarist", which was a contradictory accusation that, in Gramsci's view, was a clear indication of the direction taken by that movement, which did not confuse politics with real action simply because it did not have the educational objective of transforming it into a scientific or theoretical formula. This direction was based on the experience of "real men", shaped by a certain historical relationship, with certain feelings, perspectives, fragments of worldviews resulting from the spontaneous combination of a certain environment of material production with the incidental agglutination of different social elements.

The *L'Ordine Nuovo* group can be credited for no longer neglecting or despising those elements of spontaneity, but without fetishizing them; on the contrary, it acted tenaciously to homogenize them, make them coherent and connect them with modern theory. The organic relationship between political direction and the concrete articulation of the subaltern classes lies precisely here:

---

[18] Ibid., 328.

This combination of "spontaneity" and "conscious direction", that is, discipline, is precisely the real political action of the subaltern classes, as a mass policy and not a simple adventure of groups that mirror themselves in the mass.[19]

In Gramsci's view, a modern theory of political direction cannot be in opposition to the "spontaneous" feelings of the masses. With this expression, the Sardinian intellectual referred to the heritage created by everyday experience in relation to common knowledge, not to the denial of any systematic educational activity by an already conscious leading group. The two elements, "spontaneity" and "conscious direction", are necessary to each other to change the instinctive and aprioristic dimension of common knowledge, but without establishing a dualistic relationship between political direction and subaltern classes, which are reduced to mere mass of maneuver.

On the other hand, arrogance and contempt in the face of spontaneous movements, as well as the refusal to relate to them in order to offer them a conscious direction capable of elevating them and providing them with political content, can have serious consequences because the creation of a spontaneous movement of the subaltern classes, especially in contexts of economic crisis, is often accompanied by a reactionary movement of the ruling classes that uses general uneasiness to weaken government and promote conspiracies that inevitably end in coups d'état. Among the most "efficient" causes of coups, Gramsci highlights conscious leading groups' refusal to give the spontaneous uprisings of the subaltern classes organized and positive direction. We can say this is the main political lesson learned by Gramsci from the failure of the "red biennium", which was followed by fascism. The task of political theory should be to translate into theoretical language the elements of historical life, not, in the opposite direction, try to shape reality on the basis of abstract doctrinal schemes and plans thoroughly created in advance. Also in this case we are faced with a method that dates back to the primacy attributed by Lenin to the particular study of concrete "socioeconomic settings", against all doctrinal pretension that faces reality based on scholastic schemes predefined by the visionary intuition of intellectuals.[20]

---

[19] Ibid., 330.
[20] Gianni Fresu, *Lénin leitor de Marx: dialética e determinismo na história do movimento operário* (trans. Rita Matos Coitinho, São Paulo, Anita Garibaldi, 2016), 109.

CHAPTER 18

Permanent Transformism

The whole *corpus* of the *Notebooks* is based on a condition for scientific research: to understand the deep roots of the drama that led to fascist dictatorship, it was necessary to study the history of the Italian ruling classes and understand the contradictions inherent in the process of national unification.

In the notes of *Notebook 19*, Gramsci highlighted four preliminary thematic groups necessary to understand the origins of this set of problems: (1) the analysis of the various meanings taken on by the word "Italy" in different historical periods; (2) the study of the phases of the passage from Republic to Empire with the "nationalization" of Rome and the peninsula, a transition that led to the recasting of Italian hegemony and to the development of an imperial, supranational and cosmopolitan class; (3) the interruption of the sociopolitical development of communal civility; and (4) Italy's minor importance in the mercantilist period as opposed to other, great new modern states.

The unsuccessful establishment of a unitary Italian state in the modern era and the consequent and traditional absence of a national sentiment comparable to that which appeared in the nations interested in the consolidation of the great absolutist states are particularly important themes in the *Notebooks*. According to the Sardinian intellectual, the historical role of medieval communes and of the Italian bourgeoisie proved to be a disaggregating element of the existing unity, and no new, more advanced forms of unity were found. When other countries began to develop a

G. Fresu, *Antonio Gramsci*, Marx, Engels, and Marxisms, https://doi.org/10.1007/978-3-031-15610-6_18

consciousness aiming to organize their own national culture, Italy lost its role as an international cultural center without the emergence of its own process of national aggregation. Instead of nationalizing, its intellectuals moved abroad and took on top political and cultural roles in European courts.

The failure of the process of national integration of the Italian bourgeoisie, successively made impossible by foreign rule, was historically attributed to two external factors: (1) the Turkish invasion of the Near and Middle East, with the interruption of trade with the East; and (2) the transfer of trade relations from the Mediterranean to the Atlantic, with the great geographical discoveries. In reality, according to Gramsci, these phenomena should be considered the effect of the decline of the Italian Republics, not its cause. In general, the bourgeoisie developed better in absolutist states, exercising indirect power, while in Italy the bourgeoisie, despite having a decisive political role, underwent an involutional process. This was primarily due to the political breakdown of the peninsula, which for a long period determined its decline. Albeit very rich, neither communes nor communal lordships could be considered states, because they lacked a vast territory and sufficient population for an independent international policy. Therefore, the Italian bourgeoisie was the first to exist and create significant forms of capitalist accumulation, but it could not escape the corporate-municipal dimension and ended up undergoing a process of involution, which led it to abandon trade and the risk of productive investments in favor of land income. The bourgeoisie became ruralized, adopting the parasitic behavior typical of the old aristocracy, while the intellectuals kept their cosmopolitan character, but without becoming nationals. The cosmopolitanism of the Italian institutional and intellectual tradition—which the Church inherited from the Roman Empire—is one of the causes of Italy's subordination in international relations during the Middle Ages. In Italy, the Church, with its dual role of universal spiritual monarchy and secular principality, was neither strong enough to occupy the entire peninsula nor weak enough to allow anyone else to do so. The tradition of Roman and medieval universality prevented the development of bourgeois national forces beyond the purely economic-municipal field, which only happened after the French Revolution.

In order to continue a serious study of the historical development of Italian intellectuals, it was necessary to return to the Roman imperial era, when the Italian peninsula was a point of intellectual attraction for all the domains of the Empire. This made the leading groups, including the emperor, increasingly imperial and less Latin. In this sense, in *Notebook 3*, Gramsci speaks of a line of unitary, not national, continuity regarding the development of the Italian cultured classes, which determined an internal imbalance in the composition of the Italian population. The theme of the cosmopolitan role of Italian intellectuals is subsequently developed in *Notebook 5*. For a long period, Italy had an international cultural role, attracting to its universities scholars interested in self-improvement by assimilating culture under the guidance of Italian intellectuals. In addition to this reality, there was also a migratory phenomenon of a different nature toward Italy: from all corners of the world, travelers arrived at the peninsula, which was seen as a great open-air museum and considered, for a long time, essential in the intellectual development of the European cultured classes. Despite this, after a certain moment, Italian intellectuals (with the exception of ecclesiastics) began to emigrate, while the opposite phenomenon ceased. If, on the one hand, the Roman center became internationalized, on the other, other countries developed a national culture of their own with the decisive contribution of Italian intellectuals. This led to the disintegration of the "medieval cosmopolis"; however, the loss of the historical role of the international cultural center did not lead to the genesis of a national culture of its own.

The theme of the weakness of the Italian ruling classes has its roots distant in time, well before the nineteenth century, in the limitation of the capitalist development of communal civility, in the cosmopolitan nature of the intellectual strata, in the ill-fated establishment of a modern unitary state before a series of international events allowed such process. On the contrary, conceiving and presenting the *Risorgimento* as an essentially Italian fact combined provincialism with the little political-intellectual honesty of its interpreters. According to Gramsci, the concept of "national personality", considered outside international relations, would be a mere literary abstraction with no historical and political basis. In this sense, it would not be possible to explain the *Risorgimento* without duly recognizing the weight of the profound transformations produced in the European balance in the eighteenth century:

> There is a mutual weakening of the two great powers and a third power emerges: Prussia. Therefore, the origin of the engine of the *Risorgimento*, that is, of the process of establishing the conditions and international relations that allowed Italy to unite into a nation and international forces to develop and expand, should not be sought in this or that concrete event

recorded at one date or another, but precisely in the same historical process in which the European system itself is transformed.[1]

Among the factors behind the *Risorgimento*, Gramsci also indicated the "catastrophic" weakening of the Vatican in the eighteenth century. According to Gramsci, as Hegel explained in his lessons on *The philosophy of history*, the Holy See, given the long process of Counter-Reformation, lost much of its strength because, unable to count on the dissuasive pressure of the fanatical masses that it commanded, it gradually lost its ability to directly and indirectly influence other governments. "The royalist policy of Enlightenment monarchies was the manifestation of this loss of authority on the part of the Church as a European and therefore Italian power."[2]

Even with this weakening, the conditions for the *Risorgimento* were created because the process of Italian unification could only take place with this recasting of the Church as an Italian and overall a European power. The *Risorgimento* is the point of origin of the essential elements of the weakness of the Italian ruling classes, starting with the failure of the democratic perspectives of the Action Party and, in contrast, with the hegemonic capacity the moderates led by Cavour, "the exponent of war of position" in Italy, the most organic representative of this change produced in the expansion of the European bourgeoisie.

As contradictory as it may seem, in the *Risorgimento* the concepts of "war of position" and "war of movement" coincide, and war of movement becomes war of position. "It is a dynamic assessment [Gramsci writes] that must be made about the Restorations, which would be a cunning of providence in the sense intended by Vico."[3]

This identification was due to the complementary nature of the concept of war of movement (popular initiative), represented by Mazzini, and passive revolution (war of position), represented by Cavour, both equally indispensable. There is a fundamental difference, however, that explains the moderates' hegemony over the Action Party:

> Whereas Cavour was aware of his mission (at least to some extent) and understood Mazzini's mission, Mazzini does not seem to have been aware

---

[1] Antonio Gramsci, *Quaderni del carcere* (Turin, Einaudi, 1977), 1963.
[2] Ibid.
[3] Ibid., 1767.

of his and Cavour's; if, on the contrary, Mazzini had been aware, in other words, if he had been a realistic politician and not an enlightened apostle (that is, if he had not been Mazzini), the outcome of the convergence of the two activities would have been different, more favorable to Mazzinism: that is, the Italian state would have been built on less backward, more modern foundations.[4]

It is well known that in parallel with neo-Guelphic suggestions, a liberal orientation was also developed among the moderates in favor of national unification by consensus among the Italian states. However, the primacy of this process was attributed to the King of Sardinia, not to the Pontiff. This orientation was evidenced in *Speranze d'Italia* (1844) by Cesare Balbo, who theorized the liberation of Italy from Austrian rule by diplomatic means, with the inclusion of Piedmont in the political landscape of the great European powers interested in solving the eastern question. Balbo had predicted the definitive expansion of Austria toward the Balkan Peninsula and its abandonment of Italian lands as a result of the foreseeable collapse of the Ottoman Empire. That would ensure the European balance, leading to a solution to both the Italian and the eastern question. However, the idea of "Balkanizing Austria", reiterated in later writings, was totally unrealistic for Gramsci; it was not a work of ingenuity or political foresight, but rather a symptom of political passivity and discouragement given the difficulty of the national project.

In 1848, two of the three main political options of the *Risorgimento* failed: first, Gioberti's neo-Guelphic hypothesis failed, which for a few years had been hegemonic on the moderate front; then, with the capitulation of the Roman Republic and the resistance in Veneto, the democratic prospects of Mazzini, Carlo Cattaneo and Giuseppe Ferrari were changed dramatically. The success of Cavour's diplomatic activity led part of the democratic movement (among others, Garibaldi himself, Daniele Manin, Giacomo Medici, Giuseppe Montanelli, Enrico Cosenz) to distance itself from Mazzini and his insurrectionary perspective, which proved totally unsuccessful by forming the Italian National Party, which expressly declared in its manifesto its intention to constitute a common cause with the Savoyas. In the first months of 1859, this party became a very useful weapon in the hands of Cavour to support his diplomatic action.

[4] Ibid.

This passage seems very important because it molecularly changed the very composition of the moderate forces, facilitating the elimination of neo-Guelphism and the impoverishment of the Mazzinian movement. It was possible to identify in it the first manifestation of transformism, whose importance (as a form of historical development) had not been sufficiently investigated yet, according to Gramsci.

After 1848, Mazzini understood the transition from "war of movement" to "war of position", a radical change in the political struggle that went beyond 1871. After 1848, only moderates developed a self-critical reflection when revamping their strategy. The elimination of neo-Guelphism was the clearest proof of this. Nothing similar happened in the Mazzinian movement, which was gradually abandoned by some of its main figures, who later became "the left wing of the Piedmontese Party". "In the expression, albeit rude, of Victor Emmanuel II: 'We have the Action Party in our pocket', there is more political-historical sense than in everything Mazzini said."[5]

Based on these dynamics, Gramsci highlighted the methods of formation of the ruling classes through a process of co-opting and methodically absorbing the new elements resulting from social dynamics. Thus, even initially hostile groups were absorbed progressively and molecularly by state apparatuses until they became their support. Transformism was an integral part of these dynamics and revealed all its attractive potential for the state in the *Risorgimento* (with republican and democratic groups), as well as after the unification of Italy (with Catholics and Reformists).

In Gramsci's view, moderate hegemony over the Action Party is one of the most paradigmatic themes in the history of the Italian ruling classes, which contributes to understanding the role played by intellectuals in defining the predominant hegemony structures.[6] During the *Risorgimento*, the intellectuals of the Action Party adopted a paternalistic attitude toward the popular masses, to which they did not want to be attached, and were therefore absorbed and incorporated "molecularly" by the moderates. The essentially Italian phenomenon of "transformism" therefore originates in these dynamics between intellectuals and the two fundamental social classes, and it includes the general problem of the formation of

---

[5] Ibid., 1782.

[6] Gianni Fresu, "Moderati e Democrati Nell'ottocento. L'interpretazione di Gramsci", in Cristina Carpinelli e Vittorio Gioiello (orgs.), *Il Risorgimento: un'epoca? Per una ricostruzione storico-critica* (Frankfurt, Zambon, 2012), 207–40.

bourgeoisie-led national groups, that is, the theme of the complete failure of the democratic perspectives of the Action Party, which was unable to encompass the complexity of the agrarian question—in Gramsci's view, the only "engine" that could mobilize the popular masses.[7]

In Gramci's view, a class is dominant when it can lead the allied classes and prevail over its enemy or adversary classes; therefore, the ruling class must lead before and after the seizure of power. Thus, the moderates exercised this direction in the Action Party during the *Risorgimento*, but they also did so later, with "transformism", and due to the ability of the moderates to exert political hegemony over the shareholders [of the Action Party] the *Risorgimento* took the form of "a revolution without revolution".

> All Italian politics from 1870 to the present day is characterized by transformism, that is, by the development of a ruling class in the cadres established by the moderates after 1848, with the absorption of the active elements that emerged from the allied classes and even enemy ones. Political direction becomes an aspect of domination, as the absorption of the elites from the enemy classes leads to their beheading and impotence.[8]

In Gramsci's view, the moderates represented a relatively homogeneous social class, subject to little fluctuation, while the Action Party, not supported by any historical class, ended up constantly subject to the direction of the moderates.[9] The intellectuals on the moderate front were really the organic expression of the upper classes, and therefore they were at the same time intellectuals, political organizers, businessmen, large landowners, that is, they indeed belonged to these classes and individually managed to combine the identity of those represented with that of the representative. Precisely due to this "condensed" nature, moderate intellectuals were able to spontaneously attract the whole mass of intellectuals in Italy. These dynamics found in the history of the *Risorgimento* confirms

---

[7] Notwithstanding all the limitations identified in the *Risorgimento* process, in Marxist historiographical orientations the *Risorgimento* assumes a central value and importance that goes far beyond its results. Thus, the clandestine PCI, in line with Antonio Gramsci's historicism, ideally referred to the *Risorgimento* as opposed to fascism (not by chance he would call its partisan divisions the Garibaldi Brigades) and interpreted the Resistance as the accomplishment of the Italian *Risorgimento*.

[8] Antonio Gramsci, *Quaderni del carcere*, cit., 41.

[9] Ibid., 2010.

an extremely important historical-political rule developed in detail in the *Notebooks*: there is no independent class of intellectuals, but each class has its own organic intellectuals; however, the class that manages to take on a driving and progressive role ends up exercising hegemony, also subordinating the intellectuals of other classes.

The Action Party could not exercise this power of attraction and was subject to that of the moderates. The Mazzinians could only have resisted the hegemonic capacity of the moderates if they had incorporated into their own program the demands of the popular masses, starting with the peasants. It was necessary to contrast the "empirical attraction" of moderates with an "organized attraction", that is, an organic government program capable of mobilizing the popular masses. But the Action Party never had a government program and could not exert a political direction even among its members, limiting itself to being only a movement of agitation and propaganda of the moderates, which followed the rhetorical tradition of Italian literature and confused cultural unity with political and territorial unity.

The contradictions of national unification were also reflected on the historiographical level, and the multiple and different interpretations of this process are, according to Gramsci, a confirmation of the ambiguities, weaknesses and inconsistencies inherent in the main forces of the *Risorgimento*, of the lack of sufficiently national elements among the ruling classes. This set of interpretations has an immediately political and non-historical nature, besides being affected by a certain abstraction and underlying partiality. This literature emerges in the most acute phases of the political and social crisis, which are marked by the distance between rulers and those ruled and by fears caused by the risks of crushing national life in its conservative balances.[10] As we will see, according to Gramsci, exactly in similar phases, marked by the crisis of hegemony of the ruling classes, the intellectual classes strive to reorganize ideological currents and political forces in crisis. We find a coherent review of these interpretations in the notes of the *Notebooks*, based on the publications associated with the

---

[10] Gianni Fresu, "Il trasformismo permanente. Feticismo storico e mitologia nazionale in Gramsci", in Mauro Pala (org.), *Narrazioni egemoniche. Gramsci, letteratura e società civile* (Bologna, Il Mulino, 2014), 151–67.

historical right[11]—which was overthrown by the advent of the left—of which the famous article "Torniamo Allo Statuto!" [Let's return to the statute!], by Sidney Sonnino, is perhaps the manifesto. The change of government, after the fall of Marco Minghetti, gave rise to a trend marked by recriminations and pessimistic assessments about the fate of Italy. These publications were characterized by petulant rhetoric and defined by Gramsci as "angry, bilious, hostile, with no constructive elements, with no historical references to any tradition, because in the past there was no reactionary reference point that could be proposed for any restoration".[12]

This current condemned the parliamentary evolution of the Italian political system and called for a return to old customs in relations between monarchy, the Executive and the Legislature, but references to an alleged Italian government tradition were in fact vague and abstract. Underlying such rhetoric is the barely disguised fear felt by large landowners, the aristocracy and consortia of the historical right in the face of the slightest democratic progress capable of opening the political citadel to the popular masses.[13]

The books of the "rightists" depict political and moral corruption in the period of the left in power, but the publication of the followers of the Action Party does not present the period of the right-wing government as the best. It turns out that there was no essential change in the transition from right to left: the crisis faced by the country is not due to the parliamentary regime [...], but to the weakness and organic inconsistency of the ruling class and the great misery and backwardness of the country's population.[14]

[11] These publications included *Teorica dei governi e governo parlamentare* (1884) [The theory of governments and parliamentary government], by Gaetano Mosca, *L'Italia vivente* (1878) [Living Italy], by Leone Carpi, and even a series of in-depth analyses of periodicals, weeklies and magazines (*Nuova Antologia* and *Rassegna Settimanal*).

[12] Antonio Gramsci, *Prison Notebooks*, cit., 1976.

[13] The only exception in this gloomy scenario was, for Gramsci, Quintino Sella, one of the few Italian bourgeois protagonists in the attempt to build a modern state, a figure that differs significantly from the politicians of his generation in terms of technical skills, moral standing, culture and consistency. Moving away from the right, which was increasingly becoming a consortium of bureaucrats, generals and landowners, more than trying to create a political party, Sella approached some more progressive currents and participated in the transformism thus defined by Gramsci: "an attempt to create a strong bourgeois party beyond the personalist and sectarian traditions of the *Risorgimento* settings" (Ibid., 184).

[14] Ibid., 1978.

The Italian reality at the end of the century became even more absurd given the precariousness and insecurity of the new state because of the *non expedit*[15] and the fierce opposition to the legal state and to all modernity on the part of the Catholic world. More generally, the country was characterized by structural political weakness:

> At the center are all the liberal shades, from the moderates to the republicans, on which all the memories of the hatreds of the period act and which fight each other mercilessly; on the left, the poor, backward, illiterate country sporadically, discontinuously and hysterically shows a series of subversive-anarchic tendencies, with no consistency or concrete political orientation, which maintain a feverish state with no constructive future. There are no "economic parties" but *déclassé* ideological groups of all classes, roosters that announce a sun that never rises.[16]

In Italian historiography, all the analysis of Italy's past, from the Roman era to the *Risorgimento* and post-unification, was aimed at finding a de facto national unity, justifying the present with the historical past. This ideological operation happened due to the need to arouse the interest of the "national volunteers" with the alleged glories of Italian history, thus compensating for the shortcomings and limitations of a *Risorgimento* conducted by small elites, in the complete absence of the popular masses. With this national mythology, an attempt was made to replace the organic adherence of the popular masses to the state with the selection of "volunteers" from an abstractly conceived nation. That basically showed that no one was able to understand the problem proposed by Machiavelli in his military texts: the need to unite with the peasant masses to replace the mercenaries with a national militia, to adopt the national popular element as an alternative to voluntarism, since voluntarism is as mistaken and dangerous a solution as mercenarism is.

This way of representing historical events—which Gramsci calls "fetishistic history"—turns abstract and mythological characters into protagonists of Italian history and therefore "the problem of seeking the historical origins of a concrete and detailed event, the formation of the modern Italian state in the nineteenth century, was transformed into the problem

---

[15] See note 14 on Part Two, Chap. 14.
[16] Antonio Gramsci, *Quaderni del carcere*, cit., 1978.

of seeing this state as a unit, as a nation or generically as Italy, in the whole of previous history, just as the rooster must exist in the fertilized egg".[17]

In Gramsci's view, the idea that Italy had always been a nation was a purely ideological construct, a prejudice responsible for the anti-historical dialectical maneuvers aimed at making this unity date back to the pre-*Risorgimento* past. In nineteenth-century Italy, this national unity did not exist because it lacked a fundamental element, the people-nation, and a close connection with national intellectuals. For these reasons, historiographic reconstructions were in fact propaganda that sought to create national unity based on literature rather than history; this approach to unification was a "wish-to-be" rather than a "duty-to-be" determined by the already existing de facto conditions.[18]

Another ideological aspect of this historiographical approach is its tendency to find obstacles to the unification of Italy in the dormancy of the virtues of the Italian people and in the intervention of foreign powers that, with their domination, prevented the manifestation of what it really was: the existence of the Italian nation. This interpretation gave rise to totally abstract images. The anti-historicity of this approach derives from the fact that it prevented not only the understanding of reality, which it contradicted, but also the grasping of the true extent of the effort made by the protagonists of the *Risorgimento*.

Its little scientific reliability led to the need for a critical study of the *Risorgimento* to overcome an inconclusive and idle debate pertaining to sheer "empirical methodology":

And if writing history means making the history of the present, the history book that, in the present, helps the developing forces to become more aware of themselves and therefore more concretely active and accomplishing is great. The biggest flaw of all these ideological interpretations of the *Risorgimento* consists in the fact that they were merely ideological, that is, they did not encourage the action of current political forces. Works of men of letters, of dilettantes, acrobatic constructions of men who wanted to show talent, if not intelligence, either addressed to small intellectual groups with no future or written to justify reactionary forces hidden in traps,

---

[17] Ibid., 1981.

[18] Gianni Fresu, "Antonio Gramsci, fascismo e classi dirigenti nella storia d'Italia", *NAE: Trimestrale di Cultura*, Cuec, Cagliari, n. 21, ano 6, 2008, 31–2.

borrowing intentions that had imaginary purposes, and therefore small services such as intellectual minions [...] and mercenaries of science.[19]

The succession of different ideological interpretations of the emergence
of the Italian state, associated with the individual impulse of singular personalities, was a faithful mirror of the primitive and empirical nature of the
old political parties and therefore of the absence, in Italian political life, of
an organic and articulated movement potentially capable of promoting
permanent and continuous political-cultural development.

Thus, the dilettantism of historical literature on the *Risorgimento* would
be connected to the lack of a serious and rigorous historical perspective in
the programs of Italian political parties, whose "nomadic and gypsy"
nature received Gramsci's attention in other notes. Hence, the political-
cultural debates would not unfold following a continuous process either,
but through individual campaigns, from time to time, as the premise of
short-lived political movements affected by the same dilettantism observed
in terms of historical perspective.

> This is a very useful way of proceeding to facilitate the "operations" of the
> "irresponsible" or "hidden forces" that have "independent newspapers" as
> their spokesperson: they need to create occasional movements of public
> opinion to be kept until certain purposes are fulfilled and then be left to
> bleed and die.[20]

In Italy, according to Gramsci, only the history of intellectuals was
uninterrupted. Therefore, even the so-called national sentiment—before
and after the *Risorgimento*—was not tied to objective institutions; it was
not "popular-national", but simply a feeling of "intellectuals". In Italy,
there were no objective elements capable of having a real uniting role,
such as creating a national sentiment that was not purely subjective. This
role could be performed neither by language, which was discontinuous
given the predominance of dialects, nor by culture, which was very
restricted and used by small intellectual groups as a caste characteristic,
nor by political parties, which were not solid enough and acted only in
electoral situations. The only valid and widespread "popular-national" element was the Church, but given its traditional cosmopolitan nature and its

---

[19] Antonio Gramsci, *Quaderni del carcere*, cit., 1983–4.
[20] Ibid.

struggle against the secular state it played a disaggregating role, instead of favoring the creation of a unitary national sentiment.

French historical culture, on the contrary, had a united basis—in addition to the various political trends that ensued (from dynastic to radical-socialist)—a "popular-national" consciousness, precisely because the permanent element of that history, which was marked by changes of political nature, was the "people-nation"; there, that connection between "people-nation" and intellectuals, absent in Italian national history, actually existed. In Italy, on the contrary, intellectuals—engaged in the work of building mythological, not historical, unification—distinguished themselves from the people, put themselves on the outside, creating and strengthening among themselves a particular spirit of caste characterized precisely by distrust of the people. The Jacobins, on the contrary, fought hard to secure the link between city and countryside, achieving strong political hegemony, imposing themselves on the bourgeoisie and leading it to a much more advanced position than it actually wanted and than historical conditions themselves would have made possible.[21] In general, in the early stages of the revolution, the bourgeoisie presents only its immediate corporate interests; it "talks tough, but actually demands very little". In the French Revolution, it was the Jacobins who "took the bourgeois class forward, kicking its ass",[22] making it lose its corporate nature until it became a hegemonic class and providing a "permanent basis" to the new state. The Jacobins were the only "party of the ongoing revolution" because they represented the immediate interests not only of the French bourgeoisie but also of the revolutionary movement as a whole, and managed to lead a new revolutionary social bloc in which a role was also played by the popular and peasant masses, which were well aware of the need to establish a common bloc with the Jacobins to defeat once and for all the classes of the land aristocracy.

Historical experience thus demonstrated that if the peasants move in "spontaneous impulses", this causes oscillations in the intellectual strata and can lead part of them to adhere to the positions of the new social bloc. Thus, if the intellectuals or a part of them become the leaders of a platform that takes the demands of the peasant masses for itself, they end up attracting increasingly significant groups of masses. Consequently, even in Italy, it would have been possible to break down the reactionary bloc that united

[21] Ibid., 2014.
[22] Ibid., 2027.

the rural classes with the legitimist and clerical intellectual groups if the democratic groups had taken the lead in a new social bloc, attracting and directing the peasant masses and the intellectuals of the "middle and lower strata". This was precisely the programmatic task that Gramsci presented to the communists in the essay on the southern question.

In Italy, the weakness of liberal political parties, after the *Risorgimento*, was a result of the imbalance between agitation and propaganda and the lack of principles and organic continuity. Tendencies toward opportunism, corruption and "transformism" would be found in the narrow cultural and strategic horizon of political parties and in the absence of organic links between them and the classes represented. These parties did not develop as a political and collective expression of the interests of a class, as a con-solidated and theorized consciousness of its historical role, but as mere groups of immediate interests formed around personalities. They were electoral committees, not parties; they lacked theoretical activity or pro-grammatic vision focused on the future, accustomed to the "day to day, with its factionism and its personal clashes".[23] In Italy, political parties "were not permeated by the effective realism of national life"[24] and conse-quently they did not fulfill the historical function of building a national ruling class; for this reason, the main groups that acquired their intellec-tual skills in the academic world or in the production world were groups of "apolitical cadres" with a purely "rhetorical and non-national" mental and cultural basis.

> The main reason for this nature of the parties lies in the disaggregation of the economic classes, in the gelatinous economic and social structure of the country, but this explanation is somewhat fatalistic: in fact, if it is true that parties are only the nomenclature of classes, it is also true that parties are not only a mechanical and passive expression of the classes themselves, but they also react energetically to them to develop them, consolidate them, univer-salize them. This did not happen in Italy, and this omission is precisely mani-fested in this imbalance between agitation and propaganda—or however one may call it.[25]

The weakness of the political parties and consequently of the ruling classes in Italy, of their very nature, was largely a result of what Gramsci

---

[23] Ibid., 386.
[24] Ibid.
[25] Ibid., 387.

called "state government", that is to say, the bulk of the interests of the crown and of the bureaucracy which in Italy amounted to a political party, aiming to separate the permanent cadres of national political life from the masses and from the true national interests of the state, besides forging a paternalistic bond of a "Bonapartist-Caesarian type" between these individuals and the state government. Transformism and "the dictatorships of Depretis, Crispi and Giolitti", the misery and pettiness of cultural, parliamentary and political life in Italy, were analyzed precisely based on this phenomenon. If social classes usually produce political parties and these parties create the leading cadres of civil society and the state, in Italy the state government did not act to reconcile these manifestations with national state interests; on the contrary, it always favored disaggregation, separating individual political personalities from any social, cultural and even broader theoretical reference with regard to the fiduciary relationship, which is precisely "Bonapartist-Caesarian", with the state government.[26]

The Italian *Risorgimento* could have had a democratic result if it had encompassed the peasant question and the issue of land reform, progressively facing the dialectic between city and countryside.

[26] Ibid.

CHAPTER 19

Historical Premises and *Congenital* Contradictions in Italian Biography

It has been widely discussed that, in Gramsci's view, fascism was a complex phenomenon, full of premises and implications, whose deeper causes should be sought in the many contradictions inherent in the history of Italy and not only in the "psychosis" that preceded and followed the war. In this sense, although he rarely speaks directly and explicitly about fascism in the *Notebooks*, his prison notes are an important attempt at scientific investigation into this great historical drama. In the years following Mussolini's rise to power, this was not only Gramsci's belief. On the contrary, in several authors, close to or far from him, we find a similar historicist call for an organic analysis capable of explaining more thoroughly and satisfactorily the collapse of the Italian liberal regime. In Piero Gobetti, too, the drama of fascism[1] indicates the need for an exegesis of the *Risorgimento* able to reveal the "fundamental misconception of our history: a desperate attempt to become modern having only literati with non-Machiavellian cunning impulses or Garibaldians with emphasis on courts".[2]

According to this brilliant intellectual—who died at only twenty-five years of age in exile as a result of the beating he took from the fascists—the liberal revolution was imposed as a historical necessity to overcome the

---

[1] Gianni Fresu e Aldo Accardo, *Oltre la parentesi. Fascismo e storia d'Italia nell'interpretazione gramsciana* (Rome, Carocci, 2009), 53–70.

[2] Piero Gobetti, *La rivoluzione liberale. Saggio sulla lotta politica in Italia* (Turin, Einaudi, 1974), 9.

G. Fresu, *Antonio Gramsci, Marx, Engels, and Marxisms*, https://doi.org/10.1007/978-3-031-15610-6_19

inherent limits so often highlighted by his friend Gramsci. In Italy, liberalism had been stifled still in its cradle, both economically, with protectionism, and politically, which prevented a real parliamentary dialectic between political programs representative of social forces in dispute with one another. In opposition to the servile morality coercively imposed on the country by the fascist militias, it was necessary to reorganize the ethics of the Italian state based on the primacy of freedom. In the national historical becoming, from unification to fascism, the young liberal intellectual saw a permanent tendency to consider the plurality of democratic nuances, the dialectic of political contradictions, and social conflict to be anomalies to be excluded. Even before fascism, this occurred in two ways: (1) through the corrupted absorption of critical forces on the part of conservative balances; and (2) through the physical annihilation of groups and intellectuals that opposed the ruling power bloc. This blocked the country's progress, making it difficult to consolidate a modern economic activity and consequently disabling the social processes necessary for the creation of leading groups suitable for an advanced technical class.

As we have seen, Gramsci attributed the failure in the formation of a modern unitary state in Italy to the inability of the communal ruling classes to overcome the "corporate-municipal" phase; Gobetti, in turn, described the predominance of conservative interests and the parasitic exploitation of the agricultural economy as distinctive features that explained the limits of that reality. The political and economic primacy of *signoria* over the communes and the absence of a religious reform ultimately slowed national political development, limiting the fragmented cultural reality of the Italian states to the claustrophobic pettiness of the courts.

> Our reform was Machiavelli, a political theorist, a loner. His concepts did not find men able to give them life, or social ground to be founded on. He is a modern man because he develops a conception of the state that rebels against transcendence, conceives a political art that organizes practice, and professes civil religiosity as spontaneity of initiative and economy.[3]

Another element of great convergence, regarding the failure of the liberal revolution in the *Risorgimento*, is related to the negative assessment of the romantic and literary dimension of unitary aspiration, which found its most coherent expression in the abstract "metaphysics" of Mazzinism,

---

[3] Ibid., 12.

which is characterized by a moralistic and nebulous apostolate able to rally supporters in the environments of emigrated Italians, but unable to mobilize the great popular masses. In Gobetti's view, Giuseppe Mazzini's doctrine, which originated from ideological fragments of the circulation of ideas in Europe, was reduced to a modest religious reform which would later become unpopular and confuse propaganda with revolution, political reform with demagogy. Unlike this doctrinal abstraction, typical of the democratic movement led by Mazzini, Piedmontese liberalism was composed of leading cadres with a background in economics and in political concreteness.

With "a mediocre king like Victor Emmanuel II", the *Risorgimento* would have had an even more retrogressive result, so it turned out to be a great luck for the Italian people that Cavour had led that process, preventing it from turning into a tyranny. In the *Risorgimento* landscape, Cavour surpassed all his contemporaries due to his ability to face the most complex issues from the perspective of a statesman, his ability to speak to the people without demagogically asking it for consent or corrupting it. In a context dominated by the anti-modernist rhetoric of the Catholic world, Cavour was, according to Gobetti, the only one to lay the foundations of a liberal revolution, having as instruments of action only the dynasty and army of a small state.

> Compared to the men who came after him, except for [Quintino] Sella, he seems to belong to another race: for [Agostino] Depretis and for [Giovanni] Giolitti himself, who also has the mind of a statesman, the right term of comparison is not Cavour, but [Urban] Rattazzi, a model of juggling, of misunderstanding and of demagogy.[4]

As we have seen, in the post-war articles, Gramsci also used Cavour as a parameter to highlight the intellectual and political stature in opposition to figures such as Francesco Crispi, Giolitti, the nationalists or even the confused intellectuality of the Futurist movement. In *Notebook 8*, he once again highlighted the need to study with no prejudice or rhetoric "Cavour's realism", which was evidenced by the very preponderance of international factors in the development of the process of national unification. The Mazzinians considered the diplomatic path of unification a "monstrous deed", whereas according to Crispi, Cavour essentially limited himself to

---

[4] Ibid., 24.

"diplomatizing the revolution", involuntarily affirming how indispensable the Piedmontese politician was. Giving new meaning to Cavour's historical legacy was politically necessary because privileging the appropriate work to create international conditions favorable to unification meant acknowledging how unprepared and weak the national forces were in the face of this mission, that is, to deal with the complete failure of the Mazzinian program.

In addition to the qualities of realism, in contrast to a diplomatic tradition based exclusively on personal cunning, Cavour tried to achieve national unification through the economy and liberalism—avoiding rhetorical or religious suggestions—by reinserting the Italians into a European policy that was strange to them until then. He based his government practice and his own foreign policy on "honorably liberal" principles, gaining much more diplomatic prestige and esteem than the real conditions of Italy and its modest ruling classes did.

According to Gobetti, Cavour's true masterpiece was his ecclesiastical policy, the "free Church in a free state" principle, a demonstration of maturity and political skill, not an abstract formula of the philosophy of law. Cavour was wise to remove the state's struggle against Church interference from the dogmatic terrain—in which, in a deeply Catholic country, it would hopelessly lose—and transfer it to the terrain of freedom of conscience. Thus, he left the anticlerical tones and the political-philosophical disputes to other political subjects, forcing the Church to confront an essential premise of modernity.

In the course of a few years, the president of the Piedmontese council created a concrete situation that was incomparably more advanced regarding the real potentialities of the country; however, after his death, the contradictions of that process emerged and the new state found itself deprived of its only true direction and with no inspiring principle equal to the historical task. These limits were clearly seen in the period between 1860 and the First World War, which was marked by the corrupting practice of transformism and by a false dialectic of alternation with no alternative consortia to run the country. According to Gobetti, the greatest deficiency of the Italian liberal regime was the absence of both a true conservative party and an authentic liberal party. Nationalist radicalism—which found first in interventionism and then in fascism its most coherent objectification—was an authentic "germ of the dissolution of political customs", becoming a unanimous practice in Italian politics after the 1870s.

The existence of a serious conservative party would have indirectly played a modern and positive liberal role, basing the moral cohesion of the country on respect for laws and public security and injecting it with anti-bodies against the nationalist megalomania typical of petty-bourgeois oscillations. In this sense, according to Gobetti, the passage from Depretis to Crispi also assumed a paradigmatic importance that would later happen again even more dramatically in the history of Italy, precisely because of the absence of a true liberal foundation.

> When they got tired of Depretis's cunning and charm, the Italians indulged in the easy seductions of Crispi's megalomania and in African defeat, and the whole nation was compromised. As late as the rehabilitations may seem, Adwa[5] marks the severe condemnation of an easy romantic mentality and represents the preventive criticism of all nationalist ideology, which would emerge in Italy with the adventure mentality and the parasitic spiritual preparation of the petty bourgeoisie: imperialism is naivety when the elementary problems of existence still need to be solved.[6]

If there had been a conservative party in Italy, it would have performed a sanitary role, preemptively eliminating the radical, nationalist psychology, which eventually overcame the "*parvenus* from a bankrupt bourgeoisie".[7] While a conservative party was lacking as an expression of southern agrarian interests, all the conditions necessary for the creation of a liberal party of industrialists failed, which thus opened up a huge gap between industry and liberalism. The deplorable surrender of the ruling classes to Mussolini, which were ready to use violence to restore the social order threatened by the eruption of mass politics, was the final result of such contradiction. Giolitti, Antonio Salandra, Benedetto Croce—all the great names of Italian liberalism—indistinctly favored and supported the rise of fascism under the illusion that they could constitutionalize it, that is, absorb it and spare for the future *duce* the same fate once suffered by Mazzinian politicians, Catholic and socialist reformists, swallowed by the balance between traditional power blocs.

---

[5] In the Battle of Adwa in Ethiopia, on March 1, 1896, the Italian army engaged in the Abyssinian War—through which it intended to conquer a colonial domain—was defeated by the troops of Negus Menelik II. This defeat frustrated Italy's colonial aspirations for many years.

[6] Piero Gobetti, *La rivoluzione liberale*, cit., 33.

[7] Ibid.

After unification, Italian industry consolidated its position thanks to customs protectionism and state subsidies, rejecting economic individualism, the liberal assumption of any approach worthy of that name. Thus, industry developed in the light of a strictly national, rather than European and global, corporate spirit. Hence the defense of the system of privileges and protections guaranteed by the state and some provincialism, both economic and political, which were incompatible with liberalism. Protectionism caused enormous political damage in Italy, oppressing through corruption both the bourgeoisie and the proletariat, which resulted in the decay of the customs of both. Giolitti's system of concessions between industry and northern socialist reformism, to the detriment of the *Mezzogiorno*, confirmed that. The absence of a conservative party increased the gulf between the North and the South and made it structural. If Italian industry had developed according to liberal models, the relationship with agriculture and the *Mezzogiorno* would have relied on more organic and harmonious bases.

More generally, Gobetti challenged Italian liberalism's inability to deal with the workers' movement, which was defined by him as the natural heir to the universal function first exercised by the bourgeoisie. The failure to understand the social dynamics underlying the class struggle and the historical development of political parties was the cause of the decline of the liberal political class, which was oppressed by the emergence of the great masses onto the political scene.

As Cavour's path had reached its end, Italian liberalism developed in complete ideological confusion, accepting everything under its banner, from fervent nationalism to parasitic protectionism, and losing consciousness of its doctrinal bases and, along with them, of the meaning of its historical mission. Fragile Italian liberalism was converted into "demagogic democracy".

> After the 1870s, the Liberal Party lost its renewal function because it did not have a central libertarian passion and it was reduced to a ruling party, a balancing act for initiates who performed their duties as tutors and deceived those ruled with transactions and social policy artifices.[8]

In light of this continuity, Gobetti described fascism as a "national biography", because it was the final representation of the renunciation of

---

[8] Ibid., 55.

politics, due to the laziness of the ruling classes, which were not very interested in engaging in the slow construction of the state and therefore in
facing modernity with the political dialectic and with the social conflict
that any modernization inevitably ends up creating. The illusion of saving
the classes from the conflict, with a rhetorical idea of conciliation, in addition to the useless and abstract conception, concealed the ill-disguised
desire to prevent the effective democratization of the country. Thus, fascism inherited from the post-Cavour ruling classes the claim to "heal the
Italians from the political struggle". The *actualist*[9] ideology of fascism and
the optimistic and relaxed confidence underlying its claim to overcome
any difficulty thanks to the palingenetic power of the will were proof not
only of the innate infantilism of this movement but, more broadly, of the
political primitivism of the Italian ruling classes, which were enthusiasti-
cally seduced by Mussolini's theatrical poses.

These elements of continuity, as well as the need for the historicist
interpretation of the fascist drama starting with the failure of the Italian
liberal revolution, are found in the fundamental work *Storia del liberalismo
europeo* [History of European liberalism], by Guido De Ruggiero. Also in
this case, the need to return to the conceptual and political roots of the
European liberal movement was linked to the need to understand the
causes of what had happened and rediscover the ideal and historical reasons necessary to overcome fascist barbarism.

Despite the chasm that opened up in the country, which led many former anti-Giolittians, starting with Benedetto Croce, to lament the "democratic progression" experienced between 1900 and 1914, De Ruggiero
was not completely indifferent to Italian liberal tradition, whose modest
importance in the European context, on the contrary, was controversially

[9] Actualism, or current idealism, conceived by the main intellectual in the Mussolini
regime, Giovanni Gentile, intended to philosophically substantiate fascism through a new
idealistic synthesis of the philosophical traditions of Kant and Hegel. According to this philosophy, the only true reality lies in the pure act of thought as awareness of the present
moment, by means of which the absolute spirit of history recognized by the philosopher
is sought.

highlighted by him. Italian liberalism presented itself largely as a mere reflection of foreign doctrines and guiding lines.[10]

This limited importance was explained by multiple factors, such as: (1) the political fragmentation that prevented the creation of large currents of public opinion, which sacrificed all the development in the pettiness and rivalry of the small regional, if not municipal, fractions; (2) the submission of large swathes of Italian territories to foreign powers, which expended considerable energy in the struggle for national emancipation, but in a context of deep conceptual confusion between the principles of freedom and independence; (3) the spirit of the counterreformation that stifled the individualistic sentiment, an essential premise of modern liberalism; (4) the literary and bookish nature of a culture reduced to "dusty scholarship isolated from all vital interests of the present" which was transformed into national political culture; and (5) the economic backwardness that delayed the differentiation between social classes and the formation of a broad middle stratum.

Among the economic and social factors that limited the potential of Italian liberalism was also the minor importance of feudalism due to the rapid emergence of municipalities and landlords and the subsequent dominance of foreign powers. Elsewhere, the antithesis between the people and the prince led to the emergence of the first school of political liberalism: diets, states general, parliaments, which were, nonetheless, alien to the Italian tradition.

> In Italy, Roman law tradition was never completely extinct, since the early Middle Ages, and its persistence effectively contrasts with the exclusive domain of feudal law, [...] which made it difficult to establish a highly privileged, exclusive right, thus favoring the civil liberties of individuals. But at the same time, being a right of subjects, of men equal in submission, with its influence, it prevented the idea of the people's own, original right, independent of the state, and therefore in opposition to the right of the prince, from taking root in the consciousness of the people. This was how the Italians lacked the vital experience of the antithesis between the people and the

---

[10] That opinion was shared by Arturo Carlo Jemolo (*Chiesa e Stato in Italia. Dalla unificazione ai giorni nostri*, Turin, Einaudi, 1975), who reaffirmed how modern liberalism, grounded (albeit in many ways) on the idea of a national state with a constitutional order and a government legitimized by a parliamentary majority, did not have a great theorist among the intellectuals of Italy—at least until Cavour. Its men, according to Jemolo, were mainly apostles of the idea, missionaries or accomplishers.

prince, which in other places helped to create the sense of political freedoms and the love for them.[11]

The intellectual movement of the *Risorgimento* was very important in the history of Italy, anticipating its political unification; however, its protagonists, followers and interpreters, assigned undeserved European importance to it, which led to misconceptions and illusions that would fatally be revealed in 1848. This self-representative disproportion was attributed to the literary tradition that, in De Ruggiero's view, like Antonio Gramsci's and Gobetti's, was the only element of continuity in national life over the centuries, in the absence of national and political unity.

After the end of the Giobertian primacy of civilization and science, typical of humanism and the Renaissance, it became a "primacy of memories". The idea of self-sufficiency, typical of Italian literary culture, was based on an imaginary world in which the idea of that primacy, already dead and buried for centuries, would continue to subsist, just as in that "fictional world" the idea of a de facto national political unity was being created (painfully confused with the unity of national culture) in the history of Italy.

The narrowness of this cultural dimension, which was convinced of having all the elements to be sufficient, made it even more difficult to insert Italian intellectual currents into the general climate of European culture:

> Even when foreign influence became predominant, as in the eighteenth and nineteenth centuries, the indelible national glory tried to diminish its importance or reduce its significance with the comparisons, the parallels and the antitheses that constitute the most sickening part of Italian patriotic literature.[12]

In this sense, the work of Vincenzo Gioberti[13] was perfectly justified and seemed important in the national context, although it was "clumsy and out of tune" in a more general and European context. De Ruggiero sharply criticized the provincialism of Italian culture related to the *Risorgimento*, which revealed an attitude of "decadent gentlemen" proud of their own status and closed in their own isolation. A "false patriotic

[11] Guido De Ruggiero, *Storia del liberalismo europeo* (Bari, Laterza, 2003), 293.
[12] Ibid., 316.
[13] Vincenzo Gioberti, *Del primato morale e civile degli italiani* (Turin, Utet, 1932).

modesty" had demotivated all courage, preventing people from looking beyond their own borders and realizing their own limits, which ruined some manifestations of the national consciousness of the *Risorgimento* and mystified the understanding of future generations: "It was surrounded by a rhetorical aura, exempted from any sincere critical assessment, even when it was the subject of study and scholarly curiosity; and the less its intellectual manifestations were known in their reality, the more they were admired and praised".[14]

That explains why, in a period marked by effervescence and intellectual exchanges like the nineteenth century, none of the works of the *Risorgimento* had any European repercussions, just as none of them became familiar to the Italians themselves.

> And to notice this, it suffices to open the books by [Antonio] Rosmini, Gioberti, Mazzini, [Cesare] Balbo, [Massimo] D'Azeglio, [Niccolò] Tommaseo, to get a sense of something closed, of literary mold, which translates the narrowness of the national environment.[15]

The protagonists of the *Risorgimento* described by De Ruggiero have several points in common with the "national volunteers" discussed by Gramsci. In both cases, there is a reference to a restricted self-selected elite from several parts of Italy centered around very high moral values, but which wishes to keep distant from the participation of the popular masses, being substantially indifferent to the problems of unity, freedom and independence. This exclusively ethical and literary dimension and its claustrophobic provincial dimension underlay much of the political behavior of the ruling class of the *Risorgimento*.

The moderate party was actually a non-party, that is, it was a current with no organization or status, around which there was a consensus of very homogeneous social groups in terms of productive relations and culture. It abhorred the very idea of a party, which was defined by Rosmini as the worm that corrodes society, not only because was the question of proselytism not raised among the masses but also because there was no desire to involve them in the sociopolitical process of unification. If Machiavelli created his political science around the centrality of what can be understood as a people, according to Gioberti, the people was a

---

[14] Guido De Ruggiero, *Storia del liberalismo europeo*, cit., 317.
[15] Ibid.

non-entity, an inert and shapeless body malleable as he wished. In line with this conception, any democratic possibility not only of popular self-government but also of common political socialization aimed at expanding the social basis of a hypothetical unitary state was completely alien to the moderates. The action and the proselytizing work of the moderates were therefore aimed only at the representatives of the caste itself and at the princes of the Italian states, to whom the role of taking the initiative was assigned. In short, the political ideal of the moderates was closer to the English semi-feudal liberalism of the eighteenth century than to modern liberalism. This difference regarding the people was not resolved by the *Risorgimento* and actually reached the first decades of the new century, despite the consolidation of mass policy as a consequence of war. This theme, as we have already seen, was constantly highlighted, even somewhat ironically, by Antonio Gramsci:

> The people (oh!), the public (oh!). Political adventurists ask with the scowl of those who know what's what: "The people! But what is this people? But who knows them? But who has ever defined them?" And in the meantime they do nothing but contrive trick upon trick to obtain electoral majorities. (How many notices have been issued in Italy between 1924 and 1929 announcing new changes in the electoral law? How many proposals for new electoral laws have been presented and withdrawn? The catalog would be interesting in itself.)[16]

Historically, the absolute reluctance to involve the people had two consequences, a political and a philosophical one: the former had a clearly anti-popular character and led the moderates to positions of extreme defensiveness due to the constant terror in the context of any possible awakening of the masses and the people and of demands for freedom; in turn, the latter originated in the traditional struggle of the conservative world against modernity, in its strenuous defense of the particular against the universal produced by philosophical rationalism. Continuing a long tradition (Edmund Burke, Joseph De Maistre, Karl Ludwig von Haller), the idea of the Enlightenment revolution was understood as the consequence of a fallacious and insolent assumption, as it was not willing to recognize the binding value of historical continuity and traditions established over the centuries.

[16] Antonio Gramsci, *Quaderni del carcere*, trans. Joseph Buttigieg, *Prison Notebooks*, v. 2 (New York: Columbia University Press, 2007), 14.

Against the disruptive effect of the two terms "freedom" and "rational-ism", the Italian ruling class clung to the Church, finding an institutional barrier in restoration and a social stabilization role in religious dogmas. In Italy, this led to considering the Catholic Church a purely national institu-tion, a great misconception that did not take into account its universal and therefore cosmopolitan nature. The impossible conciliation between the values of criticism and those of dogmatism and the illusion of a non-contradictory relationship between the political unification of Italy and the centrality of the Church as a political authority were the fruits of this misconception. Italy lived only the reflections of both the revolution and the romantic counterrevolution. From the two terms of the contradiction only a confusing substitute emerged, which gave way to a bizarre, eclectic combination:

> It seemed easy to take from Catholicism its reactionary appearance and deprive liberal rationalism of its revolutionary ferment to pacify them together. That led to the idea, which stands out in the unfortunate revolu-tion of 1848, of a liberal resurgence centered on the pope [...], simultane-ously saving the old and the new, national principles and unity, Catholicism and rationalism, enlightened absolutism and freedom. That, to put things clearly, means trying to make an omelet without breaking eggs.[17]

In this blatant contradiction, the political horizon Gioberti's *Primato* would be debated, and these limits would be the basis for the fallacious claim to make the pope, in the capacity of a temporal prince, the center of an Italian tradition from which the initiative of political unification would be expected. The success of such position among the moderates is further proof of the limits of this conservative party, fatally inserted into a revolu-tionary situation.

In parallel to and against this strong moderate component, both singu-lar and avant-garde personalities capable of original intuitions emerged, such as Giacomo Durando, who opposed Gioberti's neo-Guelph attempts and the Ghibelline tradition, and so did orientations that were decidedly more modern and appropriate to the flow of European history. Under the influence of classical economics, the more advanced orientation of Italian liberalism tried to assert its principles in the dynamics of modernization in northern Italy. The doctrine of liberalism merged with the effervescence

---

[17] Guido De Ruggiero, *Storia del liberalismo europeo*, cit., 325.

of northern Italy, finding inspiration in the currents of English liberalism and offering the productive forces of Upper Italy the lion's share in the wider Italian market, which therefore meant freedom, understood first of all in its economic sense, as a new element of national unification, through the modernization of the agrarian and industrial bourgeoisie. Cavour, the only truly European exponent in the Italian *Risorgimento*, belonged to that school, and his cultural education was completely free from that literary mold and that narrow provincialism typical of the drowsy moderate intelligentsia.[18] Cavour's scientific culture and his training in Manchester liberalism led him to realize modern industrial society's potential for expansion—albeit in a context like the Italian one, in which it was yet to come into existence—and, based on it, to make the process of national unification more dynamic. What can be noticed in Cavour's work, for the first time in the history of Italy, is the spirit of the modern liberal state and, in his figure, the very embodiment of this state and the historical value of this "liberal art of governing".

Conversely, according to De Ruggiero, the basic characteristics of Mazzinian preaching were mystical abstraction and the long distance between what inspired his doctrine and the concrete reality of Italy. The long years of exile prevented Mazzini from becoming aware of what that ghostly people was and to whom its demands were directed. Moreover, the religious, political and socioeconomic reference points of Mazzini's preaching, his reflections and his pronouncements were more in line with the history of neighboring France and England than with Italian reality. Mazzini's religious-political mysticism arose from the tradition of Lamennais and Saint-Simon, from the historical matrix of the Reformation, totally alien to Italy, the country of the Counter-Reformation, par excellence. For these reasons, the binomial "God and people" did not arouse

---

[18] Arturo Carlo Jemolo also highlighted the role of true architect of national unification performed by Cavour, who is also responsible for the constitutional and administrative basis and the ecclesiastical legislation that shaped the Kingdom of Italy. Jemolo highlighted Cavour's international relations and alliances (French and English), his balanced approach to liberalism, as well as his skill in economics and administration. In the religious question, Cavour is pointed out as a rationalist, who probably calls himself Catholic more for political reasons than out of inner conviction, being sure of the demand for modernization and laicization of the fundamental institutions of civil life based on the principle "free Church in a free state". Cavour, according to Jemolo, knew how to resist the pressures of the Jacobins, on the one hand, and of the clerics, on the other, refuting both the claims of ecclesiastical interference in institutional affairs and the measures that limited religious freedom.

any enthusiasm or sense of identification in the Italian popular spirit, being confined to the meager vanguards of democratic voluntarism.

Mazzini's anathemas against the individualistic, anarchic and materialistic spirit of the liberal school were due to the Saint-Simonian orientation, to the works of Sismondi, Owen, Fourier, with their concrete social reality of nineteenth-century industrial England—where the individualistic spirit of the free market had led to enormous social conflicts and conditions of misery and exploitation for its working class. But to rage against liberal individualism in a country like Italy, still entangled by cultural traditions and feudal customs, where the Industrial Revolution was far from happening, was absurd; that meant talking about Italy while looking at England. What could be the meaning, in Italy, of the associativism that Mazzini saw emerge from the ruins of an anarchic and merciless freedom, but which the Italians did not even know? What men would associate in an agrarian country with semi-feudal agricultural techniques[19]?

Mazzini's democracy was totally alien to Italian reality, a preaching marked by moral and rhetorical duties in the realm of wishing-to-be, not even in the realm of duty-to-be, not having any basis on being. Mazzini spoke to the people, but to an imaginary and merely rhetorical people, not to the hungry masses of landless peasants of the Italian countryside. That explains the horror experienced by Mazzini and his followers when faced with the agrarian revolution in the *Mezzogiorno* and with the land occupations of 1848, a revolution that was left adrift by the democrats who did not want to exploit those disturbing events, and with the concomitant crisis of the moderates, which made way for reaction. An idea of democracy understood as an autonomous popular organization, according to De Ruggiero, would only materialize with the emergence of the socialist movement, the first movement committed (albeit in a limited and confusing way) to the attempt to create an organic relationship with the masses, by shaking them out of their centuries-old apathy and subalternity and by putting social issues, which were largely avoided by Mazzini with his statements of principles and rhetorical impulses, on the political agenda.

This insufficiency of the Action Party, fearful and reluctant to indeed involve the popular masses in the process of the *Risorgimento*, drew several times the attention of Karl Marx himself, who even wrote about it in an article published in the *New York Daily Tribune* in April 1853:

---

[19] Guido De Ruggiero, *Storia del liberalismo europeo*, cit., 333.

Now, it is a great progress for the Mazzinian Party to have finally convinced itself that, even in the case of national uprisings against foreign despotism, there is what we often call class differences and that, in today's revolutionary movements, it is not at the upper classes that one should look. Perhaps the Mazzinians will take another step forward and understand that they need to seriously deal with the material conditions of the rural population if they want their God and his People to resonate. [...] the material conditions in which most of the rural population finds itself have made it, if not reactionary, at least indifferent to Italy's national struggle.[20]

In a subsequent article of May 11, 1858, "Mazzini and Napoleon", Marx censured the Mazzinians for remaining completely attached to the political forms of the state (republic versus monarchy), *without* looking at the social organization that supports the political superstructure:

Proud of their false idealism, they deemed it below their dignity to pay attention to economic reality. Nothing is easier than being idealistic on behalf of others. A stuffed man can mock the materialism of the hungry who ask for a small piece of bread instead of sublime ideas. The triumvirate of the Roman Republic of 1848, which left the peasants of the Roman countryside in a state of slavery that was more exasperating than that of their ancestors in imperial Rome, did not think twice when it came to discussing the degradation of rural mentality.[21]

Thus, the Mazzinian strategy was reduced to conspiratorial action and agitation, to the coup d'état of the "national volunteers", without trusting—unlike the democratic movements in Germany, England and France—any concrete historical social class. An idea of democracy in which there was nothing organic and permanent, which was apart from the instantaneous explosion of the revolutionary gesture. However, according to De Ruggiero, Mazzini's democratic tradition had a positive role, forcibly leading the reluctant world of the moderates into the field of action of the *Risorgimento*. The success of democratic action is therefore entrusted to the wisdom of Cavour's moderates, who were able to provide a conservative state framework to what was achieved on the streets. That explains

---

[20] Karl Marx and Friedrich Engels, *Sul Risorgimento italiano* (Rome, Editori Riuniti, 1959), 109.
[21] Ibid., 142.

the apparent paradox that Italy, the work of the so-called democrats, is also organized against them by the parties of order.[22]

> The fear aroused by the people therefore conditioned the formation of the unitary Italian state. It was formed with the masses taking no part whatsoever, being kept distant, against them. Such circumstance would be decisive for the whole life of the new state, from its foundation to our days.[23]

The internal weakness of the bourgeoisie forced it into continuous conspiracies in order to remain in power; in Italy there was no way to develop a dialectic between industrial entrepreneurs and landowners and, therefore, the corresponding alternation (Gramsci calls it "rotation") of the ruling classes; on the other hand, a conciliatory pact was made between them, the cost of which was paid by the whole country, especially the *Mezzogiorno*, which was forced into underdevelopment and a condition of "quasi-colonial regime". Even the failure to define actual and specific political parties of the ruling classes as a real alternative, from a liberal or conservative perspective, was a consequence of these social dynamics. Hence the indistinct and swampy nature of liberal consortia and the consolidation of transformist practices. The only real glue in the country was the bureaucratic apparatus, which was led, however, by groups with no objective basis in society.

---

[22] Guido De Ruggiero, *Storia del liberalismo europeo*, cit., 335.
[23] Ibid., 9.

CHAPTER 20

"The Old Dies and the New Cannot be Born"

As we have seen in Part One, Antonio Gramsci's work has been translated (in a philosophical, not only linguistic, sense) into realities profoundly different from those with which he dealt for the most part. Thus, for example, although he paid little attention to the relationship between the North and the South of the world, as well as to the specificities of Latin America and Brazil, in particular, the dissemination and study of his work found in these places a more widespread and branched diffusion than in Europe itself, with the obvious exception of Italy. This success is due to the centrality, in his thinking, of two categories essential to reading the political and social history of that continent: the East/West binomial, which we have already discussed, and the concept of passive revolution. In *Notebook 10*, Gramsci defined the concept of "passive revolution" as the historical fact of the absence of unitary popular initiative in the progress of Italian history, in which effective historical development presents itself as a reaction of the ruling classes to the sporadic, elementary, non-organic subversivism of the popular masses. This happens through the "progressive restorations" that accepted and incorporated some demands coming from below, thus avoiding the insurrection of the popular masses. However, to dispel misconceptions, the political fulcrum of passive revolutions is not the acceptance of part of the demands emerging from social dialectics, but rather the political sterilization of the great masses of the people.

In this sense, Gramsci speaks of "revolution-restoration" or even of "passive revolution" when referring to the Italian *Risorgimento* precisely

G. Fresu, *Antonio Gramsci*, Marx, Engels, and Marxisms, https://doi.org/10.1007/978-3-031-15610-6_20

because it happened as a revolution without a revolution, that is, without any attempt, not even by the Mazzinian democrats, to promote wider popular mobilization and participation. Nonetheless, even if passive revolutions find the maximum level of centralization on the ideological ground, they can always result in very high levels of crisis of hegemony of the ruling classes for different reasons, such as a severe economic crisis or the disruptive effects (depressive effectives and at the same time mobilization ones) typical of a war.

From this point of view, the notes of *Notebook 13* and also those in *Notebook 7* about Caesarism are particularly useful, as Gramsci indicates the goal of compiling a catalog of historical events that culminated in the advent of a charismatic personality. In generic terms, Caesarism, which should be understood as a "formula of ideological polemic" and not as a "canon of historical interpretation", would result from a situation in which the dialectic between the fighting forces takes on a "catastrophic form", to the point that it can only come to a conclusion with the mutual destruction of the subjects in conflict. Faced with the balance of forces from a "catastrophic perspective", Caesarism is an arbitrated solution, whose progressive or retrogressive nature can be understood with the historical study of concrete reality, not with abstract sociological schemes: it is progressive when it helps, even if through arrangements and conciliations, the progressive force to triumph; it follows the opposite direction when its intervention favors the triumph of the retrogressive force. Caesar and Napoleon would be examples of progressive Caesarism, while Napoleon III and Bismarck would exemplify retrogressive Caesarism: "it is a question of seeing whether, in the 'revolution-restoration' dialectic, the element of revolution or the element of restoration prevails, for it is certain that there is no turning back in history and there are no restorations '*in toto*'".[1]

In the modern world, Caesarism has encountered problems because of the presence of new means available and the greater complexity of civil society, which makes the phenomenon very different from that of the time of Napoleon III:

Until the time of Napoleon III, the regular military forces constituted a decisive element for the advent of Caesarism, which occurred with very precise coups d'état, with military actions, etc. In the modern world, union and political forces, with the incalculable financing mechanisms that small groups of citizens can use, compound the problem. Party and trade union officials

---

[1] Antonio Gramsci, *Quaderni del carcere* (Turin, Einaudi, 1977), 1619.

can be corrupted or terrorized with no need to resort to large-scale military action typical of Caesar or of 18 Brumaire.[2]

Again, the theme of hegemonic articulation in civil society becomes central, just as the analysis of the changes produced in modern politics from the war of movement to the war of position assumes particular importance. It was a radical turn in the history of the bourgeoisie, after 1870, which made the Jacobin formula of "permanent revolution" obsolete. The development of parliamentarism and the consolidation of associativism through parties and trade unions, with large public and private bureaucracies, transformed the very function of the police controlled by the state, no longer aimed only at the repression of crime, but put at the service of political society and civil society to ensure dominance. Gramsci once again reinforces this concept, maintaining that the political parties themselves and the economic organizations of the ruling classes should be considered "political police bodies, of a preventive and investigative nature".[3] Given this complex articulation, even a social form in crisis can develop and improve organizationally, being able to count on the relative weakness of the "antagonistic progressive forces" that represent its negation. In this sense, modern Caesarism would be more police-like than military precisely because it uses all the preventive and investigative tools necessary to keep hostile forces in a condition of inferiority.

The organic nature of the post-war Italian crisis was a result of its double meaning, because it was not just a problem of imbalances and setbacks in the economic structure but also a "crisis of hegemony" of the ruling classes.[4] There is absolute continuity in Gramscian thought concerning this theme, so much so that paragraph 80 of *Notebook 7* develops a conception of the force and consensus theme that was already present in his articles of 1919 on the reactionary radicalization of the petty bourgeoisie. "How to rebuild the hegemonic apparatus of the dominant group, an apparatus that was disaggregated as a result of war in all the states of the world?"[5]

---

[2] Ibid., 1620.

[3] Ibid., 1621.

[4] In the past, I had the opportunity to address these topics in several publications, particularly after an essay published in 2008: Gianni Fresu, "Antonio Gramsci, fascismo e classi dirigenti nella Storia d'Italia", *NAE: Trimestrale di Cultura*, Cagliari, Cuec, N. 21, ano 6, 2008, 29–35.

[5] Antonio Gramsci, *Quaderni del carcere*, cit., 912.

However, in addition to the crisis of liberal hegemony, the collapse of the old balances had multiple causes and could not be reduced to a single factor. Gramsci focused on the following three elements: (1) the consolidation of mass politics, and hence the emergence of popular classes in the conflict, which were now willing to take on an unprecedented role; (2) the collapse of the petty and medium bourgeoisie, which, after historically losing its productive function, was the main backbone of the reorganization of the country's defenses only to soon afterwards be downgraded again with the end of the war; (3) the limits of Italian socialism, which was immobilized and paralyzed by a distressing internal dialectic and deprived of a strategy that could lead the working class and the peasantry to a synthesis, and was therefore unable to take advantage of that unique phase in history. This contradiction between the decadence of the liberal order and the incapacity of the forces oriented toward socialism is very well summarized in the already famous expression: "the old dies and the new cannot be born".[6]

Given this condition of unstable equilibrium, the regeneration of the hegemonic apparatus could not occur with the usual instruments of the liberal state. Real change is achieved through the political use of violence with a combination of legal and illegal methods of force. From this perspective, fascism lent itself perfectly to this operation because, in a context of crisis of hegemony of the old ruling classes and of great popular mobilization, this new ideology was presented with a new, nonconformist content. Fascism assumed the function of restoring order by force, presenting itself as a revolutionary movement and opposing both the old liberal ruling classes and the socialist movement. The relationship between domination and hegemony, according to Gramsci, varies depending on the level of development of a civil society: "the greater the apolitical mass, the greater the weight of illegal forces should be. The greater the politically organized and educated forces, the more it is necessary to 'protect' the state of law etc."[7]

In a situation of high development of productive forces and with a developed civil society, the members of the leadership (intellectuals and apparatuses devoid of hegemony) are preponderant or, if we prefer, more decisive in relation to those associated with the exercise of force. This interpretative model has already been discussed and is central in the notes

---

[6] Ibid., 311.
[7] Ibid., 913.

of *Notebook 13*, in which Gramsci defines public opinion as a point of contact of the dialectic between political society and civil society, between force and consensus, or even as "the political content of the public will".

One of the main functions in the exercise of power consists precisely in shaping public opinion before the state makes certain unpopular choices, in organizing and centralizing certain elements of civil society. The struggle for the monopoly of the organizations of public opinion, through control over newspapers, parties and Parliament, precisely seeks to prevent a contradiction and, thus, a split between the two levels. When such split occurs, we are faced with a condition of "crisis of hegemony": social groups distance themselves from their traditional parties, no longer recognizing in their own leaders the political expression of their class interests. In situations of this kind, the possible solutions of force and the risks of reactionary subversivism, of obscure operations under the leadership of charismatic leaders, multiply. Such split between representatives and those represented leads, as a reflex action, to the strengthening of all those institutions relatively independent of the oscillations of public opinion, such as the military and civil bureaucracy, high finance, the Church. Underlying the crisis of hegemony of the Italian liberal regime was the futile war effort, with its vaunted and unfulfilled promises and the emergence of hitherto passive social subjects.

> And the content is the crisis of hegemony of the ruling class, which arises either because the ruling class has failed in some of its great political intentions, for which it demanded or forcefully imposed the consensus of the great masses (such as war), or because large masses (especially of peasants and petty-bourgeois intellectuals) suddenly changed from political passivity to a certain activity and made claims that, in their complex disorganization, constitute a revolution. Some call it a "crisis of authority", and this is precisely a crisis of hegemony, or crisis of the state as a whole.[8]

If the ruling classes have hegemonic apparatuses (newspapers, universities, publishing houses) and a better equipped political staff, able to change men and programs in emergency situations, the subaltern groups, which lack this robust arsenal, are at greater risk because in crises or in a historical about-face they tend to lose their own leaders. That is exactly what happened in the post-war crisis, when a significant part of the ruling classes

---

[8] Ibid., 1603.

moved from liberalism to fascism, from Giolitti to Mussolini, unifying their different factions into a single political center. As we have seen, this is a topic already addressed by Gramsci in the *Lyon Theses*, revisited and developed organically here: we are witnessing the transition of the mass of maneuver of several organizations to a single party that synthesizes the interests of the whole class and centralizes its direction, which is understood as the only direction able to overcome the mortal danger contained in the crisis. "Perhaps it will make sacrifices, expose itself to a gloomy future and with demagogic promises, but cling to power, strengthen it at that moment and use it to crush the opponent and disperse its ruling group, which cannot be too large or too trained."[9] When the situation of unstable equilibrium produces a condition in which neither the traditional group nor the progressive one can win, after the disappearance of both, a third force arises and dialectically overcomes the contradiction through a Caesarist solution to the crisis.

The centralization of the entire social group behind a single political direction can take the form of a single party or of the "charismatic leader". In Gramsci's view, this latter solution, central to Caesarism, corresponds to a still primitive phase in the development of mass parties, in which the doctrine is inconsistent and inorganic and the masses need an "infallible pope" able to interpret it and adapt it to different circumstances. This condition is dominated by poorly developed political conceptions that win over the field, stirring the emotions of its social base through the theatricals, demagogy and oratory skills of the leader. A leader of this kind, however, would have been opposed by the rise of a party that were the expression of some historically essential and progressive class, which has a unitary conception and is highly developed, on which the theme of board leadership and of the horizontal participation of private spheres was imposed. One does not need to go too far to understand what kind of organization and worldview Gramsci alludes to in these notes.

The theme of the charismatic leader is revisited in the notes dedicated to Gabriele D'Annunzio's relative political popularity. Among the elements that contributed to D'Annunzio's popularity, Gramsci listed, firstly, the apolitical nature of the Italian people and above all of the petty bourgeoisie, an apolitical nature defined as restless and disorderly, easily seduced by any kind of adventure and adventurer, especially if the established order did not oppose him strongly and methodologically; and secondly, the

---

[9] Ibid.

absence of a dominant and strong tradition, which can be attributed to a mass party, able to influence popular passions with historical-political guidelines, that is, the absence of a true bourgeois mass party. In the post-war context, the presence of two elements increased.

Four years of war freed the most restless elements of the petty bourgeoisie from all state discipline, making them even more "morally" and "socially vagrant". But Gramsci identified on these factors, although they were occasional, a permanent element, the character of the Italian people, its tendency to be seduced by the charisma of the tribune considered intelligent.[10]

In both historical research and political thought, a preliminary distinction seemed elementary to understand whether certain political enterprises and organizations were composed of "volunteers" or the expression of homogeneous social groups. As for the emergence of a figure like D'Annunzio and the rise of Mussolini, who was able to attract not only the radicalized petty bourgeoisie but also decisive segments of the national ruling classes, Gramsci identifies some features inherent in national reality at the time: the passivity and the apolitical nature of the masses, which facilitated the recruitment of volunteers and made them easily manipulated; Italian social composition, marked by the disproportionate and "unhealthy" presence of the non-productive rural bourgeoisie, of the petty and middle bourgeoisie, where restless intellectuals emerge, who are easily influenced by any initiative, "even the most bizarre one, as long as it is vaguely subversive", and who are therefore "volunteers"; the long-standing presence of the urban subproletariat and of paid agricultural workers. As in the aforementioned article of April 1921, entitled "Forze elementari" [Elementary forces], in these notes Gramsci highlighted, among the characteristics of the Italian people, a certain apolitical individualism, in which other organizational forms, such as the *cricche* [gangs]—which had more of a criminal or a gang-related nature—were preferred to political parties and trade unions. Each level of civilization had its own type of individualism, and this corresponded to the stage when economic needs were not regularly and permanently met because of misery and unemployment. The origins of this condition were deep and the responsibility lay with the national ruling class which, by excluding the great popular masses from the *Risorgimento* process, had prevented the new state from emerging from below, embracing and incorporating into

---

[10] Ibid., 1202.

the national spirit even the lowest layers, from the economic and cultural perspective. According to Gramsci, unlike what had occurred in France with eighteenth-century rationalist philosophy, or in Germany with Lutheran Reformation and nineteenth-century German philosophy, in Italy there was no intellectual and moral reform that could embrace not only the higher classes but also the popular ones. Despite being a reform, Croce's modern idealism did not have, for example, this nature, while it was precisely in this field that the capacity and diversity of historical materialism should have been assessed, for which Gramsci indicates a "totalizing function" not only regarding the organic and coherent worldview but also due to its ability to encompass the whole of society down to its roots:[11] "The historical error of the ruling class was to systematically prevent such a phenomenon from occurring in the *Risorgimento* period and to base its historical continuity on the maintenance of a crystallized situation after the *Risorgimento*".[12]

Once again, "the old dies and the new cannot be born": this famous phrase of the *Notebooks* therefore expresses the sense of the crisis of modernity and of authority witnessed in Italy in the first post-war period: to a certain extent, the ruling class is still the only one to have coercive power and thus the subordinate classes separate from traditional ideologies and "no longer believe in what they previously did".

Gramsci sees Croce and Giolitti as two most representative exponents of this ruling class and attributes the same mistake to both: they did not understand the changes produced in society as a result of the entry of the great popular masses into the landscape of Italian political life. In light of these criticisms, even the defeat of Caporetto[13] was not seen by Gramsci as a mere military event, but above all as a political and social one. Right after the defeat of the Italian Army, the conviction spread that political responsibilities should be attributed to the military mass and the "military strike"; however, even if this had actually happened, the political responsibility for such an event should be attributed to the rulers. Indeed, in war,

[11] Ibid., 515.
[12] Ibid., 817.
[13] The Battle of Caporetto, during the First World War, had been the largest and most dramatic defeat in the history of the Italian Army until then, and led to a very serious political and governmental crisis in the country. On October 24, 1917, the general of the Italian army launched the offensive against the Austrians, but soon, because of the general's misguided tactics, the offensive turned out to be a disaster that forced the Italians to strategically retreat to the interior regions of Veneto.

it is the political class that should predict how certain facts could lead to a "military strike" and deal with these fact, thus preventing the strike.

Therefore, for instance, in a war, the political class may take into account the inevitably large number of victims, but it cannot fail to take action to prevent human lives from being unnecessarily sacrificed. The masses cannot be expected to bear the brunt of an entire war without taking into account their "social character" and without meeting their demands. Hence, if the responsibility cannot be attributed to the masses, it cannot be attributed entirely to the great technical-military and political responsibilities of Luigi Cadorna, a general that represents well the mentality and capacity for political understanding of the forces ruling the country. The ruling class proved even more inept in the immediate post-war period, when it ultimately proved unable to sense the direction of the historical current and actually enabled what it wished to have—and should have— avoided: fascism.

But when the old dies and the new cannot be born, there can be ineptitude not only in the ruling class in power but also in what arises—or should present itself—as its historical negation: despite the crisis of authority of the post-war liberal regime, the spread of Marxism in Italy was limited, and the party of the proletariat proved unable to take on any positive role, being a victim of its own inertia.

Gramsci saw Claudio Treves's speech delivered in Parliament on March 30, 1920 as the epitome of that. According to Treves, the "regime crisis" was a consequence of the impasse between the opposing social forces. The old order could no longer be imposed on the masses, while the masses could not impose their order because revolution is not something done at a certain moment, but is rather like a slow natural process of erosion that manifests itself in a feverish state of restlessness of the masses.

However, the agony of the existing economic and political systems could not be ended by an immediate revolution; rather, it would have to go through a long, painful *via crucis* that would last years, and that would be the atonement for the bourgeoisie's own guilt. In Gramsci's view, underlying Treves's apocalyptic representation was the fear of accepting some concrete responsibility and, with it, the lack of any connection between the Italian Socialist Party (PSI) and the masses, the inability to understand their basic needs, aspirations and latent energies: "there was a priestly grandeur in this speech, a crescendo of curses that should have petrified us with terror, but instead were a great consolation because they showed that the gravedigger was not ready yet and Lazarus could rise again".[14]

In Gramsci's view, the PSI—even in its most radical components—was dominated by a fatalistic and mechanical conception of history, by political confusion, by the polemical dilettantism of its leaders. The socialist leaders—reformists or maximalists—all proclaimed themselves sworn enemies of voluntarism;[15] however, they detested spontaneity, which was seen as something unworthy of being considered and analyzed. In reality, for Gramsci, the spontaneity of the masses in the "red biennium" was hard evidence of the ineptitude of the Socialist Party, of the distance between its program and the concrete facts. Indeed, spontaneity had led the subaltern masses out of their state of inertia, making them protagonists of a movement and able—precisely because it was done spontaneously—to question the parasitic privileged position of union leaders and of socialists themselves.

> It was, above all, a denial that anything having to do with the movement might be reckless, fake [or not historically necessary]. It gave the masses a "theoretical" consciousness of themselves as creators of historical and institutional values, as founders of states. This unity of "spontaneity" and "conscious leadership", or "discipline", is precisely the real political action of the subaltern classes, insofar as it is mass politics and not a mere adventure by groups that appeal to the masses.[16]

Once again Gramsci returned to the themes of his youthful reflections, exactly when historical development confirmed how fragile and antidialetic the theoretical positions of socialist positivism were. In order to effectively combat the "childish" and "primitive" conceptions of misguided historical materialism, it was necessary to reconsider more carefully Marx's historical works, such as *The Eighteenth Brumaire, Revolution and Counter-Revolution in Germany, The Civil War in France* among others. These texts contain the theoretical statements present in all of Marx's work and, above all, they are important because in them it can be noticed how carefully the relations between structure and superstructure are

---

[14] Antonio Gramsci, *Prison Notebooks*, cit., 2592.

[15] In these notes, Gramsci recalls he was accused of Bergsonism at the meeting of the revolutionary maximalist faction in Florence in November 1917.

[16] Antonio Gramsci, *Quaderni del carcere*, trans. Joseph Buttigieg, *Prison Notebooks*, v. 2 (New York, Columbia University Press, 2007), 51.

treated, which have no place in Marx's more general works. It is no simple task to identify the structure, in each case, statistically and accurately: a "structural period" can only be studied in scientific terms after it has overcome its entire development process; before that, it is only possible to formulate hypotheses. The little attention given to the distinction between what is organic and relatively permanent and what is occasional and contingent led to two tendencies: that of "pedantic" and "ideological doctrinarism", which is prone to exalt the individual voluntarist element; and the opposite tendency, of vulgar economicism, tendentially inclined to overrate mechanical "structural" causes. To clarify which forces act in the history of a given period, it is necessary to distinguish organic from occasional, relying on two essential principles of the *philosophy of praxis*, which are part of the preface to Marx's *Critique of political economy*:

No social formation is ever destroyed before all the productive forces for which it is sufficient have been developed, and new superior relations of production never replace older ones before the material conditions for their existence have matured within the framework of the old society. Mankind thus inevitably sets itself only such tasks as it is able to solve, since closer examination will always show that the problem itself arises only when the material conditions for its solution are already present or at least in the course of formation. [17]

It is necessary to establish the dialectical link between "organic movements and facts", on the one hand, and "situational movements and facts", on the other, not only in terms of historiographical reconstruction—when it comes to reconstructing the past—but also and above all in political art—when it comes to constructing the present and the future—and care must be taken not to do so on the basis of merciful wishes and one's own passions, rather than on the basis of real data.

A priori, aversion to conspiracies, of which "Bordigism" was a perfect example, as well as economism, is based on the belief that in historical development there are objective laws which will develop relentlessly. Like the most deterministic conceptions, even the stubborn unwillingness to conspire has, at its core, a matrix of "fatalistic finalism", which is very similar to the religious one, for which every subjective intervention prepared according to a plan is not only useless but harmful, in comparison to the

---

[17] Karl Marx, *A contribution to the critique of political economy*, in MECW (New York, International Publishers, 1996, vol. 29, 263).

fatal course of things, with the triumphal march that, by itself, will lead to the "favorable conditions", to the fateful "H-hour" of economic and social palingenesis. If Eduard Bernstein had declassified the theme of the "end", giving "movement" the full meaning of socialist action, in turn, maximalism, in Bordiga's view, and even in Bukharin's, had transformed the final goal into a mystical moment capable of contradicting the whole dialectical nature of Marxism.

> An erroneous interpretation of historical materialism that is made into a dogma and its quest is identified with the quest for the ultimate or single cause, etc. History of this problem in the development of culture: the problem of the ultimate cause is precisely thwarted by dialectics. The history of this problem in the development of culture: the problem of ultimate causes is, in fact, dispelled by dialectics. Engels had warned against this dogmatism in some of the things he wrote during his final years.[18]

The radically uncompromising approach assigns a positive role to the will only at the time of destruction, which is separated from reconstruction and mechanically conceived; for this reason, it blindly and foolishly clings to the "regulatory virtue of weapons". According to this view, "mass ideological facts" are always behind mass economic phenomena because they are harnessed and mixed by the intervention of the ruling class, which fragments and prohibits any possible form of coordination of social forces that can counter it.[19]

Politics in fact is not always immediately attributable, in all its aspects, to the development of the structure, as a mere mechanical reflex. A certain political act may be the result of an error of assessment on the part of the

---

[18] Antonio Gramsci, *Quaderni del carcere*, trans. Joseph Buttigieg, *Prison Notebooks*, v. 2 (New York, Columbia University Press, 2007), 166.

[19] The appropriate political initiative, and therefore also the agreement, is always necessary to release certain social forces from the direction that the ruling class exerts on them. Again, in Gramsci's view, the essential issue is that a subordinate social group, willing to become dominant, must be able to lead related and allied groups, absorbing them within a new homogeneous historical socioeconomic bloc, which can be attained either through an alliance and a series of agreements or by the force of arms: that is, by either allying with this social force or subordinating it. However, for Gramsci, "if the union of two forces is necessary to conquer a third one, the use of weapons and coercion is mere methodological hypothesis and the only concrete possibility is agreement, since force can be employed against enemies, not against a part of oneself that one wishes to assimilate quickly and whose goodwill and enthusiasm are necessary" (ibid., cit., 1612).

ruling groups, just as it may be an attempt by a specific group to assume hegemony within the ruling class. These attempts can fail, and in turn, errors can be reabsorbed and overcome by historical development, but in both cases we are not faced with immediate manifestations of the economic structure, with its real and permanent modification. Often, the acts in question arise from internal organizational needs, from the need to give coherence to a political party, group or society, from sectarian needs.[20] When considering each political act as the reflection of the economic structure, these and many variables are not taken into account.

Gramsci's critique of mechanical determinism, despite having been refined, clarified and defined over time, maintains the basic historicist approach of the writings of his youth and is fully expressed in this very important concluding passage from the notes on "Structure and superstructure":

> In fact, every real historical phase leaves traces of itself in the succeeding phases, which in turn become its best document, in a certain sense. The process of historical development is a unity in time, in which the present contains all the past and, from the past, what is essential is realized in the present, without the residue of an unknowable that would be its true essence. What was lost, that is, what was not transmitted dialectically in the historical process, was in itself irrelevant, it was random and contingent scum, chronic and not history, superficial episode, despicable, ultimately.[21]

The economic factor is one of the many ways in which the deepest historical process presents itself, but the philosophy of praxis intends to explain the totality of this process in its complexity, precisely because it is a philosophy, an "anthropology", not a mere standard of historical research. The superstition of scientific progress created such ridiculous, childish illusions and conceptions to the point of "dignifying religious superstition", leading to the expectation of a new messiah who would create "The land of Cockaigne"[22] on Earth without the intervention of

---

[20] From this point of view, the history of the Catholic Church was enlightening for Gramsci because it would be absolutely absurd to pretend to track down changes in the economic structure behind any internal ideological struggle—such as the East-West schism.

[21] Antonio Gramsci, *Quaderni del carcere*, trans. Joseph Buttigieg, *Prison Notebooks*, v. 3 (New York, Columbia University Press, 2007), 175.

[22] According to the oral tradition of the Middle Ages, Cockaigne was an imaginary country, a kind of mythological paradise, where it was not necessary to work and all pleasures were allowed.

human effort, but only through the work of the forces of nature and through the increasingly perfected mechanisms of progress. This childish passion for the sciences, in fact, hid the greatest ignorance of scientific facts under the specialization of its disciplinary branches, and therefore ended up filled with expectations, turning the myth of scientific progress into "higher witchcraft".

CHAPTER 21

The Double Revision of Marxism and Similarity with Lukács

Fatalistic and mechanistic determinism is typical of a phase still defined by the subalternity of certain social groups, constituting a sort of "immediate ideological aroma", a necessary religion or excitement precisely due to the subaltern character of the social group. The mechanistic conception is, in Gramsci's view, "the religion of the subaltern". In Marxism, the division between theory and praxis corresponds to the separation between intellectual leaders and the masses, that is, to a phase in which initiative is not in the struggle yet, and determinism and belief in the rationality of history become a force of moral resistance and cohesion. But all this changes when the subaltern become leaders, historical subjects, protagonists of their emancipation process. Mechanical determinism can be explained as the "naive philosophy" of the mass, but when it is elevated to the status of philosophy by intellectuals, "it becomes the cause of passivity, of imbecilic self-sufficiency, with no expectation that the subaltern might lead and be responsible".[1]

According to Gramsci, it was precisely the residues of mechanicism—the consideration of theory as an "incidental supplement" to praxis, as a "servant of practice"—that prevented in Marxism a full development of the question concerning the unity between theory and praxis. Gramsci presents the problem in the considerations on how the development of a new thought intervenes to usher in and inaugurate a historical era and a

---

[1] Antonio Gramsci, *Quaderni del carcere* (Turin, Einaudi, 1977), 1389.

© The Author(s), under exclusive license to Springer Nature Switzerland AG 2023
G. Fresu, *Antonio Gramsci*, Marx, Engels, and Marxisms, https://doi.org/10.1007/978-3-031-15610-6_21

production that is oriented philosophically according to an original *Weltanschauung* [worldview].

In parallel with Gramsci's reflection, a similar process of intellectual and political clarification also characterizes the evolution of the young György Lukács, who was involved in a constant polemic with both positivist and revisionist Marxism. In contrast to the double revision that Marxism underwent,[2] the Hungarian philosopher also repeatedly emphasized the centrality of German classical philosophy among the essential sources of historical materialism and the absolute importance of dialectics, which he considered the heart of Marxism. This similarity was addressed several times by Michael Löwy, an attentive expert on the two intellectuals.

> The reference to idealistic thought—mainly Bergson and Croce—is in Gramsci, in 1917–1918, a means to oppose the positivist, scientific and economic-deterministic orthodoxy of Claudio Treves and Filippo Turati, official representatives of the Marxism of the Second International in the direction of Italian socialism. An attempt that finds its precise equivalent in the sui generis revolutionary ideology of Lukács at the same time, composed of a combination Hegel-Ady-Dostoevsky-Sorel radically opposed to Kautskism. [...] In this first attempt to formulate a non-positivist revolutionary Marxism, both Gramsci and Lukács will make extensive use of Sorel, a representative of an anti-capitalist romantic socialism.[3]

According to the young Lukács, Marxism is characterized by its revolutionary dialectic *method* able to overcome the distinction between theory and praxis and the mechanicism of doctrinarism. In it, the concepts are not strict and immutable schemes or rational apparatuses isolated from each other, which would only be understood through abstraction; Lukács speaks of living realities that produce an uninterrupted procedural passage, in which individual concepts are reversed as the opposite of their original formulation. According to Eduard Bernstein, the protagonist of one of the two revisions that Marxism underwent, which are countered by Gramsci and Lukács, dialectics would violate reality for the love of method, proving inadequate to understand modern science based on "facts". In other words, dialectics would be an outdated residue of Hegelian

---

[2] On the "double revision of Marxism", see Part I, Chap. 2, in this volume.

[3] Michael Löwy, "Gramsci e Lukács: verso un marxismo antipositivista", in Nicola Badaloni (org.), *Gramsci e il marxismo contemporaneo* (Rome, Editori Riuniti, 1990), 304.

philosophy, from which one had to free oneself to adopt a scientific method "without prejudice".

In Gramsci's view, on the one hand, deterministic interpretations derived from the concrete needs of the emerging labor movement, but on the other, the simplifications of the inevitability of the end of the capitalist mode of production as a "historical necessity" seemed to offer an adequate explanation for the great depression of those years. The state of instability and vulnerability of bourgeois society, created by the greatest crisis of capitalist production until then, combined with the worsening of the living conditions of workers for almost twenty years, seemed to materialize the theories of "growing misery" and "final crisis".[4]

For all these reasons, the strong new economic recovery beginning in 1896 and the disillusion with the imminent collapse of bourgeois society led to a serious theoretical crisis of the socialist workers' movement. Until then, the dominant approach within the international socialist movement focused on a tactic in which the course of events would exactly make the explosion of capitalist contradictions coincide with the uncontrollable growth of the workers' movement, all inserted into a progressive and ascending process, which was considered irreversible. The clash of this new situation with the orthodox convictions of Marxist determinism doomed this tactic to paralysis due to the inability to adequately deal with the new phenomena associated with a scenario characterized by the emerging imperialism of the great capitalist powers.[5]

In this context of theoretical crisis, between 1896 and 1898, Bernstein began to publish in *Neue Zeit* a series of articles entitled "Problems of socialism", later revisited and enlarged in 1899 in the most famous work of Marxist revisionism, *The preconditions of socialism and the tasks of social*

---

[4] The second half of the nineteenth century was marked by a series of such rapid and profound changes that led to an unprecedented development of the productive forces in the history of humankind. Between 1860 and 1870, the zenith of free competition was reached; with the crisis of 1873, the cartel system began to emerge; then, between 1890 and 1903 (the year that, in turn, marked the beginning of a new crisis), there was an increase in business and trade that led to an increasing concentration and centralization of capital, which transformed the organization of cartels into a fundamental basis of all economic life—no longer a transient phenomenon linked to the conjuncture. According to Lenin, "capitalism has turned into imperialism".

[5] Gianni Fresu, *Lénin leitor de Marx: determinismo e dialética na história do movimento operário* (trans. Rita Matos Coitinho, São Paulo, Anita Garibaldi, 2016), 28–60.

democracy.[6] According to the author, the erroneous predictions of Marx and Engels were the logical consequence of the limits of historical materialism. The mistakes made about timing and the possibilities of development of the capitalist mode of production were therefore the consequence of a certain apriorism of historical materialism, because in it historical progress would be forced into the straitjacket of a metaphysical process animated by a movement of dialectical antithesis. The social-democrat philosopher defined the materialist one as a "Calvinist without God, [...] if he does not believe in a predestination ordained by a divinity, he does and must believe that, starting from any moment in time, all subsequent events are determined beforehand by existing matter and the dynamic relations between its parts.".[7]

The accusation of apriorism was associated with the relationship between consciousness and being, which he considered unilateral, mechanical and anti-scientific. As we will see, this is the same criticism made by Benedetto Croce against Marx. In both cases, according to Gramsci, the need for "revision" arose from the inability to distinguish the work of Marx and Engels from that of their positivist interpreters, who were refuted and shaken by concrete historical development.

With the autonomy of political and ideological factors in relation to the development of economic bases, Bernstein reassesses eclecticism (emphasizing the influence of non-economic factors against the overrating of the production technique), which in his view is a "natural and common-sense reaction" against the doctrinal tendencies "of those who intend to derive everything from a single cause and to treat everything according to one and the same method", those who intend to "confine thought in a straitjacket".[8]

These theories had a clear political goal, which was transparently outlined in the title of the work: to revise the theoretical preconditions of socialism so as to redefine the tasks of social democracy. Therefore, the analysis was all aimed at demonstrating the inadequacy of historical materialism, reshaping social democracy and thus resolving the contradiction Bernstein identified between a reformist practice based on parliamentary activity and a utopian and revolutionary theory. He attributed this

---

[6] Eduard Bernstein, *I pressupposti del socialismo e i compiti della socialdemocrazia* (Bari, Laterza, 1968).

[7] Ibid., 31.

[8] Ibid.

contradiction to a supposed Blanquist influence on Marx and to Hegelian dialectics, which would have been particularly fatal in the context of the general effervescence of the years around 1848. The questioning of the relationship between the workers' movement and Marxism should therefore entail the denunciation of its utopian apriorism, the overcoming of the Hegelian dialectic and especially of Blanquism.

Thus, the mistakes made by Marx and Engels in the *Manifesto* were due to the adoption of the Hegelian dialectic—albeit "upside-down"—as a dynamic and cardinal principle of historical materialism. The Hegelian dialectic was for Bernstein "the most treacherous element in Marxist doctrine, the pitfall that prevented any coherent consideration of things",[9] and the responsibility for the apriorism inherent in the philosophy of praxis was attributed to him. Moreover, in Bernstein's view, "placing the dialectic upside-down" was not an easy operation "because whatever the true relation between things and reality, as soon as we leave the solid ground of experimental facts and start to think beyond them, we are faced with the world of logical concepts, and if we then follow the laws of the Hegelian dialectic, we will be, before we know it, once again enmeshed in the spontaneous development of the concept; herein lies the great scientific danger of the Hegelian logic of contradiction"[10] and, therefore, although the Hegelian dialectic was of great use to lead to important discoveries, when the attempt was made at deductively anticipating the developments of reality on the basis of these principles, Marxism created an abstract doctrinarism full of arbitrary constructions.

In this sense, the deductive relationship inserted in the *Manifesto of the Communist Party* between the advanced conditions of European civilization and the impending proletarian revolution constituted a "historical self-deception" worthy of a "visionary". However, in Bernstein's view, underlying this error was not only a simple overrating of some contingent political factors (as Engels had stated in the preface of 1895); it was rather an arbitrary, purely speculative and deductive anticipation of the maturity of a development whose first signs could, at most, be glimpsed. It was an inevitable result, when trying to translate the dialectic of the world of concepts into that of reality, attributed to the influence of Hegelian philosophy on Marx.

[9] Ibid., 58.
[10] Ibid., 52.

These theoretical assumptions were therefore challenged in relation to the negation of some of Marx's predictions about the evolutionary modalities of the capitalist mode of production; such negation, in turn, was useful for the transformation in concrete action and in the objectives of social democracy. Thus, Bernstein negated or re-signified some of the fundamental theories of Marxism: the theses on the contradiction between the social character of production and the private form of appropriation of profits; those related to the polarization of society into two extreme classes, with the increasing proletarianization of the petty and middle bourgeoisie, and, therefore, with the increase in the gap of economic inequality between capitalists and workers; the theses on the increasing centralization and concentration of capital, and the relation between this fact and the increased exploitation of the labor force; finally, the theses on crises related to the tendency of the rate of profit to fall. All these "inaccurate predictions" would be only the result of the theoretical apriorism of Marxism.

Objections to the fundamental theoretical principles of Marxism found their political translation in the controversy over Marx's mistakes in dealing with the theme of the relationship between socialism and democracy. In Bernstein's view, with the progress of the productive forces and the pressure of the organizational and political force of the workers' movement, representative institutions would have ceased to be an organ of bourgeois government, giving rise to a progressive and inexorable expansion of the spheres of real democracy. The development of social legislation, especially the protection of labor rights and the democratization of institutions in modern countries, would naturally end the class struggle, which would reduce the opportunities and the need for major political catastrophes. In Bernstein's view, there is a contradiction between political democracy and capitalist exploitation; the development of political equality would naturally lead to the reabsorption of economic inequalities and class differences. Therefore, social democracy should, without hesitation, embrace the banner of universal suffrage and parliamentary growth, abandoning not only the idea of the revolutionary seizure of power but also the revolutionary phraseology that survived, but now had no concrete meaning. After this theoretical and political turning point, the development of an increasingly strong reformist current, which opposed a maximalist approach, began in the Second International. The essential difference between the two views lay in the primacy attributed either to reformist practice or to the revolutionary strategy.

Even the phrase that epitomizes Bernstein's thought ("what is usually termed the final goal of socialism is nothing to me, the movement is everything"[11]), which contrasts the moment of reform with the final goal of social-democrat action, has its basis in the "rebellion" against Marxist apriorism. Preconceived theories about the outcome of the movement, which predetermined its direction and character, led the movement itself to utopianism, paralyzed any real progress and compromised the scientific nature of Marx's work.

In the last chapter of his essay, emblematically entitled "Kant against Cant", the influence of the neo-Kantian vulgate is explicit, which in those years was consolidated among a minority of German social democracy and openly aimed to maintain a scientific core to Marxism, reducing it to a mere canon of historical interpretation, and in this sense reconciling it with Kant, as it frees scientific socialism from the negative influence of the Hegelian dialectic.

Bernstein evokes Kant's spirit against the *Cant*[12] concealed in the labor movement, that is, the conservative and dogmatic tendency of tradition among the revolutionaries. For those who wish to follow real development, criticism is indispensable, while tradition can become an overwhelming burden and turn from a driving force into a brake that withholds it; in this sense, the invocation to Kant amounts to the critical battle against scholasticism, which would be mainly supported by Hegel's legacy on historical materialism.[13]

Strongly opposing this neo-Kantian revision, but also the deterministic revision of official Marxism, Gramsci and Lukács devoted themselves to profound critical reflections in their youth and adulthood.[14]

According to the Hungarian philosopher, the elimination of the dialectical method of Marxism would deprive it of its rigor and revolutionary strength. The mere, crude gathering of facts would not make the complexity of history intelligible because only dialectics shows how each mode

---

[11] Eduard Bernstein, *I presupposti del socialismo e i compiti della socialdemocrazia*, cit., 244.

[12] The word "Cant" indicates the fanatical chant of the Puritans, the pure and simple ritual repetition of a formula, and more generally, according to Bernstein, insincere rhetoric.

[13] In clear opposition to this approach, during the war, Lenin devoted himself to an in-depth study of Hegel's work to demonstrate its importance in Marxism. From this study emerged his *Philosophical notebooks*. I covered this extensively in my monograph *Lénin leitor de Marx: dialética e determinismo na história do movimento operário*, cit.

[14] Gianni Fresu, *Il diavolo nell'ampolla. Antonio Gramsci, gli intellettuali e il partito* (Naples, Istituto Italiano per gli Studi Filosofici/La Città del Sole, 2005), 21–48.

of production creates in itself the elements of its ruin and of its overcoming. Only through dialectics does the role of the contradiction inherent in each stage of history become clearer. According to Lukács, without dialectics, the researcher would grope around in a maze of disorganized facts, with no criterion, and would get lost expecting to receive from the facts the indication of action. Once again, we find a central element of the philosophical controversy already identified in Antonio Labriola and Gramsci: if eclecticism found its justification in the rejection of the dialectical method, in turn, even the vulgar reduction of orthodox Marxism was attributed precisely to the abandonment—albeit not evident or manifest—of dialectics. "While Bernstein openly declared that the final goal did not exist for him, but movement was everything, Kautsky and his followers assigned the final goal a role of a heavenly god, enveloping it in an aura of sublimity alien to all immediate reality."[15] Thus, the final goal became just an empty formula, which was useful for embellishing the conclusions of speeches, books or manifestos.

Revolution in Marx has a procedural nature—using Gramsci's lexicon, we could say "molecular"—and at some point the continuous growth of quantitative differences turns into a qualitative difference. In the dialectical unity of individual moments, therefore, the revolutionary process is expressed, and it is in it that one must seek maturity or the possibility of revolution:

> Every moment of the regular course of the labor movement, every increase in wages, every reduction in working hours etc. are, therefore, a revolutionary action, because it is precisely at these moments that the process is formed, which, at some point in time, becomes a qualitatively new element, an element that makes capitalist production impossible. But these singular moments can only become revolutionary in the unity of the dialectical method. For those who recognize only individual moments, the labor movement is diluted in reformist wage claims.[16]

Marx, thanks to Hegel, came to understand the unity-totality of the dialectical process; he did understand how the whole prevails over the parts and how one should get to the singular parts starting from the whole, not the opposite. Therefore, he was able to unmask the "false consciousness" inherent in classical political economy, which considers in isolation

[15] György Lukács, *Scritti politici giovanili 1919–1928* (Bari, Laterza, 1972), 28.
[16] Ibid., 30.

the individual elements of the economic process, then arriving at the economic system. For Lukács, because of this reversal, political economy makes certain assumptions of the mode of production emerge (the origin of private property and private law) as eternal natural laws, as necessary prop for human existence. Political economy can describe the functioning of the mode of production, within certain relations, but it cannot explain how these relations of production emerge and how the production process arises historically. For Lukács, both political economy and sociology were unable to conceptually go beyond the scope of the assumptions that govern production as it occurs in bourgeois society.

It is exactly this unitary, totalitarian conception (not in the sense that this term took on later, after the Second World War) of the historical process that makes Marx's method deeply linked to action and life; thus, even the so-called conceptual contrast between abstract and concrete collapses before a vision in which concrete means concrete as a composition of different determinations, a unity of the multiple.

If Marx was the first to grasp the historically determined and non-eternal nature of the *economic laws*, it was also precisely because of this method that Hegel was able to recognize world history as a unitary process driven by a continuous dialectical movement, in which transformations did not arise from inscrutable divine or natural laws, but from the interweaving of objective and subjective contradictions arising within society itself. As Domenico Losurdo repeatedly showed in his works, if the uprisings related to the French Revolution were once explained by resorting to conspiracy theories or by comparing them to natural disasters and epidemics, Hegel was the first to provide a conceptual framework that allowed the rational historical understanding of revolutionary processes.

> Hegel identifies the genesis of the revolution in a complex, in an interweaving of contradictions, and the decisive importance of *Logic* lies in providing the conceptual tools essential to the understanding of this fact: the violent uprisings that swept the old feudal world and, more generally, an order that was decrepit are not the result of a conspiracy or of stealthy approaches, as counterrevolution theorists would claim, nor are they the result of the conflict, of the fury of a moral consciousness against an order considered to be contrary to the natural rights of humankind, as not only the theorists, but also the protagonists, of the French Revolution would or tended to affirm. But the category of negation is of great importance. Hegel celebrates "the immanent power of negation", and negation is a central category of logic, whose genesis or centrality cannot be adequately understood if one does not

consider the experience behind the French Revolution, the most intense and dramatic historical movement of negation.[17]

According to Lukács, the dialectical method was the only one able to avoid both the utopianism of the reformist approach and the inert messianism of "vulgar Marxism", which were both united by the repudiation, abandonment or, more simply, lack of acknowledgement of the central role of Hegelian dialectics in historical materialism. This centrality was also reaffirmed by Lukács in the review of the new edition of Ferdinand Lassalle's letters:[18]

> The young Marx's evolution was marked by criticism of Hegel, by overcoming Hegel internally, which is carried out in such a radical way that Marx will never explicitly return to this topic, although the intention of giving continuity to dedicating a volume to the usable core of Hegelian logic occasionally appears, and this demonstrates that the core of Hegelian philosophy, which was overcome and preserved by Marx in his thinking, is more important than vulgar Marxists usually admit.[19]

The essence of Marxism would not be so much in the predominance of economic motivations, but in the category of "totality", that is, the predominance of the whole over individual parts, the essential method of Hegelian philosophy reworked in an original way by Marx and transformed into the basis of a completely new historical science.

Marx preserved the essence of the Hegelian method and, through its materialistic inversion, turned it into the basis of a revolutionary science, which considers every partial phenomenon an element of the whole and conceives the dialectical process as "unity of thought and history". Historical materialism interprets society as a whole, admits the cognizable delimitation of its individual parts, but does not conceive of a conceptual autonomy from them: for Marxism, disciplinary delimitation is inevitable in study, but there can never be an autonomous science of law, economics, history and so on. For Marxism, there is only a unitary "historical-dialectical" science of the development of society as a whole.

---

[17] Domenico Losurdo, *L'ipocondria dell'impolitico. La critica di Hegel ieri e oggi* (Lecce, Milella, 2001), 25.

[18] György Lukács, "La nuova edizione delle lettere di Lassalle", em *Scritti politici giovanili 1919–1928*, cit., 225.

[19] Ibid., 206.

Liberal tradition, on the contrary, always considers society's phenomena from the individual perspective; thus, classical political economy has always considered the laws of capitalist development from the point of view of the *singular capitalist*. Marx, on the other hand, analyzed "the problems of the whole capitalist society as problems of the classes on which it is structured, understood as totality".[20]

Consistent with this epistemological-political approach, in the essay *The young Hegel and the problems of capitalist society*, Lukács set himself the task of showing the specific German roots of Marx's complete work, showing the organic relationship between his worldview and the progressive evolution of Germany from Lessing to Heine, from Leibniz to Hegel and Feuerbach. "An appropriate historical analysis of Hegel, which from the beginning examines and interprets him from Marx's perspective, can also be a contribution to accomplishing this task."[21]

Among the coincidences that are revealed between the themes discussed by Gramsci and Lukács in the polemic against "the two revisionisms", the respective critical notes on the writings of Bukharin in 1922, *Historical materialism: a system of sociology*, are particularly important. Both considered him the heir of a metaphysical and "vulgar" materialism, almost a posthumous revenge of the positivist determinism of the Second International at the heart of the Soviet state.

According to Lukács, the intention of creating a popular work on historical materialism met a real need; however, Bukharin's *Historical materialism*, which from the start had the problem of resorting to "second-hand" sources, trivialized the great questions concerning art, literature and philosophy, without making them more accessible to laypeople. If on the surface the account seemed clear and linear, in reality all the most problematic connections were omitted and were, in the end, less intelligible. Thus, the intention of making historical materialism more understandable to the majority ended up translating into a shallow equalization of all the problems that concerned him. In this essay, for instance, the analysis of the relations between the economy and the spiritual sphere seemed to follow more the caricatures made by Marx's detractors than his work by asserting an absolute identity relationship between the relations of production and the state, which was totally out of touch with reality. Contrary to this

---

[20] György Lukács, *Storia e coscienza di classe* (Milan, Sugar, 1970), 38.

[21] Idem, *O jovem Hegel e os problemas da sociedade capitalista* (trans. Nélio Schneider, São Paulo, Boitempo, 2018), 40.

simplification, history has shown how the possibility of balancing economic forces between competing classes could enable the temporary
emergence of a state apparatus not fully dominated by either of the two
fighting classes (this was the case with absolute monarchy at the beginning
of the modern era). Similarly, a class could achieve economic power without being able to create political and legal institutions that fully corresponded to the new era. That was the case of the German bourgeoisie in
its phase of maximum economic development, when it abruptly interrupted its liberal reforming action and left control over the state apparatus
in the hands of the agrarian aristocracy of the Junkers.

In general, *Historical materialism* abandoned the tradition of historical
materialism without, however, reaching the conceptual levels of the revisionist works that preceded it and, above all, without finding reason in the
facts. In particular, the philosophical study of the introductory chapter
completely ignored the contributions of German classical philosophy, just
as the passing reference to Feuerbach was most superficial.

> Bukharin's theory, which comes considerably closer to the bourgeois mate-
> rialism of the natural sciences, thus takes on the appearance of a science
> (according to the French use of the term) and, in its concrete application to
> society and history, not rarely ends up nullifying the decisive element of the
> Marxist method: that of *bringing all the phenomena of economics and sociol-
> ogy back to the social relations of men*. The theory has a hint of a false objectiv-
> ity: it becomes fetishistic.[22]

Dealing with social evolution, Bukharin attributed to technique an
overarching meaning, stating that every system of social technique also
determines the system of labor relations between men, to the point of
defining the close dependence between the level of development of the
forces of production and the technical evolution of society as "fundamental normativity". Explaining the development of productive forces through
technique inevitably leads to falling into a new "fetishism", just as arguing
for the centrality of factors such as "nature", the weather and the environment in the political-philosophical studies of the eighteenth and nineteenth centuries did. On the contrary, the technique should be conceived
as a moment of each of the productive systems, and its development
should be explained by the evolution of social productive forces, not the

---

[22] Idem, *Scritti politici giovanili 1919–1928*, cit., 191.

opposite. The level reached by the technique, determined by the development of the productive forces, can exert influence on it, but it would not be correct to decontextualize the technique from the set of ideological forms in order to assign it autonomous existence.

These errors were a direct consequence of Bukharin's generalist approach and of the understanding of Marxism as a "general sociology", that is, of the attempt to "flirt" with the natural sciences.

> The entire philosophical foundation of Bukharin's theory is still attached to the point of view of materialism of *intuition*; instead of subjecting the natural sciences and their method to a historical-materialistic critique, that is, understanding them as products of capitalist development, he applies the method to the knowledge of society recklessly, in an uncritical, antihistorical and antidialetic fashion.[23]

As for Gramsci, in *Notebook 4* he identifies some lines of research useful for the study of materialism and idealism in order to build a history of Marxism with two stated goals: (1) to clarify its evolutionary processes and its limits; and (2) to develop a new ideological framework able to focus on reality and transform it. These philosophical reflections on Marxism are based on the methodological criteria necessary to frame the work of its main inspirer. When one intends to study an author, whose worldview has never been systematically exposed and in which theoretical and practical activities are closely intertwined, one must carefully reconstruct his biography by analyzing all the works, minor writings, and letters according to a chronological sequence that is able to capture his *leitmotiv*. In the study of an author, it is necessary to distinguish the works that he completed and published from those that were not completed and remained unpublished since the content of the latter must be examined much more carefully and thoroughly, precisely because of their nature as materials that were temporary and still in preparation, to which the author would probably return later. In these notes, the Sardinian intellectual seems to outline how to advance in the *mare magnum* of Karl Marx's thought, but he also provides some guidelines that prepare the study of his own work, particularly the *Prison Notebooks*. In these notes, again, Gramsci delves into the process of philosophical involution and vulgarization of Marxism after Marx and Engels. If original Marxism constituted the overcoming of the highest

---

[23] Ibid., 201.

cultural manifestation of its time, German classical philosophy, Marxism after Marx proved incapable of embracing and understanding man in all his aspects; therefore, it was necessary to resort to the contributions of other philosophies. Gramsci sees a merit to positivism: that of having promoted a new connection between European culture, which was stuck to "old rationalist ideologies", and a reality whose meaning had been lost. At the same time, however, it was limited by including the same reality in predefined self-referential schemes, trapping it in the sphere of "still life". That resulted in the impoverishment of philosophical research, which was transformed into a new form of "materialistic theology".[24]

In sharp contrast to this approach, Lenin developed a brutal theoretical confrontation in the global Marxist movement;[25] however, despite its proximity to the Russian revolutionary, Bukharin's work was strongly affected by the influence of the social and natural sciences, according to the superficial and positivist theoretical approach characteristic of the Second International.

For Gramsci, there is already a contradiction between the title and the content of Bukharin's work. A book entitled *Historical materialism* should have systematically and organically exposed the fundamental philosophical concepts of Marxism, also providing a critical review of all the spurious concepts of strange origin, which were often erroneously brought together under the term "historical materialism". On the contrary, in *Historical materialism*, the only philosophical considerations in the introductory chapter were very schematic and superficial. Even the apodictic assertion that "true philosophy" is philosophical materialism, while the philosophy of praxis would be "pure sociology", whose meaning Bukharin does not

---

[24] Antonio Gramsci, *Quaderni del carcere*, cit., 85.

[25] "All this leads, as a practical consequence, to *attendiste* and almost messianic trends in the labor movement: the subjective element assumes a marginal and totally subordinate function in relation to the objective sphere; the class struggle is a law of social evolution that Marxists must limit themselves to explaining, as Newton explains gravitation. Therefore, the task of the socialist forces was simply to increase their strength, waiting for history to take its course, to the point of indeed determining—as an inevitable natural law—the demolition of the capitalist mode of production and the establishment of a socialist society. [...] All these trends and interpretations were connected with the general part of the 1891 Erfurt program—which was not only voted by German social democracy, but which soon became an important theoretical assumption for all other socialist parties—and were completely theorized in the essays of such important intellectuals as Karl Kautsky, for whom the task of social democracy was not to organize the revolution, but organize itself for the revolution; not to make the revolution, but use it" (Gianni Fresu, *Lénin leitor de Marx*, cit., 41–2).

explain, is the fruit of this impoverished understanding of Marxism. The discussion does not clarify, first of all, what Bukharin means by sociology, whether it is a science of politics and historiography or a systematic gathering of empirical observations on politics and historical research. The assessment of the author of the *Notebooks* is extremely harsh, identifying at the root of sociology the pretentious ambition to achieve an "exact" science of social facts, politics and history. When commenting on sociology's inability to know the dialectical principle of quantitative-qualitative change, Gramsci exposes a conception that has many similarities with the reflections of Lukács:

> Sociology was an attempt to create a method of historical-political science, depending on a philosophical system already formed—evolutionary positivism—to which sociology reacted, but only partially. Sociology has therefore become a trend in itself; it has become the philosophy of non-philosophers, an attempt to schematically describe and classify historical and political facts according to criteria built on the model of the natural sciences. Thus, sociology is an attempt to derive *experimentally* the laws of the evolution of human society in order to predict the future as certainly as an oak is expected to develop from an acorn. Vulgar evolutionism is the basis of sociology that cannot know the dialectical principle with the passage from quantity to quality, a passage that disturbs all evolution and all laws of uniformity understood in the commonly evolutionist sense.[26]

Gramsci contrasted the subjectivism of Bukharin's *Historical materialism* with historicism, which was reaffirmed with the well-known Hegelian proposal "what is real is rational and what is rational is real", often misinterpreted as a philosophical legitimization of everything that exists, including despotic and reactionary governments. As a matter of fact, Hegel applies the "real" attribute only to what is also "necessary"—thus, not all governmental measures can be understood in this way—and what is "necessary" is also "rational". As Engels explains in one of his most important philosophical essays, such proposition applied to the Prussian state entity means that this state corresponds to reason insofar as it is proposed as necessary: "if it appears to be evil, but still, despite its evil character, continues to exist, then the evil character of the government is justified and

---

[26] Antonio Gramsci, *Quaderni del carcere*, cit., 1432.

explained by the evil character of its subjects. Today's Prussians have the government they deserve".[27]

Thus, for Hegel, the "real" attribute does not apply to all historical contexts and to all social or political states of affairs, so the Roman Republic was as real as the Empire that supplanted it, while the French monarchy was so devoid of necessity, and therefore irrational, that it ended up destroyed by the revolution, whose rationality and historical necessity were defended only by Hegel. The whole core of the Hegelian proposition lies in the dialectic of the *thesis* that transforms into its opposite: in historical becoming, what was once real ends up ceasing to be necessary and becomes unreal; the dying reality is replaced with a new vital reality, and its violent or peaceful rise depends on the understanding of the old, of its greater or lesser opposition to the new necessity. If everything that is real in human history can cease to be necessary and become irrational, and everything that is rational in men's minds is destined to become real, Hegel's proposition on the rationality of the real means to Engels that "all that exists is doomed to perish". According to Engels, the revolutionary nature of Hegelian philosophy is due to the fact that it eliminates, at once, the dogmatism of any philosophical theme, putting an end to the "definitive character of all products of human thought and action":

> Truth now lay in the process of cognition itself, in the long historical evolution of science, which rises from lower to ever higher levels of consciousness without ever reaching, through the discovery of the so-called absolute truth, a point at which it can no longer advance and all it can do is fold its hands in its lap and contemplate the absolute truth attained. [28]

This discourse applies both to philosophy and to any practical activity: just as cognition evolves from a lower to a higher level, history cannot stop, reaching a definitive conclusion, a perfect condition. The state and perfect and definitive society exist only in fantasy. Every historical situation is only a phase of an ascending process of development of human society. Each stage is historically determined and, as such, necessary, but it ceases to be so when the conditions for a successive higher stage are created within it, entering the cycle that leads it from decay to death. Thus, the

---

[27] Friedrich Engels, *Ludwig Feuerbach e il punto di approdo della filosofia classica tedesca* (trans. Palmiro Togliatti, Rome, Rinascita, 1950), 12.
[28] Ibid., 14.

same discourse concerns philosophical systems and the process of development of thinking, whose essence Bukharin does not reach, limiting himself to denying its rationality. Thus, Gramsci explains, "the history of philosophy becomes a historical treatise on teratology because it starts from a metaphysical point of view". Again, the Sardinian intellectual contrasts mechanistic determinism with Hegel's dialectic, indicating its centrality among the essential sources of Marxism:

> Seeing the entire philosophical past as delirium and madness is not only an error of anti-historicism, because it entails the anachronistic claim that in the past one should have thought as we do today, but it is a real vestige of metaphysics, because it supposes a dogmatic thought that is valid in all times and countries, through which the whole past is judged. Methodical anti-historicism is nothing more than metaphysics. The fact that past philosophical systems are outdated does not exclude the fact that they were once historically valid and that they performed a necessary function: their expiration must be considered from the point of view of complete historical development and real dialectics; the fact that they deserved to collapse is no moral judgement or hygiene-of-thought judgement, made from an "objective" point of view, but a dialectical-historical judgment. One can confront Engels's presentation of Hegelian propositions, according to which "everything that is rational is real, and real is rational", a proposition that will also be valid for the past.[29]

Notwithstanding their philosophical intentions, the issues dealt with in *Historical materialism* have, for Gramsci, no theoretical nature, perhaps only an immediately political one, halfway between philosophy and everyday practice, and above all they are a chaotic and inorganic juxtaposition of reflections on disconnected historical facts. The attempt to reduce Marxism to a sociology was in line with the most deteriorated positivist tendencies of the late nineteenth century, which we discussed in Part One of this volume, the same tendencies that led so many neophytes of Marxism to unforgivable theoretical confusion, which led them to the "most bizarre journalistic improvisations". It was the same propensity to schematically translate historical materialism with the claim of "having the whole of history in the pocket" already criticized by Labriola, which generated the most general and mechanical forms in which the only systematic element was improvisation. Marxism, on the other hand, is based on the totality of

[29] Antonio Gramsci, *Quaderni del carcere*, cit., 1416–7.

the historical process, that is, on an experience that cannot be schematized or organized into a "hard science", but can lead to "philology", as a research method to study specific empirical facts, or to "philosophy, understood as the general methodology of history".

Philology can lead to the identification of more general tendencies, but the statistical law of large figures cannot be used in the study of human and political facts, as is the case in the natural sciences; at most, it can be of (limited) value only while the masses "remain essentially passive". On the contrary, the schematic adoption of statistics as an essential law of science and of political art can have serious and catastrophic results because, in addition to promoting "intellectual laziness" and "programmatic superficiality", it can lead not only to a scientific error (remediable with new research, as in the case of the use of statistics in the natural sciences) but also to a much more serious "ongoing practical error". "Political action tends precisely to make the crowd overcome passivity, that is, destroy the law of large figures; so how can this be considered a sociological law?"[30] Moreover, even the economic claim that follows a plan is fated to disrupt the mechanically understood statistical laws, and the same is true of the predominance of the collective directive function of political parties instead of individual or "charismatic" leaders. "Human consciousness replaces *naturalistic spontaneity*", Gramsci writes; therefore, the random gathering of arbitrary individual acts (so-called statistical data) becomes the norm for economics and political art, which creates a "naturalistic scheme" disturbed by the conscious intervention of man, which destroys what until then was considered a "natural law".

For Gramsci, as for Lukács, the philosophy of praxis is the "general philosophy", a totality created by the organic interweaving of history, economics and politics. To be consistent with its title, in *Historical materialism*, after a systematic treatment of the philosophy of praxis as a general philosophy, Bukharin would also have to deal with its individual parts, but in this regard it lacks, first of all, a clear and precise definition of what philosophy of praxis itself is, and moreover its discussions about the individual parts are chaotic and random.

Thus, in *Historical materialism* a minimal exposition of dialectics is also lacking, and Gramsci attributes this fact to Bukharin's intention to divide the philosophy of praxis into two distinct parts: a sociology, understood as the science of politics and of history, after the fashion of the natural

---

[30] Ibid., 1430.

sciences; and a systematic philosophy proper. This division, which for Gramsci is the origin of all errors of *Historical materialism*, makes dialectics lose its nature, its very purpose, because as a central element of history and politics, it is downgraded to formal logic. One can only understand its meaning when one conceives Marxism as an integral, new and original philosophy, as Labriola did, in which dialectics is the driver of the totality of a historical, political and economic process. In Gramsci's view, Marxism ushers in a new phase in the development of world thought, due to which idealism and old bourgeois materialism are overcome—into which Bukharin definitely falls by making such distinction.

> When separated from the theory of history and politics, philosophy can only be metaphysical because the great achievement in the history of modern thought, which is represented by the philosophy of praxis, is precisely the concrete historicization of philosophy and its identification with history.[31]

The intention of writing *Historical materialism* based on a doctrine still being defined and developed was weak from its premises. When a world-view has not reached a "classical" phase yet, so as to allow a clear and thorough exposition of a given topic, why not frame the question in the correct theoretical and historical terms, simply making an introduction to the scientific study to deal monographically with its essential problems? That is, a more serious and reliable work from a scientific point of view, in contrast to the vulgar idea of science, which also derives from positivism, according to which science means "system", even if the system does not have organic coherence, but only "mechanical exteriority". This also happens in *Historical materialism*, defined as a "mechanical juxtaposition of disparate elements, which remain inexorably disconnected, despite the veneer of unity given by literary writing".[32]

According to Gramsci, Bukharin proved unable to understand the historical movement, becoming and dialectics itself, and for this reason his work failed to critique speculative philosophy. Bukharin should not have "conceived philosophy as historicity", that is, he should not have understood a philosophical statement as a necessary expression of a certain historical action, but this is exactly what he did by falling into the dogmatic schematism already followed by Kautsky and the theorists of the Second

---

[31] Ibid., 1426.
[32] Ibid., 1424.

International. This will be based on a casuistry of specific historical examples, of issues solved dogmatically, through a metaphysical and anti-historical empiricist approach, such as speculative idealism:

> If speculative idealism is the science of categories and the a priori synthesis of the spirit, that is, a form of anti-historical abstraction, the philosophy implicit in *Historical materialism* is reverse idealism, in the sense that empirical concepts and classifications replace speculative categories, as abstract and anti-historical as they are.[33]

The concept of science present in *Historical materialism* takes natural science as science proper, or the only one at all, and therefore historical methodology can only be defined as scientific if it is able to "abstractly" predict the future of society, the future of history, just as in the natural sciences the laws of evolution allow one to predict the outcome of the evolution of natural processes. Historical materialism, on the other hand, can only scientifically predict the presence of class struggle, not its outcome, since it is always the outcome of contrasting forces in continuous motion, which cannot be reduced to predetermined, fixed amounts in test tubes. In Gramsci's view, the only real prediction is made by action, insofar as it contributes with voluntary intervention to creating the conditions for the hypothetical outcome. All this means that the "prediction" of socialism, as a result of the struggle between classes, is not a "scientific act of knowledge", it is not the "prediction" of an inevitable and already written law, but rather it refers to the practical effort to form a collective will in this sense; it pertains to the possibilities created by the interweaving of objective and subjective causes, in which the latter greatly contribute to determining the outcomes of the "prediction". Prediction cannot be a cognizable act because one can only know what was, not what will be.

Like Lukács, Gramsci also counters Bukharin for wanting to make the philosophy of praxis depend on a general theory of vulgar materialism, while Marxism, as Labriola clarified in his essays, would be able to "suffice by itself", already having all the fundamental elements for a "total" and "integral" conception of the world that is "vivified" by reorganizing the whole of society, that is, in "total and integral civility".[34] The error was to seek a general philosophy on the basis of Marxism and confuse, in Marx's

---

[33] Ibid., 1403.
[34] Ibid., 1434.

personal philosophical culture, the philosophical currents and philosophers that interested him during his development and the origins or constituent parts of his philosophy. Marx's philosophical development and culture are useful as long as it is clear that the philosophy of praxis constitutes the original overcoming of all the old philosophies to which Marx referred and opens up a completely new path capable of totally transforming the very way of conceiving philosophy.

In the notes on the *Objectivity of the external world* of *Notebook 11*, which deal with the dialectic between human history and the history of nature and in which there is also a passing reference to Lukács, Gramsci is led to a statement often used instrumentally to reinforce the thesis (in our view, erroneous) that Engels is a positivist desecrator of Marx's work: "Surely in Engels (*Anti-Dühring*) there are ideas that can lead to deviations from [Bukharin's] *Historical materialism*".[35] The reflection, however, does not take into account the nature of this work and the fact that it did not intend, in the least, to be a systematic exposition of historical materialism, but it overall met the needs of political controversy.

In the political climate marked by the consolidation of Marxism as the predominant doctrine of the workers' movement, new waves of socialism tried to find both in the social sciences and in Marx a unitary conception of the world, a "philosophy of history". For a long time, this work involuntarily responded to this "encyclopedic" need for a systematic synthesis of the philosophy of praxis, having been the main text in Marxist studies for many generations of revolutionaries. *Anti-Dühring* is the first systematic presentation of the theories of scientific socialism. The three main aspects of Marx and Engels's work—philosophy, economics, politics—are present for the first time in an overview in which the different elements intersect. Precisely due to its unitary and general nature, *Anti-Dühring* had an important influence on the consolidation of Marxism as the theory of the workers' movement.

Anti-Dühring is that important not so much because of the controversy with Dühring, but because of the positive exposition it provides. According to Valentino Gerratana,[36] this work, which lent itself to both eclectic and "orthodox" interpretation, was celebrated from the very first moment as a handbook or compendium of socialism and was defined as

[35] Ibid., 1449.
[36] Valentino Gerratana, "Introduzione", in Friedrich Engels, *Antidühring* (Rome, Editori Riuniti, 1971).

the first systematic and complete work of the theoretical principles of scientific socialism, which were closely connected with all the main aspects of modern sciences. But it was a misunderstanding. In Gerratana's view, *Anti-Dühring* was not a summary of the thought of Engels and Marx, but required the reading and in-depth study of the work of these authors. Only involuntarily did *Anti-Dühring* meet that need for synthesis, and in general Engels himself was always very critical of the tendency toward encyclopedic synthesis that was typical of that historical period. To be more precise, this "mania", which was clearly present in Dühring, was one of the main polemical targets of the text, since the preface to the first edition, of 1878, in which Engels challenged precisely the systemic and pseudoscientific tendency of most intellectual productions of that time.[37] After all, Antonio Labriola himself, certainly not suspicious of positivist sympathies, defined *Anti-Dühring* as "the most comprehensive book on critical socialism", which was able to provide "all the philosophy necessary for the intelligence of socialism".[38] In the preface to the second edition, Engels himself explains why this work was taken as the unitary representation of the Marxist dialectical method, although it was created exclusively from the need to respond to Dühring's theories. Dühring's thought, extending over a very wide theoretical field, made Engels follow him in all the areas covered and contrast Dühring's theses with his. Thus, negative criticism became positive exposition, and mere polemics became a unitary compendium of the theories of Marx and Engels. The need for synthesis and the prominence of certain parts in relation to others, essentially due to the

---

[37] "The 'system-creating' Herr Dühring is by no means an isolated phenomenon in contemporary Germany. For some time now, in Germany, systems of cosmogony, of philosophy of nature in general, of politics, of economics, etc., have been springing up by the dozen overnight, like mushrooms. The most insignificant *doctor philosophiae* and even the *studiosus* will not take anything less than a complete 'system'" (Friedrich Engels, *Antidühring*, cit., 4).

[38] Antonio Labriola, *La concezione materialistica della storia* (Bari, Laterza, 1965), 191.

needs of the contingent political battle,[39] transformed *Anti-Dühring* into the fundamental text to favor the assimilation and consolidation of Marxism in the workers' movement. However, at the same time, precisely because of its "involuntarily systemic" nature, *Anti-Dühring* lent itself to superficial generalizations, which ended up favoring (or at least not preventing) the deterministic internalization of Marxism itself.

[39] On this issue, Engels's letter to Bloch of September 21, 1890 is particularly enlightening. "The fact is that young people sometimes attach greater importance to the economic side than it deserves; this is partly my fault and Marx's. In the face of adversaries, we should highlight the essential principle denied by them, and then we did not always find the time, place, and occasion to do justice to the other factors participating in reciprocal action. But as soon as the exposition of a period of history was reached, that is, the practical application, things changed, and no error was possible. However, unfortunately, we also very often happen to believe that we have perfectly understood a new theory and can undoubtedly deal with it as soon as we appropriate the essential principles—and, moreover, not always in a precise manner. I cannot help but address this criticism to more than one of the last-minute *Marxists*, and so a strange confusion was created from time to time" (Friedrich Engels, *Sul materialismo storico* (Rome, Editori Riuniti, 1949), 78).

CHAPTER 22

Translatability and Hegemony

As we have seen, Gramsci's political biography, between 1921 and 1926, was marked by the dramatic failure of revolutionary attempts in the West and the beginning of a phase of reflux that enabled a radical reactionary turn that culminated in the advent of fascism. Therefore, the fundamental question in the *Prison Notebooks* is why, despite a deep economic and hegemonic crisis of the ruling classes and an objectively revolutionary context, it was not possible to "translate", in the West, the victorious experience of Russian Bolsheviks and, on the contrary, it was reaction that triumphed.

Albeit often omitted, the theme of political translatability in different national languages is present in Lenin and that deeply influenced Gramsci, who was one of the first to be aware of this fact. We can find several confirmations in the prison notes. In *Notebook 11* in particular, he recalls that in 1921 the Russian revolutionary highlighted the inability to translate the Russian language into European languages, that is, to give national content to universal values arising from specifically national conditions, from the October Revolution. He returned to the concept in *Notebook 19*, in which he highlights the limits of Giuseppe Mazzini's democrats in the *Risorgimento*, mainly their misconception of the role of the Jacobins in the French Revolution, and therefore of the centrality of the agrarian question as an incentive to a democratic revolution in Italy through the uprising of

G. Fresu, *Antonio Gramsci*, Marx, Engels, and Marxisms, https://doi.org/10.1007/978-3-031-15610-6_22

the popular masses in the process of national unification: Ferrari[1] did not know how to translate from French into Italian, and therefore his own insight became an element of confusion and led to new sects and small schools, but did not affect the real movement".[2]

Gramsci diffusely addressed the theme of the reciprocal translatability of different philosophical languages, starting from a premise (included in *Notebook 11*) that recognizes the value of the gnosiological superiority of historical materialism: only in the *philosophy of praxis* is translation "organic and deep", whereas in other worldviews we usually find a simple game of "generic schemes". The concept of translatability lies in the dialectic between the universality and national peculiarities of all socio-economic formations:

> Translatability presupposes that a given phase of civilization has a "fundamentally" identical cultural expression, even if the language is historically different, and is determined by the particular tradition of each national culture and each philosophical system, by the predominance of an intellectual or practical activity, etc.[3]

In the following note, entitled *Giovanni Vailati and the translatability of scientific languages,* he further develops the reasoning, explaining how scientists studying within the same culture can affirm truths considered different or opposite simply by using different scientific languages. Likewise, similar national cultures (Germany and France, in this specific case) can be considered different and opposite, or one superior to the other, because they employ different languages of tradition, which are created by the historical-cultural specificities of each of them. Although the translatability of national philosophical languages can never be perfect (in the case of language either), these civilizations can find translation in each other, at least in the background and essential elements. That would be the meaning of Marx and Engels's statement in *The Holy Family* that French political language amounts to the language of classical German philosophy. This remark can also be found in the lessons of Hegel's *History of philosophy*, according to which the philosophy of Kant, Fichte and Schelling contained revolution in the form of thought. If in Germany the new principle is asserted as spirit and concept, in France it manifests itself

---

[1] Giuseppe Ferrari (1811–1876), an important philosopher and democratic politician engaged in the process of Italian National Unification.

[2] Antonio Gramsci, *Quaderni del carcere* (Turin, Einaudi, 1977), 2016.

[3] Ibid., 1468.

as effective reality; however, the two countries would be part of the same universal historical progress. Conceptually, Gramsci finds a connection between Hegel's statement and Marx's eleventh *Theses on Feuerbach*, according to which, in order to become true, philosophy must become political and find practical translation into the effective reality of things. In this sense, the philosophy of praxis is historically conceived as a transitional phase of philosophical thought, to the point of interpreting historical development as the passage from the domain of necessity to that of freedom.

Every philosophy arises from the internal historical contradictions of which it is part, and every philosophy conceives itself as a unity between history and nature, that is, as the development and overcoming of what preceded it; however, in the history of philosophical thought, Hegel's work is a different case because it understands what reality is in a single philosophical system as awareness of contradictions. In this note, Gramsci addresses the problem, which had always been a subject of controversy, of Hegelianism as a source of Marxism:

> In a certain sense, therefore, the philosophy of praxis is a reform and the development of Hegelianism; it is a philosophy free (or that seeks to be free) of any unilateral and fanatic element; it is the full consciousness of the contradictions in which the philosopher himself, understood individually or as a group, not only understands the controversy, but also places himself as an element of contradiction, elevating this element to principle of knowledge and, therefore, of action.[4]

This is the premise of Marxism's concreteness (understood in its authentic form, not brutalized by positivist determinism), that is, of its ability to escape any abstract systemic generalization. For this reason, he concludes: "Man in general, even if he presents himself, is denied, and all dogmatically unitary concepts are disrespected and destroyed as an expression of the concept of 'man in general' or of the human nature immanent in every man".[5]

The translation of the philosophical terrain to that of praxis would be the essence of historical materialism and one of the reasons for its superiority over other philosophical views, which is why Gramsci adopts Labriola's definition: philosophy of praxis. But this level does not exhaust the field of translatability of the philosophy of praxis; on the contrary, its main

[4] Ibid., 1487.
[5] Ibid., 1488.

implementation field lies in the translation of the theory into the conditions of each specific and original national socio-economic formation.

The philosophy of praxis emerges in the concrete terrain of historical contradictions; for this reason, it is mainly linked to "need" rather than "freedom", which has not had the chance to manifest itself historically yet. In this sense, the programmatic indication of the contradictions that prevent the passage from need to freedom also means overcoming the philosophy of praxis, which emerged based on these contradictions and, therefore, on the need to fight against them.

In Gramsci's view, the division between theory and praxis in Marxism thus corresponds to the distinction between intellectual leaders and the masses and is typical of a phase marked by the complete subordination of the latter; the development of the philosophy of praxis can be achieved if it elevates its own intellectuals within the class of which it is the worldview, that is, by overcoming this rupture and the deterministic conception, which is its theoretical expression. As we have seen, the issue of relations between intellectuals and masses is the theme present with greatest continuity in Antonio Gramsci's work; in the prison notes it takes on center stage, both in historical-analytical terms and in political-philosophical thinking, and it is in *Notebook 12* that it produces the most organic set of reflections.

When approaching the systematic study of the history of intellectuals, the first problem to be investigated is whether intellectuals constitute an autonomous and independent social group or whether each social group produces its own specialized category of intellectuals.

According to Gramsci, each "essential" social group, arising within certain relations of economic production, tends to create one or more classes of intellectuals that give the group homogeneity and consciousness, in the economic, social and political field: thus, for example, the consolidation of the bourgeoisie coincides with the emergence of specialized intellectual functions in economic and political sciences, in the law, in the organization of culture, in production techniques themselves.[6]

However, in this phenomenon of emergence, the new class usually finds not only pre-existing, consolidated social groups but also intellectual classes that tend to present themselves as a social group per se, that is, these various categories of traditional intellectuals tend to assert themselves and exist according to a "spirit of corporation"; consequently, they

[6]Ibid., 1513.

consider themselves autonomous and independent from the dominant social group and its functions, as a result of a historical continuity of their particular "status".[7] Italian idealist philosophy represents the most coherent ideological expression of this uninterrupted historical continuity of intellectuals as a "class" and of their alleged autonomy from the dominant social classes.

An example of that is the ecclesiastics, who can monopolize for a long time some "intellectually" important functions, such as religious ideology, school, education, morality, justice, charity and so on. On the basis of what has been said, the ecclesiastics remained the intellectual category organically linked to the landed aristocracy, to which they were legally equated and with which they shared the exercise of feudal ownership of land and state privileges associated with property. Historically, the centralization of powers in the monarch, with the rise of modern states, led to the emergence of new secular categories of organic intellectuals, such as the so-called togated aristocracy, in charge of administrative and jurisdictional management in territories on behalf of the sovereign.

The relationship between intellectuals and the world of production is mediated by the social fabric, which articulates the set of superstructures where intellectuals are the employees. This set is essentially twofold: "civil society", which corresponds to the function of hegemony that the ruling class exercises over the whole of society, and "political society or state", which corresponds to the direct domain that is expressed in the functions of command and in "legal government".[8] According to Gramsci, the common concept of state is one-sided and inevitably leads to great errors

---

[7] In the notes entitled *Nomenclature and content issues*, present in *Notebook 11*, Gramsci dealt with this phenomenon in general terms: "One of the characteristics of intellectuals as a crystallized social category (that is, one conceived as uninterrupted continuity in history, therefore regardless of the struggle of groups, not as an expression of a dialectical process, for which each dominant social group creates its own category of intellectuals) is precisely the union, in the ideological sphere, with a previous intellectual category by means of the same nomenclature of concepts. Every new historical organism (type of society) creates a new superstructure, whose specialized representatives and standard-bearers (intellectuals) cannot but be conceived as, they too, *new* intellectuals arising from the new situation, not the continuity of the previous intelligentsia. If the *new* intellectuals place themselves as a direct continuation of the previous *intelligentsia*, they are not at all *new*, that is, they are not linked to the new social group that organically represents the new historical situation, but they are rather the conservative and fossilized remnants of the social group that has been historically overcome" (ibid., 1406).

[8] Ibid., 1518.

regarding its nature simply because it refers exclusively to the institutional-coercive apparatus, while a state should not be understood only as the government apparatus, but also as the apparatus deprived of hegemony or civil society. Intellectuals are thus "employees of the dominant group for the exercise of the subaltern functions of hegemony and of political government",[9] and this exercise happens in two ways: through the spontaneous adherence of the masses to the fundamental dominant group's direction of social life; or through the legal coercive apparatus, with which the ruling class firstly guarantees for itself the legal discipline of groups from which it cannot obtain consensus, either active or passive, and, secondly, prepares for the future in view of the crises of the functions of hegemony and domination, at times when the spontaneous consensus of society is reduced.

The organizational function of social hegemony and of state domination determines a complex hierarchy of qualifications and a stratification of hierarchical competencies that is quite similar to the military institution. The development of the productive forces and the evolution of capitalist societies in a democratic and bureaucratic sense expand the systems of the hegemonic and domination apparatus and make them more sophisticated, extending and diversifying the essential intellectual functions, to the point that it can be said that the higher the degree of development of the productive forces, the greater the importance of the hegemonic functions in civil society.

According to Gramsci, one of the most characteristic themes of Lenin's theory of revolution is the need to nationally translate the principles of historical materialism, that is, to reject superficial statements about capitalism and revolution in general, to build a new theory of transformation from the concrete conditions of each socio-economic formation.[10] In line with this general issue, Russia's path to socialism should have been different from that imagined for western countries. Because of this diversity, Lenin developed a conception of relationship with the peasant masses that is not found in the other members of the Russian Social Democratic Labor Party (RSDLP), and that, in the course of 1917, surprised many Bolsheviks, who still clung to the old program. Indeed, in the conception of social

---

[9] Ibid., 1519.

[10] Gianni Fresu, "Gramsci e a revolução nacional", in Ana Lole, Victor Leandro Chaves Gomes e Marcos Del Roio (orgs.), *Gramsci e a Revolução Russa* (Rio de Janeiro, Mórula, 2017), 157–78.

democracy, it was understood that the role of the peasant masses was limited to the bourgeois-democratic phase of the revolution, so there was no hegemonic plan of action directed to them by the workers' party. This was actually another theme developed by Gramsci in his constant controversy with the Italian Socialist Party (PSI). Against all this, Lenin did a first about-turn between 1901 and 1908, proposing the inclusion, in the program of the revolutionary party of the proletariat, of the claims of the peasant masses, because the Russian party could only succeed if it faced the problem of guiding these masses.[11] This intuition, which would be decisive in 1917 and would lead to the reception of Marxism in rural countries with limited development of productive forces, is not found in any other Marxist author of the time. It was a position that Rosa Luxemburg herself criticized as a "petty-bourgeois" solution to the peasant question.

Nonetheless, in *The development of capitalism in Russia*, of 1898,[12] land reform is the cornerstone to lead the Russian proletariat to have a hegemonic role in the face of the immense and amorphous masses of landless peasants. Gramsci was quite sure of this conception when he analyzed the positive role of the Jacobins in the French Revolution and cited this kind of guidance when reflecting on the role of the Italian working class in the progressive solution to the southern question.

Polemicizing with both Kautsky's orthodox positions and Bernstein's revisionism, Lenin was the protagonist of a tough theoretical-political dispute within the international socialist movement. According to the then prevailing guidelines, it was not possible to do without the only western modernization and transition scheme. As a result, a backward country like Russia could not even think of a socialist revolutionary process without first going through all the stages of the "*via crucis* of capitalism" and through the evolutionary stages of bourgeois society. This antidialetical interpretation of Marxism showed all its contradictions in the face of a major theme for the European workers' movement at a time marked by

---

[11] This battle waged by Lenin has its most important synthesis in the text *The agrarian question and the critics of Marx* (*La questione agraria e i critici di Marx*, Rome, Editori Riuniti, 1976). The first nine chapters were written in 1901, and the last three in 1907. The clandestine publication of the first nine chapters took place in 1901, and then they were republished in 1905 and 1906, being subsequently joined to the last three chapters in an edition of 1908.

[12] Vladimir Ilitch Lenin, *Opere complete*, v. 3: *Lo sviluppo del capitalismo in Russia* (Rome, Editori Riuniti, 1956).

deep inter-imperialist contradictions: the colonial question. Between 1905 and 1907, in the context of Germany's growing expansionist ambitions and the rise of nationalism, social democracy found itself divided between two antithetical positions: on the one hand, there was aversion and strong opposition to imperialism; on the other, there was support for a positive colonial policy. In the Stuttgart Congress of August 1907, prominent figures of social democracy such as Eduard Bernstein, H. H. van Kol and Eduard David followed this latter line, according to which the forced Europeanization of the colonial domains would accelerate the evolutionary process of those countries and rid them of the archaic socio-economic structure, of the despotic and feudal institutions. Thus, colonialism and the expansion of western productive relations, with industrialism, would hasten socialism.

Although there is a widespread tendency to present the work of the *Notebooks* and more specifically the theories on hegemony as a point of great discontinuity between Gramsci and Lenin, in the notes concerning the passage from the "war of movement" to the "war of position" in *Notebook 7*, the Sardinian intellectual attributes precisely to Lenin the merit of having understood the complexity of the structures of domination of western societies of advanced capitalism, indicating for the first time to the subaltern classes the great historical task of hegemonic conquest. On the contrary, for Gramsci, Trotsky's theory of "permanent revolution" was a reflection of the theory of war of movement, of immediate assault, that is, a reflection of a country where the general economic, social and cultural conditions were embryonic and poorly developed, so the ruling class was not in a position to exercise its own political and social hegemony.

The formula of the "permanent revolution" first appeared in 1848, as a scientifically based expression of the Jacobin experience, and more generally corresponds to a phase of extreme backwardness of urban and rural society, with the limited development of civil society and of the hegemonic apparatus of the ruling classes. At this stage, there were no major political parties and trade unions, and there was greater national autonomy of the economy and of the state and military apparatus. This phase changed radically in 1870, with European colonial expansion, when the internal and international organizational relations of the states became more complex and intertwined; in this phase, in politics, changes also occurred in military art, and the formula of the "permanent pevolution" was overcome by civil hegemony, that is, it went from the war of movement to the war of position. In modern democracies, the articulation of both the state and civil society is comparable, in political art, to the "trenches" and permanent fortifications of the "war of position". It can be said that a state wins a war to the extent that it prepares it, both at the military-technical and at the political level, during the years of peace. Of course, this discussion concerns only modern and advanced states, not backward countries and colonies.

Thus, in Gramsci's view, Trotsky's theory was the fruit of a superficial approach, both at the national and at the European level, and only his obstinacy led him to believe that fifteen years later it would be possible to realize what had been theorized at the time of the 1905 revolution.[13] Lenin, on the other hand, had understood that in the West, in March 1921, after the failure of the revolutionary prospects and given the beginning of a phase of reactionary offensive, there was a shift from the war of movement to the war of position. The former had succeeded in the Russian Revolution of 1917, but the latter was, at that time, the only one possible in the West, where civil society was over-developed, and the hegemonic capacity of the ruling class was very strong. In Gramsci's view, this is the most immediate and important meaning of the "united front" theory. Lenin did have the intuition, but he did not have time to develop it, not least because, according to Gramsci, he could only do it on the theoretical level, while the task was essentially "national", that is, western parties were responsible for a reconnaissance of the terrain and the identification of trenches and fortresses:

---

[13] Gramsci was referring to Trotsky's memoirs, in which Trotsky stated that the close connection and continuity between the bourgeois revolution and the socialist revolution created a condition of permanent revolution from which one could no longer escape until the outbreak of social revolution. Based on this, Trotsky aimed to skip all stages and force the situation to immediately move from the bourgeois to the socialist revolution, stating that even if in 1905 nothing had been achieved and the revolution had been stifled, his predictions were eventually confirmed fifteen years later. Gramsci concluded that Trotsky's theory was not very good, "neither fifteen years earlier, nor fifteen years later", and ironically derided his so-called heavenly gifts by affirming that these gifts were, at most, able to guess "at the wholesale level": "It's like predicting that a four-year-old girl would become a mother and then saying, 'I had guessed it,' when at the age of twenty she does indeed become a mother— forgetting about wanting to rape the girl when she was four, out of the conviction that she would become a mother" (Antonio Gramsci, *Prison Notebooks*, cit., 866, trans. Joseph Buttigieg, *Prison Notebooks*, v. 3 (New York, Columbia University Press, 2007), 168.).

In the East, the state was everything, civil society was primordial and gelatinous; in the West, there was a proper relation between state and civil society, and when the state tottered, a sturdy structure of civil society was immediately revealed. The state was just a forward trench; behind it stood a succession of sturdy fortresses and emplacements. Needless to say, the configuration varied from state to state, which is precisely why an accurate reconnaissance on a national scale was needed.[14]

In *Notebook 14*, paragraph 68, dedicated to Machiavelli, Gramsci writes that the task of the "international class" was therefore to study exactly "the combination of national forces" (what in other notes he defined as the elements of trench and fortress) and to develop them also according to international requirements. One can define as such only the ruling class able to interpret this combination; therefore, Gramsci concludes, the accusations of nationalism from Leone Davidovici to Giuseppe Bessarione[15] "are inept when it comes to the core of the issue".[16] In the study of the entire effort, between 1902 and 1917, of the "majority" (the Bolsheviks), Gramsci continues, one understands that its originality was precisely in "purging internationalism of all vague and purely ideological elements (in the bad sense) to give it a realistic policy content".[17] Hegemony is based on the requirements of a national character; therefore, to direct strictly national social strata, an international class must nationalize itself because, according to the Sardinian intellectual (and this is also the cause of the failure of the revolutions in the West), the world conditions for socialism were not objective, and thus several phases should occur in which the singular national combinations could be very different.

It is interesting to note that Gramsci links "non-national" attitudes to the mistakes already made by deterministic mechanicism in the Second International, which produced inertia and passivity in the labor movement, when no one believed in the international conditions to start the revolutionary process and, while some waited for others, the movement was limited to accumulating forces. Now the same "non-national" attitude reemerged in the theory of permanent revolution, which he defined as the result of an "anachronistic and unnatural Napoleonism":

[14] Ibid.
[15] These are the semi-encrypted forms that Gramsci used, to escape prison censorship, to refer to Liev Davidovich Bronstein (Trotsky) and Joseph Vissarionovich (Stalin).
[16] Antonio Gramsci, *Quaderni del carcere*, cit., 1729.
[17] Ibid.

The theoretical weaknesses of this form of old mechanicism are masked by the general theory of permanent revolution, which is nothing more than a generic prediction presented as a dogma that destroys itself due to the fact that it does not manifest itself effectively.[18]

According to Gramsci, Rosa Luxemburg's theory also treated the events of 1905 superficially and deterministically, with reasoning that bordered on "historical mysticism". Just as, in war, field artillery, after making room in the enemy ranks, erupts and obtains a strategic victory, according to Rosa Luxemburg, the immediate moment of the economic crisis would lead to the strategic victory of the proletariat by means of three devastating effects: (1) the crisis would create a gap in the class consciousness and self-confidence of the bourgeoisie; (2) the subaltern classes would be able to form, shape and coordinate their own cadres, hitherto dispersed; and (3) ideological focus on the goal pursued would prevail.

In fact, the attack was immediately only tactical, both in war and in political science: in the former case, indeed, the war is not made up just by the trenches, as such, but by the industrial apparatus underlying them, by the abundance of supplies—ultimately, by the ability to resist after advancing and retreating, to quickly replace the elements lost during the enemy's offensive; likewise, in the more advanced states, civil society developed an articulated, complex structure that can resist the "assaults" and the destruction produced by sudden economic crises.

The superstructures of civil society are like the trench system of modern warfare. Just as in modern warfare, in a violent artillery attack, one has the impression that the entire opposing defense system has been destroyed, but in fact only the outer surface has been destroyed and, during the attack and the advance, the attackers are faced with a defensive line that is still efficient, so it also happens during the great economic crises.[19]

In fact, two of the three effects of incursions into the enemy ranks predicted by Rosa Luxemburg do not occur because, on the one hand, neither can the attacking troops organize and coordinate the attacks over time and space, developing an aggressive spirit, nor, on the other, do the attacked troops lose their cohesion and self-confidence.

[18] Ibid., 1730.
[19] Ibid., 1616.

If Lenin is pointed out by Gramsci as the protagonist of a "realized hegemony", Benedetto Croce, in turn, is presented as the greatest scholar of hegemony in Italian philosophy. Thus, Croce's work is credited with having directed scientific interest to the study of cultural and philosophical elements as an integral part of the structures of domination of a society, which underlies the understanding of the function of great intellectuals in the life of states, in the construction of hegemony and consensus, that is, of the "concrete historical bloc". More generally, in Gramsci's view, attention to the functions of intellectuals in political science is primarily due to Hegel. With the German philosopher, there is indeed the passage from the patrimonial conception of the state, the state of castes with no mobility of the *ancien régime*, to the design of the ethical state. Without understanding this fact, it would be historically difficult to understand modern idealism and its social origins. What distinguished the bourgeoisie the most in its revolutionary phase was its ability to include other social classes and guide them through the state, to exercise political and social hegemony. While in feudalism the aristocracy, organized as a "closed caste", did not attempt to encompass the other classes, the bourgeoisie is much more dynamic and mobile, aiming to assimilate the rest of society at the economic and cultural level. This profoundly changes the function of the state, transforming it into an "educator", also through the hegemonic function of law in society. The bourgeoisie historically works to make the ruling classes homogeneous (in customs, morals, common knowledge) and to create a social conformism able to consolidate its power through a combination of force and consensus. It is thus able to organize and manage, with its own cultural schemes, even the ruling classes. Every state is ethical to the extent that it acts to elevate the population as a whole to a cultural and moral level in line with the development of productive forces and the interests of the ruling classes. This very important function identifies the fundamental state activities, even if they are not the only ones, in courts and schools. The concept of the ethical state must also include all the private initiatives that constitute the apparatus of political and cultural hegemony of the ruling classes. Gramsci reflected deeply on the functioning of these apparatuses of hegemony, and Marx had the great merit of revealing how the bourgeoisie uses all ideological instruments (the economy, philosophy, politics, etc.) to transfigure concrete reality by presenting its own interests as if they were universal.

On the conception of "ethical-political history", Benedetto Croce built the history of the moment of hegemony. In Crocean historiography, the juxtaposition of the terms "ethics" and "politics" indicates two essential terms of "political direction" and "domination": in the former case (ethics), the reference is hegemony, the activity of civil society; in the latter case (politics), the reference is state-government initiative, the institutional and coercive dimension. "When there is this contrast between ethics and politics, between demand for freedom and demand for force, between civil society and state-government, there is a crisis, and Croce goes so far as to affirm that the true state, that is, the driving force of the historical impulse, must be sought where it is least expected",[20] to the point that at certain times, although it seems paradoxical, the political and moral direction of the country can be exercised even by a revolutionary party, not by the legal government. For the Sardinian intellectual, Croce's greatest limitation is his belief that Marxism does not acknowledge the moment of hegemony and does not attach importance to cultural direction. In his righteous reaction to positivist mechanicism and economic determinism, Croce confuses historical materialism with its vulgarized form. This issue has already been very clearly highlighted by Marco Vanzulli, quoted in Chap. 2 of Part I of this book: Croce, the ambiguous curator of Antonio Labriola's philosophical heritage, was the protagonist of the arbitrary transfiguration of Labriola's thought, which was the basis for his critique of Marx. Contrary to what Croce stated, according to Gramsci, for the philosophy of praxis, ideologies have nothing arbitrary, but are instruments of political direction. For the mass of those ruled, these are instruments of domination through mystification and illusion; for the ruling classes, a "deliberate and conscious deception". In the relationship between the two levels, what emerges is the essential function of the hegemonic struggle in civil society and the non-arbitrary nature of ideologies:

> These are real historical facts, which must be fought and revealed in their nature as instruments of domination, not for reasons of morality etc., but precisely for reasons of political struggle: to make those ruled intellectually independent from rulers, to destroy one hegemony and create another, as a necessary moment of the reversal of praxis. [...] For the philosophy of praxis, superstructures are an objective and operational reality.[21]

---

[20] Ibid., 1302.
[21] Ibid., 1319.

Moreover, it is in the field of ideologies, of the so-called superstructure, that men become aware of their social being and of the passage from the "class in itself" to the "class for itself". For historical materialism, therefore, between structure and superstructure (between the economy and ideologies), there is a necessary and vital link, which allows us to speak of the former tending to move toward the latter, which does not exclude a mutual relationship between the two terms and also the function of superstructures, which is all but secondary.

But Gramsci does not limit this awareness of historical materialism to the work of its two founders; on the contrary, he writes that recent developments in the *philosophy of praxis*—the reference is again Lenin—place the moment of hegemony as an essential moment of state conception itself and of the work of transforming the social relations of production, valuing the factors of cultural direction, of the creation of a "cultural front", alongside purely economic and political factors.

> The proposition made in the "Introduction" to *Critique of political economy* that men become aware of structure conflicts on the basis of ideologies should be considered a gnosiological statement, not a purely psychological and moral one. Hence, the theoretical-practical principle of hegemony also has a gnosiological objective and, therefore, it is in this field that one can find Ilyich's most important theoretical contribution to the philosophy of praxis. Ilyich effectively advanced philosophy as he advanced in doctrine and political practice. The realization of a hegemonic apparatus, to the extent that it creates a new ideological terrain and leads to a reform of consciousness and of the methods of knowledge, is a philosophical fact.[22]

Among the paradigms of ethical-political history present in *Storia dell'Europa nel secolo XIX* [History of Europe in the nineteenth century], by Benedetto Croce, Gramsci identified a political use of categories as an "instrument of government", a faithful mirror of this self-representation of bourgeois ideology that Marx defined as "false consciousness". The main limitation of the representation made by Croce of the liberal era would be the maintenance of two distinct levels (one for the intellectuals and the other for the great popular masses) of what is understood by religion, philosophy, freedom. "Freedom as an identity of history and of spirit and freedom as a religion-superstition, as a detailed ideology, as a practical

---

[22] Ibid., 1249–50.

instrument of government."[23] The supposed ethics of the liberal state clashes against its little inclination for expansion and inclusion.

[Croce] believes he is dealing with a philosophy, and he is dealing with an ideology; he believes he is dealing with a religion, and he is dealing with a superstition; he believes he is writing a history in which the class element is to be exorcised, and he describes, with great clarity and merit, the political masterpiece through which a certain class introduces the conditions of its existence and of its class development and makes them accepted as a universal principle, as a worldview, as a religion, that is to say, he describes the development of a practical approach to government and domination. [...]

However, for the great governed and ruled masses, the philosophy or religion of the dominant group and its intellectuals always presents itself as fanaticism and superstition, as an ideological motive typical of a subservient mass. And does the ruling group not intend to perpetuate this state of affairs? Croce must explain why the freedom worldview cannot become a pedagogical element in the teaching of primary schools and how he himself, as a minister, introduced in elementary schools the teaching of confessional religion. This absence of "expansiveness" in the great masses attests to the restricted and immediately practical character of the philosophy of freedom.[24]

In these notes, the central problem of Gramsci's work reemerges with all its strength: the distinction between manual and intellectual work, understood as a paradigm of the distinction between rulers and those ruled, the organic dimension of all the structures of domination and exploitation of liberal society—a conception whose supposedly natural origin Gramsci countered by demonstrating its historicity and contrasting it with the statement that "every man is a philosopher".

That said, Gramsci attached fundamental importance to Croce's philosophy, to the point of suggesting, in his work, a work similar to what was done by Marx and Engels on Hegel and, at the same time, the creation of an *Anti-Croce* able to perform the same role *Anti-Dühring* had had for new Marxists before the war. His polemical and nihilistic nature in the face of historical materialism was, for Gramsci, a reaction to the fatalistic mechanicism of determinism, but apart from the confusion made by the philosopher between Marxism and some of its degenerative tendencies, he acknowledged the merit of his reassessment, in the field of political

---

[23] Ibid., 1231.
[24] Ibid., 1231–2.

struggle and organization, of the "cultural struggle front" by developing the doctrine of hegemony and expanding the conceptual field of political science beyond the simple identification of the state-force relationship.

Confusing Marxism with its deterministic degenerations, Croce criticized in Marx the idea of a supposed mechanical succession, naturally inscribed in the laws of historical evolution, from one social mode of production to another.

> By developing the contradictions of the capitalist or bourgeois era, which came after feudalism, and by giving birth, from the core of that era, to those generated and educated by it, who will bury and succeed it—the proletarians—he extracted the communist synthesis that he wished these executors of historical necessity to accomplish, and based on this dialectical scheme, he wrote and formulated, toward the end of 1947, the *Communist Manifesto*. [25]

His originality as a "creator of ideologies" lay in all that, in the sense that the intellectual from Trier gave the communist movement a more articulated theoretical foundation, with a philosophical and historical basis, in his most important work, *Capital*, with which Marx ended "moralism and sentimentalism" and turned to "simpler and more elementary motivations". Marx, says Croce, replaced the motto given by Wilhelm Weitling to the League of the Just, "all men are brothers", by introducing the perspective of the union of one portion of humankind based on hatred of the other portion and the destruction of the latter: "proletarians of all countries, unite". If through Hegel's dialectics historical materialism seemed to reach "the rational certainty of the future", both the utopianism of the early socialists and the insurrectional conception of violent onslaught of old Jacobinism were immanent in this doctrine. The novelty lay in providing these premises with a philosophical and dialectical view that showed the path, the goal of accompanying the relentless development of the historical process with the union between theory and praxis, which would opportunely lead to the revolutionary intervention of violence that would enable "the reaping of the ripe fruits".

> Marx devoted himself to the doctrinal elaboration of economics and historiography that he had sketched in the *Communist Manifesto* and began that series of works that, through the *Critique of Political Economy* led him to

---

[25] Benedetto Croce, *Storia d'Europa nel secolo decimonono* (Bari, Laterza, 1965), 129–30.

Capital. Practically, the doctrine that prevailed in him was determinism or naturalistic fatalism.[26]

It must be said that Croce's accusation of positivist popularization was not limited to socialism; he considered it a degenerative trend of European culture in the historical phase of the Second Industrial Revolution. According to Croce, everything that concerned the liberal movement and the national order of European society was closely linked to the idealistic and historical thought developed in the first decades of the nineteenth century, until it was objectified in the constitutions and institutions of its various nations. In spite of that, the Italian philosopher did not conceal a progressive reduction of the driving impulse originating in liberalism; in this sense, he wrote that "if the waters had bathed and fertilized the earth, which had been covered with a good harvest, the source from which they had sprung gradually depleted and almost died.".[27] After 1870, in liberalism itself there were still few traces of its great philosophical and historiographical tradition, which was replaced with the primacy of the natural sciences and hard sciences, which led to an extremely poorer positivist conception of historical and social development.[28] Historiography was reduced to "simple erudition and philologism" or converted into historical determinism, crushed by the predominance of this or that naturalistic cause to which everything should conform. This approach negated the value of the spiritual moment, of the creative force of the will, of freedom as a principle driving ideas and ideals that move men in history. The confusion between natural sciences and historical and philosophical sciences, and therefore the intention of transforming the latter into positive sciences, produced a mechanical and primitive determinism unable to understand both the former and the latter:

> Science, as it is established, does not and should not consider anything but force or forces, with no moral or aesthetic or intellectual qualification, physical force or vital force, and must treat it deterministically so as to measure it and provide it with laws; the philosophy of that time placed this scientific concept of force above life and spirit and transformed it into its source; hence the philosophical pseudo-theories, mechanistic in many ways, and the pseudo-hermeneutics of history based on these fanciful theories, and hence,

[26] Ibid., 184.
[27] Ibid.
[28] Ibid.

through a sort of sympathetic correspondence between theory and practice, the elevation of simple and abstract vital and ideal energy as the law of the strongest and the value of action as action and of fact as fact. Darwinism, at that time, was the epitome of this transition from simple observations and conjectures of natural science to a general interpretation of life, reality, and history, and ultimately to dictating practical living, to a supreme rule of conduct.[29]

Croce shows that one of the perverse consequences of this conception is found in the delusions of the theory of races created, among others, by Arthur de Gobineau, who converted some natural empirical classifications into real entities, ultimately attributing to one or the other the right to rule over society. This sentence, which could not be appealed against, belonging to a work created in 1931—hence in the phase of maximum expansion of fascism, which would enact racial laws a few years later—has an even deeper meaning.

[29] Ibid., 226–7.

CHAPTER 23

The Philosopher Man and the Tamed Gorilla

As we have seen, the enlarged conception of the concept of state and political domain in Gramsci is not reduced to coercive apparatuses, but rather encompasses the instruments through which the hegemonic apparatus of a ruling class is articulated, which is responsible for defending and developing the "theoretical or ideological front". Understanding the cultural articulation (press, publishers, libraries, schools, circles etc.) of domination structures is vital to any theory that aims to change the existing state of affairs, either by providing a living historical model of such structure, or by enabling a more realistic and sensible assessment of the forces acting in society to ensure some stability. Undoubtedly, paragraph 49 of *Notebook 3* is the one in which Gramsci most clearly outlines the historical task of a hegemonic conquest of the "elements of trenches and fortifications" underpinning the articulation of civil society, based on a process of material and spiritual self-determination of subaltern groups that, to use a typical expression of Georges Sorel, Gramsci identifies as the "spirit of cleavage".

> What can be contrasted, on the part of an innovative class, with this formidable set of trenches and fortifications of the ruling class? The spirit of cleavage—that is, the progressive acquisition of the consciousness of one's historical identity—a spirit of cleavage that must aim to extend itself from the protagonist class to the classes that are its potential allies: all of this

© The Author(s), under exclusive license to Springer Nature Switzerland AG 2023
G. Fresu, *Antonio Gramsci*, Marx, Engels, and Marxisms, https://doi.org/10.1007/978-3-031-15610-6_23

requires complex ideological work, the first condition of which is an exact knowledge of the field that must be cleared of its element of human mass.[1]

Thus, the political understanding of the hegemonic scope is fundamental to study the crisis of hegemony of the bourgeoisie after the First World War, and hence the advent of fascism. It is precisely this complex articulation of advanced civil society that makes the study of the historical function assumed by intellectuals in it essential. Hence the need for an in-depth analysis of the distinction between intellectuals understood as an "organic category of every social group" and intellectuals understood as a "traditional category". Historically, the consolidation of a new social mode of production is always marked by the struggle of the emerging social group to "hegemonize traditional intellectuals", a struggle that proves all the faster the more the social group in question can simultaneously produce its own organic intellectuals.[2]

An example of that is the consolidation of modern industrial production in England, in which the emerging class gains surprising economic-corporate predominance, but limited consolidation in the intellectual and political field. With the consolidation of the new system of industrial production, the bourgeoisie produces a large number of organic intellectuals, but the old aristocracy, having lost its economic supremacy, maintains its monopoly in the higher theoretical and political dimension. In its struggle for domination, the industrial bourgeoisie ends up absorbing the political-intellectual dimension of the old ruling class, which "is assimilated as traditional intellectuals and as the ruling stratum of the new social group in power. The old agrarian aristocracy joins the industrialists with a kind of sewing that, in other countries, is precisely the one that unites the traditional intellectuals with the new ruling classes".[3]

Upon identifying the figure of the intellectual, the grossest mistake consists in seeking its distinctive and characteristic element, the intrinsically intellectual nature of its activity, rather than the "system of relations in which they position themselves in the general set of social relations", that is, in the social position that intellectuals assume on the basis of existing production relations. To explain this concept, Gramsci uses precisely

---

[1] Antonio Gramsci, *Quaderni del carcere* trans. Joseph Buttigieg, *Prison Notebooks*, v. 2 (New York, Columbia University Press, 2007), 53.
[2] Antonio Gramsci, *Quaderni del carcere*, cit., 1541.
[3] Ibid., 1526.

the example of the industrial worker: indeed, the fundamental characteristic is not the intrinsically manual or instrumental nature of his labor activity—if so it would not be different from previous forms of labor, equally manual and instrumental—but rather this work in relation to certain conditions or social relations. Similarly, although the entrepreneur must have some qualifications of intellectual nature, his social figure is given by the general social relations that characterize his own position as owner in industry.

All men are intellectuals, one might say; but not all have, in society, the function of intellectuals (just as it may happen that everyone at some point fries a couple of eggs or repairs a tear on their coat, but it cannot be said, because of this, that all are cooks and tailors). Thus, historically, specialized categories for the exercise of intellectual function are formed; they are formed in connection with all the most important social groups and undergo more extensive and complex elaborations in connection with the dominant social group.[4]

This theme was revisited in the notes dedicated to *Fordism* and to its strategic objective: the creation of a new type of worker, shaped to the requirements of production.[5] The reflections of *Notebook 22*, however, were not limited to Fordism, linking the technical-productive goals of Taylorism to Americanism, of which Rotary's ideology was, in its own way, representative. As for paragraph 2 of *Notebook 5*, Gramsci highlights the particularity of and the essential differences between Rotary and traditional Freemasonry, highlighting the importance of this modern form of bourgeois ideology. Gramsci suggested a study of the ideological, practical and organizational aspects of this reality, questioning whether the great crisis of 1929 would not have re-signified its prestige and, more broadly, that of Americanist ideology.

First of all, Rotary is not denominational, anticlerical, or Masonic, being able to adhere to everything in a clear way, assuming the conception of industrial and commercial activity as a "social service" capable of overcoming "capitalism of plunder". Rotary found in the United States the natural seat of its development and in Americanism ideological support for the development of the productive forces in line with the new habits of

---

[4] Ibid., 1516.
[5] Gianni Fresu, "Americanismo e fordismo: l'uomo filosofo e il gorilla ammaestrato", *NAE: Trimestrale di Cultura*, Cagliari, Cuec, n. 18, ano 6, 2007, 53–4.

honesty and fairness in business. Thus, Rotary cannot be confused with Freemasonry; it is rather its overcoming, an expression of "concrete and precise interests". Freemasonry had a bourgeois-democratic character associated with secularism, while Rotary had a popular projection only indirectly, being essentially a modern organization of the upper classes. Gramsci pointed out that the Church, not holding Rotary on high esteem, could not have the same opposing stance traditionally taken against Freemasonry, because this would have entailed hostility against capitalism itself.

The exception to this orientation is the Jesuit world, due to the repeated attempts of ideological offensive of *La Civiltà Cattolica*[6] against Rotary, which was considered a disguised emancipation of traditional Freemasonry.[7] The underlying idea is that traditional Freemasonry used the religious agnosticism of Rotarians to promote its own secular worldview. However, the Sardinian intellectual points out a contradiction in its attitude that prevents a more direct fight against Rotary. If the attitude of indifference and therefore of religious tolerance is a reason for open hostility in Catholic countries, on the other hand it becomes a reason for interest in non-Catholic or Protestant countries, in which, in order to be able to spread and conduct an offensive of conquest, the Catholic world needs "amorphous institutions" from a religious point of view. This explains why the stance toward Rotary is one of ideological criticism, but with no excommunications, prohibitions, or other international combat practices.

Always confirming this close link between the technical and ideological domain, the rationalization of work and prohibitionism had moments of deep convergence, such as investigations into the lives of workers and inspections in companies to check their morality, obviously understood as the need for a new work method. Those who attribute such an offensive to a simple manifestation of hypocritical puritanism did not understand the extent of the "American phenomenon", which for Gramsci is the greatest collective effort ever made, with an unprecedented "awareness of goals" in history, that of creating a new type of worker and man. Taylor's

---

[6]Founded in 1850 by a group of churchmen, such as priests Carlo Maria Curci and Antonio Bresciani (often critically cited by Gramsci), and still active, *La Civiltà Cattolica* is the magazine of the Society of Jesus, the order of the Jesuits. Historically, this publication represented the most conservative and anti-modernist positions of the Church, which were engaged in the struggle against liberalism, socialism and the tradition of Freemasonry.

[7]Antonio Gramsci, *Quaderni del cárcere*, cit., 593.

phrase, "tamed gorilla", perfectly expresses, albeit in a brutal and cynical way, this goal of American society:

> To develop to the maximum level, in the worker, automatic and mechanical attitudes, in order to break the old psychophysical link of qualified professional work—which required some active participation of the intelligence, the imagination, the initiative of the worker—and reduce productive operations only to the mechanical physical aspect.[8]

However, in Gramsci's view, we are not facing a completely original reality, but rather the point of arrival of a long process of transformation that is consolidated by industrialism.

Attention to the worker's behavior was certainly not dictated by concern for his "humanity" and "spirituality", but aimed only at keeping a psychophysical balance beyond work that prevented the worker from collapsing in production. Human involvement in production reached its maximum level in the work of craftsmen, in which the worker's personality was reflected in the object created, but industrialism, especially Taylorism, directed brutalization in the division of labor against this humanity and spirituality of producers. The only concern of American industrialists is the physical (psycho-muscular) efficiency necessary to ensure the stability and continuity of production. Fordist industrialists take care of workers for a simple reason: the company is like a machine that, as such, "should not be disassembled and renewed in its individual parts too often, without great losses".[9] In this sense, even the prohibitionist crusade was a battle against the most dangerous agent of destruction of the productive force, a way of standardizing the lifestyle of the working class with the new division of labor that would be created by Taylorism. The same applied to sexual behavior, the irregularity of which was, along with alcohol, a dangerous enemy of nerve energies—also because induction to behaviors of alcoholic and sexual depravity would be inherent in monotonous, repetitive and obsessive work. That explains why Ford created corporate inspection organs aiming to control how workers spent their money and what their latent or private attitudes were at the sexual level. It is interesting how, in these notes, Gramsci closely connects the requirements of the mode of production with the most outstanding traits of puritanism and *American*

[8] Ibid., 2165.
[9] Ibid.

ideology, not reducing the prohibitionist crusade and the moralization of customs to a simple cultural and religious tendency. In this sense, it is a new "state ideology" grafted onto traditional puritanism, presenting itself as a "rebirth of the morality of the pioneers, of *true* Americanism [...]".

It is evident that new industrialism wants monogamy; it wants the worker not to waste his nerve energies on the disorderly and exciting search for casual sexual satisfaction: the worker who goes to work after a *night of extravaganza* is not a good worker; passionate exaltation does not fit with the timed movements of the production gestures linked to the most perfect automatism.[10]

But even if attempts to depersonalize labor, typical of Taylorist industrialism, can be extremely widespread, according to Gramsci, the goal of turning the worker into a "tamed gorilla" is doomed to failure. That is because when the division of labor functions reaches its level of improvement and technical specialization—which Gramsci calls "adaptation process"—the worker's brain is freed, not mummified. Mechanization concerns only the physical gesture: "The memory of the craft, reduced to simple repeated gestures with intense rhythm, *is accommodated to muscle and nerve bundles*, leaving the brain free and calm for other occupations".[11] Just as we walk without the brain having to participate in all the movements involved in walking, the work of the so-called "Fordized worker" does not lead to the cancellation of intellectual functions in the productive act. The attempt to brutalize industrialism therefore aims to make the separation between manual labor and intellectual functions constantly operative and insurmountable, and it is precisely in this unrealistic aspiration that its greatest limitation lies.

Thus, when we generally allude to the distinction between intellectuals and non-intellectuals, we take as a distinctive element only that which is predominant in the specific professional activity, that is, intellectual elaboration, or the muscular-nervous effort. However, even taking this very superficial classification into account, for Gramsci one can speak of intellectuals, but one cannot speak of non-intellectuals, that is, one can say that there are no non-intellectuals because, first, there is no human activity that excludes all intellectual intervention and, second, all human beings outside their professional activity perform some intellectual activity and are

---

[10] Ibid., 2167.
[11] Ibid., 2171.

philosophers who participate in a specific worldview, who contribute with their work to maintain it or modify it.[12]

Industrialists were aware of this truth: the worker "unfortunately" remains a human being and not only cannot be prevented from reasoning, but the very specialization in simple repetitive functions offers him more possibilities for thinking than the forms of work in which there is a greater component of "humanity" and "spirituality". In Gramsci's view, the latter is present with its maximum strength in craftsmanship, in which there is still a strong link between art and work. On the contrary, the dissatisfaction caused by the obsessive monotony of work, which does not allow any creative harmony between the personality of workers and the fruit of their activities, leads workers to develop "non-conformist" thoughts. The Taylorist factory, therefore, takes to extremes the phenomenon of alienation already present in the previous organizational forms of industrial production and, at the same time, increases the factors essential for the outbreak of social conflict. All this means that, although it is much more rational and progressive than previous forms of capitalist economic organization, Taylorism cannot develop its full potential precisely because of the class contradictions that interfere with the direction of this process.

In a historical phase in which workers become aware of themselves and their function and, therefore, reach full social and political subjectivity, work automation cannot go beyond the fundamental contradiction between capital and labor. Taylorism can only adequately make its programmatic nature concrete in a context dominated by the self-management of workers, when the proletariat assumes a function of economic direction. It is precisely the absence of that, besides the intention of concentrating all the effort for the development of productive forces only at the time of external coercion, that also undermined the prospect of militarization of labor proposed by Trotsky in order to face Russian economic breakdown. In Gramsci's view, Trotsky's stance on the "militarization of labor" was closely related to the problem of "rationalization of production and labor", typical of Americanism, but revealed a much more backward trend. The essential goal of this position was to give supremacy to industry, in productive and cultural terms, with the use of coercive methods able to accelerate the processes of transformation of society toward discipline and order in production, adapting customs to labor needs. Addressing the problem in these terms would necessarily entail a deleterious form of

---

[12] Ibid., 1375.

"productive Bonapartism". The concerns underlying Trotsky's positions were correct, but the solutions proposed were profoundly mistaken.

The enhancement of the Taylorist method presupposes continuity and stability in worker composition, that is, a limitation in the phenomena of workforce turnover. In Ford, that occurred through the system of high wages because social coercion alone, besides not being enough, would also have been more expensive than high wages. However, in Gramsci, it is clear that the system of high wages would be transitory, doomed to fail with the end of the technical-industrial monopoly of some companies, both in the United States and abroad. With the competition that rationalized, generalized and low-cost production inevitably creates, high profits disappear and, at this point, the limitation of turnover can only happen, at most, through the pressure of the reserve industrial army, when enlarged.

In any case, despite the high-wage system, there was still great instability of the labor force at Ford, a trend deriving from the fact that the Taylorist organization required a type of qualification that entailed levels of exploitation of the labor force much higher than it was possible to offset through high wages. In light of all these considerations, Gramsci questions whether the Taylorist system is really "rational" or whether it is a "morbid phenomenon" to be fought with union struggles and legislative limitations. In his interpretation, the Taylorist method is rational, but to be applied it requires a profound change in social conditions, customs and lifestyles. Above all, it is necessary to disseminate it through consent and persuasion, not only through coercion, as Trotsky intended, for example, that is, through a system of high wages accompanied by a general improvement in the quality of life, to compensate for the heavy expenditure of muscle and nerve energy that this method of work implies. The continuity and stability of work must be ensured so as to promote in every way the creation of a set of skilled workers, which is not shaken even by a cyclical crisis or by a temporary interruption of production:

> It would be uneconomical [Gramsci adds] to disperse the elements of a constituted organic whole with effort, because it would be almost impossible to regroup them, to the extent that their reconstitution with new elements, if successful, would involve considerable attempts and expenses.[13]

---

[13] Ibid., 2174.

However, as we have already mentioned, although Gramsci defines Americanism-Fordism as rational and progressive, that does not prevent him from identifying its limits, especially the impossibility of overcoming the social contradictions inherent in the organic crisis of capitalism. Americanism-Fordism based its programmatic economy project on the attempt to make workers a simple extension of machines, to the point of intending to adapt their attitudes and lifestyles to the needs of production. However, as we have seen, for Gramsci, in the struggle between the "tamed gorilla" and the "philosopher man", it is the latter that prevails, and therefore the other necessary condition for the homogenization of society for the purposes of Fordist production—the overcoming of the capital-labor conflict—is not reached either.

The materialization of new social relations of production should therefore have as an essential premise the overcoming of the distinction between manual and intellectual labor, which is an unnatural distinction, but historically determined, as a consequence of a division of labor imposed on the masses of instrumental workers. The subordinate classes' creation of their own organic intellectuals is the key element, but as we have seen this task is hindered by the very conditions of the subordinate classes, whose history is necessarily disaggregated and episodic. In them, there is a tendency toward unification, but that can only be fully accomplished after victory; otherwise, the subordinate classes will depend on the initiative of the ruling class, even when they rebel.

For Gramsci, the great intellectuals that emerged in the context of Marxism, besides not being many, were not connected with the people, let alone came from the people, but rather were always an expression of the ruling class to which they returned during historical changes. As for those who remained in the field of Marxism, they did so by subjecting it to a profound revision, rather than by favoring its autonomous development.

The interpretation of transformism is also used by Gramsci to explain the irresistible attraction held by the ruling classes on the leaders of the Italian socialist movement; hence the cyclical tendency toward its absorption into the conservative balances of the country. The Italian socialist movement created entire strata of intellectuals who then joined the class whose social domination they contested. It is a question that, according to the Sardinian intellectual, could be explained by the low adherence of the upper classes to the people:

In the struggle between generations, the young get closer to the people, but when crises reach the turning point, the young people return to their class (this happened in the cases of the nationalist-syndicalists and the Fascists). Deep down, it is the same general phenomenon of transformism in a different context. "Classic" transformism is the phenomenon that brought the parties together in the *Risorgimento*; this transformism brings into sharp relief the contrast between culture, ideology, etc., and class power. The bourgeoisie is unable to educate its youth (generational struggle); the young allow themselves to be culturally attracted by the workers, and they even become [or try to become] their leaders (an "unconscious" desire to make themselves the bearers of the hegemony of their own class over the people), but during historical crises they return to the fold.[14]

Thus, the creation of its own organic intellectuals becomes central to avoiding the systematic beheading of the political movements of the popular masses in times of crisis; however, such creation should not consist in separating the individual proletarians from their classes of origin to make them leaders of the movement, but rather in radically transforming the conception, role and function of intellectuals and, above all, in completely changing the relation between manual and intellectual activity:

> The problem with creating a new intellectual class therefore lies in critically developing the intellectual activity that exists in every one to some extent, by changing its relationship with the muscle-nerve effort toward a new equilibrium, and transforming the same amount of muscle-nervous effort, as part of a general practical activity, which continually innovates the physical and social world, into the basis of a new and comprehensive worldview.[15]

Gramsci contrasts this new idea of intellectual function with the "traditional" and "vulgarized" type, that is, the scholar, the philosopher, the journalist, the artist, all those categories of individuals who manage to have the exclusivity of intellectual activity. In fact, this is a fossilized residue of the past, because in modern industrial society a close connection between technical-practical activity and intellectual activity is already spontaneously created.

---

[14] Antonio Gramsci, *Quaderni del carcere*, trans. Joseph Buttigieg, *Prison Notebooks*, v. 2 (New York, Columbia University Press, 2007), 115.
[15] Antonio Gramsci, *Quaderni del carcere*, cit., 1551.

The production of "organic intellectuals" and their close connection with "traditional intellectuals" take on particular importance for the modern party. If we take into account the predominant function that the members of a party perform, that is, the managerial and organizational function, we must conclude that they are all, in a sense, intellectuals. Individuals from different social groups join a political party with a different perspective and role from those of the trade union, because in the party they become agents of the general activities, national and international, of the party.

For Gramsci, Machiavelli's *The Prince* is the metaphor for the modern political party, in which a collective will likely to become "universal and total", that is, to found the state itself, is concentrated. The notes of the *Notebooks* evoke the creation of a "modern Prince", understood as an organism that plastically embodies the collective will of the popular masses. The "modern Prince" must necessarily have a part dedicated to Jacobinism, an example of how a collective will, in some respects original, was concretely formed and operated; he must also investigate what conditions must exist to awaken and develop a collective will that is an *ex-novo* creation.

According to Gramsci, Machiavelli's *The Prince* is not a cold utopia, but a "living book", because it manages to merge ideology and political science through myth, because in it the political conception is not abstractly doctrinal at all, but is aimed at an ideal leader who, despite not having immediate historical reality, represents the collective will of a scattered and pulverized people. Through its fantastic and artistic form, *The Prince* has the ability to stimulate, convince and arouse the organization of this collective will. If in his exposition Machiavelli identifies, with rigor and scientific detachment, the qualities necessary for the prince to guide a people and found a state, in the conclusions he becomes a people, fuses into it, and becomes its consciousness and organic expression. According to Gramsci, the strength and modernity of *The Prince* lie in all that, in the understanding that the creation of a national popular collective will is not possible without the irruption of the great masses into political life. This intuition is present in the idea of the reform of the militia, in which Gramsci sees in Machiavelli's "primitive Jacobinism" the germ of his revolutionary conception that later translated historically into the role played by the Jacobins in the French Revolution.

The idea of a "modern Prince", the construction of a party that is the real expression of the popular masses, has as its main objective precisely the end of any "passive balance" through a profound "intellectual and moral reform", that is, a worldview that coincides with the subsequent development of this collective will toward a "superior and total form of civilization", a radical transformation of society based on its social mode of economic production. Just as, for the young Marx, in his polemic with Bruno Bauer about the *Jewish question*, human emancipation cannot be limited to political emancipation, according to Gramsci, there cannot be a cultural reform, a civil elevation of the exploited classes, if it is not preceded by a radical economic transformation capable of putting an end to their condition of subalternity.

> Therefore, an intellectual and moral reform cannot but be linked to an economic reform program so that the economic reform program is precisely the concrete way all moral and intellectual reforms are presented.[16]

This core issue is critical to correctly understand the notes of the *Notebooks* about school and education without making Gramsci an educationalist.[17] Reducing the pedagogical problem present in his reflections to educational techniques or to the cultural problem means misunderstanding, underestimating or omitting the organic nature of the issues and the radical nature of the solutions proposed.[18]

In Marx, the political and educational dimensions are inextricably intertwined in a relationship of reciprocity: on the one hand, a profound transformation of social conditions is essential to create a different school system; on the other, it is necessary to change the nature of education to change social conditions.[19]

The educational perspective in Marxism lies in the need to enable the full development of human personality, overcoming the conditions imposed by the division in the classroom and the specialization of labor. On his path of intellectual development, Marx went from philosophical

---

[16] Ibid., 1561.

[17] Gianni Fresu, "De Marx a Gramsci: educação, relações produtivas e hierarquia social", em Anita Helena Schlesener, André Luiz de Oliveira e Tatiani Maria Garcia de Almeida (orgs.), *A atualidade da filosofia da práxis e políticas educacionais* (Curitiba, UTP, 2018), 19–62.

[18] Mario Alighiero Manacorda, *L'alternativa pedagogica in Gramsci* (Rome, Editori Riuniti, 2012), 43–101.

[19] Idem, *Marx e a pedagogia moderna* (trad. Newton Ramos-de-Oliveira, São Paulo, Cortez, 1991), 36.

criticism to a critique of political economy, while maintaining a dialectical organic relationship between the two spheres, which also relates to the educational problem and the question of the complete liberation of man. If the development of industrial society produces maximum dehumanization, labor alienation, and the transformation of workers into commodity and machine prosthesis, the very division of labor responsible for that denial of humanity can become a determining factor for the integral development of the individual.

For Marx, and for Gramsci, in bourgeois society, the school plays an increasingly important role in consolidating relations between rulers and those ruled, providing labor for material production and intellectually producing the future representatives of the ruling class. Free, public education, free from the social conditions of exploitation of bourgeois society, would allow the participation of young people in the entire production system, making it possible to alternate from one sector to another due to social demands or their own inclinations.

The possibility of choosing the direction of one's own existence, of disabling the predestination of old class relationships, would represent the premise of the omnilateral development of man, in which the passage from the domain of necessity to that of freedom materializes. In this sense, socialism would find one of its fundamental reasons in guaranteeing equal opportunities for all, which concretely means the possibility of choosing (in Hegel the passage from necessity to freedom is already expressed in these terms) consciously, and with no conditions, one's own field of activity. Only when this freedom of will ceases to be the patrimony of the few and becomes a collective condition for the integral development of the personality, according to Marx, "can society write on its flag: 'From each according to his abilities, to each according to his needs!'".[20]

This set of problems, already dealt with by the young Gramsci in some articles published between 1916 and 1920, found in the *Notebooks* a more organic in-depth analysis, connected to the question of the relationship between intellectuals and subaltern groups and to that of the absence of an Italian national-popular culture.

In the paragraph *About Italian universities*, in *Notebook 5*, this problem is addressed with the analysis of universities' inability to influence and regulate national cultural life, while in *Notebook 12* the reflection focuses directly on the historical role of the school and its increasingly specialized

---

[20] Karl Marx, *Critica del programma di Gotha* (Rome, Editori Riuniti, 1976), 32.

evolution, parallel to modernization and proportional to the degree of development of productive forces.

> The great development of activities and school organization (in a broad sense) in the societies that emerged from the medieval world shows the importance of intellectual categories and functions in the modern world: just as it was sought to deepen and expand the "intellectuality" of each individual, it was also sought to increase the specializations and refine them. That results in educational institutions of varying degrees, even organs to promote so-called "high culture", in all fields of science and technology. The school is the instrument for producing intellectuals of different degrees. The complexity of the intellectual function in various states can be objectively measured by the number of specialized schools and their hierarchy: the larger the school area and the more numerous the "vertical" "degrees" of the school, the more complex the cultural world, the civility, of a particular state.[21]

Thus, the level of industrial and social development can be measured by the degree of articulation of the structures of intellectual production and selection. The formation of intellectual classes does not take place in an "abstract democratic terrain", but rather in line with certain social relations of production, according to "very concrete traditional historical processes" that, through the school, guide the division and specialization of labor. School orientations have the precise function of shaping society, separating the intellectual ruling classes from the social mass of instrumental workers. The close interweaving between technical-productive needs and the conformation of the formative orientation is also found in the differences in intellectual selection between city and countryside, therefore, between the North and the South of Italy:

> The different distribution of the various types of school (classical and professional) in the "economic" terrain and the different aspirations of the various categories of these classes determine or shape production in different branches of intellectual specialization. Thus, in Italy, the rural bourgeoisie produces especially state officials and liberal professionals, while the city bourgeoisie produces industry technicians: therefore, northern industry produces mostly technicians, and southern Italy mostly civil servants and liberal professionals.[22]

[21] Antonio Gramsci, *Quaderni del carcere*, cit., 1517.
[22] Ibid., 1518.

In this articulation, Gramsci continues, the division between classical school and vocational school performed a role in line with the productive needs of bourgeois society. However, the emergence of a new system of specialized schools of varying degrees shook the traditional school structure. This later specialization was related not only to so-called vocational schools but also to the selection of intellectual classes with an increasingly specialized and less universalist education. For instance, if the political-bureaucratic personnel had a general technical-legal education before, later they moved on to an increasingly detailed disciplinary specialization, with the creation of professional figures built around a specific need (technical-administrative, fiscal, economic-political, etc.). The crisis of the old educational system led to the overcoming of any kind of "disinterested" and purely formative school. The solution could have been found in a single initial school of general, humanistic and formative culture, capable of harmoniously balancing manual labor skills and intellectual functions. From this first level, after repeated experiences of professional orientation, students would go to a secondary school of specialization, according to students' attitudes and inclinations.[23]

According to Gramsci, the school had to be public, recipient of an economic and organizational commitment of the state to create an educational network from kindergartens to universities, because only public schools can involve all generations with no differences of group, stratum or class. Gramsci speaks of an "active school", referring to a first phase in which it must be disciplinary and prepare in the direction of dynamic conformism, and a "creative school", in which, based on the level shared by students, it is possible to encourage the specific development of each personality, which is made autonomous and responsible and marked by a solid and homogeneous moral-social consciousness: a full-time school and collective life day and night, free from the old hypocritical and external forms of discipline, in which study must be done collectively. By identifying it as "creative", Gramsci did not intend to propose a school of inventors and discoverers, but rather to indicate a specific phase characterized by a research and training method capable of stimulating students' spontaneous effort, in which teachers are only guides: "to discover for oneself, without suggestions and external help, a truth and creation, because the truth is old and demonstrates the process of the method; it indicates that, in any case, we entered the stage of intellectual maturity, in which new

---

[23] Ibid., 1531.

truths can be discovered"[24] through seminars, experimental work and bibliographic research.

In Gramsci's view, the old school was deeply oligarchic, perpetuating and consolidating the old dualistic relations between classes and the condition of subalternity of the simple. Although it might seem like the fruit of democratization, even the professional specialization of the school actually contributed to making social differences permanent. Once again, the solution to this contradiction required changing the old "naturalistic schemes" in the relationship between rulers and those ruled. The new way of being an intellectual should encompass organically working techniques, scientific techniques and a humanistic worldview, transforming each individual into a "specialist + politician".[25]

> Intrinsically, the democratic trend cannot only mean that manual workers get qualifications, but that every citizen can become a "ruler" and that society gives them, albeit "abstractly", the general conditions to be able to do it; democracy tends to make rulers and those ruled coincide (in the sense of government with the consent of those governed), ensuring that each and every person governed can freely learn the skills and techniques generally required for such purpose.[26]

[24] Ibid., 1537.
[25] Ibid., 1551.
[26] Ibid., 1547.

CHAPTER 24

Michels, the Intellectuals and the Issue of Organization

The theme of the instrumental use of the law by ruling groups, which were transformed, due to a relationship of passive delegation, into a priestly caste of experts in politics, presents some essential points for our debate in the notes dedicated by Gramsci to Robert Michels.[1]

Political Parties: A Sociological Study of the Oligarchical Tendencies of Modern Democracy, by Michels, a successful work published for the first time in 1911, represents an essential moment in the considerations on the contradictions between political direction and the masses in the history of the labor movement. Obviously, this is not the place for a systematic study of this text, nor will we delve into Michels's controversial and paradigmatic political-intellectual biography.[2] Here we will limit ourselves to recalling only some elements that are useful (from our point of view) to develop a more general and organic reasoning about some Gramscian categories and conceptions addressed in this work. As we will see, Gramsci dealt extensively with Michels's work in the *Notebooks*, drawing from it reflections and critical assessments that help define his view of Marxism as an organic solution to the separation between intellectual and manual functions.

---

[1] Gianni Fresu, *Il diavolo nell'ampolla. Antonio Gramsci, gli intellettuali e il partito* (Nápoles, Istituto Italiano per gli Studi Filosofici/La Città del Sole, 2005), 201–18.

[2] Robert Michels's biography, with his parabolic passage from German social democracy to fascism, is emblematic of the epic contradictions of those years.

G. Fresu, *Antonio Gramsci*, Marx, Engels, and Marxisms, https://doi.org/10.1007/978-3-031-15610-6_24

In this sense, two themes in Michels's discourse are essential among many others: the so-called "iron law of oligarchy" and the "law of the distortion of ends", that is, the study of the dynamics that lead the organized structure of a mass party to fall prey to the dictatorship of a ruling minority until it transforms the organization itself from a means to an end. Both aspects arise from the processes of growth and development of the political organization of workers, and both inevitably lead to the total distortion of the purposes, of the ends and, more generally, of the very nature of the revolutionary party of the proletariat. According to Michels, when a class intends to achieve the purposes and ideals derived from the economic roles it has, it needs organization in the economic and political field as a means of constituting a collective will.

In general, democracy cannot exist without organization, and this is even more true of the working class, whose only weapon, in the fight against the privileged classes, is organization. The tendency toward unification among individuals in the same socio-economic condition is an increasingly typical feature of modern societies, but the working class needs even more "solidarity among the interested parties" because, if isolated, the proletarian is completely at the mercy of economically stronger classes. According to Michels, the popular masses have numerical strength, but this will only have a real weight—by multiplying, from simple disaggregated numerical strength, into political and social strength—with its structured and disciplined organization at mass level.

Once established, this organization can keep the physiognomy of a struggle party and face the highest level of centralization of the economy, only structuring itself according to a line of command marked by agility and hierarchy, in which the members are to obediently follow their leader so that the whole organization may seem to be a hammer in the hands of the president. Centralization is the only guarantee for rapid decision-making, and only a certain degree of "Caesarism" guarantees the rapid transmission and the timely execution of orders in everyday struggles. For Michels, internal democracy in a political party is counterproductive for the immediate availability for the struggle. But this need also brings along the equally inevitable disadvantage of the dictatorship of the leading groups over the organized masses:

> In fact, the source from which the conservative currents flow over the plain of democracy, where they sometimes lead to disastrous floods and render the plain unrecognizable, goes by one name, that is, organization.

Organization implies the tendency toward oligarchy. A deeply aristocratic element integrates the nature of organization. While creating a solid structure, the mechanism of the organization causes serious changes in the organized mass, completely inverting the relationship between the rulers and the mass and dividing each party into two: a minority, whose task is to lead, and a majority led by it.[3]

For Michels, there is an inversely proportional relationship between democracy and organization; therefore, in advanced societies, the degree of democracy is doomed to decrease with the evolution of socio-political organization. This deeply pessimistic perspective cannot be shaken even by systems of political participation not mediated by representation. According to Michels, the self-government of the masses, the overcoming of leadership through forms of direct democracy, and the emanation of the popular will are in fact unachievable because, first of all, direct democracy cannot operate without the aid of the representative system. Moreover, even if popular assemblies can limit the delegated participation of representative democracies, they are actually more subject to the formation of an oligarchic leadership.

The "crowd" leads to the "law of reduction of responsibility", that is, in the indistinct mass, individuals and their personalities tend to disappear. In popular assemblies, crowds are more susceptible to the speaker's eloquence and are therefore easier to dominate than in a traditional Parliament. The small audience guarantees a more sensible and reflective membership, which allows greater respect for the occasional emergence of minorities or individuals in opposition to the majority, while the deliberations by acclamation in popular assemblies are determined by enthusiasm or irrational panic, that is, by more tumultuous and elementary forms of adherence.

In turn, the inversely proportional relationship between organization and democracy, which leads the majority to be tyrannized by an eminent minority, finds its most typical form of expression in the modern political party. In his analysis, Michels refers to the large Social Democratic Party of Germany (SPD): the tendency toward technical specialization of the main functions of a party or trade union, a logical consequence of its growth, leads to the need for "leadership by competence" and ends up transferring all the decision-making powers of the participating mass only to the

---

[3] Robert Michels, *La sociologia del partito politico nella società moderna* (Bolonha, Il Mulino, 1966), 55–6.

leaders. If initially they are executive bodies of the will of the mass, later, with the development into complex organization, the leaders emancipate themselves from the masses, become independent and ultimately dominate them. Also in this case, the degree of organization inevitably tends to increase with the growth of the party itself, but at the same time the technicalization of its leading functions leads to the creation of a caste of officials and leaders who tend to become an oligarchic leadership; in conclusion, for Michels, the establishment of a professional leadership in the party is the end of its democracy.

Among the ruling oligarchies of a party inserted into the system of parliamentary representation, institutional representatives play an absolutely prominent role. Michels emphasizes very effectively that the delegation relationship produces a kind of "moral right" to the perpetuation of this function, that is, to remain in office continuously and for as long as possible, transforming it from a fixed-term election into an election that lasts a lifetime. When a leader holds the office of delegate for some time, he tends to consider it his property. If later the delegation is questioned, the leader will use all possible and imaginable reprisal techniques to wreak havoc on the organization and finally come out fortified in his role. Faced with criticism over his performance, the leader threatens to resign, with the sole objective of maintaining and strengthening his power, obtaining from the assembly a new plebiscite investiture capable of embodying the vicarious function of a competent court. Obviously, such maneuver is successful when the leader in question is irreplaceable at that particular moment or, in any case, skillful and cunning to the point of seeming to be irreplaceable.

This process, analyzed by Michels also in the relationship between the parliamentary group and the whole militant body in the Italian Socialist Party (PSI), is a determining factor behind that phenomenon that makes the leaders free themselves from the conditioning of the organized mass in the party. The beautiful democratic gesture of resignation would conceal, most of the times, an ill-disguised authoritarian spirit of pressure on his followers in order to obtain a new irrevocable mandate.

Closely linked to the phenomena described thus far is another degeneration of political parties (central to Gramsci's reflections) analyzed by Michels both in its historical genesis in relation to states and in reference to its manifestation in democratic parties: "Bonapartism". For Napoleon I, his power was founded on the will of the mass, so much so that he called himself "the first representative of the people"; Napoleon III, in turn, based his "Caesarism" on the principle of popular sovereignty. "Bonapartism" relates any violation of the law to the principle of the popular will and does not acknowledge any intermediary body between the will of the prince and the will of the people. "Bonapartism is the theorization of individual will originating in the collective will, but emancipated over time to become sovereign",[4] since precisely the original democratic nature constitutes the legitimacy of its anti-democratic present too. Through plebiscite, democracy and autocracy end up being connected. For "Bonapartism", even independence and possible opposition to an act of intermediary bodies, such as the judiciary or the public administration, are an attack on the popular will that placed the power of the prince above any other body by voting. Parliament, the judiciary and the public administration must be instruments subject to the will of the prince and, through him, to the will of the people.

The history of modern parties and trade unions reveals numerous affinities with the aspects described thus far and, as we have seen, the young Gramsci, still deeply influenced by Sorel, develops an important aspect of his controversy against Italian socialism around this issue. In parties, the intangible authority (due to democratic origins) is the leading committee or the leader, whom the mass of members must obey unhesitantly. For Michels, discipline is the submission of the collective to its collective will. Also in this case, the tendency to consider any opposition to the work of the leader as anti-democratic is determined by the democratic nature of his mandate. This ultimately ends up making party leaders demand mechanical and military adequacy from the masses, with no need for further explanation. They issue orders based on science and consciousness, firmly believing that the work done, as a consequence of a freely voted mandate, is beyond criticism.

Thus, it is no coincidence that, in socialist parties, any current of critical opinion regarding the leadership is considered the work of saboteurs and enemies committed to demagogically breaking the unity of the party:

In the general conduct of the leaders of modern democratic parties [...], "the grace of the people" became "the grace of God", a theory typical of that system which in French history we know by the name of Bonapartism.[5]

---

[4] Ibid., 295.
[5] Robert Michels, *La sociologia del partito politico*, cit., 305.

For these reasons, in the revolutionary workers' movement, both tactics and attitudes related to conflicts of internal opposition would not be different at all from the political action of a bourgeois government. According to Michels, when a certain degree of partisan development is reached, it ends up being dominated by oligarchic dynamics made autonomous by the mass of the organized. The leaders end up identifying the organization, as well as its property, with themselves, interpreting any criticism against the party as directly and personally directed at them. The bureaucrat's identification with the party is so perfect and absolute that it makes each leader a small Sun King, whose motto could easily be *Le parti c'est moi* [The party is me].

The structure of the political party has a pyramidal configuration, and the decision-making power is inversely proportional to numbers. Its structure moves from the electoral body, above which is the mass of members, followed by the set of participants of the general assemblies and, finally, the group of employees and the restricted steering committee. This structure makes the participatory and decision-making base very narrow, while the mass of the organized becomes, to use Gramsci's classic expression, mere "mass of maneuver". Within the hierarchical configuration, militants from the city—among whom the leaders are chosen—tend to clearly take precedence over affiliates from the countryside or from provincial sections, who are largely destined to have a merely passive role in party life.

In addition, there is also the problem of the social composition of those who participate in discussions and in the main governing bodies of the working-class political party, who are largely of bourgeois origin:

> The regular attendees at meetings, especially in smaller cities, are not proletarians, who sleep early, exhausted from work, but rather middle-class individuals of all sorts: from petty bourgeois, through those who sell newspapers and illustrated postcards, to young intellectuals with no position in their own circle, who are all glad to speak as authentic proletarians and as the class of the future.[6]

For Michels, this dualistic condition between leaders and the masses is greatly facilitated by the mindset of the masses, which need preliminary preparation by their leaders and, more generally, guidance to move. Michels speaks of the "innate impotence of the masses", which is

[6] Ibid., 87.

confirmed by the condition of disintegration they experience when they are suddenly deprived of their leaders: they leave the countryside in a chaotic escape, not showing the ability to quickly reorganize, and behave like a "terrified ant colony", and the only way out of this paralysis is the spontaneous emergence of new leaders able to replace the old ones. In Gramsci's view, on the contrary, the impotence of the masses is not innate, but a consequence of proletarian parties' organization modalities, which largely reproduce the most typical ruptures of bourgeois society. To avoid this phenomenon, it is necessary to combat any conception that considers political direction too complex a function for the people—therefore, an activity to be delegated to a specialized caste—to make as horizontal as possible (to recall the Gramscian metaphor of the party as a coral reef) the formulation and direction, or at least the creation, of intermediate organs able to constantly keep in touch the different levels of the party.

The impotence shown by the masses when they are suddenly beheaded, albeit not innate, but induced, is also a fundamentally important problem in Gramsci. The history of the labor movement in Italy had already offered several examples of this phenomenon, but the advent of fascism is perhaps the most emblematic:

> The working class is like a great army suddenly stripped of all its junior officers; in this army, it would be impossible to maintain discipline, the structure, the fighting spirit, the unity of direction with the mere existence of a general staff. Each organization is an articulated complex that works only if there is an adequate numerical relationship between the mass and the leaders. We have no cadres, we have no connections, we have no services to embrace the great mass with our influence, to strengthen it and to make it an effective tool for the revolutionary struggle.[7]

According to Michels, the tendency of the masses to be guided is also increased by another factor of a psychological nature that contributes to determining leaders' supremacy: gratitude for those who write and fight in the name of their interests, which creates the reputation of defenders and advisers of the people, who may be imprisoned, exiled or persecuted. This "sacred duty of gratitude" practically translates into an unlimited mandate of representation, to the point of elevating the leader above all else and never subjecting his work to verification in the name of battles long fought.

[7] Antonio Gramsci, "Il nostro indirizzo sindacale", *Lo Stato Operaio*, 18 out. 1923, em *La costruzione del Partito Comunista 1923–1926* (Turin, Einaudi, 1971), 5.

For Michels, with the growth of the party, the proletarians' voluntary and provisional work is replaced with political technicians' professional work, a problem particularly central to Gramsci's reflections on the relationship between intellectuals and the masses. At a certain level of party development, skills specialize, and the division of labor triumphs to the point of determining a complex organizational structure constantly directed by professionals and employees independent from the organized mass. The emergence of this professional leadership further increases the differences between leaders and followers in the party, and the formal education obtained, "intellectual superiority", is precisely one of the most determining factors in the supremacy of minorities over majorities.

This phenomenon produces two different consequences: in some countries, such as Italy, the so-called bourgeois intellectuals or "deserters of the bourgeoisie" (lawyers, university professors, doctors), due to their intellectual superiority and specific skills, join the party and become its guides. In other countries, such as Germany, due to some general conditions—such as the severity of class conflict and also the workers' higher educational level—a large majority of former manual workers started to perform to the technical and political functions of the party, alongside a limited number of intellectuals of bourgeois origin. However, even in this case, according to Michels, the result is the same, because the level of education obtained by these former manual workers and the attendant social—and also economic—liberation make them profoundly different from their former classmates.

In these reflections by Michels, apart from some approximation and instrumentalization, it is possible to grasp one of the main problems for Gramsci and, even before, for Marx: the separation between intellectual and manual work. Michels indeed notes the great attraction exerted by the party—with its abundance of paid positions and the possibility of making a career—on intellectually gifted proletarians. This phenomenon can molecularly modify the very proletarians who became party leaders or officials, turning them into officials with petty-bourgeois characteristics:

> While their occupation and the needs of daily life make it impossible for the masses to have a profound knowledge of political processes, and above all the working of the political machine is inaccessible for the masses, the leader is nonetheless enabled, given his new position, to make himself intimately familiar with all the technical details of political life. Thus, the worker elevated to a leadership position increasingly assimilates the notions […]

that in the long run lead to his growing superiority over those who are led by him.[8]

Therefore, with the evolution of social legislation, the greater the difficulty in orienting oneself in political life and the greater the complexity of political functions themselves, the more this distance between leaders and class increases, "to the point that the former lose consciousness of their class origin, and a true division is created between ex-proletarians and proletarian followers".[9]

Assuming leadership functions at the professional level then determines an economic and status dependence on the party, which makes leaders cling with all their might to this role even when, over the years, the passion for the socialist future and for the proletarian brotherhood is gone. Michels describes this phenomenon and finds it both in the "deserters of the bourgeoisie", who often destroy the bridges with their classes of origin and with their previous professional activities, and in those of proletarian origin, now accustomed to the social and economic status arising from their political and organizational duties and no longer able or, in any case, no longer willing to resume their previous occupation as manual workers. This representation, albeit perhaps overly schematic, even so raises very interesting questions. Among them is certainly the analysis of the dynamics that lead the deserters of the bourgeoisie to change sides to become leaders of the proletariat. This tendency, as we have seen, is very present at the center of Gramsci's reflections.

The so-called "deserters of the bourgeoisie", who became leaders of the workers' parties, often find their connection with the proletariat at an early age, either as an act of rupture and ethical rebellion against the state of affairs in their own family, or because of their scientific adherence to the postulates of historical materialism. Often, the transition from a class to the leadership of an antagonistic one derives from youthful instincts, from the nihilistic enthusiasm that drives the immediate attack against the reality that one is escaping.

On the other side of the barricade, the "deserters of the bourgeoisie" often act and fight over a lifetime, but quickly tire. They join the workers' organizations and soon become leaders when they are still young, but over time the weight of physical and mental tensions pertaining to this kind of

---

[8] Robert Michels, *La sociologia del partito politico*, cit., 127.
[9] Ibid.

life leads to disillusion, to formal but disinterested adherence to socialism, and finally, as Gramsci writes, they "return to the flock":

> With the passing of youth, their ideals have also passed [...]. The mass loses, in their eyes, the glorious charm; the love of the neighbor and ideals grow pale in reality. Thus, many leaders are estranged from the essential components of socialism. Some offer a little resistance to skepticism; others even, consciously or not, return to the ideals of their (non-socialist) childhood or of their native background. [10]

In Antonio Gramsci's view, this phenomenon is typical of the so-called "historical turning points", of the phases of reflux that force the workers' movement toward defensive positions or strategic retreats, and it is precisely this phenomenon, which is present in the history of Italian socialism, that cyclically determines the beheading of the workers' movement and the impossibility, for several years, of reconstituting its bases in strong positions. But for Gramsci, unlike Michels, this phenomenon is not an inevitable natural law, but one of the most decisive and complex challenges of socialism: the production of organic intellectuals themselves; not party employees with petty-bourgeois employment roles, but manual workers able to perform political leadership functions, especially in the workplace, without ever losing contact with their historical role.

The goal should not be the social promotion of some workers with particular attitudes toward the role of intellectuals, but the cultural and political elevation of the popular masses as a whole and their transformation into conscious protagonists.

This rupture has historically led to an unavoidable contradiction in the process of shaping the proletariat's class consciousness because, in the so-called passage from the "class in itself" to the "class for itself", the fundamental role is played by the bourgeoisie, which, in its constant class struggle, mobilizes and strengthens its interests, hegemonizing the proletariat. But the bourgeoisie is acting not only as a "master of arms" of the proletariat, but also as the protagonist of another phenomenon: the tendency for groups to disengage from it, to put their skills and energies at the service of the working class and to encourage it to fight back against their own social class and the state of things it represents.

---

[10] Ibid., 283.

This phenomenon is never particularly significant in numerical terms—the number of "deserters from the bourgeoisie" is always quite limited—but it is remarkable in terms of quality, because these individuals are usually above the average of their own class when it comes to moral strength, theoretical skill and spirit of sacrifice. At the beginning of its political history, the proletariat did not yet have the cultural means to disengage from the complex labyrinth of social relations of production, to gather its interests again and shape its worldview coherently. As Lenin had already done in *What is to be done?*, Michels points out that socialist theory originated from the philosophical, economic and historical formulations of bourgeois science and that the very progenitors of socialism were, first and foremost, scholars and, secondly, political men.

The recruitment of the workers' parties among the ranks of the bourgeois intelligentsia is absolutely central in the formation of their leading groups; however, it indeed leads to the domination of real oligarchies, in most cases socially estranged from the masses they intend to lead. Revolutionary syndicalism and various currents of socialist thought historically sought to eliminate this problem, proposing the exclusion of intellectuals from the leadership of the workers' movement to entrust it directly and without mediation to worker leaders in order to maintain strong affinity between worker leaders and their followers.

Proletarian leadership undoubtedly has advantages, according to Michels, first of all because a former proletarian leader, despite no longer practicing in this post, can better understand the economic needs of the masses, and therefore can express expert opinions on specific issues related to labor, production and working life in general. He has a much deeper knowledge of the psychology of the masses than a deputy or a leader of bourgeois origin and can thus stay in much more constant contact with them.

But according to Michels, these reasons can apply to trade union activity, in which the cadre of leaders really remains connected with their profession, while within the sphere of political struggle the situation would be completely different. In the political struggle, the "iron law of oligarchies" manifests its ruthless nature even among the ranks of the proletariat because when the manual worker professionally assumes a leading position within a political party and thereby is paid, he ceases to belong to the working class to join that of the employees, until he is organically absorbed by the oligarchic tendencies that distinguish every leading group:

The proletarian leader then ceases to be a manual worker, not only in the technical sense [...], but psychologically and economically as well, and becomes an intermediary just like his colleague the lawyer and the doctor. In other words, as a delegate and a representative, the leader of proletarian origin is subject to the same oligarchical tendencies we have discussed in relation to the bourgeois refugees who become labor leaders. [11]

As in much of his work, also when dealing with this theme, Michels remains insistently and somewhat arbitrarily in the schematism of a petty sociology, which intends to map collective attitudes and behaviors based on supposed psychological characteristics of social groups. For Gramsci, this is the "purely descriptive character and external mode of classification of old positivistic sociology":

He does not have any methodology which is intrinsic to the facts, no critical point of view other than the amiable skepticism of the salon or the reactionary coffee shop which has replaced the equally superficial unconventionalities of revolutionary syndicalism and Sorelism.[12]

Thus, even when dealing with the leading cadres of proletarian origin, the German sociologist makes use of lengthy explanations and numerous practical examples in order to demonstrate how they, once freed from their occupation, would generally be more power-hungry, stubborn, selfish, vain, subject to self-satisfaction and lazy, less open to criticism and even prone to innate cowardice, if compared to bourgeois intellectuals. In Michels, in some cases there were in-depth and quite current analyses coexisting with schematic representations of social and individual dynamics, often no different from the commonplaces about the southerners' immutable indolent nature and their proclivity to crime, or about the Jews' notorious avarice.

For Michels, the history of the workers' movement generally shows that a socialist party is all the more exposed to the demands of the environment—therefore, more corruptible and prone to opportunism—the more pronounced its proletarian nature is. Hence, the idea that the proletariat can rely only on itself, thus ensuring the protection of its interests, without

---

[11] Ibid., 408.
[12] Antonio Gramsci, *Quaderni del carcere*, trans. Joseph Buttigieg, *Prison Notebooks*, v. 1 (New York, Columbia University Press, 2007), 325.

the intermediation of third parties from other social classes, would be nothing more than a mere illusion.

The inevitable oligarchic tendency of leadership in the political party is therefore a dead-end situation. To demonstrate that, Michels denies, as viable alternative solutions, both the hypothesis of revolutionary syndicalism and that of anarchism. Moreover, in the degenerative processes of the revolutionary political party of the masses, Michels also includes the equally inevitable tendency toward a progressive conservative transformation. Even in this case, the disease that leads the organization to the loss of its revolutionary impetus—and to become increasingly prudent, until it is lost in laziness, inertia and the immobility of its ordinary institutional tasks—would derive from the growth of the organization.

The revolutionary party emerged with the ambition of being superior to the centralized force of the bourgeois state and, for this reason, it organizes itself with a powerful and articulated organizational structure that has its own authority and is guided by strict discipline. The mass revolutionary party is a state within the state, born with the stated goal of emptying and destroying the existing one to replace it with something completely different. However, as this organization expands and consolidates to take on an imposing physiognomy, rather than gaining revolutionary momentum, it ends up being the victim of an opposite phenomenon.

For Michels, also in this case there is a very close relationship between the growth of the party and the increase in prudence in the policy adopted:

> In other words, the conservative tendencies typically associated with possession also manifest themselves in the socialist party. For half a century, members of the party have been struggling and sweating over the creation of a model organization. [...] what was organized was a bureaucracy which can rival—due to its consciousness of its duties, its zeal, and its obedience ·to superiors—that of the state itself; the coffers are full; a complex of financial and moral interests has taken shape throughout the country. A bold and harsh tactic would endanger all this: the work of thousands of leaders and sub-leaders; in short, the whole party.[13]

In the end, the organization ends up being transformed from a means to an end, and the love for the creature makes its leaders avoid any risky policy that could compromise its existence. An excessive and continuous

---

[13] Robert Michels, *La sociologia del partito politico*, cit., 495.

revolutionary offensive could make the state decide to dissolve the party, which becomes the main concern and ends up guiding the political line.

With that, Michels also describes the "law of distortion of ends", completing the framework of his analysis of the socialist organization of the masses, which ultimately does not offer particular solutions regarding its *duty to be*. Michels essentially limits himself to an ontological assessment, continuing and developing the analysis of the decadent and decompositional tendencies of Marxist organizations initiated by Sorel. Once accounts have been settled with his limits, there remains an indisputable fact: this work revealed a series of real problems that the workers' political movement, throughout its long history until today, has not been able to solve completely.

In *Prison Notebooks*, Gramsci expresses serious and sarcastic criticism of Michels's studies on political parties, devoting to them some reflections of considerable importance. The notes concerning the German scholar have their starting point in Max Weber's definition, according to which the political party is a spontaneous association of propaganda and agitation, whose propensity for power is linked to the need to obtain, for its members, the moral and material advantages that power entails and to pursue and achieve objective ends. In Gramsci's view, the personal party, which grants the protection of a *powerful man* to its *inferior* members, was quite common, especially with the emergence of modern political parties. Examples of political groups identified by the names of their leaders abound. Even in the labor and socialist movement, this tendency still exists. The most obvious example was the distinction between Lassalleans and Marxists in German socialism, and between Guesdists and Jauresists in French socialism.[14] Therein lies an analogy between modern parties, religious sects and monastic orders.

In Gramsci's view, the definition of "charismatic leader", that is, of a leader who exercises power over his subordinates due to qualities that seem supernatural, was not created by Michels, but rather by Weber.

The general characteristics of this party are manifold and the Lassallean movement itself provides a first emblematic example:

---

[14] Gramsci refers to the articulation of the French socialist movement and German social democracy around the strong personality at the political level, which led to the emergence of currents named after their respective intellectual reference points: Jules Bazile, known as Guesde (1845–1922), and Jean Jaurès (1859–1914) in France; Ferdinand Lassalle (1825–1864) and Karl Marx (1818–1883) in Germany.

He [Lassalle] took pleasure in bragging to his supporters about the idolatry he enjoyed from the delirious masses and from virgins dressed in white who sang him praises and offered him flowers. This charismatic faith was not only the result of an exuberant and somewhat megalomaniacal psychology, but it also corresponded with a theoretical conception. We must—he told the Rhenish workers while explaining to them his ideas on the organization of the party—forge a hammer out of all our dispersed wills and put it in the hands of a man whose intelligence, character and devotion can guarantee us the ability to strike hard. It was the dictator's hammer.[15]

Another emblematic example discussed by Gramsci is Mussolini himself, who took on the functions of the sole head of a party and of a state. The fascist party is fully identified with the figure of Mussolini. However, this having become the flesh and blood of individual charismatic leadership is also linked to the prohibition against forming groups or taking stances that could question it. In this sense, Mussolini used the state to dominate the party, and in turn the party to dominate the state. However, the devastating effect of charismatic leaders upon the masses is "infantile": "To those who are familiar with the susceptibility of Italian crowds to sentimental exaggeration and 'emotional' enthusiasm". Thus, the longevity of charismatic parties, which for Gramsci can be both authoritarian and anti-authoritarian, "is often dependent upon the longevity of their energy and enthusiasm, which sometimes provide a very fragile situation".[16]

According to Gramsci, Michels's theoretical production on political parties is simplistic and superficial, his ideas are often confusing and schematic, the categories and definitions included in them are not immune to trivial errors, the analytical and narrative plot is oppressed by an idle and complicated plethora of redundant bibliographic citations.[17] However, in Gramsci's view, some aspects of this work can be interesting and useful as

---

[15] Antonio Gramsci, *Quaderni del carcere*, trans. Joseph Buttigieg, *Prison Notebooks*, v. 1 (New York, Columbia University Press, 2007), 319.

[16] Ibid., 321.

[17] "He also supports even the most banal truisms with the authority of the most disparate writers. One often gets the impression that it is not the line of thought that determines the citations, but the heap of ready citations that determines the line of thought, giving it a disjointed and improvised character. Michels must have compiled an enormous card index, but in the manner of a dilettante, an autodidact [...]; he does not have any methodology intrinsic to the facts, no critical point of view other than the amiable skepticism of the salon or the reactionary coffee shop which has replaced the equally superficial unconventionalities of revolutionary syndicalism and Sorelism" (ibid., 324–5).

raw materials and empirical observations. Thus, for example, despite harshly criticizing the arguments on the theory of the "charismatic leader" and the assertions about the "iron law of oligarchy", about the problems of relations between democracy and the tendency toward oligarchy in political parties described by Michels, Gramsci recognizes that these ideas have a precise meaning when there is, in the organization, a class division between bosses and members. In this case, the problem is not one of the many classifications of sociological schematism, which often make Michels's work unreliable, but the encounter with a real problem, a deep political contradiction with clear practical effects on the history of trade unionism and of social democratic and communist parties. And this is precisely the topic we will address in the last chapter of this book.

CHAPTER 25

The Dismantling of the Old Schemes of Political Art

As thoroughly explained, the dualistic nature of relations between rulers and those ruled is a central theme in Gramsci's theory for several reasons, especially because within this contradiction lie both the origins and the persuasive force of the relations of exploitation and domination typical of bourgeois society.

In *Notebook 2,* Cadornism is defined as a paradigmatic category capable of synthesizing the relationship between intellectuals and masses, and therefore the passive nature of Italian social and political relations. According to Gramsci, demanding from Cadorna[1] great political skills would not be generous since at that time the leading politicians in power had no military skill at all. The Italian ruling classes proved inadequate to politically prepare military leaders; thus, Cadorna's inability to play a motivating political role in relation to officers, non-commissioned officers and soldiers corresponded to that of the government (and politics in general) in relation to the popular masses. Cadorna's evident aversion to parliamentary political life was no different from that of the royal house and that of the liberals who led the country.[2] But as we have seen in this

---

[1] Luigi Cadorna (1850–1928) was the Italian general associated with the defeat of Caporetto in the First World War, which was caused by his firm and expensive strategy (in terms of human lives sacrificed) based on the so-called *spallate* [frontal attacks], the military offensive against the tight Austrian defense lines, which ended with the failure of the troops and the withdrawal of the Italian army to the Piave River Valley.

[2] Antonio Gramsci, *Quaderni del carcere* (Turin, Einaudi, 1977), 259.

© The Author(s), under exclusive license to Springer Nature Switzerland AG 2023
G. Fresu, *Antonio Gramsci*, Marx, Engels, and Marxisms, https://doi.org/10.1007/978-3-031-15610-6_25

biography, Cadornism was not only a problem of the national ruling classes; on the contrary, it also profoundly marked the movement that fought them.

The organizations of the labor movement proved inadequate to eliminate the old standards of political art, eventually applying them internally and once again assigning the working classes the role of "mass of maneuver". In Gramsci's view, all human groups have their own "optimal principle of defined proportions", and this can be seen both in the army and in political parties, in trade unions and in factories. This principle consists in relations between the different elements of the social group in question,[3] which are necessarily balanced and harmonious relations, in which change in one of the elements makes a new balance in the whole necessary.

The presence of cadres of different levels and with different skills reveals how a movement of opinion turns into a political party, because the party essentially has the function of producing skilled leadership cadres for their various functions. The effectiveness of a party lies in its existence as a "mass function", which develops and multiplies the main leading cadres of a social class, transforming it from a disintegrated and amorphous group into an "organically predisposed political army". The qualitative or even quantitative deficit of leading functions at the different levels of a political party ends up making its action sterile and ineffective even in the presence of favorable conditions for its useful functioning. In Gramsci's view, the post-war history of the socialist party, and that of the communist party, bears ample testimony to this.

Associated with the discussion on the principle of defined proportions is the production, during historical development, of the career employee technically trained in bureaucratic work, a question of "primordial" significance in political science and in the history of state employees, a topic dealt with extensively in the previous pages devoted to Michels. The issue of employees tends to coincide with that of "organic intellectuals" in the essential social group: the consolidation of a new social and state form creates the need for a new type of employee, but it cannot do without (at least for some time) the employees inherited from pre-existing social and political relations.

This problem had extraordinary importance for Russia after October 1917 due to the difficulties encountered by the emerging Soviet state in

---

[3] In a political party, this is associated with relations between the ruling group, institutional representatives, mid-level cadres, militant cadres and the mass of members.

directing production and public administration itself toward workers, and it was necessary to seek a solution in a new inspiration, to which the entire state machine should be directed: unity between manual and intellectual labor. This problem was not solved by the Russian Revolution, neither in practice nor theoretically. In the paragraph entitled *The concept of organic centralism and the priestly caste*, in *Notebook 3*, Gramsci seems to refer to the problem of the doctrinaire and dogmatic crystallization of an ideology and to the question of the formation of an official priesthood entrusted with its administration. Against this tendency, he writes that ideology should be conceived historically, as a manifestation of a ceaseless struggle, not as something artificial and mechanically superimposed. The intention to forge once and for all an organism already objectively perfect would be a disastrous illusion of organic centralism because it could "drown a movement in a quagmire of personal academic disputes".[4]

The issue of employees and the organization of a new social state order are closely connected with the theme of "organic centralism" and "democratic centralism". "Organic centralism" is a concept according to which the political group is chosen through cooption around a personality, a "charismatic leader" who considers himself the bearer of "infallible truths" and the guardian of "infallible natural laws" of historical evolution. Within "organic centralism", it is necessary to distinguish whether the dominance of a part over the whole is concealed or explicitly implemented, that is, whether it is the result of a unilateral conception of fanatical and sectarian groups. In this case, one should not speak of "organic centralism", but of "bureaucratic centralism"; organicity is rather "democratic centralism": organic because it is the result of a continuous adaptation of the organization to the real movement of things, not their bureaucratic crystallization. "Democratic centralism" is for Gramsci "a balance between impulses from below and command from above, a continuous insertion of the elements stemming from the depths of the mass into the solid structure of the steering apparatus, which ensures continuity and the regular accumulation of experiences".[5] It is a flexible formula that consists in the constant critical pursuit of what is equal amidst apparent diversity, in which the pursuit of organic unity does not entail general uniformity, let alone the result of a cold rationalist process; organic unity is a practical and experimental

---

[4] Antonio Gramsci, *Quaderni del carcere*, trans. Joseph Buttigieg, *Prison Notebooks*, v. 2 (New York, Columbia University Press, 2007), 56.
[5] Antonio Gramsci, *Quaderni del carcere*, cit., 1634.

necessity, and it is the organic unity between theory and praxis, between the intellectual classes and the popular masses, between the rulers and those ruled. The predominance of "bureaucratic centralism" in a state indicates, instead, that its leadership group is "saturated"; it has become a consortium of interests committed to perpetuating its privileges, stifling new vital forces at birth, even when they are aligned with the interests of the dominant group.

The "law of defined proportions" varies depending on the social group taken into account and also on the level of culture, mental independence and spirit of initiative of its more backward and peripheral members. In this sense, the most stagnant and brutal forms of "bureaucratic centralism" occur precisely because of the absence of initiative and responsibility coming from below, due to the limits and still primordial nature of the peripheral element, even when it is homogeneous with the hegemonic territorial group.

The attainment of a complete and perfect form by the parties is difficult because any development entails new tasks and responsibilities for them. In the case of the party driven by the ambition to eliminate class distinction from society, it can be said that it reaches the condition of perfection when it loses its historical necessity, ceasing to be a subject that is real while rational and vice versa. Each party is a class nomenclature, and therefore if classes no longer exist, the need to organize themselves into a party is also reduced. Thus, the complete accomplishment of classless society and of the communist party must occur with the end of the communist party itself.

That said, however, among the various forms of human groupings, the political party is one of the examples in which the rule of the "optimal principle of defined proportions" can be best understood. A party becomes historically necessary when the conditions for becoming a state begin to take shape and allow us to glimpse possible developments; when that happens, the party is formed and articulated by three fundamental elements: first, the diffuse element of the mass, whose participation depends on discipline and loyalty, without which the party could not exist. However, the strength of this element is closely connected with the ability of the leading element to perform a cohesive and centralizing role, in the absence of which the diffuse element of the mass would be dispersed, devoid of discipline and eventually powerless.

Gramsci understands discipline as the organic, continuous, and permanent relationship between rulers and those ruled, which tends to lead to a collective will, not the passive and mechanical acceptance of orders to be executed without debate. If thus conceived, discipline does not nullify through its existence, limits "irresponsible impulsiveness and arbitrariness". Freedom and personality are called into question not by discipline itself, but by the nature of the source of the direction to be implemented: if it is of democratic origin, that is, if it is a specialized technical function, not an arbitrary act or an external imposition, discipline becomes a necessary element of democratic order and freedom. But the democratic origin of leadership is achieved if it is exercised within a homogeneous social group; if on the contrary it is exercised by one social class over another, the social group enforcing order may speak of discipline, but the group affected by it may not.

The second fundamental element of the party examined by Gramsci is the "main cohesive" element, the national leadership group, which gives cohesive strength and centralization to all members and proves even more decisive for the existence of the party than the diffuse element of the mass. Gramsci writes:

> There is talk of captains without an army, but in reality it is easier to produce an army than to produce captains. So much so that an army is destroyed if it lacks captains, while the existence of a group of captains, united, agreeing with each other, with common purposes, soon produces an army, even where it does not exist.[6]

Finally, the third element is the so-called intermediate cadres, whose role is to articulate the leading element with the mass and keep them in physical, moral and intellectual contact, thus ensuring the continuity of political direction. The political effectiveness of a party and its efficient functioning are therefore closely linked to the existence of "defined proportions" among these three elements.

The distinction between leaders and those led and between rulers and those ruled is a primordial and unyielding element of political art, whose origin has its own causes that must be analyzed in detail. The problem of "defined proportions" in the political party is related to the best and most effective way of leading and forming leading groups. In the revolutionary party, the fundamental issue, associated with the formation of the leading groups, is the will to reduce the division between rulers and those ruled.

[6] Ibid., 1734.

On the other hand, one of the most classic flaws of the leading groups is the belief that, once orientation is identified, it must be applied with military obedience, so that one does not even feel the need to explain its necessity and rationality.

The belief that something will be done because the leader considers it correct and rational, and for this reason is affirmed as an indisputable fact, is exactly what Gramsci means by "Cadornism". In parties, the tendency toward "Cadornism" and, along with it, "the criminal habit of neglecting the means of avoiding unnecessary sacrifices" are part of a misguided way of conceiving political direction, although it is clear that the worst collective political disasters occur when "playing in someone else's shoes".

> Everyone has heard of front officers describing how soldiers really risked their lives when it was necessary, but how they rebelled when they saw themselves neglected. For instance: a company could fast for many days upon realizing that food would not be enough, but it would mutiny if a single meal were denied due to negligence or bureaucracy.[7]

Overcoming "Cadornism"—the predominance of collective and broad organizations of political direction—leads to overcoming the old "naturalistic" schemes of political art and, more generally, the relationship between rulers and those ruled in society. The spread of mass parties and their organic adherence to the most intimate life of the popular classes, together with the shaping of their critical class consciousness, understood as the overcoming of a disorganized, casual and mechanical form of popular sentiment, are the two essential elements of this change in which the germs of future society can already be glimpsed.

Cadornism is therefore the metaphor of an unresolved historical problem: the instrumental use of the masses by the leading groups, the fact that they turn out to be a raw material in the hands of the "charismatic leader" of the day. In an article written on the occasion of Lenin's death in 1924,[8] Gramsci already asked himself some questions about the necessary relations between the party and the masses in the context of the dictatorship of the proletariat, in which we can read that, preliminarily, every state is a dictatorship. As long as there is a need for a state, the problem of direction,

---

[7] Ibid., 1753.
[8] Antonio Gramsci, "Capo", *L'Ordine Nuovo*, mar. 1924, in *La costruzione del Partito Comunista 1923–1926* (Turin, Einaudi, 1971).

of the "leader", will arise. However, in the context of the transition to socialism, the essential problem is not the existence or not of a "leader", but the nature of relations between him and the masses, that is, whether they are purely hierarchical and military relations or, on the contrary, relations of an organic nature. In order for the "leader" and the party not to be an aberration, an unnatural and violent superimposition on the masses, both must first be part of the class, or at least represent its most vital interests and aspirations. In Gramsci's view, Benito Mussolini perfectly represented all the most negative characteristics of the so-called "charismatic leader", as he intended to lure the masses with his brilliant oratory and theatrical performances, but with no organic connection with them.[9]

This theme is revisited in the notes of *Notebook 6*, in which the Sardinian intellectual deals with the distorted meaning of the terms "ambition" and "demagogy", as he affirms the need not to confuse "lofty" and "petty ambition". When this difference is clear, one can say that politics without ambition is not conceivable; however, when the difference is not clear, ambition is associated with base opportunism, with the betrayal of one's principles and social group, to gain a greater immediate profit.

Just as politics cannot exist without ambition, neither can there be a "leader" that is disinterested in the exercise of power, but even in this case the problem is not so much ambition itself, but rather the nature of the relationship between the "leader" and the mass with which this "lofty ambition" is pursued. The problem is when the leader's ambition increases after he has created a desert around him, or if this feeling is associated with the elevation of an entire social stratum; in other words, if the ambitious leader sees his elevation as a function of overall elevation.

---

[9] "In Italy, we have the fascist regime, we have Benito Mussolini as its leader, we have an official ideology in which the leader is deified, declared infallible, proclaimed the organizer and inspirer of a Holy Roman Empire reborn. Let us look at the photographs: the most hardened face we have ever seen at socialist rallies. We know this face: we know this rolling of the eyes in the orbits, which in the past, with their mechanical ferocity, threatened the bourgeoisie and today threaten the proletariat. We know this whole mechanism, all this paraphernalia, and we understand it can impress and move the guts of the youth of the bourgeois schools; up close, it is really impressive and surprising. But a leader? [...] He was then, like today, the concentrated type of the Italian petty bourgeoisie, an angry and fierce mixture of all the debris left on national soil by several centuries of domination by foreigners and priests: he could not be the leader of the proletariat; he became the dictator of the bourgeoisie, which loves the fierce face when it again becomes Bourbon, which expects to see in the working class the same fear he felt of those rolling eyes and that menacing clenched fist" (ibid., 15).

The same observations apply to so-called demagogy, which is associated with the general tendency to use the masses by sparking their enthusiasm, which is consciously generated and nourished with the sole aim of pursuing their particular "petty ambitions". But if the "leader" does not consider the mass "cannon fodder", that is, an instrument for achieving his own goals and then being discarded, but rather gives it a historical leading role in an organic and general, not particular, political end, demagogy itself can be positive. The tendency of the reprehensible demagogue is to present himself as irreplaceable, to make people believe that the only thing behind him is the abyss. To this end, he eliminates all possible competitors, placing himself directly in instrumental relationship with the masses, through his attractive features and the use of all the spectacular instruments necessary to obtain passive consent, not active participation:

> The political leader with a lofty ambition, on the other hand, is inclined to create an intermediate stratum between himself and the masses, to foster potential "rivals" and peers, to elevate the capabilities of the masses, to produce individuals who can replace him as a leader. His thinking is in line with the interests of the masses, who do not wish to see an apparatus of conquest [or domination] dismantled by the death or incapacitation of a single leader, which would plunge the masses back into chaos and primitive impotence.[10]

Replacing "Cadornism" and changing the old "naturalistic" schemes of political art means, first of all, combating the prejudice underlying the view of philosophy as something excessively difficult and the preserve of a specialized category of intellectuals and sages. Every man, whatever his professional activity, is a philosopher[11] who participates in a certain worldview. The problem does not lie in having more or fewer intellectual faculties, but rather in understanding whether that conception is purely spontaneous or mechanical or, on the contrary, critical and coherent—that is, if it responds to the real needs of those who have them or if it is the result of an exogenous and imposed formulation, absorbed unconsciously

---

[10] Antonio Gramsci, *Quaderni del carcere*, trans. Joseph Buttigieg, *Prison Notebooks*, v. 3 (New York, Columbia University Press, 2007), 83.

[11] In the article "Socialism and culture", published in *L'Ordine Nuovo* in 1919, Gramsci wrote that "every man is a philosopher", addressing this topic in terms not very different from those he used in the *Notebooks*.

from the social environment in which it emerges onto the world.[12] As we have seen, according to Gramsci, the subaltern groups were constantly directed by the ruling classes, and therefore even in the various manifestations of popular philosophy (language, common knowledge, common sense, popular religion, folklore), fragments and characteristics of the ruling group's worldview can be found. The unreflected or spontaneous adherence to the idea of civility of the ruling class is actually the most effective guarantee of the preservation of its domination relations, which leads the exploited to accept the very laws of exploitation on which their subalternity is based. In an advanced society, with stratified private apparatuses of civil hegemony, the cornerstone of passive balances lies not so much in the concentration of force in the hands of the state as in the gravitational capacity for ideological and cultural regimentation.

In order for subaltern groups to be able to break free from this domination, a "spirit of cleavage" is necessary. The subaltern must be self-determined materially and spiritually, overcoming the fragmentary and episodic forms of the "spontaneous philosophy" that inhibits their consciousness.

Is it preferable to think without critical consciousness, in a disaggregated and occasional way [...] or is it preferable to formulate one's own worldview consciously and critically and, based on that, in connection with the work of one's own brain, choose one's own sphere of activity, actively participate in the production of world history, be one's own guide and no longer accept, passively and indifferently, that one's personality trait is determined exogenously? [...] Thus, criticizing one's own worldview means making it unitary and coherent and elevating it to the point reached by the most advanced thinking in the world. It means, therefore, also criticizing all the philosophy hitherto existing, to the extent that it left stratifications consolidated in popular philosophy. The beginning of critical thinking is the awareness of what really exists, that is, knowing oneself as a product of the historical process

---

[12] In the notes on Bukharin's *Popular essay*, Gramsci defines the "philosophy of common sense" as the "philosophy of non-philosophers", that is, the worldview uncritically absorbed from the various social and cultural environments in which the moral individuality of the average man develops. For Gramsci, this philosophy is not always identical in time and space and is characterized by being a "disaggregated, incoherent, inconsequential conception, according to the social and cultural position of the crowds where this philosophy is found" (Antonio Gramsci, *Quaderni del carcere*, cit., 1396).

hitherto developed, which provided one with a multitude of accepted traits without the benefit of inventory. This initial inventory needs to be made.[13]

A critically coherent worldview requires full awareness of its historicity (the critical worldview must respond to certain problems posed by reality), is historically determined, arises from a specific development of productive forces, and is in contradiction with other worldviews, which are, in turn, the expression of other historically determined interests.

But the creation of a critically coherent worldview must necessarily assume a unitary character, finding a way out, for the premises of this philosophy, in socialization and in collective participation. Creating a new culture able to position itself critically in relation to the past also means socializing the discoveries already made and turning them into the foundation of concrete action, making this culture an "element of coordination" and of the "intellectual and moral" order of the masses. In itself, Gramsci writes, the fact that a mass of men is led to think of the present and of reality in a united and coherent way is philosophically more important than any philosophical discovery or novelty that remains in the closet of the restricted intellectual elites. For any worldview that becomes a cultural movement and produces a practical activity and a conscious and consequent political direction,[14] the real problem is to maintain the ideological unity of the social bloc united by it.

Thus, for example, one of the main elements of strength, meaning and persistence among the religious masses, especially the Catholic masses, is precisely the fact that they constantly fought for the doctrinal union of the entire religious mass, so as not to create one religion of intellectuals and another of "simple souls", so that the upper intellectual strata were not separated from the lower ones.

The Church managed to keep its faithful community through the coherent repetition of its apologetics and the maintenance of continuity between it and the faithful. Whenever this continuity was interrupted—as in the times of the religious reformation and in the French Revolution— the Church suffered incalculable damage. The *philosophy of praxis* should have learned a lesson from that example. Every new worldview that seeks to replace common knowledge and old conceptions must necessarily act in

---

[13] Ibid., 1376.
[14] Gramsci refers to ideology, that is, to a worldview that manifests itself in art, law, economic activity and all manifestations of life, both intellectual and collective.

two ways: first, never tiring of repeating its own arguments, giving them coherence and continuity; second, working to "intellectually elevate ever wider popular strata, which means working to arouse intellectual elites of a new kind that arise directly from the masses and remain in contact with them to become their basis.".[15]

One of the greatest limits of the philosophies before the *philosophy of praxis* was precisely not having succeeded in creating an "ideological unity from top to bottom", "between ordinary men and the intellectuals". Thus, for example, idealism opposed the cultural movement of "going toward the people" manifested in the phenomenon of popular universities, although this was, with its several flaws, a phenomenon worth studying and worthy of interest, not deserving to be simply downgraded, because it demonstrated the enthusiasm and will of ordinary men given the possibility of rising to a higher worldview.

However, if one of the strengths of the Catholic Church lies in its intention to maintain, in doctrinal unity, the contact between the higher intellectual strata and the masses, this goal was never achieved with a work aimed at elevating the masses to the level of intellectuals, but rather by imposing iron discipline on intellectuals, so that they do not exceed certain limits in the distinction between them and the masses. For Gramsci, Marxism should be methodologically (not just ideologically) antithetical to this worldview, since it should not withhold the masses in their

---

[15] Antonio Gramsci, *Quaderni del carcere*, cit., 1392.

primitive philosophy of common knowledge, but aim to elevate them to a
higher conception of life.[16]

> If he affirms the need for contact between intellectuals and ordinary people,
> it is not to maintain unity at the lowest level of the masses, but precisely to
> build an intellectual-moral bloc that politically enables the intellectual prog-
> ress not only of scarce intellectual groups, but also of the masses.[17]

---

[16] In this approach, we can notice the great influence of Lenin's *What is to be done?*, in
which the issue is discussed extensively. In this work, we read, for example: "our very first and
most pressing duty is to help train working-class revolutionaries to be, in regard to party
activity, on the same level as the intellectual revolutionaries [...]. Therefore, our attention
must be devoted chiefly to elevating the workers to the level of revolutionaries, instead of our
descending to the level of the 'working masses' as the 'economists' wish to do [...]" (Vladimir
Ilyich Lenin, *Che fare?*, Turin, Einaudi, 1979, 151. And, again in this sense, Lenin quotes
Karl Kausty: "Modern socialist consciousness can only arise on the basis of profound scientific knowledge. [...] The vehicle of science is not the proletariat, but the *bourgeois intelligentsia*: it was in the minds of individual members of this stratum that modern socialism
originated, and they were the ones who communicated it to the more intellectually developed proletarians [...]" (ibid., 47), to which the Russian revolutionary later adds in a footnote: "This does not mean, obviously, that the workers have no part in such creation. But
they have a part not as workers, but as socialist theoreticians [...]; in other words, they take
part only when they are able, and to the extent that they are able, more or less, to master the
science of their era and make it advance. And so that workers may succeed in this more often,
every effort must be made to raise the level of consciousness of workers in general; it is necessary that workers do not confine themselves to the artificially restricted limits of 'literature for
workers', but that they increasingly learn how to master literature in general. It would be
fairer to say 'are not confined', instead of 'do not confine themselves', because the workers
themselves do read and want to read everything written for the intelligentsia, and only some
(bad) intellectuals think it is enough 'for workers' to be told about factory conditions and to
repeat what they have long known" (ibid., 47–8).

[17] Antonio Gramsci, *Quaderni del carcere*, cit., 1384.

CHAPTER 26

Epilogue

*It is necessary to eliminate the widespread prejudice underlying the
view that philosophy is something very difficult because it is the
intellectual activity of a certain category of specialists or of systematic
professional philosophers.*
—Antonio Gramsci (*Quaderni del carcere* (Turin, Einaudi,
1977), 1375.)

In Gramsci's view, achieving a critical consciousness able to transform subaltern groups into self-aware historical subjects is possible only with the
subversion of the "old naturalistic schemes" of political art, with the total
abandonment of a dualistic way of understanding the relationship between
political direction and the masses. Thanks to this traditional conception,
the intellectual becomes a kind of priest guarding the flask with the devil
inside, in charge of interpreting the feelings of the popular masses and
then translating them into political guidelines that they must apply
mechanically, if not militarily. On the contrary, the process of material and
spiritual self-determination causes elaboration and direction to result from
an "active and conscious involvement" of the collective organism, no longer being the result of the intellectual intuition of the leader or of the
ruling group, which the chain of command translates unilaterally, from
top to bottom, into an idea-force necessary for the action of the masses.
Gramsci describes this whole system of "living philology", in which there

G. Fresu, *Antonio Gramsci*, Marx, Engels, and Marxisms,
https://doi.org/10.1007/978-3-031-15610-6_26

remains a relationship of definite proportion between "the great mass, the party, the leading group and the whole, well articulated, [which] can move like a collective man".[1]

Gramsci attributes the contradiction in the relationship between intellectuals and masses to background incommunicability. Due to its subalternality, the popular element can "feel", but is not always able to understand and, above all, to "know", whereas the intellectual element can "know", but is rarely able to "feel". For the Sardinian philosopher, the error of intellectuals lies in the belief that it is possible to "know" even in the total absence of empathy, without "feeling and falling in love"; therefore, through a process of distinction, not by means of an organic relationship with the "people-nation" able to understand its elementary passions. The pure intellectual, an expression of the historical dualistic relationship between knowledge and instrumental activity, which for Gramsci unites dissimilar figures such as Benedetto Croce and Amadeo Bordiga, connects with the people only to interpret its feelings, not to understand it and to be in tune with it in order to place it in a dialectical relation with a higher, scientific and coherently devised worldview. The pure intellectual leans toward the people only with the purpose of building scientific schemes; he connects with the people as a zoologist who observes the world of insects:

> Knowledge does not become politics-history without this sentimental connection between intellectuals and the people-nation. In the absence of such bond, relations between intellectuals and the people-nation are reduced to relations of a purely bureaucratic, formal order; intellectuals become a caste or a priesthood. If the relationship between intellectuals and the people-nation, between leaders and those led, between rulers and those ruled is an organic adherence in which the feeling-passion becomes understanding and, thus, knowing (not mechanically, but in a living way), only then do the relationship of representation and the exchange of individual elements between those ruled and rulers, between leaders and those led take place, that is, the life of the whole that is the only social force is materialized, the historical bloc is created.[2]

Gramsci spoke repeatedly of the iron dictatorship of intellectuals on the set of instrumental functions of society, a dualistic relationship so organic that it makes the barrier between leaders and those led insurmountable, condemning the masses to an unchanging and violent condition of

[1] Ibid., 1430.
[2] Ibid., 1,505–6.

subalternity. In it all the relations of bourgeois domination and exploitation are concentrated and summarized, all the bonds of command and obedience of the eternal distinction between leaders and those led are legitimized. Such dictatorship exemplifies the interested representation of knowledge by the intellectual strata: philosophy, knowledge and political direction are represented as concepts that are not transferable to "ordinary men", as something too complicated, the preserve of a specialized priesthood. Preserving, in relation to knowledge, the same widespread amazement among the people, just like a miracle (humanly unattainable), was useful to the existing state of affairs and to the passive social balance. Gramsci's entire intellectual and political biography originated and remains closely linked to a historical problem: removing from the shoulders of the "ordinary man" the unbearable weight of political subalternity, which is inextricably intertwined with exploitation and the consequence of the domination of man over man.

> A good part of Italians, when discussing a problem, do not pay attention to what is essential in this problem; they only examine the most prominent details and present them as essential. They are like the citizen who went to the fields to offer the peasants patriotic help in threshing, bagged the chaff and left the wheat in the field. He was a poet, a good citizen, and the chaff had bewitched him with its divine lightness, with his gentle dance in the fields under the shimmering rays of the sun, and also because his shoulders preferred a sack of chaff to a sack of wheat.[3]

In the figure of Antonio Gramsci, different demands and perspectives coexist, but in his theoretical production a framework of deep continuity develops. That does not mean that he always remains identical; on the contrary, on many issues his reasoning develops, becomes more complex, takes new directions, changes some initial judgments. The Gramsci of the *Notebooks* cannot be objectively superimposed on the young director of *L'Ordine Nuovo*, or the communist leader, because his thinking does not develop in a condition of intellectual rigidity without evolution.

Therefore, there is no contrast between a political Gramsci and a "man-of-culture" Gramsci, nor can one speak of a supposed ideological rupture in his intellectual production, to the point of dividing it into before and after. Gramsci was a young revolutionary, a political leader and a theorist:

---

[3] Antonio Gramsci, *La difesa dello Schultz*, 27 novembre 1917, "Avanti edizione Piemontese, XXI, n. 329. em *Scritti giovanili 1914–1918*, cit., p 133.

however, this tripartite division only makes sense to help organize the different phases of his life chronologically. In the reflections of the *Prison Notebooks*, he did not reject his youthful ideals; likewise, the strong need for theoretical questioning, typical of the prison notes, characterized his entire existence, even when he was a young revolutionary or the political leader of the international communist movement.

REFERENCES

Agosti, Aldo (Org.). *Gli anni del fascismo, l'antifascismo e la Resistenza*. Bari, De Donato, 1980.

———. *La Terza Internazionale*. Storia documentaria (1929–1943). Rome, Editori Riuniti, 1979.

Ajmone, Fiorella. *Lelio Basso nel socialismo italiano*. Milan, Franco Angeli, 1981.

Albanese, Giulia. *La marcia su Roma*. Rome/Bari, Laterza, 2006.

Aliaga, Luciana. *Gramsci e Pareto*: ciência, história e revolução. Curitiba, Appris, 2017.

Angioni, Giulio. *Rapporti di produzione e cultura subalterna*. Contadini in Sardegna. Cagliari, Edes, 1982a.

———. *Sa laurera*. Il lavoro contadino in Sardegna. Cagliari, Edes, 1982b.

Antonini, Francesca. Gramsci, il materialismo storico e l'antologia russa del 1924. *Studi Storici*: Rivista Trimestrale dell'Istituto Gramsci, v. 59, n. 2, 2018. p. 403–36.

Amoretti, Biancamaria Scarcia. *Il mondo musulmano*. Quindici secoli di storia. Rome, Carocci, 1998.

Badaloni, Nicola. *Il marxismo di Gramsci*. Turin, Einaudi, 1975.

——— (org.). *Gramsci e il marxismo contemporaneo*. Rome, Editori Riuniti, 1990.

Baldussi, Annamaria; Manduchi, Patrizia. *Gramsci in Asia e in Africa*. Cagliari, Aipsa, 2009.

Banti, Alberto Mario et al. *Storia contemporanea*. Rome, Donzelli, 1997.

Baratta, Giorgio. *Le rose e i Quaderni*. Saggio sul pensiero di Antonio Gramsci. Rome, Gamberetti, 2000.

© The Author(s), under exclusive license to Springer Nature Switzerland AG 2023
G. Fresu, *Antonio Gramsci*, Marx, Engels, and Marxisms,
https://doi.org/10.1007/978-3-031-15610-6

————; Catone, Andrea (orgs.). *Tempi moderni*. Gramsci e la critica dell'americanismo. Rome, Edizioni Associate, 1989.

————; Liguori, Guido (orgs.). *Gramsci da un secolo all'altro.* Rome, Editori Riuniti, 1999.

Bernstein, Ernst. *I pressupposti del socialismo e i compiti della socialdemocrazia.* Bari, Laterza, 1968.

Bertolissi, Sergio; Sestan, Lapo (orgs.). *Da Gramsci a Berlinguer.* La via italiana al socialismo attraverso i congressi del Partito Comunista Italiano, v. 2: *1944–1955.* Venice, Edizioni del Calendario/Marsilio, 1985.

Birocchi, Italo. Considerazioni sulla privatizzazione della terra in Sardegna dopo le leggi abolitive del feudalesimo. *Archivio Sardo del Movimento Operaio, Contadino e Autonomistico,* n. 11–13, 1980.

————. *Per la storia della proprietà perfetta in Sardegna.* Provvedimenti normativi, orientamenti di governo e ruolo delle forze sociali dal 1839 al 1851. Milan, Giuffrè, 1982.

————. Il Regnum Sardiniae dalla cessione ai Savoia alla "fusione perfetta". In: Guidetti, Massimo (org.). *Storia dei sardi e della Sardegna.* L'Età contemporanea. Dal governo piemontese agli anni sessanta del nostro secolo. Milan, Jaca Book, 1990.

Bordiga, Amadeo. Partito e azione di classe. *Rassegna Comunista,* ano I, n. 4, 31 maio 1921.

————. Il pericolo opportunista e l'Internazionale. *l'Unità,* 30 set. 1925.

————. *Struttura economica e sociale della Russia d'oggi.* Milan, Contra, 1966.

————. *Le lotte di classi e di stati nel mondo dei popoli non bianchi.* Storico campo vitale per la critica rivoluzionaria marxista. Naples, La Vecchia Talpa, 1972.

————. *Testi sul comunismo.* Naples, La Vecchia Talpa, 1972.

————. *Economia marxista ed economia controrivoluzionaria.* Milan, Iskra, 1976.

————. *La sinistra comunista nel cammino della rivoluzione.* Rome, Edizioni Sociali, 1976.

————. *I fattori di razza e nazione nella teoria marxista.* Milan, Iskra, 1976.

————. *Drammi gialli e sinistri della moderna decadenza sociale.* Milan, Iskra, 1978.

————. *Dalla guerra di Libia al Congresso socialista di Ancona, 1911–1914.* Org. Luigi Gerosa. Genoa, Graphos, 1996.

————. *La guerra, la Rivoluzione russa e la nuova Internazionale, 1914–1918.* Org. Luigi Gerosa. Genoaa, Graphos, 1998.

————. *Mai la merce sfamerà l'uomo.* La questione agraria e la teoria della rendita fondiaria secondo Marx. Org. R. Camiris. Rome, Odradek, 2009.

————. *Scritti 1911–1926.* Genoa, Graphos, 2010.

————. *Scritti scelti.* Milan, Feltrinelli, 1975.

Boscolo, Alberto. *I viaggiatori dell'Ottocento in Sardegna.* Cagliari, Editrice Sarda Fossataro, 1973.

_____; Brigaglia, Manlio; Del Piano, Lorenzo. *La Sardegna contemporanea.* Cagliari, Edizioni della Torre, 1974.

Brigaglia, Manlio. *Sardegna perché banditi.* Milan, Carte Segrete, 1971.

_____ (org.). *L'inchiesta Salaris e la relazione Pais Serra.* Sassari, Edes, 1990.

Burgio, Alberto. *Gramsci storico.* Una lettura dei Quaderni del Carcere. Bari, Laterza, 2003.

_____. *Per Gramsci.* Crisi e potenza del moderno. Rome, Derive Approdi, 2007.

_____; Santucci, Antonio (orgs.). *Gramsci e la rivoluzione in Occidente.* Rome, Editori Riuniti, 1999.

Cafiero, Salvatore. *La questione meridionale.* Florence, Le Monnier, 1980.

Canfora, Luciano. *Gramsci in carcere e il fascismo.* Rome, Salerno Editrice, 2012.

Cardia, Umberto. *Autonomia sarda.* Un'idea che attraversa i secoli. Cagliari, Cuec, 1999.

_____ (org.). *Gramsci e la svolta degli anni trenta.* Cagliari, Edes, 1976.

Cardia Marci, Susanna. *Il giovane Gramsci.* Cagliari, In. E.S., 1977.

Carteggio Marx-Engels. Rome, Editori Riuniti, 1972.

Catone, Andrea; Susca, Emanuela (orgs.). *Problemi della transizione al socialismo in URSS.* Naples, La Città del Sole, 2004.

Cerroni, Umberto. Introduzione. In: Lênin, Vladímir Ilitch. *Stato e rivoluzione.* Rome, Newton Compton, 1975.

Chabod, Federico. *L'Italia contemporanea (1918–1948).* Turin, Einaudi, 1961.

Chambers, Iain (org.). *Esercizi di potere.* Gramsci, Said e il postcoloniale. Rome, Universale Meltemi, 2006.

———; Curti, Lidia (orgs.). *La questione postcoloniale.* Naples, Liguori, 1997.

Civile, Giuseppe. *I volti dell'élite.* Classi dirigenti nell'Ottocento meridionale. Naples, Libreria Dante & Descartes, 2002.

Cole, George Douglas Howard. *Storia del pensiero socialista,* v. 5: *Socialismo e fascismo.* Rome/Bari, Laterza, 1968.

Colombi, Arturo. *Nelle mani del nemico.* Rome, Editori Riuniti, 1971.

Coutinho, Carlos Nelson. *Gramsci.* Porto Alegre, L&PM, 1981.

———. *Democracia e socialismo*: questões de princípio e contexto brasileiro. São Paulo, Cortez, 1992.

———. *Marxismo e política*: a dualidade de poderes e outros ensaios. São Paulo, Cortez, 1994.

———. *Contra a corrente*: ensaios sobre democracia e socialismo. São Paulo, Cortez, 2000a.

———. *Cultura e sociedade no Brasil*: ensaios sobre ideias e formas. Rio de Janeiro, DP&A, 2000b.

———. *Il pensiero politico di Gramsci.* Milão, Unicopli, 2006a. [Ed. bras.: *Gramsci*: um estudo sobre seu pensamento político. 3. ed., Rio de Janeiro, Civilização Brasileira, 2007.]

———. *Intervenções*: o marxismo na batalha das ideias. São Paulo, Cortez, 2006b.

——. *De Rousseau a Gramsci*. São Paulo, Boitempo, 2011a.

——. *O leitor de Gramsci*. Rio de Janeiro, Civilização Brasileira, 2011b.

Cortesi, Luigi (org.). *Amadeo Bordiga nella storia del comunismo*. Naples, Edizioni Scientifiche Italiane, 1999.

Critica Marxista. Il pensiero di Gramsci. Rome, n. 6, ano 25, 1986.

——. *Oltre Gramsci, con Gramsci*. Rome, n. 2–3, ano 25, 1987.

Croce, Benedetto. *Due anni di vita politica italiana (1946–1947)*. Bari, Laterza, 1948a.

——. *Teoria e storia della storiografia*. Bari, Laterza, 1948b.

——. *Scritti e discorsi politici*. Bari, Laterza, 1963.

——. *Storia d'Europa nel secolo decimonono*. Bari, Laterza, 1965.

Dal Pane, Luigi. *Antonio Labriola nella politica e nella cultura italiana*. Turin, Einaudi, 1975.

Daniele, Chiara (org.). *Gramsci a Roma, Togliatti a Mosca*. Il carteggio del 1926. Turin, Einaudi, 1999.

De Clementi, Andreina. *Amadeo Bordiga*. Turin, Einaudi, 1971.

De Felice, Franco. Introduzione al Quaderno 2. In: *Americanismo e fordismo*. Turin, Einaudi, 1978.

De Felice, Renzo. *Il fascismo*. Le interpretazioni dei contemporanei e degli storici. Bari, Laterza, 1970.

——. *Le interpretazioni del fascismo*. Bari, Laterza, 1995.

De Luna, Giovanni. *La passione e la ragione*. Fonti e metodi dello storico contemporaneo. Florence, La Nuova Italia, 2001.

De Micheli, Mario. *La matrice ideologica del fascismo*. Milan, Feltrinelli, 1975.

Del Piano, Lorenzo (org.). *I problemi della Sardegna da Cavour a Depretis (1849–1876)*. Cagliari, Fossataro, 1977.

Del Roio, Marcos. *Gramsci e a emancipação do subalterno*. São Paulo, Editora Unesp, 2018.

Del Roio. *I prismi di Gramsci*. La formula politica del fronte unico (1919–1926). Naples, La Città del Sole, 2010.

——. (org.). *Gramsci: periferia e subalternidade*. São Paulo, Edusp, 2017.

De Ruggiero, Guido. *Storia del liberalismo europeo*. Bari, Laterza, 2003.

De Simone, Cesare. *Soldati e generali a Caporetto*. Rome, Tindalo, 1970.

Degras, Jane (org.). *Storia dell'Internazionale comunista attraverso i documenti ufficiali*, t. 1: *1919–1922*. Milan, Feltrinelli, 1975a.

——. (org.). *Storia dell'Internazionale comunista attraverso i documenti ufficiali*, t. 2: *1923–1928*. Milan, Feltrinelli, 1975b.

——. (org.). *Storia dell'Internazionale comunista attraverso i documenti ufficiali*, t. 3: *1929–1943*. Milan, Feltrinelli, 1979.

D'orsi, Angelo. *1917*. L'anno della rivoluzione. Rome/Bari, Laterza, 2016.

——. *Gramsci*. Una nuova biografia. Milan, Feltrinelli, 2017.

Dubla, Ferdinando. *Gramsci e la fabbrica*. Bari, Lacaita, 1986.

————; Giusto, Massimo (orgs.). *Il Gramsci di Turi*. Manduria, Chimienti, 2008.

Ellenstein, Jean. *Storia dell'URSS*. Rome, Editori Riuniti, 1976. 2 v.

Engels, Friedrich. *La guerra dei contadini in Germania*. Rome, Rinascita, 1949a.

————. *Sul materialismo storico*. Rome, Editori Riuniti, 1949b.

————. *Ludwig Feuerbach e il punto di approdo della filosofia classica tedesca*. Trad. da edição original alemã de 1888 de Palmiro Togliatti. Rome, Rinascita, 1950.

————. *Sulle origini del cristianesimo*. Rome, Rinascita, 1954.

————. *La situazione della classe operaia in Inghilterra*. Rome, Edizioni Rinascita, 1955.

————. *Antidühring*. Rome, Editori Riuniti, 1971.

————; Marx, Karl. *Sul Risorgimento italiano*. Rome, Editori Riuniti, 1959.

Ferrara, Marcella; Ferrara, Maurizio (orgs.). *Conversando con Togliatti*. Note biografiche. Rome, Editori di Cultura Sociale, 1953.

Filippini, Michele. *Una politica di massa*. Antonio Gramsci e la rivoluzione della società. Rome, Carocci, 2015.

Fiori, Giuseppe. *Vita di Antonio Gramsci*. Rome/Bari, Laterza, 1989a.

————. *Vita di Enrico Berlinguer*. Rome/Bari, Laterza, 1989b.

————. *Gramsci, Togliatti, Stalin*. Rome/Bari, Laterza, 1991.

————. *Antonio Gramsci*. Vita attraverso le lettere. Turin, Einaudi, 1994.

Fovel, N. Massimo. *Economia e corporativismo*. Ferrara, S.A.T.E., 1929.

Francioni, Gianni. *L'officina gramsciana*. Ipotesi sulla struttura dei "Quaderni del carcere". Naples, Bibliopolis, 1984.

————. *Tre studi su Gramsci*. Naples, Bibliopolis, 1988.

————; Giasi, Francesco; Paulesu, Luca (org.). *Gramsci*. I quaderni del carcere e le riviste ritrovate. Rome, MetaMorfosi, 2019.

Fresu, Gianni. *Il diavolo nell'ampolla*. Antonio Gramsci, gli intellettuali e il Partito. Naples, Istituto Italiano per gli Studi Filosofici/La Città del Sole, 2005.

————. *Americanismo e fordismo: l'uomo filosofo e il gorilla ammaestrato*. *NAE: Trimestrale di Cultura*. Cagliari, Cuec, n. 18, ano 6, 2007.

————. *Lenin lettore di Marx*. Determinismo e dialettica nella storia del movimento operaio. Naples, La Città del Sole, 2008a.

————. *Antonio Gramsci, fascismo e classi dirigenti nella storia d'Italia*. *NAE: Trimestrale di Cultura*. Cagliari, Cuec, n. 21, ano 6, 2008b.

————. *La prima bardana*. Modernizzazione e conflitto nella Sardegna dell'Ottocento. Cagliari, Cuec, 2011.

————. *Moderati e democratici nell'Ottocento*. L'interpretazione di Gramsci. In: Carpinelli, Cristina; Gioiello, Vittorio (orgs.). *Il Risorgimento: un'epoca?* Per una ricostruzione storico-critica. Frankfurt, Zambon, 2012.

————. *Eugenio Curiel*. Il lungo viaggio contro il fascismo. Rome, Odradek, 2013.

————. *Gramsci e a revolução nacional*. In: Lole, Ana; Gomes, Victor Leandro Chaves; Del Roio, Marcos (orgs.). *Gramsci e a Revolução Russa*. Rio de Janeiro, Mórula, 2017a.

———. *Nas trincheiras do Ocidente*: lições sobre fascismo e antifascismo. Ponta Grossa, Editora UEPG, 2017b.

———. De Marx a Gramsci: educação, relações produtivas e hierarquia social. In: Schlesener, Anita Helena; Oliveira, André Luiz de; Almeida, Tatiani Maria Garcia de (orgs.). *A atualidade da filosofia da práxis e políticas educacionais.* Curitiba, UTP, 2018.

———; Accardo, Aldo. *Oltre la parentesi.* Fascismo e storia d'Italia nell'interpretazione gramsciana. Roma, Carocci, 2009.

Garin, Eugenio. *Cronache di filosofia italiana.* Bari, Laterza, 1959.

———. *Intellettuali italiani del XX secolo.* Rome, Editori Riuniti, 1974.

———. *Con Gramsci.* Rome, Editori Riuniti, 1997.

Garosci, Aldo. *Storia dei fuoriusciti.* Bari, Laterza, 1953.

Gemelli, Francesco. *Rifiorimento della Sardegna.* Cagliari, Fossataro, 1966.

Gentile, Emilio. *Fascismo e antifascismo.* I partiti italiani fra le due guerre. Florence, Le Monnier, 2000.

———. *Fascismo.* Storia e interpretazione. Rome/Bari, Laterza, 2002.

———. *Il culto del littorio.* La sacralizzazione della politica nell'Italia fascista. Rome/Bari, Laterza, 2008a.

———. *La via italiana al totalitarismo.* Il Partito e lo Stato nel regime fascista. Rome, Carocci, 2008b.

———. *E fu subito regime.* Il fascismo e la marcia su Roma. Rome/Bari, Laterza, 2012.

Giacomini, Ruggero; Losurdo, Domenico (orgs.). *Lenin e il Novecento.* Naples, La Città del Sole, 1997.

———; ———; Martelli, Michele (orgs.). *Gramsci e l'Italia.* Naples, Istituto Italiano per gli Studi Filosofici/La Città del Sole, 1992.

Gilpin, Robert. Attori nell'economia globale. In: BATINI, Elisabetta; RAGIONIERI, Rodolfo (orgs.). *Culture e conflitti nella globalizzazione.* Florence, S. Olschki, 2002.

Gioberti, Vincenzo. *Del primato morale e civile degli italiani.* Turin, Utet, 1932.

Gobetti, Piero. *Camilla Ravera in carcere e al confino.* Parma, Guanda, 1969.

———. *La rivoluzione liberale.* Saggio sulla lotta politica in Italia. Turin, Einaudi, 1974.

Gramsci, Antonio. Il Partito si rafforza combattendo le deviazioni antileniniste. *l'Unità,* 5 jul. 1925.

———. *L'Ordine Nuovo 1919–1920.* Turin, Einaudi, 1972.

———. *Scritti giovanili 1914–1918.* Turin, Einaudi, 1975a.

———. *Il Vaticano e l'Italia.* Rome, Editori Riuniti, 1961.

———. *Scritti politici.* Rome, Editori Riuniti, 1969.

———. *La costruzione del Partito Comunista 1923–1926.* Turin, Einaudi, 1978a.

———. *Lettere dal carcere.* Turin, Einaudi, 2020.

———. *Scritti 1915–1925.* Milan, Moizzi, 1976.

———. *Quaderni del carcere*. Turin, Einaudi, 1975b [trans. Joseph Buttigieg, *Prison Notebooks*, 3 v. New York: Columbia University Press, 2007).

———. *Socialismo e fascismo*. Turin, Einaudi, 1978b.

———. *Il rivoluzionario qualificato*. Rome, Delotti, 1988.

———. *La questione meridionale*. Rome, Editori Riuniti, 1991.

———. *Lettere dal carcere 1926–1930*. Palermo, Sellerio, 1996.

———. *Lettere a Tatiana Schucht*. Turin, Einaudi, 1997.

———. *Quaderni del carcere*. I Quaderni di traduzione (1929–1932). Rome, Treccani, 2007. 2 v.

———. *Quaderni del carcere*: edizione anastatica dei manoscritti. Cagliari, Società Editrice L'Unione Sarda, 2009. 18 v. (Biblioteca Treccani)

———. *Il giornalismo, il giornalista*. Scritti, articoli, lettere del fondatore de "l'Unità". Org. Gianluca Corradi. Florença, Tessere, 2017.

———.*Scritti* (1910–1926), volume I (1910–1916), Istituto della Enciclopedia Italiana, Roma, Treccani, Roma, 2019.

———*Epistolario*, volume 2, gennaio novembre 1926, Istituto della Enciclopedia Italiana Treccani, Roma

Grieco, Ruggero. *Scritti scelti*. Rome, Editori Riuniti, 1966.

Gruppi, Luciano. *Il pensiero di Lenin*. Rome, Editori Riuniti, 1971.

———. *Storicità e marxismo*. Rome, Editori Riuniti, 1976.

———. *La teoria del partito rivoluzionario*. Rome, Editori Riuniti, 1980.

———. *Il Partito Comunista Italiano*. Rome, Salemi, 1981.

———. *Per un avvio allo studio di Gramsci*. Rome, Salemi, 1987.

Haupt, Georges. *L'Internazionale socialista dalla comune a Lenin*. Turin, Einaudi, 1978.

Hegel, Georg Wilhelm Friedrich. *Fenomenologia dello spirito*. Florence, La Nuova Italia, 1960.

———. *Lineamenti di filosofia del diritto*. Bari, Laterza, 1965.

———. *Enciclopedia delle scienze filosofiche in compendio*. Bari, Laterza, 1967.

———. *Scienza della logica*. Bari, Laterza, 1968.

———. *Filosofia del diritto*. Florença, Vallecchi, 1969.

———. *Filosofia della storia*. Florence, La Nuova Italia, 1975.

———. *Filosofia dello spirito*. Turin, Unione Tipografico Torinese, 1980.

———. *Introduzione alla storia della filosofia*. Bari, Laterza, 1982.

Hobsbawm, Eric. *I rivoluzionari*. Turin, Einaudi, 1975.

———. *Il secolo breve*. Milan, Rizzoli, 1994.

———. *Intervista sul nuovo secolo*. Bari, Laterza, 1999.

———. *Anni interessanti*. Autobiografia di uno storico. Milan, Rizzoli, 2002a.

———. *I banditi*. Il banditismo sociale nell'età moderna. Turin, Einaudi, 2002b.

———. *Nazioni e nazionalismi dal 1780*. Programma, mito, realtà. Turin, Einaudi, 2002c.

——— (org.). *Storia del marxismo*. Turin, Einaudi, 1979–1981. 3 v.

————; Bairoch, Paul (orgs.). *L'età contemporanea*. Turin, Einaudi, 1996.

Holz, Hans Heinz. *Marx, la storia, la dialettica*. Naples, La Città del Sole, 1996.

————; Abendroth, Wolfgang; Kofler, Leo. *Conversazioni con Lukács*. Bari, De Donato, 1968.

Irde, Pierino. *Dalla terra di nessuno alla proprietà perfetta*. Cagliari, Edizioni Castello, 1999.

Isneghi, Mario. *Il mito della grande guerra*. Bologna, Il Mulino, 1989.

————. *L'Italia in piazza*. I luoghi della vita pubblica dal 1848 ai giorni nostri. Milan, Mondadori, 1994.

Jemolo, Arturo Carlo. *Chiesa e Stato in Italia*. Dalla unificazione ai giorni nostri. Turin, Einaudi, 1975.

Kautsky, Karl. *Etica e concezione materialistica della storia*. Milan, Feltrinelli, 1958.

————. *La questione agraria*. Milan, Feltrinelli, 1959.

————. *Introduzione al pensiero economico di Marx*. Bari, Laterza, 1972.

————. *La questione coloniale*. Milan, Feltrinelli, 1977.

————. *L'imperialismo*. Bari, Laterza, 1980.

La Fondazione del Partito Comunista. Documenti. Naples, Laboratorio Politico, 1996.

La Questione italiana al Terzo Congresso della Internazionale Comunista. Rome, Libreria Editrice del Partito Comunista d'Italia, 1921.

Labriola, Antonio. *Discorrendo di socialismo e di filosofia*. Org. Benedetto Croce. Bari, Laterza, 1947.

————. *Opere*. Milan, Feltrinelli, 1962. 3 v.

————. *La concezione materialistica della storia*. Bari, Laterza, 1965.

————. *In memoria del Manifesto dei comunisti*. Rome, Newton Compton, 1973a.

————. *Scritti filosofici e politici*. Turin, Einaudi, 1973b. 2 v.

————. *Epistolario*. Rome, Editori Riuniti, 1983. 3 v.

Le Lannou, Maurice. *Pastori e contadni in Sardegna*. Cagliari, Edizioni della Torre, 2006.

Lênin, Vladímir Ilitch. *Opere complete*. Rome, Editori Riuniti, 1955–1970. 45 v. [trans. Lenin Collected Works, Moscow, Progress Publlishers, 1973]

————. *Sul movimento operaio italiano*. Rome, Editori Riuniti, 1970.

————. *Stato e rivoluzione*. Rome, Newton Compton, 1975.

————. *Che fare?*. Turin, Einaudi, 1979.

————. *L'imperialismo fase suprema del capitalismo*. Naples, La Città del Sole, 1994.

Leonetti, Alfonso. *Note su Gramsci*. Urbino, Argalia, 1970.

Lepre, Aurelio. *Gramsci secondo Gramsci*. Naples, Liguori, 1978.

————. *Il prigioniero*. Vita di Antonio Gramsci. Bari, Laterza, 1998.

Liguori, Guido. *Gramsci conteso*. Interpretazioni, dibattiti e polemiche 1922–2012. Rome, Editori Riuniti/University Press, 2012.

————. *Sentieri gramsciani*. Rome, Carocci, 2006.

————; Voza, Pasquale (orgs.). *Dizionario gramsciano, 1926–1937*. Rome, Carocci, 2009.

Livorsi, Franco (org.). *Amadeo Bordiga*. Il pensiero e l'azione politica 1912–1970. Rome, Editori Riuniti, 1976.

Lole, Ana; Gomes, Victor Leandro Chaves; Del Roio, Marcos (orgs.). *Gramsci e a Revolução Russa*. Rio de Janeiro, Mórula, 2017.

Lombardo Radice, Lucio; Carbone, Giuseppe. *Vita di Antonio Gramsci*. Rome, Edizioni di Cultura Sociale, 1952.

Longo, Luigi. *Continuità della resistenza*. Turin, Einaudi, 1977.

Losurdo, Domenico. *Democrazia o bonapartismo*. Trionfo e decadenza del suffragio universale. Turin, Bollati Boringhieri, 1993.

————. *Antonio Gramsci dal liberalismo al comunismo critico*. Rome, Gamberetti, 1997.

————. *Il revisionismo storico*. Bari, Laterza, 1998.

————. *Il peccato originale del Novecento*. Bari, Laterza, 1999.

————. *L'ipocondria dell'impolitico*. La critica di Hegel ieri e oggi. Lecce, Milella, 2001.

————. *Dai Fratelli Spaventa a Gramsci*. Per una storia politica della fortuna di Hegel in Italia. Naples, La Città del Sole, 2006.

————. *Guerra e revolução*: o mundo um século após outubro de 1917. Trad. Ana Maria Chiarini e Diego Silveira Coelho Ferreira. São Paulo, Boitempo, 2017a.

————. *Il marxismo occidentale*. Come nacque, come morì, come può rinascere. Bari/Rome, Laterza, 2017b.

Lukács, György. *Il giovane Hegel e i problemi della società capitalistica*. Turin, Einaudi, 1960.

————. *Storia e coscienza di classe*. Milan, Sugar, 1970.

————. *Scritti politici giovanili 1919–1928*. Bari, Laterza, 1972.

Lupo, Salvatore. *Il fascismo*. La politica in un regime totalitario. Rome, Donzelli, 2005.

Luxemburgo, Rosa. *L'accumulazione del capitale*. Contributo alla spiegazione economica dell'imperialismo. Turin, Einaudi, 1960.

————. *Scritti politici*. Rome, Editori Riuniti, 1967.

————. *Introduzione all'economia politica*. Milan, Jaca Book,1975.

Manacorda, Mario Alighiero. *Marx e a pedagogia moderna*. Trad. Newton Ramos-de-Oliveira. São Paulo, Cortez, 1991.

————. *L'alternativa pedagogica in Gramsci*. Rome, Editori Riuniti, 2012.

————. *O princípio educativo em Gramsci*: americanismo e conformismo. Trad. William Laços. Campinas, Alínea, 2013.

Manconi, Francesco (org.). *Le inchieste parlamentari sulla Sardegna dell'Ottocento*. L'Inchiesta Depretis. Cagliari, Edizioni della Torre, 1984.

Maquiavel, Nicolau. *Il Principe*. Turin, Einaudi, 1995.

Marx, Karl. *Per la critica dell'economia politica*. Rome, Editori Riuniti, 1974.

————. *Critica del programma di Gotha*. Rome, Editori Riuniti, 1976.

————. *Il capitale*. Rome, Editori Riuniti, 1994.

————; Engels, Friedrich. *L'ideologia tedesca*. Rome, Editori Riuniti, 1958.

————; ————. *Sul Risorgimento italiano*. Rome, Editori Riuniti, 1959.

————; ————. *Opere complete*. Rome, Editori Riuniti, 1972 [MECW, New York, International Publishers, 1996].

————; ————. *Carteggio*. Rome, Editori Riuniti, 1972.

Mauro, Walter. *Invito alla lettura di Gramsci*. Milan, Mursia, 1981.

Melchiorre, Virgilio; Vigna, Carmelo; De Rosa, Gabriele (orgs.). *Antonio Gramsci. Il pensiero teorico e político*. La "questione leninista". Rome, Città Nuova, 1977.

Melis, Guido (org.). *Gramsci e la questione sarda*. Cagliari, Edizioni della Torre, 1977.

Merli, Stefano. *Fronte antifascista e politica di classe*. Socialisti e comunisti in Italia (1923–1939). Bari, De Donato, 1975.

Michels, Robert. *La sociologia del partito politico nella società moderna*. Bologna, Il Mulino, 1966.

Mustè, Marcello. *Marxismo e filosofia della praxis*. Da Labriola a Gramsci. Rome, Viella, 2018.

Noce, Teresa. *Rivoluzionaria professionale*. Milan, La Pietra, 1974.

Nolte, Ernst. *La crisi dei regimi liberali e i movimenti fascisti*. Bologna, Il Mulino, 1970.

————. *I tre volti del fascismo*. Milan, Mondadori, 1971.

Paggi, Leonardo. *Le strategie del potere in Gramsci*. Rome, Editori Riuniti, 1984.

Pala, Mauro. *Americanismi*. Sulla ricezione del pensiero di Gramsci negli USA. Cagliari, Cuec, 2009.

————. *Narrazioni egemoniche*. Gramsci, letteratura e società civile. Bologna, Il Mulino, 2014.

Paulesu Quercioli, Mimma (org.). *Gramsci vivo*. Milan, Feltrinelli, 1977.

Pavone, Claudio. *Una guerra civile*. Saggio storico sulla moralità della Resistenza. Turin, Bollati Boringhieri, 1994.

————. *Alle origini della Repubblica*. Scritti su fascismo, antifascismo e continuità dello Stato. Turin, Bollati Boringhieri, 1995.

Pecchioli, Ugo (org.). *Da Gramsci a Berlinguer*. La via italiana al socialismo attraverso i congressi del Partito Comunista Italiano, v. 1: *1921–1943*. Venice, Marsilio/Edizioni del Calendario, 1985.

Petronio, Giuseppe; Musitelli, Marina Paladini (orgs.). *Marx e Gramsci*. Memoria e attualità. Rome, Manifestolibri, 2001.

Pillon, Cesare. *I comunisti nella storia d'Italia*. Rome, Edizioni del Calendario, 1967. 2 v.

Pirastu, Ignazio. *Il banditismo in Sardegna*. Rome, Editori Riuniti, 1973.

Pistillo, Michelle. *Vita di Ruggero Grieco*. Rome, Editori Riuniti, 1985.

Poitier, Jean-Pierre. *Piero Sraffa*. Biografia. Rome, Editori Riuniti, 1990.

Ragionieri, Ernesto. *Socialdemocrazia tedesca e socialisti italiani 1875–1895*. Milan, Feltrinelli, 1961.

———. *Il marxismo e l'Internazionale*. Rome, Editori Riuniti, 1968a.

———. *Alle origini del marxismo della Seconda Internazionale*. Rome, Editori Riuniti, 1968b.

———. *Il marxismo e l'Internazionale*. Studi di storia del marxismo. Rome, Editori Riuniti, 1972.

———. *Palmiro Togliatti*. Rome, Editori Riuniti, 1976.

———. *La Terza Internazionale e il Partito Comunista Italiano*. Saggi e discussioni. Turin, Einaudi, 1978.

Rao, A. M. (org.). *La crisi politica del regno di Sardegna dalla rivoluzione patriottica ai moti antifeudali (1793–96)*. Rome, Carocci, 1999.

Rapone, Leonardo. *Cinque anni che paiono secoli*. Antonio Gramsci dal socialismo al comunismo. Rome, Carocci, 2011.

Renda, Francesco. Contadini e pastori nella Sardegna moderna. *Archivio Sardo del Movimento Operaio, Contadino e Autonomistico*, n. 11–13, 1980.

Rigola, Rinaldo. *Storia del movimento operaio italiano*. Milan, Domus, 1947.

Robotti, Paolo; Germanetto, Giovanni. *Trent'anni di lotte dei comunisti italiani, 1921–1951*. Rome, Edizioni di Cultura Sociale, 1952.

Romano, Salvatore Francesco. *Gramsci*. Turin, Einaudi, 1965.

Rossi, Pietro (org.). *Gramsci e la cultura contemporanea*. Atti del Convegno internazionale di studi gramsciani (Cagliari 23–27 aprile 1967). Rome, Editori Riuniti, 1967.

Roveri, Alessandro. *Dal sindacalismo rivoluzionario al fascismo*. Florence, La Nuova Italia, 1972.

Said, Edward W. *Orientalismo*. Turin, Bollati e Boringhieri, 1991.

———. *Cultura e imperialismo*. Rome, Gamberetti, 1998.

Salaris, Francesco. Atti della Giunta per la Inchiesta Agraria. In: *Le inchieste parlamentari sulla Sardegna dell'Ottocento*. Sassari, Edes, 1984.

Salinari, Carlo. *I comunisti raccontano*, v. 1: *1919–1945*. Milan, Teti, 1975.

———; Spinelli, Mario. *Il pensiero di Gramsci*. Rome, l'Unità, 1977.

Salvadori, Massimo. *Gramsci e il problema storico della democrazia*. Turin, Einaudi,1970.

———. *Storia del pensiero comunista da Lenin a Gorbaciov*. Bari, Laterza, 1992.

Salvati, Mariuccia. *Il Novecento*. Interpretazioni e bilanci. Bari, Laterza, 2001.

Salvatorelli, Luigi. *Pensiero e azione del Risorgimento*. Turin/Rome, Einaudi, 1944.

———; Mira, Giovanni. *Storia d'Italia nel periodo fascista*. Turin, Einaudi, 1964.

Salvemini, Gaetano. *Memorie di un fuoriuscito*. Milan, Feltrinelli, 1960.

Salvucci, Pasquale (org.). *Tra marxismo e idealismo*. Urbino, Montefeltro, 1981.

Santarelli, Enzo. *Storia del fascismo*. Rome, Editori Riuniti, 1973. 3 v.

———. *Il mondo contemporaneo*. Rome, Editori Riuniti, 1974.

398   REFERENCES

Santucci, Antonio. *Nuove lettere di Antonio Gramsci, con altre lettere di Piero Sraffa*. Rome, Editori Riuniti, 1986.

Silone, Ignazio. *Il fascismo, origini e sviluppo*. Milan, Mondadori, 2002.

Smith, Denis Mack. *Da Cavour a Mussolini*. Catania, Bonanno, 1968.

———. *Storia d'Italia*. Bari, Laterza, 1975.

———. *Mussolini*. Milan, Rizzoli, 1990.

———. *Le guerre del Duce*. Milan, Mondadori, 1997.

———. *A proposito di Mussolini*. Bari, Laterza, 2004.

Sole, Carlino (org.). *La Sardegna di Carlo Felice e il problema della terra*. Cagliari, Fossataro, 1967.

Sorel, Georges. *Scritti politici*. Turin, Unione Tipografico-Editrice Torinese, 1968.

Sotgiu, Girolamo. *Alle origini della questione sarda*. Note di storia sarda del Risorgimento. Cagliari, Fossataro, 1967.

———. *Lotte sociali e politiche nella Sardegna contemporanea*. Cagliari, Edes, 1974.

———. *Movimento operaio e autonomismo*. Bari, De Donato, 1975.

———. *Storia della Sardegna sabauda (1720–1847)*. Bari, Laterza, 1984.

———. *Storia della Sardegna dopo l'Unità*. Bari, Laterza, 1986.

Spinetti, Gastone Silvano. *Bibliografia degli esuli politici sotto il fascismo*. Rome, Solidarismo, 1959.

Spivak, Gayatri Chakravorty. *Critica della ragione postcoloniale*. Verso una storia del presente in dissolvenza. Rome, Meltemi, 2004.

Spriano, Paolo. *Gramsci e L'Ordine Nuovo*. Rome, Editori Riuniti, 1965.

———. *Gramsci*. Milan, C.E.I., 1966.

———. *Storia del Partito Comunista Italiano*. Turin, Einaudi, 1967–1979. 4 v.

———. *L'Ordine Nuovo e i Consigli di fabbrica*. Turin, Einaudi, 1971.

———. *Gramsci e Gobetti*. Turin, Einaudi, 1977a.

———. *Gramsci in carcere e il Partito*. Rome, Editori Riuniti, 1977b.

———. *Sulla rivoluzione italiana*. Turin, Einaudi, 1978.

———. *Togliatti segretario dell'Internazionale*. Milan, Mondadori, 1980.

Sullam, Simon Levi. Dio e il popolo. La rivoluzione religiosa di Giuseppe Mazzini. In: Banti, Alberto M.; Ginsborg, Paul. *Storia d'Italia*. Turin, Einaudi, 2007.

Tasca, Angelo. *Nascita e avvento del fascismo*. Bari, Laterza, 1972.

Terracini, Umberto. *Quando diventammo comunisti*. Conversazione con Umberto Terracini tra cronaca e storia. Milan, La Pietra, 1976.

———. *Intervista sul comunismo difficile*. Rome/Bari, Laterza, 1978.

———. *Al bando dal Partito*. Carteggio clandestino dall'isola e dall'esilio, 1938–45. Milan, Rizzoli, 1981.

Thomas, Peter D. Cosa rimane dei subalterni alla luce dello Stato integrale?. *International Gramsci Journal*, v. 2, n. 4, 2015. p. 82–92.

Togliatti, Palmiro. *Il Partito Comunista Italiano*. Rome, Editori Riuniti/Rinascita, 1971.

———. *Gramsci*. Rome, Editori Riuniti, 1972a.

————. *Opere*. Rome, Editori Riuniti/Rinascita, 1972b–1979. 4 v.

————. *La formazione del gruppo dirigente del Partito Comunista Italiano (1923–24)*. Rome, Editori Riuniti, 1984.

Tranfaglia, Nicola. *Dallo Stato liberale al regime fascista*. Milan, Feltrinelli,1973.

————. *Labirinto italiano*. Il fascismo, l'antifascismo, gli storici. Florence, La Nuova Italia, 1989.

————. *La prima guerra mondiale e il fascismo*. Milan, TEA, 1996.

————. *Un passato scomodo*. Fascismo e postfascismo. Bari, Laterza, 1999.

————. *Fascismi e modernizzazione in Europa*. Turin, Bollati Boringhieri, 2001.

Vacca, Giuseppe. *Gramsci e Togliatti*. Rome, Editori Riuniti, 1991.

————. *Vita e pensieri di Antonio Gramsci*. 1926–1937. Turin, Einaudi, 2012.

————. *Modernità alternative*. Il Novecento di Antonio Gramsci. Turin, Einaudi, 2017a.

———— (org.). *Gramsci e il Novecento*. Atti del convegno internazionale di studi del 1997. Rome, Carocci, 1997.

————; Manduchi, Patrizia; Marchi, Alessandra (orgs.). *Studi gramsciani nel mondo*. Gramsci nel mondo arabo. Bologna, Il Mulino, 2017b.

Valiani, Leo et al. *Fascismo e antifascismo*. Lezioni e testimonianze. Milan, Feltrinelli, 1962. 2 v.

Vanzulli, Marco. *Il marxismo e l'idealismo*. Studi su Labriola, Croce, Gentile e Gramsci. Rome, Aracne, 2013.

Villa, Nora. *Camilla Ravera*. La piccola grande signora del PCI. Milan, Rizzoli, 1983.

Zanelli, Antonio. *Condizioni della pastorizia in Sardegna*. Relazione al Ministero dell'Agricoltura, Industria e Commercio (Direttore dello stabilimento in zootecnia di Reggio Emilia). Cagliari, Tipografia Editrice dell'Avvenire di Sardegna,1880.

Žižek, Slavoj. *Tredici volte Lenin (per sovvertire il fallimento del presente)*. Milan, Feltrinelli, 2003.

————. *Lenin oggi*. Milan, Ponte delle Grazie, 2017.

Index[1]

---

[1] Note: Page numbers followed by 'n' refer to notes.

© The Author(s), under exclusive license to Springer Nature   401
Switzerland AG 2023
G. Fresu, *Antonio Gramsci*, Marx, Engels, and Marxisms,
https://doi.org/10.1007/978-3-031-15610-6

Printed by Printforce, the Netherlands